Race and Ethnic Relations
Sociological Reading

GW00703197

Gordon Bowker

Gordon Bowker was born in 1934 in Birmingham
and served in the RAF from 1952 to 1955. In 1960 he
graduated in Sociology from Nottingham University
and obtained an MA in Sociology and Philosophy of
Education at London University Institute of Education
in 1966. Since 1966 he has taught Sociology at the
University of London, Goldsmiths' College where he
is now Principal Lecturer and Deputy Head of
Department. For two years he lived and worked in
Australia and travelled widely in North America and
Europe. His publications include *Under Twenty*
(1966), *Education of Coloured Immigrants* (1969),
Freedom: Reason or Revolution? (1970). He has also
written extensively for educational television and
radio as well as for magazines, journals and
newspapers.

John Carrier

John Carrier was an undergraduate and postgraduate
student at LSE and now lectures there in Social
Administration, having taught at Goldsmiths' College
for eight years. He has taught a wide variety of Social
Policy courses at university and professional training
level. His research work 'A Jewish Proletariat' led him
on to consider theoretical approaches to minority
groups in general and he has published various articles
on this theme. John Carrier is a life-long Londoner,
except for National Service and a spell in the
Merchant Navy. He is married and has four children.

Race and Ethnic Relations
Sociological Readings

Edited by

Gordon Bowker
*Principal lecturer in Sociology,
University of London, Goldsmiths' College*

John Carrier
*Lecturer in Social Administration in the
London School of Economics*

Introductory essay by

Percy Cohen
*Professor of Sociology in the
London School of Economics*

Hutchinson of London

Hutchinson & Co (Publishers) Ltd
3 Fitzroy Square, London W1

London Melbourne Sydney Auckland
Wellington Johannesburg and agencies
throughout the world

First published 1976

Printed and bound in the United States of America

ISBN 0 09 125750 6 (cased)
ISBN 0 09 125751 4 (paper)

Note the following abbreviations for journals are used in the reference lists and select bibliography:

A.J.S.   *American Journal of Sociology*
A.S.R.   *American Sociological Review*
B.J.S.   *British Journal of Sociology*
S.F.   *Social Forces*
S.P.   *Social Problems*
S.R.   *Sociological Review*

Contents

Part three Institutions   228

Percy Cohen, Race Relations as a Sociological Issue

A number of vexed questions such as those of race and intelligence, arouse strong feelings among students of race relations. However, there are some other matters which fall more clearly into the area of sociological discussion which, though they may arouse less intense feelings, are considered at least intellectually problematic. Four of these lie at the very heart of the sociological study of race. The first is the question of whether the various elements of what we call 'racial problems'—prejudice, intolerance, discrimination and antagonism—can be explained largely in terms of a theory of domination or stratification. The second concerns the part played in race relations by *ideas* about race. The third concerns the part played by other psychological states associated with racial consciousness. And the fourth concerns the importance which sociologists should attach to the facts of *racial* differences as such.

It will be noted, at the outset, that the whole area of the sociology of race relations is thought to exist by virtue of what are considered to be signs of potential or actual social antagonism between racial groups. This is, of course, a curious situation. For why should sociologists not ask why relationships are amicable unless they expect them not to be? Or, why indeed should sociologists bother to ask why relationships are not amicable? Why do they not take for granted that hostility sometimes exists, just as they so commonly take it for granted that it sometimes does not exist? Why, for that matter, do social scientists study the causes and characteristics of war but not those of peace? (The fact that 'war studies' are often described by the euphemism 'peace studies' deceives few social scientists.) The answer to all of this is very simple and should surprise no one—social scientists study things which disturb them and many, though not all, of the things which disturb them are those which are experienced by other men, as well as by themselves, as problems. They study industrial relations because industrial conflict which goes beyond a certain point is widely considered a problem; they study war because they share the view of many other people that it is a state of affairs that men could best do without but which they have, till now, been unable to do without; they study social inequality when some men no longer take it for granted that they must tolerate those features and consequences of it which they find undesirable. Of course, social scientists study not only those things which are considered social problems, but also those which are experienced as merely puzzling. But they need to be either puzzled or morally disturbed, or both, in order to be motivated to ask specific questions and to give answers to them. And most sociological questions which are rooted in social problems are no less intellectually challenging than are those which are merely considered puzzling. It is wise to acknowledge the routes of all our sociological enquiries—for at least that way we come to recognize what it is we are asking. Also, we are better enabled to provide answers which approximate best to the truth, regardless of their implications for our policies of social well-being.

One of the best known theories which purports to explain the phenomena of racial differentiation and antagonism in social life—and the latter is thus seen as following almost directly from the former—is that which attempts to account for them in terms of social stratification. The theory comes in a number of forms, the first of which might be called a simple, Marxian–type explanation. According to this theory, the problems of race relations arise when colonists employ a conquered people, either on their own soil or elsewhere, to exploit the resources which they have acquired through conquest or so-called discovery. In these circumstances a structure emerges in which the members of different racial groups constitute separate classes, a dominant class and a labouring class. Here, the freedom of the one group to exploit the other as fully as possible is facilitated by a clear demarcation of the boundaries around each group; and the most obvious line of demarcation is that of racial difference. This accounts for the exclusion of the lower-status racial group from almost all forms of social interaction with members of the dominant group.

   This is, of course, a gross simplification of this variant of the theory; however it will do as a starting point, for it is supported by facts which are quite unrelated to those of race relations. As is well-known, some of the characteristics of racialist societies are also to be found, at certain periods of history, in those class-stratified societies whose populations are homogeneous. In both types of society the superior class not only enjoys both economic and political power over the other, as well as higher prestige, but also possesses a culture which is distinguishable from that of the inferior class; in addition, the members of the superior class hold highly unfavourable, stereotypical views of their social inferiors, who are commonly thought of as dirty, lazy, morally lax and sexually unrestrained. Further, men of the dominant class will have sexual access to women of lower status—though they will not, as a rule, marry them. However, they will forbid any such access to their own women on the part of men of lower status and will certainly not countenance marriages between lower status men and higher status women.

   These parallels between racial and class stratification are meant to show that the so-called characteristics of racialism, since they can occur in racially homogeneous societies must, really, be the characteristics of social contempt which derive from certain forms of class domination. There is something to be said for this argument and the facts certainly do show that what are thought to be typically racial forms of social perception and practice do appear also in racially homogeneous societies. However, if one is to stretch one's conception of racialism to say that members of a lower class are treated, in certain circumstances, as though they were members of a different race, then one could argue that some forms of social stratification are a special case of a more general phenomenon which also includes racial stratification; indeed, one could account for the similarities by arguing that some forms of class stratification exemplify the same social processes as racialism. In short, on the strength of this evidence alone it is hardly more plausible to explain the facts of racialism in terms of social stratification than it is to explain some of the facts of social stratification—especially the stereotypes of social inferiors and the rules concerning sexual privilege—in terms of some of the elements which are to be found in racialism.

Another variant of the Marxian-type explanation of racialism and racism—using the former term to refer to a type of social structure, the latter to refer to a set of ideas about racial differences which are used to justify racialism—puts much greater emphasis on the historical significance of slavery. According to this theory, slavery, which involves the buying and selling of whole men, not just their labour power, leads to the treatment of those men as mere objects. This process of dehumanization results in the perception of slaves as lesser beings; however, since they are still dimly recognized as human they come to be classed as humans who are different in nature from their owners; and, insofar as they are racially different from their owners, their race is taken as a physical representation of their different and inferior nature. According to this theory true racialism and racism—that is, the emphasis on racial differences in maintaining social hierarchies and forms of domination and exploitation and the use of ideas about race to justify this emphasis—then spread from situations of slavery to other situations of colonialism. It is the image of the inferior slave which is then stamped on all men who are colonized. Of course, the extension of these practices, perceptions and beliefs functions to maintain a system of imperial or colonial domination within which the colonized can be exploited in a variety of forms.

A recent variant of this theory seeks to bring it up to date by arguing that, as a result of slavery and of colonialism, there is now a system of internal colonialism within certain capitalist societies in which members of racially inferior groups are treated as though they were not truly members of that society and can therefore be made to submit to practices of discrimination, exclusion and exploitation which no other members of that society could be expected, by its dominant sections, to tolerate. The blacks in the United

States, for example, are seen as an internal, colonial population, as are the blacks in the Republic of South Africa and of Rhodesia. The gist of this theory is not just that blacks in white-dominated societies occupy a lower social status or a particular class position just because this is a relic of past colonial history and/or of slavery, but that they continue to occupy this status in a society in which they are treated in the way in which a colonial power treats those indigenous or imported subjects who are prevented from enjoying the privileges of the colonizing classes who are their oppressors, exploiters and superiors. It is, of course, assumed in this argument, that there is an economic advantage to some of those who perpetuate the internal colonial status of men of other races.

The final version of the stratification theory of race explains the occurrence of racially structured societies simply in terms of conquest and domination and treats explanations which emphasize exploitation, and the specific historical significance of slavery in particular, as special instances of the more general theory. On this view it does not really matter whether the conquerors have anything much to gain by exploiting the conquered; for the fact of conquest itself will always result in racial stratification and, therefore, in discrimination and prejudice. The opportunities for exploitation will, of course, give rise to special forms of race relations which would otherwise not occur; but the non-existence of exploitation will not necessarily make for racial absorption or even for a kind of egalitarian pluralism. This theory can then explain the existence of a racialist society in Australia or in parts of Central and South America, where the aboriginal populations were not economically or otherwise exploited but were rather dispossessed and/or excluded from participation in the new economy; while it can also explain the forms of racialism to be found in East and Southern Africa, in North America and elsewhere, where exploitation did occur.

Proponents of this last theory—and even of the Marxian versions of the stratification theory—acknowledge the existence of the so-called plural societies, such as colonial Malaya, in which not all of the racial groups are clearly stratified in relation to one another; they would recognize that different racial or ethnic populations coexisted in rather separate cultural and institutional worlds, interacting only in the market place; but they would hold that such relationships, which are not themselves ones of racial dominance and submission, can exist only in societies in which some other racial group dominates all of the others. It is the dominance of the colonizing race which prevents any one of the other racial groups from attempting to dominate, or succeeding in dominating, any of the others.

In contrast to the stratification theories of race, there is the segmental theory. According to this it is the mere coexistence of potential rivalry between different racial groups which produces a racially antagonistic society; there is no need for stratification or any form of domination to promote this.

In short what is at work is the fundamental tendency of all racial groups to treat other such groups as strangers and to continue to do so. This is partly a consequence of and, in part, a condition of the existence of solidarity within such groups which cuts across any other division within them. Given this solidarity, given the tendency to exclude others, given the maintenance of identity and cohesion through endogamy and the confinement of a variety of forms of activity and interest within each racial group, there will be a jealous guarding of the interests of members of that group vis-à-vis other such groups. And, insofar as members of any one racial group are perceived as intruding into the domains of other such groups, racial conflict will occur; and the occurrence of such conflict will tend to strengthen the resolve of each group to discriminate against the other in whatever practices permit this.

We must now take a more critical look at these theories in the light of those factual and theoretical considerations which might have a bearing on them. The first theory, which almost, but not quite, reduces the social phenomena of race to those of stratification, does not fully answer the questions relating to race. For, if an exploited racial group happens to con-stitute a social class—as it may well do—then why is it necessary for that class to be additionally treated as an inferior racial group? The fact that it is so treated seems to suggest that there is something additionally racial in such structures of social relationship and that this additional element is not ac-counted for when simply reduced to an aspect of class. This point can be made most tellingly by considering what would happen if racial barriers to occu-pational mobility and educational opportunity were lifted in those societies, like those of Southern Africa, in which race and class membership overlap almost completely. In time some blacks would be employed on merit and there would be an expansion of the number of occupational positions higher up the salary and status scale, so that more and more blacks would come to be socially equal, in at least some respects, to whites. Later on, some blacks would come to occupy positions which are higher on the occupational scale than those occupied by some whites, while some of these blacks would them-selves become administrators and employers of blacks and of whites. All of this would mean that some blacks would displace some whites from positions previously reserved for whites and that some whites would have to acknow-ledge the superior status and power of some blacks. These changes are feared most by those whites whose welfare and status are protected by existing racial barriers, though they may also be feared by whites who do not, themselves, have much to lose as a result of them; hence, what all of this shows is that the vested interest which whites have in this system inheres less in the opportunity to exploit the labour of others than in the preference which these whites have for preserving higher social statuses for themselves or for other whites like themselves. Changes which would permit greater equality of opportunity for blacks would hardly threaten a system of capitalist exploitation of labour! On the whole, the true beneficiaries of racial discrimination are those lower status whites who would lose their claim to reserved statuses and occupations which they have in a system of racial oppression.

The final argument that is sometimes used to defend the stratification theory is that racial discrimination is supported, if not created, by a ruling class so as to discourage other members of its own racial group from rebelling against it. Even where this is the case it shows how powerful the racial element itself can be.

The 'slavery' theory of racialism does, in fact, go further in explaining the racial element as a phenomenon in itself. For it seeks to show how a particular form and process of social domination and exploitation results in the perception of men of a particular race as either less than human or as belonging to a distinctly inferior breed of men. Some support is given to this theory by the evidence of Arab history which seems to show that a more clear-cut view of black men as inferior developed among the Arabs after they had begun to enslave these men in Africa. Prior to this, men who were lighter than Arabs were viewed as no less inferior to them than those who were darker. After the Arabs had begun to enslave black men they treated them as distinctly inferior to themselves while they began to treat men lighter than themselves as more nearly their equals. But while this evidence may show that racialism and racism are intensified by slavery, it does not show that it is created by it. The fact that men tend more often than not to enslave those who are strangers, in preference to those who are considered part of their own moral community, indicates that strangeness, as such, contributes to the likelihood of enslavement. The availability of those who can be initially perceived as lesser breeds, acts as an incentive to engage in activities which can make use of the most extreme forms of dehumanized enslavement.

The general conquest theory lacks some of the strengths of the slavery theory in explaining the peculiarly modern form of racialism and racism but it also lacks some of its weaknesses in that it acknowledges that since the conquest is of one race over another the conquerors must be disposed to exclude the conquered from positions of power and prestige by virtue of their being members of a race which has succumbed to the invader.

The segmentary theory does acknowledge that racial strangeness is, itself, a factor in creating racially differentiated societies. What it does not explain is the common association between racial differentiation and some form of stratification. To do this requires a reformulation of one or more of these theories so that they can subsume some of the others. But before we can attempt that we must look at other matters which have a bearing on our task.

Much ink has been spilled in the debate over the role played by ideas about race. At the one extreme there has been the predictable attempt to explain everything in terms of ideas, while at the other there has been the equally predictable attempt to treat ideas about race as the product of a particular structure of race relations. It is, of course, almost unnecessary to add that there have been attempts to find an intermediate position.

The arguments have, in fact, been about different sets of ideas. The first debate concerns the relevance of religious ideas and is really about a specific set of cases. The question that it centres on is whether Catholicism has had a more benign influence on race relations than has Protestantism, and whether this explains what has been sometimes described as the non-racist nature of Brazil as contrasted with the racist nature of North America. The simplest version of this historical hypothesis asserts that Catholicism always treated all men as more or less immediately ready for conversion, while Protestantism, with its greater emphasis on an individual sense of salvation has not done so; therefore, in a Catholic country such as Brazil, the Church and its doctrines influenced the Portuguese colonizers into treating black slaves as the potential equals of white men, at least in the eyes of God. Another version of this hypothesis states that Catholics were less prone to feelings of guilt concerning their sexual liaisons with black slave women than were Protestant men, so that the former recognized their racially mixed offspring as their own, while the latter either did not do so or did so half-heartedly or secretly so as to avoid public censure for openly acknowledging those things of which almost everyone knew.

Whether or not social relations were influenced in this way by religious ideas and sentiments or whether they were more influenced by other factors, such as the nature of colonization—many Portuguese men came out to the colony of Brazil without wives and children, while the whites in the southern states of North America were local settlers who married local women—or by the nature of the plantation system, is a difficult question to settle. But there is no doubt that there were differences between the two societies and that some of these have persisted up to the present time. To begin with, Portuguese men did give some recognition to their mixed and illegitimate offspring. As a result, there was a tendency in Brazilian society to rank the offspring of mixed unions as less black than the offspring of unions between blacks, and as less white than the offspring of unions between whites. This has produced a graded racial hierarchy with pure whites at one end and pure blacks at the other; whereas, in North America all men who were not white were classed as coloured, since the illegitimate offspring of mixed unions were not, as a rule, differentiated from other coloured children.

Religious ideas may or may not have played a role in all of this. But the outcome of the debate should concern us only insofar as we wish to explain the differences between societies with respect to their social structures; it will not concern us in our assessment of why race constitutes a basis of social differentiation in racially heterogeneous societies. For Brazil has been and is, though to a lesser extent than before, a racialist society, though possibly in some respects, less racialist and certainly less racist than some parts of the United States have been—can a society be described as non-racialist in which social status is affected by the degree of blackness or whiteness which a man exhibits? It is certainly a society with a subtle form of racialism; but that hardly makes it non-racialist. It is also true that in Brazil other factors, like wealth, can militate against racial status: money, as they say, lightens. But one should note that money is thought not to eliminate one's racial origin only to make it more bearable.

American Indians in the United States *are* differentiated in terms of the *degree* of Indian or white 'blood' which they possess. Nowadays neither whites nor Indians simply differentiate between the one and the other but class some Indians as part-white and some whites as part-Indian. Such racial gradations are recognized in this Protestant society because white men could take Indian wives and therefore create legitimate offspring; so that later, all such mixed offspring, whether of unions that were originally legitimate or not, could be treated as neither purely Indian nor purely white. It is, therefore, true to say that Brazil could permit without legitimate unions what North America could permit only with such unions; and this difference is indicative of a different degree or form of racialism. But whether this difference can be attributed to religion is still debatable.

The second set of beliefs that is sometimes thought to have played an all-important role in creating and maintaining racialism are those biological ideas concerning racial differences which emerged in the nineteenth century. According to these doctrines, fundamental differences between men of different races are not just anatomical but also psychological; and these latter differences are as 'natural' or 'inborn'—or genetically inherited, as we would now say—as the former. These differences account not only for differences in mental capacity but also for differences in mental style. Those who stress the importance of these doctrines argue that prior to their formulation men did not necessarily treat so-called racial characteristics as immutable, while after their formulation and enjoyment of scientific legitimacy they did.

Opponents or critics of this view argue that such doctrines could not have influenced ordinary men in their dealings with men of other races, that they emerged after the establishment of racial domination and that they are to be treated as intellectual devices for justifying racial domination and exploitation. One does not have to accept this last judgment—that theories of racial difference were and still are nothing but racist ideologies—in order to reject the view that social structures based on racial differentiation have come about because of such ideas. There is a perfectly acceptable alternative view that such doctrines are scientific hypotheses which account for certain facts although they may be no better at accounting for these facts than other hypotheses which consider racial differences to be anatomical and, possibly, in some limited respects physiological but *not* psychological. This does not preclude the possibility that some men were motivated to accept these racial theories so as to justify racial domination; and this is not inconsistent with the view that these were *bona fide* scientific ideas. After all, there were certain facts to be explained and there were current ideas which strongly emphasized the importance of biological thinking; and these racial theories did account for the fact that racial differences did correlate with differences in levels of social development and cultural achievement as measured by social scientists at that time. It was not in the least bit far-fetched to explain the social and cultural 'backwardness' of certain societies in terms of their racial characteristics.

However, accepting that racial doctrines were not merely ideologies, though they were clearly false in the form in which they were proposed, it does not follow that they had very much to do with the establishment of racialism. First, they were only, at the outset, known to a small number of people. True they could have filtered down 'through the ranks', changing their form in the process. But there was really little need for this as many white men had already invented simple racist ideas 'on the spot'. Whether ordinary men used terms like 'race' or any other terms to refer to the same phenomena referred to by their intellectual betters, who had been influenced by biological thinking, was of little consequence. If men were looking for justifications for their treatment of their racial 'inferiors' they could have recourse to other sources which were, for them, probably more persuasive: white Protestants in the southern United States like their counterparts in Southern Africa needed only to refer to the Bible; and they had good reasons for paying no heed to evolutionary biology.

The ideas which undoubtedly do play a major part in encounters between men of different races are less the full-blown doctrines of the Church or of the scientific community than those simple ideas which ordinary men develop as an inherent part of the processes of social interaction. For, all social interaction involves, to a greater or lesser extent, and in one form or another, the generation of sets of expectations, categories and other mental constructions which enable the interacting parties to deal with the social world as more or less predictable; and when men of different races encounter one another they form certain typical ways of perceiving one another and develop certain tacit assumptions regarding one another's conduct. These mental constructions do, of course, change with growing experience of such encounters; but they also serve, at each stage, to give these encounters a form which is dependent upon the meanings which the participants to them come to share. Thus, to say that racial exclusion becomes part of the pattern of race relations is to refer not just to the physically observable facts of separateness but also to the sets of categories which serve to define boundaries around social units within which certain reserved activities occur. Since men do not, from the outset, engage in such encounters without certain social and cultural dispositions to perceive them in certain ways, it can be said that the outcomes of their encounters, especially when these became crystallized as particular forms of social structure, are a function of the course of inter-action and of the ideas which develop within them, and that these last are themselves influenced by those predispositions which precede the encounters themselves.

It is, clearly, extremely difficult to apprehend the nature of these pre-dispositions and of the ideas which inhere in processes of racial encounter. They can be inferred from what is observable and observed. But to infer sub-jective states from observable conduct renders such factors almost useless in explaining what has been observed. It is probably for this reason that social scientists and historians either attempt to avoid all reference to ideas or are content to refer to well formulated, recorded doctrines whose existence can be known independently of the process of social interaction. It is also not surprising that in most discussion of race relations the reference to ideas is almost always to those of the conquerers, since it is to them that social scientists have easiest access.

Theories of race relations which refer to other psychological characteristics and dispositions have, on the whole, been treated even less hospitably by sociologists than have those theories which emphasize every-day ideas. The main objection to them has been that such things as racial prejudice are learned in situations in which racial differentiation and its other social con-comitants occur; so that their existence is a product of the very things which they are often proposed to explain. There is a good deal of evidence to support this: witness, for example, the increasing intensity of racial hostility in the northern cities of the United States and the decreasing intensity of it in many parts of the South, despite the so-called 'ingrained prejudice' of southern whites.

The defence of those theories which give some importance to psychological processes can take several forms. The first is to concede that while some kinds of racial prejudice may be psychologically superficial and highly situational so that they may, therefore, disappear where there is a change in the social conditions which sustain them, other forms of prejudice may be far more deeply rooted in the personalities of those who carry them, and will, therefore, function so as to resist those social changes which reduce inequality between races while supporting other changes which might serve to maintain racial inequality. These deeper sources of prejudice would not only be learned earlier in life, but would be rooted in the unconscious in such a way as to give them great affective power. The inner representation of the other race would be part of a larger system of unconscious symbols relating to such things as loved and hated objects, hostile forces invading the body, vengeful fantasies of aggressive sexuality, and so on. In this way relations with members of other races could be partly governed by those unconscious forces which strengthen other motives which produce racial antagonism.

A different, and more plausible version of this theory, would argue not that the processes of early childhood experience somehow link together race with other elements of unconscious anxiety and aggression, but rather that the existence of particular kinds of racial differentiation and, especially, discrimination would *activate* unconscious anxiety and aggression or that they would provide a socially acceptable set of objects on which to project fantasies linked with these complex affects. The difficulty with the one version of the theory is that it presumes far too much about the way in which the inner representation of racial strangers in the unconscious coincides with the inner representation of other feared and hated objects. The weakness in the second, more plausible version, which makes no such assumptions, is that it must take as given a structure of race relations in which typical encounters between members of races will activate these unconscious processes. This means that the second version of the theory can not explain the actual structure of race relations, though it may well explain why, given such a structure, some other things are likely to occur: for example, that women of 'other' races will be sexually desirable but possibly treated with contempt for their possession of this characteristic; or, that men of other races will be seen as sexually threatening to women and, possibly, to men of one's own race. These aspects of racialist societies, which have been emphasized by psychoanalysts whose experience has been of white patients with racist feelings and fantasies, have also, more recently, been emphasized by black, radical and other writers who have, in turn, been influenced by Franz Fanon, himself a psychoanalyst from Martinique. The fact that blacks now concur in emphasizing the importance of these matters does not, in itself, mean that these theories are correct, nor even that they are relevant to the analysis of other aspects of race relations. But it is worth considering why some blacks should find these particular insights into the psychosexual aspects of race relations of such central importance. This is not a matter to be pursued here. One can only remark that there does seem to be some evidence to support the earlier psychoanalytic assertions that, at least in some conditions of racial antagonism and sexual domination, other unconscious anxieties and hostilities will play a part in influencing the forms which racial encounters take and in informing the imagery of racism.

In all of this discussion it should be remembered that there are some more tangible social processes with which to start. If urban whites in the cities of northern United States resent the intrusion of blacks, we need not immediately speculate about the psychosexual and other unconscious fantasies

which whites may have about black intrusion; we need only remember that
blacks are viewed as social and cultural inferiors whose presence reflects on
the social and cultural status of lower class whites who experience these newcomers as intruders.

Furthermore, if we are to inquire into the internal processes of the mind
and into the way in which they affect social interaction we should start with
those processes which seem most likely, in terms of our theories of human
behaviour, to be both socially standardized and causally significant in con-
tributing to social processes themselves. Thus, we can assume that people
who are stigmatized do, to some extent, internalize the image which others
have of them. We can then go on to ask how and whether this internalized
image affects conduct in varying circumstances. When perspectives of race
relations exclude the possibility of change in the real world, this self-depreciation may contribute to self-abasement; when such perspectives include the
possibility of change then an internal state of self-depreciation may produce
ambivalent motivations and ambiguous models of what is possible: the wish
to escape a despised status coupled with the fear of failure may produce the
reaction of outrage accompanied by a symbolic rejection of the depreciated
self. The function of this rejection is two fold: it does serve to counter the
collective sense of self-depreciation; and it proves a temporary substitute for
real change. Perhaps it is only by serving the second function that symbolic
rejection of self can, in the circumstances, serve the first: the function of the
outrage is to express the ambivalence and ambiguity which inhere in the perception of the world as it is.

One should not, of course, assume that these two factors—racial self-
perception and the circumstances with which it interacts—can be treated as
simply independent of one another; in reality the change in circumstances is
experienced also, in part, as a change in self-perception.

Of course there are limits to the internal change which can occur without
a large-scale change both in the perceptions which others have of one as
well as of their modes of conduct towards one. And these limits are, to some
extent, set by the degree of unchangeability of those characteristics that mark
one as racially recognizable. This is where physical characteristics of race
may demonstrate their importance, not least at the level of perception and
self-perception.

There are two principal views concerning the importance of racial characteristics in the study of race relations. One is that there is nothing particularly
distinctive about race as such, so that there is, therefore, no important difference between race relations and ethnic relations, or between racial identification and ethnicity. The proponents of this view argue that what matters is
that men recognize or claim to recognize differences in behaviour between
themselves and others. Because of the importance which is attached to

culture which informs and makes possible men's lives with one another, noticeable differences in culture will be emphasized in order to affirm the utility and symbolic value which that culture has for any collectivity or group. What counts then, is the tendency to demarcate one's own cultural boundaries and to identify with the members who conduct themselves within them. This leads to the treatment of cultural strangers as potential rivals in whatever spheres men compete for what is scarce. It is not assumed, on this view, that ethnic identity and the demarcation of cultural boundaries necessarily precede ethnic interaction; rather, it is assumed that there is a two-way process in which ethnic identity and cultural boundary-maintenance affect the potential for ethnic rivalry, while the latter reinforces ethnic identity. Further, it is assumed that both sets of processes are affected by the wider system in which they occur, and whose characteristics may be such as to strengthen or weaken the degree of ethnicity or to modify it. Nor is it assumed that race, as such, is completely irrelevant to the processes of cultural identification and ethnic interaction; it is assumed only that race will be used as a convenient sign for the recognition of ethnic identity, but that other such readily observable differences between ethnic groups could do just as well, and that even where these are not initially present or salient that they will emerge, in one way or another, if circumstances encourage this.

The opposing view is that race is not just another sign of ethnicity, but is something qualitatively different from other such signs, so much so that it may be used to emphasize cultural differences which scarcely exist, or even to create some which are non-existent. Those social scientists and historians who emphasize the distinction between ethnicity and racialism propose one or other of a number of historical or theoretical hypotheses to explain how race comes to assume the importance that it does have or is thought to have in social life. The first explanation attributes racial consciousness to certain peculiarities of Western civilization arguing that it, above all others, has embodied a colour consciousness in its linguistic and other symbols so that its bearers have been predisposed toward colour consciousness. For example, the forces of lightness are thought of as good, those of darkness as bad; whiteness is used to symbolize purity, blackness is used to represent evil; white is the colour for a bride to wear, black the colour for a mourner. It is assumed here that awareness of racial differences can be more or less equated with awareness of differences in skin colour; and the evidence in support of this is that the reference is always to men who are black, red, brown, yellow or just coloured, rather than to men who are broad-nosed, slant-eyed, curly-headed, hairy, or non-hairy.

A second, more general theory, which can take account of the existence of racial consciousness in a number of civilizations, asserts that darkness of skin activates infantile nocturnal fears and other unconscious mechanisms associated with them; while an associated theory suggests that even the slightest 'natural' darkness of skin colour arouses ambivalent feelings and fantasies concerning dirt.

According to another theory which puts the emphasis on differences in skin-colour, but which is non-specific with respect to the colours themselves, a man's skin is perceived as containing his body and, within it, the essence of his self, so that the character of his skin tells one something of that which it encloses, rather as the wrapping on a package may be thought to tell one something of the nature or quality of the things which it contains. This theory might explain why differences in skin-colour are assumed to signify differences in mental processes and forms of behaviour even when these last are not actually observed. It also suggests that where men react to the skin-colour of those of another race they assume that the real or imputed differences which lurk in the 'dog beneath the skin' are liable to erupt, perhaps when one is least expecting them to do so.

Finally, there is a theory which puts no emphasis on skin-colour at all but only, in more general terms, on visible racial differences. The burden of this theory is that men who are markedly different from one another in their observable physical characteristics are difficult to classify. On the one hand, their physical strangeness makes them somewhat non-human; however, on the other, their physical familiarity makes them human or near-human: consequently, their racial distinctiveness makes them cognitively anomalous. This does not, of itself, mean that they will be thought of as inferior. If their actions create a favourable impression, then their physical peculiarities are taken to signify their superiority or, at least, their worthiness; if their actions make an unfavourable impression, then their physical peculiarities are taken as signs of their inferiority or unworthiness. Putting it another way, one might say that men who are physically anomalous are perceived as either more than or less than fully human in terms of the categories of any one moral community.

Whatever the truth of these theories, it can safely be said that there is some evidence to support most of them. This, in itself, says very little, for supporting evidence can almost always be found for any theory. What none of these theories can explain is why the psychological tendencies to which they refer manifest themselves far more strongly in some sections of a society than in others, and in some sets of circumstances within a society than in others.

It is also safe to say that theories which emphasize racial differences receive some factual support, as do theories which make little or no distinction between racial and ethnic relations. One can show that ethnic groups which belong to the same race and, what is more important, which *treat* one another as members of the same race, can be no less antagonistic, discriminatory and exclusive in their relations with one another than groups which are 'recognized' as racially different from one another: witness the ethnic-regional antagonisms in newly-independent African and Asian societies and the religious-ethnic hostilities of Cyprus and Northern Ireland. (It should be remembered that the opposition between Northern Ireland Catholics and Protestants is no less ethnic than religious: Catholics identify themselves as Irish as much as Protestants identify themselves as British, just as Cypriot Greeks identify themselves as Greek no less than as Christian, while Turks identify themselves as Turkish no less than as Muslim.) Further, one can show that where cultural differences are small or even non-existent—such as those between middle-class black men and middle-class white men in the United States—race consciousness will still serve to separate the one group from the other.

Few of these issues in the study of race relations can be resolved within the framework of any one existing theory; what is needed is a reformulation of existing theories to provide a better explanation of the variety of facts.

It has become a theoretical commonplace in sociology to argue that social cohesion is strengthened by the existence of intersecting ties within any social group or collectivity. The underlying reasoning is that if the differences between groups or social sectors within a society do not coincide with one another—for example, if the ties of class pull against those of local community—then, assuming that one tie is not so powerful as to more than offset the effects of others, antagonisms between different groups or sectors will tend to remain within 'manageable' limits. What has been less considered in sociology is the corollary to this theory: that if the differences between sectors of a society coincide then the division between such sectors will be great. This, I suggest, provides us with a starting point for a theory of ethnic relations and, in turn, for a theory of race relations.

Consider the situation created by the coexistence of several ethnic groups or collectivities in the same society. The members of each group share, by definition, a common culture, and common characteristics which enable them to identify one another by such things as language or dialect, habits of dress, etc. The members tend to marry within their ethnic group: if most of them did not the group could not continue to have a distinct culture of group identity. In addition the members may share a common territory or at least live in particular neighbourhoods. In some societies the members of each group may have a single occupation or set of occupations from which other such groups are excluded. Let us now assume that there is little cause for competition between these groups since each lives a more or less autonomous life. In such circumstances ethnic relations will not necessarily be those of friendship—there may be little more than a formal cordiality between them—but they will also not be those of enmity. If the ethnic groups interact only in the marketplace and there is a division of labour between them, then the process of bargaining between them may be the sole source of conflict. What keeps the groups clearly separate from one another is that they are different in a number of respects.

Let us say, now, that the members of one group do invade the domain of another, or that the members of different groups compete with one another in a common domain, for example that of politics. In such circumstances, there is a strong likelihood that the conflicts of interest will be defined not simply as those between individuals, but as those between ethnic groups, especially where the members of a particular ethnic group share a common interest, or see themselves as having a common interest in opposing the interests of another such group. This process of conflict will have come about partly because distinct ethnic groups can be recognized by one another and partly because they have ceased to observe the limits of their own ethnic domains.

Clearly what makes such group solidarity and inter-group rivalry ethnic, rather than anything else, is the fact that each group possesses a distinct culture. In addition, what makes ethnic persistence possible is the confinement of marriage and procreation largely within the ethnic group. The key to ethnic preservation is the maintenance of an internal culture including the social controls which prohibit others from having marital access to one's women; hence inter-ethnic sexual exclusion comes to possess strong symbolic significance. Thus, each group will define its identity in terms of certain key cultural symbols and will define its limits in terms of the permissibility of sexual access; so that, in time, sexual exclusion and jealousy become part of a larger set of sentiments and ideas which inform ethnicity.

All of this assumes a segmental structure of ethnic relations and the absence of race. Let us now introduce the element of status inequality: this, in its mildest form, may constitute a ranking of ethnic groups, so that some enjoy higher prestige than others by virtue of their culture, length of residence or occupation; while in its most extreme form it may involve a combination of political domination, inequality of wealth and prestige and exploitation of the inferior group by their superiors in the control of labour and resources and in sexual relations. What the introduction of a greater or lesser degree of status inequality does is to add another dimension of difference which also, by its very nature, creates a conflict of interest in which the parties have unequal bargaining power. However, in addition to providing a further element or elements of difference between the groups, inequality also provides the means whereby it itself can be perpetuated.

Furthermore, something occurs at the psychological level which makes for yet another change. In all situations of ethnic differentiation there is some degree of mutual stereotyping containing unfavourable characterizations. However, in segmental structures it is unlikely that either party will internalize the image which the other has of it. In all situations of social ranking there is a tendency for the lower classes or status groups to internalize, to some extent, and in some forms, some of the negative images which superiors have of them; and where social ranking is associated with ethnic difference, the tendency is even stronger for a negative self-perception to be internalized by those of lower status.

We have then, three sets of changes which accompany the introduction of ranking to our model of ethnic differentiation and rivalry. First, there are new elements of difference between the ethnic groups in power, prestige and wealth. Each of these is a powerful behavioural and cognitive difference in itself. The second set of changes is that the possession of higher rank, especially when associated with greater political and economic power, enables the dominant ethnic group to use every means to perpetuate or even to increase the nature and scope of its privileged status, and to foster an image of self-depreciation among the lower status groups which also contributes to the maintenance of its own position by discouraging changes or opposition to it. The third set of changes is the process whereby some ethnic groups come to take for granted the valuation which is placed on them by others.

These characteristics and consequences of ethnic ranking, especially where its structure overlaps and is congruent with that of a class system, are, as we have noted earlier not altogether different from some kinds of class system which are not associated with ethnic ranking. And the reason for this should now be clear. For, in certain forms of class structure the cultural differences and social barriers between classes—the differences in internal culture and the prohibitions on exogamy—are very much the same as those between ethnic groups. If each class lives a life-style which is markedly different from that of the other, if the upper class perceives itself as a special and different breed of men, if social distance is not just a matter of prestige rankings but also of preservation of life-styles, one might say that there is something in such a class system very much akin to ethnic differentiation. Of course, this parallel is greater in some conditions of class stratification than in others. For one thing, there must be a clear line of demarcation between the life-styles of the classes and there must be little incentive to or possibility of legitimate unions across the lines of class. Naturally, no system of class does more than approximate to this set of conditions; but then few systems of ethnic ranking do more than approximate to it.

Introducing the element of race into our model—whether into a model of segmented ethnic relations or into one of ethnic stratification; and usually, it is the latter—adds a new element to the process whereby group differences are characterized. First, it introduces an additional difference; second, it introduces one which is associated with the natural rather than the cultural order of things. Whether or not Clause Lévi-Strauss is right in arguing that one of the fundamental tensions in all human cultural and social systems is that which inheres in defining the boundaries between the natural and the cultural orders and of establishing the relationship between them, it seems likely that all societies and social systems have some cognitive and other means for, at the very least, indicating an awareness of the importance of this division. When men of different races encounter one another and experience a possible ambiguity of recognition and an ambivalence of feeling concerning the full humanity of the other, then clearly an element is added which is qualitatively different. But to say that it is qualitatively different is not to say that the recognition makes for a more powerful drive towards antagonism than is produced by the recognition of cultural differences or than by the establishment of domination or status differences. Certainly, the addition of a new and, let us concede, qualitatively different element, adds force to the powers of antagonism and differentiation. But does it add more force than is added by other elements? If one believes that perceptions of natural difference arouse greater responses of differentiation and opposition, then clearly one must argue that racial difference is a quantum shift from ethnic difference. If one does not believe this, then one takes a more conservative view of the difference added. It really amounts, in any case, to a question of degree. For no one doubts that the degree of emphasis on racial difference which may activate the most powerful psychological responses will depend on a host of cultural and social factors which mould and channel such responses and even, to some extent, not only elicit but even create them.

Part one Sociological Perspectives

This opening section includes theoretical material exemplifying three distinctive approaches in sociology—those employing paradigms or perspectives of order, conflict and interaction.

The distinction between order and conflict perspectives within the field of race relations has figured prominently in a number of recent publications (Horton, 1966; Van den Berghe, 1967; Schermerhorn, Extract 7). The *order perspective* stresses an image of society as a natural boundary-maintaining system transcending man and acting to sustain existing institutions. Man himself is seen as a naturally hierarchical creature, a product of a socialization process by means of which society restrains him from disorderly behaviour. This perspective also entails a value system emphasizing stability, authority and order.

The history of this approach in modern sociology has its roots in the early work of Emile Durkheim (1933; 1938)*, and its development in recent times culminated in the social theories of Talcott Parsons, structural-functionalism and the so-called systems perspective (Parsons, 1951). Firmly rooted in the positivistic tradition, this kind of theory commits the sociologist to regarding the subject-matter of sociology as what Aaron Cicourel (1968) has called 'hard' data and what Durkheim called 'social facts', that is, observable social phenomena, external to the individual and susceptible to measurement. Exponents of this approach are likely to define problems in terms established by official agencies of social control and hence to regard certain forms of behaviour as pathological and disorderly. A research strategy modelled on that of the classical natural sciences is then adopted in an attempt to isolate the *causes* of the pathology. Implicit in this approach is the notion that, having isolated the *causes*, action may be taken to eliminate the problem by means of carefully directed social policies.

Those employing the *conflict perspective,* on the other hand, regard society as characterized by struggle between competing interest groups and prone to change through the creative activities and efforts of men. Man is seen as both coerced by impersonal external factors (especially economic

*Full references appear, throughout the text, at the end of the relevant extract or introduction.

factors) and yet able to redefine and restructure them by overcoming false beliefs about the true nature of his situation. The values implicit in such a model are autonomy, change, action and qualitative growth. This approach owes more to Karl Marx (1957) and Max Weber (1947), each of whom recognized that the struggle between interest groups was a fundamental feature of modern complex societies, although Marx gave it a more central place in his sociology than did Weber.

The conflict theorist defines his problem in different terms from the order theorist, regarding social order and disorder as largely a consequence of society's economic arrangements and the ideologies which legitimate them. Relevant 'hard' data would be that indicating the relative distribution of wealth, status and power between groups—what Marx called the economic substructure. But, in addition, due attention is given to the superstructure of ideas to which this substructure is seen as giving rise. This involves considering the historical process whereby such economic arrangements and world views have been generated and which, especially in capitalistic and bureaucratically organized societies, tend to alienate men from themselves and others. The elimination of alienation or the false consciousness which leads men to endure domination and exploitation lies in men acting together to gain greater control of their social, political and economic lives to ensure an equitable distribution of society's products and resources.

A third approach, closely related in some ways to the conflict perspective, is what may be called the *interactionist perspective*. Here the notion that sociology's subject-matter is some supposedly external and coercive structure of social norms or economic arrangments is rejected. Rather, the 'true' subject-matter of sociology is seen as the system of meanings with which human actors operate and by means of which they define social situations as 'real'. This approach stems more directly from Max Weber's later work (Weber, 1947) and more recently from the writings of George Herbert Mead (1934) and Alfred Schutz (1962).

The interactionist attempts to produce a 'value-free' definition of his problem, that is to say he is not primarily concerned with maintaining social order nor with imposing control upon his fellow men. Nor does he regard the alienation of man nor his exploitation in a capitalist or colonialist world as his prime concern. He is therefore not committed to *explaining* order and disorder in cause-effect terms. Rather, he sees his problem as that of revealing and *understanding* the systems of meanings and rules which are implicit in men's actions, whether or not regarded by others as orderly or disorderly. For him, data are any expression of such meanings (either linguistic or paralinguistic) and the key to sociological understanding is therefore the 'language' by means of which men transmit and receive them. Man on this view is existential man, creator and innovator whose existence has meaning only by virtue of his ability to construct and reconstruct his own social reality. Not that man exists in subjective isolation from all others, however, for the meanings with which he operates are socially given. One form which this approach has taken is symbolic interactionism (Manis and Meltzer, 1967), another is phenomenological sociology (Schutz, 1962). Ethnomethodology, a more recently developed alternative to positivistic sociology, attempts to develop the empirical possibilities implicit in phenomenological sociology (Garfinkel, 1967).

There have been several attempts to synthesize these various approaches. The classic attempt to reconcile order and action theories was that of Talcott Parsons (1937), but, as many of his critics have pointed out, Parsons gradually lost sight of the 'voluntaristic' character he originally assigned to social action in the course of developing a model of the social system in which the normative structure was seen as the major source of order and disorder (Scott, 1963). There have also been attempts to reconcile order and conflict perspectives among which Lewis Coser's *The Functions of Social Conflict* (1956) stands out. But if this attempt fails in the eyes of some critics, it is because it tends to focus only upon those forms of conflict which may be accommodated within the Parsonian scheme, and then demonstrating (paradoxically) how these contribute towards the *maintenance* of 'order'.

Perhaps less publicized have been efforts to synthesize conflict and action theories. One finds such an attempt in embryonic form in Berger and Luckmann's discussion (1967, Part 2) of the social world experienced as objective reality. Here Marxist and Schutzian notions are brought together in an analysis of the use to which 'conceptual machineries' designed to maintain a particular 'symbolic universe' are often put by competing interest groups. It seems unlikely that Marx would have disagreed with their conclusion that 'He who has the bigger stick has the better chance of imposing his definitions of reality' (p. 127).

Our selection of race relations theories attempts to reflect each of the mainstream theoretical positions discussed above. Not all are 'pure' examples of the three approaches outlined, nor do the syntheses exactly parallel those mentioned, but it is hoped that the preceding analysis will enable the reader to locate them within the wider realm of sociology. The inclusions from Robert Park, Gunnar Myrdal, and S. N. Eisenstadt, therefore, may be seen as illustrating applications of an order perspective to race and ethnic relations situations. Oliver Cromwell Cox exemplifies the conflict approach from an admittedly Marxist position and, although written in the mid-1940s, *Caste, Class and Race* can be regarded as a classic statement of that position. Alfred Schutz's paper, 'The Stranger', while not a fully articulated phenomenological theory of race relations, may be taken as a possible starting-point for such an account. R. A. Schermerhorn attempts to produce a synthesis between 'order' and 'conflict' theories, while John Rex incorporates both 'conflict' and 'interactionist' components into his analysis of racism.

Robert Park (Extract 1) was perhaps the first to produce a comprehensive and systematic theory of race relations from the standpoint of modern sociology. The key to locating him theoretically seems to lie in his contention that 'In the relations of races there is a cycle of events which tends everywhere to repeat itself...' and 'which takes the form...of contacts, competition, accommodation and eventual assimilation...' which 'is apparently progressive and irreversible'. Park, however, failed to take structural features (the relative distribution of wealth, status and power) into consideration in implying that the stage of competition would inevitably give way to the stage of accommodation.

Gunnar Myrdal (Extract 2), in his classic study of race relations in the United States, has also been criticized for failing to take account of such factors. His conclusion was that the American black–white situation was in effect a moral dilemma resulting from a conflict between the liberal American creed of egalitarianism and the unequal treatment of the Negro within a context of shared goals and norms, a conclusion which must have seemed extremely persuasive in the relatively quiescent American society of the mid-1940s when Myrdal's study was first published.

In his work on the absorption of immigrants in Israel, S. N. Eisenstadt (Extract 3) attempted an anatomy of the migration and absorption process which, like Park's race relations style, assumes the assimilation of one group by another as the ultimate outcome of racial and cultural contact. Once again the emphasis is on order and integration while the conflict of vested interests tends to be ignored. When he addresses himself to the migration–absorption process from the point of view of the individual immigrant, for example, it is seen in terms of his being required to learn new values and play new roles in order to adjust and participate.

In 1947, Franklin E. Frazier (1947, pp. 265–71), the distinguished black American sociologist, concluding an overview of U.S. research, argued the need for 'a dynamic sociological theory of race relations, which will discard all rationalizations of race prejudice and provide the orientation for the study of the constantly changing patterns of race relations in American life'. He noted the emergence of 'a new school of thought, utilizing the concept of caste and class...which has undertaken new studies in race relations...' and which 'has focussed attention upon the neglected phase of race relations —the structural aspects' (Frazier, 1947, pp. 41–2).

Perhaps the most explicit exposition of the new approach which Frazier had detected came from Oliver Cromwell Cox (Extract 4) who reformulated the American black–white problem in Marxist terms. On his analysis, 'the struggle has never been between all black and all white people—it is a political –class struggle'. However, fear of the prospect of violence had led even black scholars like W. E. B. Du Bois to refrain from seeing the situation as a clash of interests between capitalists and proletariat. Cox rejects the possibility of the emergence of a black Lenin and maintains, ironically enough, that 'A great leader of Negroes will almost certainly be a white man, but he will also be a leader of the white masses of this nation; and, of course, whether they are permitted to recognize him or not, he will eventually prove to be the emancipator of the poor whites of the South'. He concludes that 'The problem of racial exploitation...will most probably be settled as part of the world proletarian struggle for democracy; every advance by the masses will be an actual or potential advance for the coloured people. Whether the open threat of violence by the exploiting classes will be shortly joined will depend upon the unpredictable play and balance of forces in a world-wide struggle for power'.

Cox's classic statement of the Marxist perspective on race relations is neatly complemented by Andrew Asheron's (Extract 5) treatment of racial ideology in South Africa. Asheron is primarily concerned to challenge the reformist thesis of Horwitz and Macrae, summarized in Horwitz's terms as, 'Economic rationality urges the polity forward beyond its (racial) ideology'. Asheron rejects this view on the grounds that white supremicist ideology, reinforced by legislation and the socialization process, is now far too persistent for such an outcome to be possible. It is now an essential part of the white man's 'social definition of reality', a definition which can only be changed by a fundamental structural revolution and the overthrow of the capitalist system which South African racialism currently legitimates.

A new, and increasingly pervasive, variation on the 'conflict' perspective, is exemplified by Robert Blauner's (Extract 6) scholarly treatment of the 'Third World Movement' in the United States. He argues that, 'The orthodox Marxist criticism of capitalism...often obscures the significance of patterns of labor status,' and goes on to point out that, 'Since, by definition, capitalism is a system of wage slavery and the proletariat are "wage slaves", the various degrees of freedom within industry and among the working-class have not been given enough theoretical attention'. Blauner suggests that Max Weber's treatment of capitalism, by emphasizing the 'formally free' status of labour in a capitalist system enables us to highlight the contrasting status histories of those minorities incorporated into a society as a result of voluntary migration and those incorporated through conquest and slavery.

A subtle and persuasive attempt to reconcile order and conflict approaches to ethnic relations is made by R. A. Schermerhorn (Extract 7). Following a critical review of 'systems analysis' as expounded by Talcott Parsons and Marion J. Levy, and an equally critical analysis of 'conflict theory' as expounded by Gerhart Lenski and Ralf Dahrendorf, Schermerhorn takes the view that the two perspectives are inseparable, each entailing the other. Systems analysis applied to ethnic relations situations, he argues, focusses on the functions the ethnic group performs within the total structure of society and their fitting into that society by a process of gradual adaptation and adjustment whereby the dominant group's values and norms become internalized. Conflict theory, on the other hand, regards the ethnic group as an embattled minority, struggling for life, identity and prestige in a precarious and threatening world. But, he goes on, 'neither perspective can exclude the other without unwarranted dogmatism'. The argument is then illustrated by reference to European expansion from the fifteenth- to the nineteenth-centuries, the East German uprising of 1953, the colonial conquest of South Africa, and relations between the indigenous population and the Chinese community of Thailand. He then shows diagramatically how he conceives that conflict and integrative processes may be linked together. Emphasizing one process may be more fruitful in one situation than in another, and the relationship between the two will be dialectical in character. The Schermerhorn approach, of course, involves a positivistic view of the nature of social reality as something *external* and *coercive* rather than a construct which has its origins within the inter-subjective world of existential man, the view held by Alfred Schutz and the phenomenologists.

Schutz's paper, 'The Stranger' (Extract 8), looks at a specific type of situation, that in which a stranger approaches a group seeking admission to it, the outstanding example being that of the immigrant. The key to his approach is to be found in his conception of the 'cultural pattern of group life' (folkways, mores, laws, habits, customs, etiquette, fashions, values and systems of orientation). This, he argues, 'like any phenomenon of the social world, has a different aspect for the sociologist and for the man who acts and thinks within it'. The social scientist is the detached observer, observing, describing, classifying and ordering his observations according to established procedures and criteria. For the actor, however, the social world is experienced primarily as a field of actual or possible actions rather than as an object of his thinking. He organizes knowledge of his social world not in terms of a scientific system but in terms of its relevance to his actions. The approaching stranger does not share this system of relevances. He will, therefore, need to question what to the in-group seems unquestionable and trust to second-hand knowledge about the system when his immediate need is for first-hand experience of it. This will lead to a dislocation of his habitual system of relevance. Prior to any possible adjustment he will need to modify thoroughly his system of categories for interpreting the world and his recipes for acting within it. Although this paper limits itself to one confrontation situation between alternative systems of relevance the scheme of analysis could well be extended to a wide range of group and individual relationships, and while it does not attempt an account of the historical circumstances giving rise to such typical confrontations the approach need not necessarily preclude it.

The value of this approach is recognized by John Rex (Extract 9) who argues that 'The Schutzian perspective is especially important for us, in that we are concerned in the study of racism precisely with the role of ideas in everyday life'. He is particularly interested in the role which commonsense assumptions about the nature of the everyday world play in the perceptions of one group by another, and the ways in which racist perceptions may be intellectualized for respectability's sake or redefined by the positive efforts of militant minorities. He goes on to develop his account of racism by introducing notions from Marx and Pareto, each of which, he argues, emphasize part of the truth.

What we have in intergroup relations is a succession of the following elements (a) a process of conflict, competition or struggle for survival between groups, (b) psychological reactions of aggression and hostility on the part of members of one group against members of the other, (c) verbal expressions of this hostility asserting that the other group has undesirable qualities or demanding that in some way it should cease to exist.

The action perspective on race relations initiated by Schutz has not been developed by the school most committed to operationalizing his sociology, the ethnomethodologists. Perhaps Rex's analysis of racism will indicate the direction in which this kind of substantive research might proceed.

References

Banton, M. (1967), *Race Relations*, London.
Berger, P. and Luckman, T. (1967), *The Social Construction of Reality*, London.
Cicourel, A. (1968), *The Social Organisation of Juvenile Justice*, New York.
Coser, L. (1956), *The Functions of Social Conflict*, London.
Durkheim, E. (1933), *The Division of Labour in Society*, London.
Durkheim, E. (1938), *The Rules of Sociological Method*, Glencoe, Ill.
Frazier, E. F. (1947), 'Sociological theory and race relations', *A.S.R.*, vol. 12, no. 3.
Garfinkel, H. (1967), *Studies in Ethnomethodology*, Englewood Cliffs, N.J.
Horton, J. (1966), 'Order and conflict theories of social problems as competing ideologies', *A.J.S.*, vol. 71, pp. 701–13.
Manis, J. G. and Meltzer, B. N. (1967), *Symbolic Interaction*, Boston, Mass.
Marx, K. and Engels, F. (1957), *Manifesto of the Communist Party*, Foreign Languages Publishing House, Moscow.
Mead, G. H. (1934), *Mind, Self and Society*, Chicago.
Parsons, T. (1937), *The Structure of Social Action*, Glencoe, Ill.
Parsons, T. (1951), *The Social System*, London.
Schutz, A. (1962), *Collected Papers*, 3 vols., The Hague.
Scott, J. F. (1963), 'The changing foundations of the Parsonian Action Scheme', *A.S.R.*, vol. 28, pp. 716–35.
Van den Berghe, P. (1967), *Race and Racism*, New York.
Weber, M. (1947), *The Theory of Social and Economic Organization*, Glencoe, Ill.

1 *R. E. Park,* Race and Culture

The race relations cycle

The impression that emerges from this review of international and race relations is that the forces which have brought about the existing inter-penetration of peoples are so vast and irresistible that the resulting changes assume the character of a cosmic process. New means of communication enforce new contacts and result in new forms of competition and of conflict. But out of this confusion and ferment, new and more intimate forms of association arise.

The changes which are taking place on the Pacific Coast—'the last asylum', in the language of Professor Ross, 'of the native-born'—are part of the changes that are going on in every other part of the world. Everywhere there is competion and conflict; but everywhere the intimacies which participation in a common life enforces have created new accommodation, and relations which were merely formal or utilitarian have become personal and human.

In the relations of races there is a cycle of events which tends everywhere to repeat itself. Exploration invariably opens new regions for commercial exploitation; the missionary, as has frequently been said, becomes the advance agent of the trader. The exchange of commodities involves in the long run the competition of goods and of persons. The result is a new distribution of population and a new and wider division of labor.

The new economic organization, however, inevitably becomes the basis for a new political order. The relations of races and people are never for very long merely economic and utilitarian, and no efforts to conceive them in this way have ever been permanently successful. We have imported labor as if it were a mere commodity, and sometimes we have been disappointed to find, as we invariably do, that the laborers were human like ourselves. In this way it comes about that race relations which were economic become later political and cultural. The struggle for existence terminates in a struggle for status, for recognition, for position and prestige, within an existing political and moral order. Where such a political and moral order does not exist, war, which is the most elementary expression of political forces, creates one. For

R. E. Park, *Race and Culture*, The Free Press, 1950, pp. 150–1.

the ultimate effect of war has been, on the whole, to establish and extend law and order in regions where it did not previously exist.

The race relations cycle which takes the form, to state it abstractly, of contacts, competition, accommodation and eventual assimilation, is apparently progressive and irreversible. Customs regulations, immigration restrictions and racial barriers may slacken the tempo of the movement; may perhaps halt it altogether for a time; but cannot change its direction, cannot at any rate, reverse it.

In our estimates of race relations we have not reckoned with the effects of personal intercourse and the friendships that inevitably grow up out of them. These friendships, particularly in a democratic society like our own, cut across and eventually undermine all the barriers of racial segregation and caste by which races seek to maintain their integrity.

It was the intimate and personal relations which grew up between the Negro slave and his white master that undermined and weakened the system of slavery from within, long before it was attacked from without. Evidence of this was the steady increase, in spite of public opinion and legislation to the contrary, of the number of free Negroes and emancipated slaves in the South. Men who believed the black man fore-ordained to be the servant of the white were unwilling to leave the servants they knew to the mercy of the system when they were no longer able to protect them.

In spite of the bitter antagonism that once existed toward the Chinese, the attitude of the Pacific coast is now generally amiable, even indulgent; and this in spite of the nuisance of their tong wars and other racial eccentricities. The Chinese population is slowly declining in the United States, but San Francisco, at any rate, will miss its Chinese quarter when it goes.

There has never been the antagonism toward the Japanese in this country that there once was toward the Chinese. Even such antagonism as existed has always been qualified by a genuine admiration for the Japanese people as a whole. Now that the exclusion law seems finally to have put an end to Japanese immigration, there is already a disposition to relax the laws which made the permanent settlement of Orientals on the Pacific coast untenable.

It does not follow that because the tendencies to the assimilation and eventual amalgamation of races exist, they should not be resisted and, if possible, altogether inhibited. On the other hand, it is vain to underestimate the character and force of the tendencies that are drawing the races and peoples about the Pacific into the ever narrowing circle of a common life. Rising tides of color and oriental exclusion laws are merely incidental evidences of these diminishing distances.

In the Hawaiian Islands, where all the races of the Pacific meet and mingle on more liberal terms than they do elsewhere, the native races are disappearing and new peoples are coming into existence. Races and cultures die—it has always been so—but civilization lives on.

2 *Gunnar Myrdal,* An American Dilemma

The American Negro problem is a problem in the heart of the American. It is there that the inter-racial tension has its focus. It is there that the decisive struggle goes on. This is the central viewpoint of this treatise. Though our study includes economic, social, and political race relations, at bottom our problem is the moral dilemma of the American—the conflict between his moral valuations on various levels of consciousness and generality. The 'American Dilemma', referred to in the title of this book, is the ever-raging conflict between, on the one hand, the valuations preserved on the general plane which we shall call the 'American Creed', where the American thinks, talks, and acts under the influence of high national and Christian precepts, and, on the other hand, the valuations on specific planes of individual and group living, where personal and local interests; economic, social, and sexual jealousies; considerations of community prestige and conformity; group prejudice against particular persons or types of people; and all sorts of miscellaneous wants, impulses, and habits dominate his outlook. [...]

The Negro problem in America would be of a different nature, and, indeed, would be simpler to handle scientifically, if the moral conflict raged only between valuations held by different persons and groups of persons. The essence of the moral situation is, however, that the conflicting valuations are also held by the same person. *The moral struggle goes on within people and not only between them. As people's valuations are conflicting, behavior normally becomes a moral compromise. There are no homogeneous 'attitudes' behind human behavior but a mesh of struggling inclinations, interests, and ideals, some held conscious and some suppressed for long intervals but all active in bending behavior in their direction.*

The unity of a culture consists in the fact that all valuations are mutually shared in some degree. We shall find that even a poor and uneducated white person in some isolated and backward rural region in the Deep South, who is violently prejudiced against the Negro and intent upon depriving him of civic rights and human independence, has also a whole compartment in his

Gunnar Myrdal, *An American Dilemma,* Harper and Row, 1944, 1962, pp. lxxi–lxxiii, lxxiv–lxxv.

valuation sphere housing the entire American Creed of liberty, equality, justice, and fair opportunity for everybody. He is actually also a good Christian and honestly devoted to the ideals of human brotherhood and the Golden Rule. And these more general valuations—more general in the sense that they refer to all human beings—are, to some extent, effective in shaping his behavior. Indeed, it would be impossible to understand why the Negro does not fare worse in some regions of America if it were not constantly kept in mind that behavior is the outcome of a compromise between valuations, among which the equalitarian ideal is one. At the other end, there are few liberals, even in New England, who have not a well-furnished compartment of race prejudice, even if it is usually suppressed from conscious attention. Even the American Negroes share in this community of valuations: they have eagerly imbibed the American Creed and the revolutionary Christian teaching of common brotherhood; under closer study, they usually reveal also that they hold something of the majority prejudice against their own kind and its characteristics.

The intensities and proportions in which these conflicting valuations are present vary considerably from one American to another, and within the same individual, from one situation to another. The cultural unity of the nation consists, however, in the fact that *most Americans have most valuations in common* though they are arranged differently in the sphere of valuations of different individuals and groups and bear different intensity coefficients. This cultural unity is the indispensable basis for discussion between persons and groups. It is the floor upon which the democratic process goes on.

In America as everywhere else people agree, as an abstract proposition, that *the more general valuation—those which refer to man as such and not to any particular group or temporary situation—are morally higher*. These valuations are also given the sanction of religion and national legislation. They are incorporated into the American Creed. The other valuations—which refer to various smaller groups of mankind or to particular occasions—are commonly referred to as 'irrational' or 'prejudiced', sometimes even by people who express and stress them. They are defended in terms of tradition, expediency or utility.

Trying to defend their behavior to others, and primarily to themselves, people will attempt to conceal the conflict between their different valuations of what is desirable and undesirable, right or wrong, by keeping away some valuations from awareness and by focusing attention on others. For the same opportune purpose, *people will twist and mutilate their beliefs of how social reality actually is*. In our study we encounter whole systems of firmly entrenched popular beliefs concerning the Negro and his relations to the larger society, which are bluntly false and which can only be understood when we remember the opportunistic *ad hoc* purposes they serve. These 'popular theories', because of the rationalizing function they serve, are heavily loaded with emotions. But people also want to be rational. Scientific truth-seeking and education are slowly rectifying the beliefs and thereby also influencing the valuations. In a rationalistic civilization it is not only that the beliefs are shaped by the valuations, but also that the valuations depend upon the beliefs. [...]

When we thus choose to view the Negro problem as primarily a moral issue, we are in line with popular thinking. It is as a moral issue that this problem presents itself in the daily life of ordinary people; it is as a moral issue that they brood over it in their thoughtful moments. It is in terms of conflicting moral valuations that it is discussed in church and school, in the family circle, in the workshop, on the street corner, as well as in the press, over the radio, in trade union meetings, in the state legislatures, the Congress and the Supreme Court. The social scientist, in his effort to lay bare concealed truths and to become maximally useful in guiding practical and political action, is prudent when, in the approach to a problem, he sticks as closely as possible to the common man's ideas and formulations, even though he knows that further investigation will carry him into tracts uncharted in the popular consciousness. There is a pragmatic common sense in people's ideas about themselves and their worries, which we cannot afford to miss when we start out to explore social reality. Otherwise we are often too easily distracted by our learned arbitrariness and our pet theories, concepts, and hypotheses, not to mention our barbarous terminology, which we generally are tempted to mistake for something more than mere words. *Throughout this study we constantly take our starting point in the ordinary man's own ideas, doctrines, theories and mental constructs.*

In approaching the Negro problem as primarily a moral issue of conflicting valuations, it is not implied, of course, that ours is the prerogative of pronouncing on *a priori* grounds which values are 'right' and which are 'wrong'. In fact, such judgments are out of the realm of social science, and will not be attempted in this inquiry. Our investigation will naturally be an analysis of morals and not *in* morals. In so far as we make our own judgments of value, they will be based on explicitly stated value premises, selected from among those valuations actually observed as existing in the minds of the white and Negro Americans and tested as to their social and political relevance and significance. Our value judgments are thus derived and have no greater validity than the value premises postulated.

3 *S. N. Eisenstadt,* The Absorption of Immigrants

Characteristics of migration and immigrant absorption

In this extract we shall analyse some of the most important fundamental social and psychological characteristics of the process of migration and of absorption of immigrants, making the postulate that despite many specific differences between various migrations, some broad features are common to all of them, or at least to those of modern times, though these common features may vary in relative importance and in their method of interconnexion. We shall first outline these characteristics, and in subsequent chapters establish their common character by a consideration of various particular cases.

We define migration as the physical transition of an individual or a group from one society to another. This transition usually involves abandoning one social setting and entering another and different one. Keeping this definition in mind, we can ascertain the basic socio-psychological components of each stage or aspect of the migratory movement.

In every movement of the kind we can find three such stages. First, the motivation to migrate—the needs or dispositions which urge people to move from one place to another; second, the social structure of the actual migratory process, of the physical transition from the original society to a new one; third, the absorption of the immigrants within the social and cultural framework of the new society.

We assume that every migratory movement is motivated by the migrant's feeling of some kind of insecurity and inadequacy in his original social setting. The literature on migration, and such sources as the letters of immigrants, interviews, and the like, abound in indications that the migrant feels some kind of frustration, of inability to attain some level of aspiration in his original society, where he is unable to gratify all his expectations or to fulfil the role of his desire. This may be due to a variety of causes—over-population, the shrinkage of economic opportunities, the opening-up of new cultural

S. N. Eisenstadt, *The Absorption of Immigrants*, Routledge and Kegan Paul, 1954, pp. 1–10.

and economic horizons and channels of communication, political oppression, and so on; it is not our concern to enumerate these at this stage of our discussion. We shall not here inquire what are the conditions in which migration is found to be the best solution for this inadequacy, as compared with others, for example, rebellion. It is this feeling of frustration and inadequacy, whatever its cause, that motivates migration, and it is the existence of some objective opportunity that makes it possible to realize the aspiration to migrate. For this reason, immigrants also tend to develop certain definite expectations in regard to the role they will fulfil in their new country. The hope of resolving some of their frustrations in that country brings it within the scope of their social or perceptual field. These expectations may be more or less definite, and the images called up by the new country may differ widely as between one type of migrant and another, but some such expectation can usually be found among them all. These provide him with his initial and predisposing attitudes towards his new country, and serve as a background for more concrete expectations concerning the part he is to play there.

Although immigration involves complete physical transition from one society to another, this does not mean that the immigrant necessarily develops expectations concerning his future role in every separate sphere of the new society. In other words, the motive for migration is not necessarily a feeling of insecurity and inadequacy in every main sphere of social life. The immigrant, as has often been pointed out, may remain 'attached' to his original society and culture in various ways. This would mean that in some spheres there had been no overwhelming feeling of inadequacy and frustration. Thus, both the feeling of inadequacy and the consequent expectations in relation to the new society may be limited to certain aspects alone of the total social field of contact between individual and society. We may here distinguish four such main spheres from the point of view of the immigrant's motives and aspirations.[1] First, he may feel that his original society does not provide him with enough facilities for and possibilities of adaptation, i.e., that he cannot maintain a given level of physical existence or ensure his, or his family's, survival within it. Secondly, and even more frequently, his migration may be prompted by the feeling that certain goals, mainly instrumental in nature (e.g., economic or other satisfactions) cannot be attained within the institutional structure of his society of origin. Many modern European overseas migrations have been motivated by such feelings of inadequacy; hence the great emphasis placed by various theories of migration upon economic problems and factors.[2] Thirdly, the immigrant may feel that within the old society he cannot fully gratify his aspirations to solidarity, i.e., to complete mutual identification with other persons and with the society as a

[1] This distinction follows in a general way that of Parsons, Shils, and Bales (1953) in their work on systems of action and group-structure.

[2] See, for instance, Fromonte (1947, pp. 174 ff) and Reinhard (1950).

whole. Migration of political refugees and *émigrés* is strongly marked by this particular feeling of inadequacy. Fourthly, he may feel that his society of origin does not afford him the chance of attaining a worthwhile and sincere pattern of life, or of following out a progressive social theory, or at any rate does so only partially. The most outstanding examples of this are the migrations of the various Utopian groups which settled in the United States, Canada, and elsewhere. Perhaps the early Puritan migrations which established the American Colonies were also thus motivated.

The distinction here made between the various spheres of society may provide an important tool for an analysis of the processes of migration and absorption. The stability of any society depends on an optimum number of its members finding satisfaction and gratification in all four of these spheres in accordance with the society's institutional arrangements. Lack of gratification in any of them necessarily upsets social stability, and gives rise to various processes of social change. Such lack of gratification need not affect all these spheres; the feeling of inadequacy may be stronger in one than in another, and migration is not necessarily motivated by the existence of such a feeling in regard to all of them. The inadequacy may be limited to one alone, or at least may be felt most strongly in relation to one sphere, while in others there may still be a strong attachment to the old setting. Hence, the immigrant's initial attraction to his new country may be limited to a single sphere (e.g., the attainment of certain economic goals), without any disposition to the performance of new roles in other fields, such as that of family relations. Consequently his integration into the new society may, at any rate at first, be impeded by the limitation of his expectations to only one, or a few, aspects of the social life and not to all of them. The initial image he develops of the new country may be focused on one aspect alone, e.g., that of economic opportunity, while as regards other aspects it may still cling to the old setting.

Thus it is obvious that the analysis of the immigrant's motives for migration and his consequent 'image' of the new country is not of historical interest alone, but is also of crucial importance for understanding his initial attitudes and behaviour in his new setting. It is this initial motivation that constitutes the first stage of the process of social change inherent in any migration and in the absorption of the immigrants, and this first stage largely influences the subsequent stages inasmuch as it decides the immigrant's orientation and degree of readiness to accept change.

The second stage is usually what we may call the physical process of migration, the actual transplantation itself. This process, however, is not merely a physical one. It involves wide social changes, and is the first *actual* stage of the re-forming of the immigrant's social field. Like the first stage, it is not merely of historical interest, but entails some important analytical elements. Firstly, all such processes carry with them a shrinkage in the individual's field of social participation and in the extent of his group life. Through the migratory process, he detaches himself from many—sometimes most—of the social roles he had previously performed, and becomes limited to a relatively restricted field and group. Migration always takes place in comparatively small groups which are taken out of their total setting. These may be either already existing groups—families, bodies of neighbours, political fraternities, etc.—or new ones brought into being with a view to the migration. The nature of these groups—their composition, values, and roles —is closely connected with the initial motive for migration. Thus, if the principal motive was economic, they may be either existing families which maintain their old culture, or relatively uncoordinated, non-cohesive groups of young unmarried men and women, who hope to amass a fortune and then return home.[3] On the other hand, if the basic motive is to establish a new pattern of life, a new type of overall society, the migrants may develop special new groupings, various kinds of closely cohesive sects and *Bunde*, unlike any of the groups existing in the original society.

However these groups are composed [...] the migratory process always involves a narrowing of the sphere of social participation. This limitation is of a twofold character: on the one hand, many of the roles which the individual had performed within his old society he can perform no longer. His life is centred in one or several restricted primary membership groups, which by their very nature make it possible for him to perform but few roles. On the other hand, the various institutional channels of communication between these groups and the whole society are largely severed. The various reference groups of the old society towards which the individual and the small groups were oriented, the various leaders, elites, and wider formal or semi-formal associations with which they kept in contact and through which they were identified with the society—all these almost cease to exist. In their place emerge the various new images of the new country, along with the images of those aspects of the old country to which the migrant is still attached. However, these various images and orientations are at this stage very general. They are mere expectations of future roles and identifications, not real institutionalized roles, groups, or symbols of identification.

Thus, the process of migration entails not only a shrinkage in the number of roles and groups in which the immigrant is active, but also, and perhaps principally, some degree of 'desocialization' (Curle, 1947, p. 117), of shrinkage and transformation of his whole status-image and set of values. Throughout the process of migration, the immigrant is in one way or another changing his values. But he does not usually attain a coherent new set, because (*a*) he may as yet have no definite new values to co-ordinate consistently into a new

[3] This was the case in many of the Eastern European migrations to the United States.

hierarchy, and (*b*) whatever his values and their order and consistency may be, they are not so far related to any definite role or institutionalized behaviour They are only general indicators of overall expectations. Hence the migrant may be said to live through the process of migration in an unstructured, incompletely defined field, and cannot be sure how far his various aspirations and expectations can be realized. This, like any non-structured and incompletely defined situation, gives rise to some feeling of insecurity and anxiety, as the literature on migration amply illustrates.[4] The need to overcome this insecurity usually becomes closely connected with the initial wish to resolve the original inadequacy which led to migration, and is important in determining the immigrant's readiness to accept new roles and his initial behaviour in his new country. Thus, the process of social change inherent in most migrations ultimately involves not only the attainment of specific goals or patterns of cultural gratification, but also, and perhaps mainly, a resocialization of the individual, the re-forming of his entire status-image and set of values.

It is from this standpoint that the main features of the process of absorption can be understood. From the immigrant's point of view, this process may be seen as one of institutionalizing his role-expectations. This involves several different though closely connected phases. First, he has to acquire various skills, to learn to make use of various new mechanisms—language, technical opportunities, ecological orientation, etc.—without which he can hardly exist for long in his new setting. Secondly, he has to learn how to perform various new roles necessary in the new society. Thirdly, he has gradually to rebuild and re-form his idea of himself and his status-image by acquiring a new set of values, and testing it out in relation to the new roles available to and required of him. We now see how the term 're-socialization' is justified. This process of learning and re-formation of concepts is in some ways not unlike the basic process of an individual's socialization in any society. The immigrant, however, starts from an already given social basis, namely, from the groups, and their role-expectations, within which the migratory process took place.

The institutionalizing of roles can thus best be seen as a process of transformation of the immigrant's primary basic groups and fields of social relations—those groups which are the ground of his active participation in society. It is by the interweaving of these groups into the social structure of the receiving country that the immigrant's behaviour becomes institutionalized, i.e., that his expectations become both compatible with the roles defined in the new society and capable of being realized in it.

To analyze the process by which the immigrant's role is institutionalized,

---

[4] See, for instance, Thomas and Znaniecki (1927) and any of the numerous collections of immigrant letters, documents, etc.

we must first set out the main general criteria of the transformation of his primary groups. What elements of social action does this involve?

Its first and fundamental aspect is the development of group values and aspirations compatible with the values and roles of the absorbing society and capable of being realized within it. At the outset the primary groups of the immigrants usually carry with them their former general aspirations and values, and the extent to which these are changed to accord with the potentialities and definitions of the new society is an important index of the degree in which roles are institutionalized.

The internal change in the values and roles of the primary group is, however, not enough to secure their full adaptation to the new social structure. Side by side with it there must also take place the formation of new channels of communication with the wider society and of orientations towards the wider spheres of activities, and the extension of social participation beyond the primary group. The following seem the main criteria of such re-formation:

1. The extension of the solidarity of these groups to the new society by the development of identification with it, i.e., with its ultimate values and symbols, and of a feeling of belonging to, and actively participating in, the new society;
2. The *scope* of the institutional and associational activities of the immigrants, extending from their primary groups—participation in various associations (parties, etc.);
3. The extent to which the immigrants' behaviour within their primary groups is directed towards wider 'reference groups' in the social structure—such as class and status groups, professional standards, etc., and is accepted by these groups; and
4. the extent to which stable social relations develop with 'older' members of the social structure, leading to the establishment of new primary groups in common with them.

Only in so far as these various channels of communication between the immigrants' primary groups and the absorbing social structure develop and continue to function smoothly may the institutionalizing of the immigrants' behaviour be said to be achieved.

This extension of the social participation and orientation of immigrants beyond their small primary groups is not, however, a one-dimensional process. During the migration, these groups usually serve as the main bearers of the immigrants' social roles and values, and the various kinds of expectations existing within them may be somewhat undifferentiated. But once the migrants and their groups are settled in the new country, this becomes less true, and the immigrants seek the fulfilment of their expectations in different directions. Here the main differentiation usually accords with the four chief spheres or aspects of the social system and its principal institutional frameworks. The immigrants have to find in the new society the settings in which these various types of expectation can be realized. This calls for a widening of the fields of social participation, not only beyond the basic primary and membership groups, but also in the direction of greater variation between the respective fields of activities. It is here that the interlinking of the immigrants' basic motivation and role-expectation with the process of their absorption becomes strongly marked. It is the basic motivation that determines the initial direction of their expectations and of the extension of social relations within the receiving country.

Within this process of extension of social participation, special importance should be attached, as we have already said, to the establishment of channels of communication with the wider society. Foremost among such channels are the leaders, whether formal or informal, of various types, thrown up by the transformation of leadership in immigrant communities; new types of leaders emerge as a result of the impact of the new social setting. The making of contact between the immigrants and these leaders is one of the most important aspects of the institutionalizing of their behaviour. (See Eisenstadt, 1951, 1952.)

To summarize then—the process of absorption, from the point of view of the individual immigrant's behaviour, entails the learning of new roles, the transformation of primary group values, and the extension of participation beyond the primary group in the main spheres of the social system. Only in so far as these processes are successfully coped with are the immigrant's concept of himself and his status and his hierarchy of values re-formed into a coherent system, enabling him to become once more a fully-functioning member of society.

As is well known, however, this process is not always either smooth or successful. Our analysis has indicated only its general direction and scope, but not how it is actually realized in any given society. In order that we may analyse the more concrete processes, an additional aspect must be considered. The institutionalization of the immigrant's behaviour takes place not *in vacuo,* but within a given social structure. Within that structure certain expectations develop with regard to the immigrants, and certain demands are made on them. Just as they themselves have certain images of the new country, so has the new society, or some of its sectors, authorities, and so on, certain images of the immigrants, however vague, and certain definite expectations with regard to them. While the migration process is one of social change, the limits and possibilities of this change are to a great extent fixed by the absorbing social structures, at any rate during the initial stage. That the immigrants want to change in certain ways so as to attain certain goals within the new society is not enough; the problem is always how far within the new society these aspirations are capable of being realized. By this we mean (a) whether the roles opened up to the immigrants and the facilities offered to them for realizing these roles will be of a special kind (e.g., whether there will be a tendency to any deliberate segregation, monopolizing of power-positions by the old inhabitants, etc.); and (*b*) whether the absorbing social structure will be content merely with those changes to which the immigrants aspire; e.g., whether pressure will be put upon them to change some of the cultural habits they wish to retain. Only in very rare instances—some of which will be discussed in later chapters—are the immigrants' expectations and the demands of the absorbing social structure fully compatible from the beginning. In most cases there is some degree of incompatibility, and this may be of two interconnected kinds: (*a*) between role-expectations and role-demands in some given (institutional) sphere of the social structure (e.g., in the economic or political field); or (*b*) in the main directions of these expectations and demands, e.g., when the immigrants want to attain economic roles while the demands made on them are mainly in the political sphere. It is obviously under varying conditions in these respects that the immigrants' behaviour becomes institutionalized; hence, it is not necessarily a smooth and even process.

References

Curle, A. (1947), 'Transitional communities and social reconnection', *Human Relations*.

Eisenstadt, S. N. (1951), 'The place of elites and primary groups in the process of absorption of new immigrants', *A.J.S.*, November.

Eisenstadt, S. N. (1952), 'Communication processes among immigrants in Israel', *Public Opinion Quarterly*, Spring.

Fromonte, P. (1947), *Demographie économique*, Paris.

Parsons, Shils and Bales (1953), *Working Papers Towards a Theory of Action*, February.

Reinhard, M. (1950), *Histoire de la population mondiale*, Paris.

Thomas, W. and Znaniecki, T. (1927), *The Polish Peasants in Europe and America*, New York.

4 *Oliver Cromwell Cox,* Caste, Class and Race

Changing social status

It seems quite evident that the status of Negroes in the United States has changed considerably since 1865. It is exceedingly infrequent, however, that we are able to observe the immediate incidence of change. Sometimes it is difficult to determine whether the race is advancing toward a more favorable position within the larger society, for the apparent solution of some one of the innumerable race problems usually precipitates a multiplicity of them. Symptoms of the changing social status are many and divergent. However, any socially significant act or condition is an index of relative readjustment of racial position only in so far as it limits or enhances freedom of participation of Negroes in the general culture. Hence it is toward the fretting away of such limitations as segregation, intergroup etiquette and deferences, economic restrictions, intermarriage prohibitions, and political ostracism that Negroes continually address themselves.

A people may derive a conception of itself only by invidious comparisons of its cultural and physical attainments and attributes with those of other competitively related groups. When the frame of reference is the general American culture, however, Negroes cannot revert to a cultural history and mythology of such a character as would inspire a significant in-group sentiment of nativistic pride (cf. Herskovits, 1941). Thus the race is not oriented toward its past but toward its present capacity and 'right' to participate freely in the culture. The American Negro's past seems to be no longer a cause. The teachings of democracy, science, and Christianity evidently afford a more consistent basis for the group's achievement of a new conception of .itself than a knowledge of the past cultural contribution of the race to world civilization. Moreover, this is largely true because American Negroes have no social urge for nationalism. René Maunier has made a similar observation in his conclusion that American Negroes are influenced by an idea of progress, while the cultural aspirations of such peoples as the Chinese, Hindus, and North African whites tend to regress toward earlier civilizations.[1]

[1] 'Among Negroes of the United States it is the idea of advancement which actuates them today. While among the Chinese and even among the whites of Africa, among the Arabs

Oliver Cromwell Cox, *Caste, Class and Race*, Doubleday, 1943, pp. 567–83.

At the basis of assimilation is the social phenomenon of persons attaining new conceptions of themselves. A people's conception of itself is a social force which constantly seeks expression, and it may be extinguished only after considerable struggle with opposing ideas. Even after this it may unexpectedly return to life, especially among those who possess a written history. 'The role of the controlling ideas, says Gustave le Bon (1917, p. 324), 'has always been so significant that peoples have never been able to change them without changing also the whole course of their history. And if in our day some benevolent divinity wanted to transform Europe, he would have only to modify the conceptions which orient certain peoples.'

Before any real increment of status advancement can be attained, therefore, the group must be able to conceive of itself as meriting it. Accommodation may be so nearly complete that even slaves may rest contented with their status. There is probably a grain of truth in Edward B. Reuter's (1915, p. 105) statement: 'Slavery did not rest upon force except in the early stages of the institution. . . . The forces that controlled the slaves were within the slaves themselves'.[2] The white masters, of course, were, in a sense, also resigned to their own position. In fact, to this day there is a degree of naïve adjustment of superordination and subordination between the races in the South. The situation, however, is extremely unstable. Both groups are constantly preoccupied with it.

An advance in social status of a subordinate group involves a concession to it, the result of which is a reciprocal redefinition of intergroup position. This concession to status may be voluntary or involuntary, but it is always an admission that the 'distanced' group merits the right to be included further in the 'we' feeling of the dominant group. In the United States, Negroes strive constantly to obtain these admissions.

A people without a culture peculiar to itself, but having only a truncated pattern of the general culture within which it lives, might be expected to rely upon decisions of the privileged group for estimates of its own achievements. In most parts of the South, therefore, the Negro leader is one who is 'liked' by white people; and the first Negro to go beyond some barrier of the status quo almost invariably has prestige within his group. He is a symbol presaging the group's formation of a new conception of itself; he has attained recognition among those having access to the vertex of the culture; he has wrested a voluntary or involuntary concession leading to wider cultural participation for his group.

---

and the Berbers, it is the idea of regress and not the idea of progress that determines their behavior. It is an aspiration toward the past, a desire to go backwards, a need for restoration and reconstruction. . . . These attitudes are especially striking in the teachings of Gandhi. We should differentiate, then, between the black and the yellow movement'. Maunier (1932), pp. 77–8.

[2] For an elaborate discussion of continuing unrest among slaves in the United States see Herbert Aptheker (1943).

Although comparatively isolated achievements of Negroes may result in some form of redefinition of group position, the situation which produces the more radical changes is success in direct competition, rivalry, or conflict. For this reason, especially in the South, some whites have found it necessary to prohibit any situation involving a direct matching of abilities between the races. At any rate, the process of assimilation involves a psychological narrowing of intergroup estimations of themselves. Hence, of major significance to a true advance in status for Negroes is a conscious realization on their part that they have an unquestionable right to some immediate social position.

Negroes in the North

It may seem paradoxical that Negroes suffer less from race prejudice and discrimination in the North where capitalism is farther advanced. A friendly critic of the writer put the question thus: 'Why does anti-Negro, anti-Semitic, anti-alien activity not attain quite the same ferocity in the highly industrialized North, with its need for an "exploitable labor force," as in the South?' The answer is, apparently, not far to seek. In the North the proletariat is farther advanced than it is in the South. In fact, we may think of advanced capitalism as a state in which the proletariat has attained some considerable degree of power. In other words, the farther the progress of capitalism, the greater the relative power of the proletariat.

In the North democracy, the proletarian system of government, is much more developed than in the South, where the white and the black proletariat has been consistently suppressed. The first great aim of the proletariat in all countries has been the capture of the ballot. In the North the workers now have the ballot, but in the South it is still limited among whites and virtually denied to Negroes. It must be obvious that if the common people, regardless of color, were as free to vote in Mississippi as they are, say, in Illinois, Mississippi could never be the hotbed of racial antagonism that it is.[3]

Industrialization creates the need for an exploitable labor force, but it is in this very need that the power of the proletariat finally resides. The factory organization not only provides the basis for worker organization but also facilitates the development of a consciousness of class power and indispensability. Social equality is not an aspiration unique among Negroes; it has been an explicit objective of the whole proletariat, regardless of color or

[3] Stetson Kennedy (1946, p. 66) puts it in this way: '... short of another civil war, the southern Negro must be emancipated economically and politically before he can be emancipated socially. This means that he must first join democratic unions and beat a democratic path to the polls. Once these two things have been accomplished—gains in one will facilitate gains in the other—the abolition of Jim Crow will be as inevitable as was the abolition of chattel slavery after civil war broke out. Once the economic and political functions of Jim Crow have been negated, its social function will vanish as the subterfuge that it is'.

country, almost from the dawn of industrial capitalism. Therefore, as the stronger white proletariat advanced toward this end in the North, Negroes have advanced also. In the South the white proletariat is weak and Negroes, almost totally proletarian,—that is to say, propertyless wage workers with a very small upper crust holding relatively insignificant productive property precariously—are weaker still. To the extent that democracy is achieved, to that extent also the power of the ruling class to exploit through race prejudice is limited.[4]

Negroes' approach to the problem

Because the racial system in the United States is determined largely by the interests of a powerful political class, no spectacular advance in status of Negroes could be expected. This, of course, might happen if the Southern oligarchy were liquidated in revolution. Revolution, however, cannot be initiated by Negroes. If it comes at all, it will be under the aegis of the democratic forces of the nation. Basically, therefore, Negroes as a whole are not radical. They tend to be conservative and forgiving, though not resigned. Their policy is that of whittling away at every point the social advantages of the whites. By continual advances, no matter how small, the Negro hopes to achieve his status of complete equality as an American citizen.

With the exception of the power philosophy of Marcus Garvey, the racial rationale of Negroes is based upon Western ideas of right and justice. Considerable reliance is put upon simple logic in exposing the inconsistencies of race prejudice. Consider, for instance, the following few sentences by Kelly Miller (1918, pp. 72–3):

They sometimes tell us that America is a white man's country. The statement is understandable in the light of the fact that the white race constitutes nine-tenths of its population and exerts the controlling influence over the various forms of material and substantial wealth and power. But this land belongs to the Negro as much as to any other, not only because he has helped to redeem it from the wilderness by the energy of his arm, but also because he has bathed it in his blood, watered it with his tears, and hallowed it with the yearnings of his soul.

Two principal ideas of racial policy seem to divide the allegiance of Negroes, the one that 'Negroes should stick together' and the other that 'Negroes should shift for themselves individually, since the individual can

---

[4] On this point Gunnar Myrdal (1944, p. 73) makes a pertinent observation: 'The South, compared to the other regions of America, has least economic security, the lowest educational level, and is most conservative. The South's conservatism is manifested not only with respect to the Negro problem but also with respect to all other important problems of the last decades—woman suffrage, trade unions, labor legislation, social security reforms, civil liberties—and with respect to broad philosophical matters, such as the character of religious beliefs and practices. . . . There are relatively few liberals in the South and no radicals'.

advance more easily than the group as a whole'. In reality, however, these two plans of action are correlated. The first is a necessity, the second an aspiration. Negroes 'stick together' when, in attempting to act as individuals, they are rebuffed or disadvantaged. Nevertheless, there is a continuing ideal that they should be free to act on their individual merits. As social pressure about them is relieved, they automatically become individualists. Negro leaders who do not perceive the latter aspiration and advocate solidarity as an ideal readily lose favor among Negroes.

The problem of Negro leadership

One of the most persistent laments among Negroes in the United States is that the race has no great leader. There is a sort of vague expectation that someday he will arise. But Negroes will not have a 'great leader' because, in reality, they do not want him. The destiny of Negroes is cultural and biological integration and fusion with the larger American society. Opposition by the latter society is generally directed against this aspiration of Negroes. Therefore, a great leader, whose function must be to bring about solidarity among Negroes, will facilitate the purpose of the opposition. The old-fashioned great leader of the post-slavery period, the almost unreserved appeaser of the Southern aristocracy, is gone forever. To develop a powerful leader Negroes must retract themselves, as it were, from their immediate business of achieving assimilation, and look to him for some promised land or some telling counterblow upon their detractors. At present, however, the most that the race can hope for is many small torchbearers showing the way upon innumerable fronts.

These leaders cannot give Negroes a 'fighting' cause. None can be a Moses, George Washington, or Toussaint L'Ouverture; he cannot even be a Mohandas Gandhi[5]—a Lenin will have to be a white man. The task of leaders of the race is far more delicate. They must be specialists in the art of antagonistic co-operation. Their success rests finally in their ability to maintain peace and friendship with whites; yet they must seem aggressive

---

[5] In commenting upon the wonderful power which Gandhi wields in India, the noted Negro publicist, George S. Schuyler (1943), inquires despairingly: 'Can the American Negro use soul force to win his battle for equal rights? Have we any leader who is ready to starve himself to death that freedom may live? Or to be beaten or shot for his convictions?' The answer is evidently yes; there are probably hundreds who will be ready to do so, if only for the glory of it. But, alas, even glory is not available to such a martyr. Unlike the East Indians, Negroes will not achieve their liberty through these methods. Leaders are in large measure produced by their followers; therefore, the question may be put thus: 'Will American Negroes arise solidly in revolt behind a Negro holy man starving to death, say, for the purpose of having the modern black codes abrogated in the South? Or will they be aroused in a body to take action against American whites because a Negro offers himself to be shot in the interest of the race?' By putting the query in this way the answer becomes obvious. Surely the Negroes might make Father Divine a universal symbol if such a prospect would not make their cause seem ridiculous.

and uncompromising in their struggle for the rights of Negroes. They dare not identify all whites as the enemy, for then they will themselves be driven together into a hostile camp.

This tentative nature of Negro solidarity presents a particularly baffling problem for the Negro leader. He must be a friend of the enemy. He must be a champion of the cause of Negroes, yet not so aggressive as to incur the consummate ill will of whites. He knows that he cannot be a leader of his people if he is completely rejected by whites; hence no small part of his function is engaged in understanding the subtleties of reaction to the manipulations of the whites of his community.

No contemporary Negro leader of major significance, then, can be totally void of at least a modicum of the spirit of 'Uncle Tom'; ingratiation, compromise, and appeasement must be his specialties. Hence, 'a great leader,' who might with one blow realize the racial dreams of Negroes, will never appear; he is destined to remain a fantasy of Negroes. Booker T. Washington symbolizes the old Southern Negro leader. He was placed between a victorious counter-revolutionary South and an apathetic North; he could not help compromising. At least the alternative of compromise must have been an unproductive, unexpressed, sullen hate. [6] Those Negro leaders who advocate Negro solidarity for purposes of nationalistic aggression will be short-lived. Indeed, in the South, the Negro who addresses his attack directly to the status quo may be feared by Negroes and marked by whites.

Probably this technique of alternate smiling and sulking will never be sufficient to reduce the obdurate racial antagonism of whites in the South. Yet it is certain that open hostility on the part of Negroes alone will not accomplish the latter end. If there is to be an overthrow of the system, it will be achieved by way of a political-class struggle, with Negroes as an ally of white democratic forces of the nation. It will not come by way of an open interracial matching of power. As a matter of fact, the struggle has never been between all black and all white people—it is a political-class struggle.

But just at this point Negro leadership seems to be weakest. Today very few of those who have the ear of the public appear to appreciate the significance of the modern political-class movement. Some, like W. E. B. Du Bois (1941), are frightened by the prospects of violence.[7] Others, like George S. Schuyler, think, as the ruling class would have them, that communism and

---

[6] Yet it should be remembered that Washington was completely void of any sense of a social mission in the common people; he stands out as the ideal Negro bourgeois, who apparently miscalculated the implacable purpose of the white ruling class in the South to keep the whole race proletarianized. He believed that Negroes, by their sweat, upon the soil especially, could unobservedly slip off their yoke of exploitation to become companion exploiters with the white oligarchy. In this, to be sure, he underestimated the intelligence of the ruling class.

[7] This citation also shows the extent to which intelligent Negroes have absorbed the comic anti-proletarian propaganda of the ruling class. See however Du Bois (1944) where the author takes a more serious attitude toward the potentialities of socialism.

fascism are bedfellows; therefore, they declare that good Negroes should have nothing to do with either. And still others, like most of the college presidents and bishops, believe that it is safer not to talk about 'isms' at all. Of course, that small group, *le petite bourgeoisie noire,* the successful Negro businessman, cannot be expected to harbor proletarian ideas. In so far as we know, none of the leading newspapers seems to realize even remotely the significance of the social movement for the future welfare of Negroes.

And yet Negroes as a whole are not anti-communist; they are indeed more decidedly potentially communists than whites. At present they seem to sense some deep meaning and value in the movement, but under the tremendous weight of anti-communist propaganda they tend to remain somewhat bewildered. Then, too, they cannot be expected to take the initiative in this movement. Probably most of them would express some such basic sympathy as the following by Congressman Adam Clayton Powell, Jr: 'Today there is no group in America including the Christian church that practices racial brotherhood one tenth as much as the Communist Party'. Indeed, in New York, communism among Negroes has made some tangible headway; they have recently elected a Negro communist to the city council of Manhattan.

The problem of white leadership

The problem of extending democracy to Negroes in the South involves one of the most frightful prospects in American social life. The Southern oligarchy has set its jaws against any such plan, which necessarily holds for them revolutionary economic consequences. The prospects are frightful because, like a true political class, the rulers of the South are prepared to hold their position even at a high cost in blood. Confronted with this terrible decision the minority of liberal whites in the South are easily overwhelmed. Here too, therefore, as in the case of the white common people, democracy involves a conquest of the bourgeois oligarchy.

To be sure, at a certain cost the articulate leaders in this region can be overthrown. Without them the masses will soon reach a satisfactory way of living, consistent with democratic principles. Modern democracy is something to be won; it has always been *withheld* by some ruling class. We should miss an understanding of the political-class interest in the racial situation of the South if we were to think as some writers (e.g. Embree, 1931, p. 201) that:

Underlying all is the great need of every man, however humble and stupid, to feel that there is some one or some group still lower than he is. Thus only can the craving for a sense of superiority be fed. In the case of the Negro, it is notoriously the poor whites who are bitterest, who most tenaciously hold to the doctrine that he must be kept down at any cost either to himself or to the community.

This kind of reasoning is common, and it has the significant—though frequently unintended—function of exculpating the Southern ruling class. But clearly, we could never explain the social order in the South by resorting to some socio-psychological constant in human nature. That which is assumed to be common to all human behavior cannot explain behavior variations; therefore, 'the craving for a sense of superiority' tells no crucial story. The attitude of the poor whites is rather more an effect than a cause. 'The Poor White, in his occasional expressions of race antagonism, acts for those Whites who tacitly condone and overtly deplore such behavior'.[8] We may take it as axiomatic that never in all the history of the world have poor people set and maintained the dominant social policy in a society.

The Civil War was a war between two dominant political classes; it resulted in a partial limitation of the scheme of life of the Southern aristocracy, yet it neither extirpated nor defeated the essential purpose of this class. The South is still very much aristocratic and fascist. 'The present white aristocratic party in the South is defending itself exactly after the manner of all aristocracies.... Having control of the government it has entrenched itself with laws.'[9] From her recent study of a Southern community Hortense Powdermaker (1939, p. 26) refers to the aristocracy as follows:

This class and the old South are inseparable, and both play an enormous part in sanctioning the beliefs by which the middle class today guides and justified its course. The superiority of the white man is the counterpart of Negro inferiority. And the aristocrat is a superior white *par excellence*, for his own qualities and because he is associated with the glory of the old days when the South was not at a disadvantage.

The present Southern aristocracy is not that natural aristocracy among men, 'the most precious gift of nature,' of which Thomas Jefferson spoke. Rather it is represented by such classic expounders of conservative, nationalistic, social philosophy in the South as Governor James K. Vardaman and Senator Theodore G. Bilbo of Mississippi, Senator Jeff Davis of Arkansas,

---

[8] Powdermaker (1939, pp. 334–5). The makers of the laws of the South ingeniously set the stage for the encouragement and perpetuation of racial antagonism. 'If there were more real contact between [poor whites and Negroes] some of the fierce hatred might be drained off, or even converted into fellow-feeling based on the similarity of their positions as agricultural workers struggling against great disadvantages.' ibid., p. 29. In these dichotomized racial situations the poor whites are always a danger to the position of the ruling class. Says Brookes: 'The economic pressure to which the Bantu has been increasingly subjected since 1924 arises principally from solicitude for the class known as "Poor Whites." The solicitude is the result ... of a feeling on the part of nationalist thinkers that the Poor Whites represent a submerged part of the South African nation. Bantu encroachment is to be resisted, not only because the Poor White may starve, but also because he may, under pressure of living conditions, betray his colour and mix his blood with the members of the Bantu proletariat. ... A great part of the driving force which leads parties and governments to restrict fields of employment for the Bantu in favour of the Poor Whites is nationalism.' Brookes (1934, pp. 28–9).

[9] Baker (1908, p. 245). See also Skaggs (1924, p. 20, 58).

Governors Hoke Smith and Eugene Talmadge of Georgia, and Senators B. R. Tillman and Ellison D. (Cotton Ed) Smith of South Carolina.

This is the same ruling class that has condoned lynching, disfranchised most Negroes, kept the Negroes confined to work as share-croppers, laborers, and domestics, retained the racial pollution laws, and used the newspapers, radio and school books to mould the minds of the white masses against equality of Negroes (Schuyler, 1942).

The 'aristocrats' maintained their power not only by their exploitation of Negroes but also by their exploitation of poor whites, who are artfully played against colored people.

It should be emphasized that the guardians of the economic and social order in the South are not poor whites; indeed, it is sheer nonsense to think that the poor whites are the perpetuators of the social system in the South. The fierce filibustering in the national Congress against the passage of an anti-lynching bill, or against the abolition of the poll tax; the hurried conferences of governors to devise means of emasculating a Supreme Court decision for equal educational opportunities; the meeting of attorneys general for the purpose of sidetracking an anti-Jim Crow decision for railroads; the attitude of Southern judges toward Negroes in courtrooms—these are obviously the real controlling factors in the Southern order.[10] The poor whites are not only incapable but evidently also have no immediate interest in the doing of such things.

Moreover, in the very amiability which upper-class whites sometimes seem to have for Negroes lies a most powerful attitude of social distance. It is a condescending, patronizing attitude, which is the complete expression of racial superiority and prejudice. This attitude is hardly available to poor whites. The Southern 'aristocracy,' as the modern capitalist ruling class of this area ·is sometimes called, could not endure without the hatred which it perpetuates among the white and black masses, and it is by no means unmindful of that fact. No single social problem, whether of war or of peace, is as important to the Southern aristocracy as that of keeping the Negro in his place.[11]

[10] On almost any day we may clip such declarations as the following from newspapers in the South: 'If the Supreme Court of the United States rules that Negroes must be admitted [to the Democratic primaries of Texas]' says W. S. Bramlett (1943) Dallas County Democratic Chairman, 'I will contribute all my experience as a lawyer and as a Democrat to nullify the ruling; and I believe most county and state party leaders will feel the same way'.

[11] It is questionable whether such off-color statements as the following by Wirth (1944, p. 305) contribute to our understanding of race relations: 'In a period of war we realize more clearly than ever . . . that racial, religious, and other prejudices constitute a danger to our national unity and it begins to dawn upon us that, however deep-seated our own internal conflicts may have been, they are as nothing compared with the conflicts between us and our enemies.' The textbooks put the latter idea in this way: The greater the intensity of conflict between two groups, the greater the internal solidarity of each. But Wirth seems

The problem of the democratic white leadership of the nation, then, is not to think of the exploitative order in the South as a Negro problem but rather as a political-class problem of the first magnitude for the nation. The Southern 'aristocrats' should be understood in the light of what they really are, and the cost of reducing them should be estimated in the light of political-class practice. The alternative is a continued divided nation, for a political class has never been known to give up its position because of logical conviction. The interest of the ruling class rests in the Negroes' and poor whites' being and feeling inferior and antagonistic. This class insists that any plan for improving Southern conditions must first satisfy the latter interest.

It is not possible to speak with any degree of comprehensiveness about the problem of white leadership without reviewing somewhat its more inclusive world context. In our chapter on race relations we attempted to develop the hypothesis that modern race prejudice is rooted in certain attitudes and economic needs of the white race and that race prejudice has been diffused throughout the world by the white race. We should reiterate, however, that we do not mean to say that race prejudice has a somatic determinant. Commercial and industrial capitalism, which involved the organized movement of Europeans to distant lands, created the cultural situation favorable for the development of white race prejudice.

In our own day this very capitalism has undoubtedly passed the noontide of its vigor and is giving place to another basic form of social organization. With the change of the dominant economic organization of the world, we should expect fundamental changes in social attitudes.

In a previous chapter [*sic*] we have attempted to show also that two major systems are contending for primacy in the suppression of the present hybrid social order: fascism and communism. Fascism must obviously be transitory; it is an aggravation of the worst aspects of capitalism. We may think of fascism as the deathbed attendant of a moribund system, or indeed as the last great spasm in the death throes of capitalism.[12] 'The chills and

---

to be very much in error when he applies this concept unrefinedly to that situation. In this war, World War II, Quislings and fifth columnists were political-class leaders and members who were natural friends of the 'enemy.' Moreover, it is misleading to say, 'We realize that prejudices constitute a danger to our national unity'. The Southern prejudice against Negroes was not given up. There was 'unity' only so long as Negroes did not demand that the South give up its prejudice. If such a demand had threatened to become effective, the ruling class in the South would have done exactly what the leaders of a number of European nations did; that is to say, make a choice between the Negroes, i.e., the proletariat, and Hitler; and the likelihood of Hitler's being chosen was great indeed. Anyone, for instance, might have tested this by trying to put through an anti-lynching bill in the national Congress. In such an event it would soon have become evident that matters concerning the war were quite secondary in importance.

[12] cf., Strachey (1945, p. 100), 'It is our fate to live in one of those times in history when a whole economic system is in decay. History teaches us that once that process has begun there is no way of saving the dying economic system. The only way out is to put a new one in its place. That is what we must, can, and will do'.

fever of capitalism, observed since its infancy, shake and burn its whole body more drastically as it approaches old age'. In degenerating into organized fascism, capitalism surrenders very much of its adopted ideals of political democracy, but it has no alternative. Fascism is the only significant device developed by the established political class for the purpose of both re-invigorating capitalism and combating the democratic forces which are naturally antipathetic to capitalism.

Fascism, then, is defensive and, to repeat, necessarily exalts the worst traits of capitalism. So far as race relations are concerned, it makes a fanatic religion of white race superiority. But this is merely a function of its im-perialistic obsession, which in turn stimulates nationalism. Those persons, then, who are honestly concerned with the elimination of race prejudice and race exploitation by the white ruling class must be concerned also with the elimination of world imperialism. It will probably not be inaccurate to state that the world stronghold of imperialism and colonialism is symbolized by the British Crown supported finally by the military and economic power of the United States.

The British Crown is a device kept sacrosanct by the great capitalists of the British Empire principally to overawe and exploit the larger part of the colored peoples of the world.[13] It is a putative institution serving as cover and shock absorber for the great imperialists and is completely without purpose in a non-capitalist democracy. As Mr Laski (1938, p. 330) puts it: 'British imperialism has deliberately elevated the prestige of the Crown as a method of protecting the ends it seeks to serve'. About fourteen out of every hundred people in the British Empire are white. Without reviewing the im-perialistic practices of other nations it should be apparent that race exploita-tion cannot be eliminated from the world without first eliminating capitalism and attacking vigorously the imperialism of Great Britain.

It should be emphasized, however, that the capitalism and imperialism of Great Britain could not survive without the sustaining hand of the American ruling class. Mr Winston Churchill, in his Fulton, Missouri, address, might have gone even farther to say that not only *must* the United States and Britain establish a permanent military alliance—which for all practical purposes is already in effect—but also an economic brotherhood. The burden of making a capitalism, collapsing all over the world, work rests squarely on the shoulders of the American ruling class; and since capitalism no longer has a morality, the people of the United States will have to keep it resuscitated and defended by pouring into it an endless stream of wealth. In a very real sense the United

---

[13] Probably no historical situation illustrates better than the semi-bourgeois interlude of the Russian Revolution the great value of a decadent and impotent monarchy to a rising bourgeoisie. Behind the controlled divinity of the royal family the bourgeoisie is able to put into effect schemes of mass exploitation, both at home and abroad, that would be otherwise unthinkable.

States today must finance world capitalism, for it cannot convince peoples by any logical argument of the social and economic value of capitalism to them. Churchill knows that the United States must pay for capitalism or speedily become aware that it is 'encircled' by a socialist world, hence he speaks with oracular confidence. Capitalism cannot offer to the masses of people that better world for which they now hunger and thirst; it can give them only reaction supported by military might and a strategic distribution of a relatively few full bellies.

The American ruling class, in its own interest, must make 'lend lease' permanent, even though it is disguised in the form of loans or outright gifts to 'suffering humanity'. This class will have to see that food and 'supplies' are rushed all over the world to strengthen the position of the various national bourgeoisies as the common people gather about them to exact an accounting of the use of their resources. In a sense, then, the United States is already fighting its own proletarian revolution on foreign battle fields.

The new economic system which will naturally supplant the old is socialism, the system whose normal emphasis is upon human welfare. The relation of socialism to racial exploitation may be demonstrated by the fact that the greater the immediacy of the exploitative practice, the more fiercely socialism is opposed. In other words, in those areas where whites live by the immediate exploitation of colored people, in those areas also socialism is most abhorred. For instance, a white communist in the Deep South is regarded in about the same light as a Negro man with a white wife. They are both threats to the exploitative system, and the ruling class has provided for their violent dispatch.[14] Indeed, the method of 'solving the race issue' is identical with the method by which capitalism is being liquidated by proletarian action.

There is an increasing number of people all over the world who are willing to accept socialism with all its implications for the abandonment of mass exploitation. Some of these people understand that there will be no possibility of giving up race prejudice while still retaining the system which produced it. They recognize consequently that the problem of white leadership is no longer that of appeasing plantation capitalists but rather that of striking decisively at the very root of the social order, and they are under no

---

[14] It may be observed further that the pith of the argument that race prejudice will not exist in a socialist society necessarily rests on the fact that this indispensable economic drive of capitalism—exploitation, and human exploitation especially—will also cease to exist. In a capitalist system human beings live and labor in the interest of private enterprise; and the fact that a goodly number of them are impersonally degraded and consumed in the latter interest is consistent with the ethics of the system. On the contrary, in a socialist system human welfare becomes the dominant purpose of production, and the ethics of that system abhor the idea of such human degradation. In other words, increasing productivity is made dependent upon increasing development of the human intellect, tastes, and ambition. Human beings are freed and elevated beyond the elevation of their material resources.

illusions about the fact that the 'capitalist power will not surrender its privileges without fighting for them'.[15]

In the process of bringing the Southern Negro into full manhood and citizenship, therefore, the white leader has a responsibility of considerable importance. It involves the liberation of the Southern poor whites as well. A great leader of Negroes will almost certainly be a white man, but he will also be the leader of the white masses of this nation; and of course, whether they are permitted to recognize him or not, he will eventually prove to be the emancipator of the poor whites of the South. For example, without any considerable attention to the 'Negro problem' particularly, President Franklin D. Roosevelt undoubtedly did more to elevate the status of Negroes in the United States than all other leaders, white and black together, over a period of decades before him. Negroes are auxiliary in the American proletarian struggle for power. James Madison probably had more vision than he thought when he referred to Negroes as that 'unhappy species of population abounding in some of the states who, during the calm of regular government, are sunk below the level of men; but who, in the tempestuous scenes of civil violence, may emerge into human character and give a superiority of strength to any party with which they may associate themselves'.

In the Deep South, ruling-class whites have taught Negroes to look to them personally for guidance; in fact, these whites have controlled Negroes through their own black leaders. The successful Negro leader has learned to be sensitive to the wishes of whites. In any political-class struggle in the South, therefore, this attitude should be capitalized by the radical white leadership.

Although Negroes have become increasingly intractable to being thus indirectly led, they have yet a certain faith in 'what the white man says'. It is this faith to which the white radical leader, interested in breaking up the Southern social order, has access. Many overcautious and conservative Negro leaders, who have no patience with militant Negroes, become readily animated when white functionaries speak to them of equal rights. When the time comes for the South to be purged of its present political-class leadership, it will surely be easier for most Negroes to follow convinced whites than to tread behind the uncertain feet of their familiar black leadership.

Moreover, it is also the responsibility of white leaders to conduct the struggle according to principles of political-class conflict. That is to say, the aristocratic Southern ruling class must be defeated not only in an open matching of power but also broken in spirit, a social aspiration which the military victors of the Civil War failed to achieve.

In this we should not be mistaken as to the source of antagonism against any serious attempt to extend democracy in the South. The standard bearers

[15] On this Guerin (1939, p. 109) remarks advisedly: 'Although socialism utilizes all the legal methods supplied by the law or the constitution, it does so, without the slightest illusion; it knows that the victory in the end is a question of force'.

of the area have repeatedly and most bluntly stated that the issue could be settled only by open violence. Thus the noted Southern writer, David L. Cohn (1944, p. 50), declares: 'I have no doubt that in such an event [that is to say, an attempt to abolish the terrible segregation laws] every Southern white man would spring to arms and the country would be swept by civil war'. Again, when the United States Supreme Court decided eight to one that Negroes should be allowed to vote in state primaries, the South Carolina General Assembly passed a number of bills to emasculate the decision, and 'the House...applauded a speech by Representative John Long...who said he was willing to "bite the dust as did my ancestors" to prevent Negroes from participating in the white Democratic primaries' (The Dallas *Morning News,* 18 April, 1944). In many parts of the modern world democracy is feverishly seeking to get such a hold of itself as to be able to say to this characteristic, anachronistic challenge: 'You shall have your wish'.

The problem of racial exploitation, then, will most probably be settled as part of the world proletarian struggle for democracy; every advance of the masses will be an actual or potential advance for the colored people. Whether the open threat of violence by the exploiting class will be shortly joined will depend upon the unpredictable play and balance of force in a world-wide struggle for power.

References

Aptheker, H. (1943), *American Negro Slave Revolts*, New York.
Baker, R. S. (1908), *Following the Colour Line*, New York.
Bramlett, W. S. (1943), Report in the Dallas *Morning News*, 1 December.
Brookes, E. H. (1934), *The Colour Problems of South Africa*, London.
Cohn, D. L. (1944), 'How the South feels', *The Atlantic Monthly*, January.
Du Bois, W. E. B. (1941), *Dusk of Dawn*, New York.
Du Bois, W. E. B. (1944), 'Prospects of a world without race conflict', *A.J.S.*, March.
Embree, E. R. (1931), *Brown America*, New York.
Guerin, D. (1939), *Fascism and Big Business*, New York.
Herskovits, M. J. (1941), *The Myth of the Negro Past*, New York.
Kennedy, S. (1946), 'Total equality and how to get it', *Common Ground*, Winter.
Laski, H. F. (1938), *Parliamentary Government in England*, New York.
Le Bon, G. (1917), *Premières Conséquences de la Guerre*, Paris.
Maunier, R. (1932), *Sociologie Coloniale*, Paris.
Miller, K. (1918), *An Appeal to Conscience*, New York.
Myrdal, G. (1944), *An American Dilemma*, New York.
Powdermaker, H. (1939), *After Freedom*, New York.
Reuter, E. B. (1915), *The American Race Problem*, New York.
Schuyler, G. (1942), Article in the Pittsburgh *Courier*, 15 March.
Schuyler, G. (1943), Article in the Pittsburgh *Courier*, 27 February.
Skaggs, W. H. (1924), *The Southern Oligarchy*, New York.
Strachey, J. (1945), *Socialism Looks Forward*, New York.
Wirth, L. (1944), Article in *The Scientific Monthly*, April.

5 *Andrew Asheron,* Race and Politics in South Africa

The origins of race consciousness

From shortly after their arrival at the Cape in 1652 the European Dutch, through superior force of arms, were in a position to dominate the indigenous Hottentot population. As a direct result of this situation, the resultant socialization process, in terms of the allocations of roles and status between the two groups, lay primarily in the hands of the European. However, in this early period of South African history, this 'naming' of roles and status was defined by the European primarily in terms of religious belief rather than skin pigmentation. Non-literate coloured races were seen by the European either as 'little lost souls', to be rescued and converted to Christianity or, alternatively, as 'pagans' who had no soul to lose and were therefore born to slavery. Thus a non-European at the Cape, once baptized into the Christian religion, was immediately accepted as a member of the white (Christian) community. And if baptized as a slave, was entitled to his freedom.

With the importation of a considerable number of slaves from the East, European attitudes with regard to race underwent a significant change. The Europeans came to associate all forms of manual labour with servility, and became increasingly reluctant to undertake this form of work. Thus economic factors gradually began to intrude and undermine the original Christian/ Heathen status differentiation. In place of the latter distinction, an economic and social hierarchy based on skin pigmentation was set up because those in the lowest economic and status groups were clearly distinguishable by their skin colour.

By the beginning of the 18th century, European agricultural expansion was taking place at the Cape; there arose the beginnings of a frontier society, and a resultant frontier mentality which was decisively to affect race attitudes in South Africa. Being intensively engaged in the struggle for survival, a frontier society can afford to give little consideration to other peoples. Under such conditions, self-identity and status, through the use of social distance,

Andrew Asheron, 'Race and politics in South Africa', *New Left Review*, vol. 53, Spring 1969, pp. 53–8.

must be kept to a maximum. In the meeting of the pastoralist Boer and African tribesman (1770 onwards), and with competition for water and grazing lands, it became imperative from the Boer point of view to dominate the Africans and to accentuate their difference. The Boers' Calvinist religion of predestination conveniently placed the 'heathen' African beyond salvation. By virtue of his religion the frontier farmer thus justified his right both to extend his own lands and to subjugate the 'heathen' by whom he was surrounded. The idea that Christians and non-Christians were in any sense equal was utterly foreign to the frontier mentality. Indeed, the Boer farmers conceived the difference between themselves and the African to be as great as that between themselves and their cattle, with the Africans in fact being named by the Boers as *Zwarte Vee* (Black Cattle). It was upon these foundations that the precursor of present-day Apartheid, the master-servant social fabric of the 19th century Boer Republics, was built up. Thus in the Transvaal Republican constitution it was specifically stated that there should be no equality of race in Church or State. Upon these determinants, the psycho-sociological and historical legacies of (racial) conflict and (racial) fear, Afrikaner Nationalism was later to build its most powerful weapon in its pursuit of the total domination of South African society—racist ideology.

The historical development of race ideology

The development of the ideology of race in South Africa, based on the historical, political and socio-psychological legacies previously outlined, arose in its overt form as a result of three fundamental and interlocking factors. Firstly, the late-19th century rise of Afrikaner nationalism in opposition to British Imperialism. Secondly, the acceptance by British Imperialism, through the mineowners, of the already existing racial master-servant social fabric. Thirdly, due to 20th century industrialization, the competition of black and white for urban employment.

Afrikaner nationalism developed out of the Boers' need both to re-establish their identity, and to create a group homogeneity through which they could ultimately rectify and overcome the humiliations and defeats which they had suffered since the events leading up to the Greak Trek of 1836 – events which culminated in their pacification by the British in the Boer War of 1899–1902. As the Boer leader General Botha remarked, 'the battle which was won and lost in the fields of war must be fought again upon the political platform.' As developed and eventually formulated (in the notorious Draft Constitution of 1941), this drive for power had as its ultimate object the total domination of South Africa in order to protect and promote the interests of Afrikanerdom.

The pivotal point of the Afrikaner–English power struggle in the period 1910–48 centred on the primarily peaceful struggle to obtain power through the white-dominated electorate. As far as the Afrikaner Nationalists were concerned, their main fear during this period lay in the possibility of a political alliance between their English-speaking opponents and the non-whites; and more particularly they feared that the English, in seeking to further this alliance, might extend the non-white vote. If this had occurred, the likelihood of Afrikanerdom ever achieving power through constitutional means was minimal. Although once or twice rather vague political overtures were made to the non-whites by Afrikaner nationalists, it can be said that their predominant tactic here centred on the elimination of the non-white from the electoral system, and hence from any 'legitimate' say in South Africa's political affairs.

In so far as the second area of attack, the white voter, was concerned, Afrikaner nationalism's task was made easier by three factors. Firstly, the Afrikaners outnumbered their English counterparts, and their birthrate was higher. Secondly, electoral delimitations and weightings have always favoured the rural, predominantly Afrikaner-speaking, areas. Thirdly, as a consequence of the growth of the mining industries and the resultant industrialization and urbanization of South Africa, large numbers of African and white workers were brought together in a common urban environment—with, however, mutually competitive interests. Thus the question of race (consciousness), rather than class (consciousness) was seen by most of the white segment to be *the* most fundamental factor in terms of their own survival.

Furthermore the Afrikaner people as a whole were much more aware than their English-speaking opponents of the significance of the race question for the future development of South Africa. Given both the historical legacy of their psycho-sociological background, and the fact that they were a predominantly rural people, the Afrikaners experienced and appreciated much more fully the harsh impact of industrialization and urbanization. They recognized more clearly the latter's consequences for Afrikaner culture, and indeed for the entire relationship between white and non-white, than did the urban-based English. The latter, secure in their exploitation of the non-white and in their overall economic domination, could afford to view the two 'racial' questions (i.e. English/Afrikaner and Black/White) in a far more lenient fashion than could Afrikanerdom. In addition racist ideology was, for Afrikaner nationalism, a two-edged political instrument. For it could be used not only to maintain and expand Afrikaner unity and solidarity, but also as a political weapon with which to attack and accuse the mining magnates and their political representatives (Smuts and the South African Party, later Smuts and the United Party) for their *laissez-faire* social and economic policy of 'selling the white man down the river for a pot of gold'.[1] Consequently

[1] After the struggle with British Imperialism over the gold-bearing reefs of the Transvaal the Chamber of Mines, with its 'economic rationality' of replacing highly paid white workers with lesser paid black labour, was seen by Afrikanerdom as the major threat to the white man's privileged existence.

Afrikaner nationalism was virtually bound to utilize the highly inflammable race issue as an ideological (political) weapon with which to obtain power.

The failure of the mining magnates and English-speaking politicians in general to withstand the onslaught of the Nationalists' strident racial ideology of 'dominate or be dominated' lies, not only in the developments outlined above, but also in the contradictions inherent in English-speaking capitalism's ends. In essence these may be said to be, and indeed remain, the implementation of a *laissez-faire* liberal (modelled on 19th century English politics) and individualist (i.e. ultimately colour-blind) policy upon the foundations of a racially authoritarian capitalist system. That is, the initiators of South Africa's industrial economy, the English mineowners, readily accepted the South African master-servant (dominant/subordinate) racial social structure that already existed prior to the opening up of the mining industry. In fact, they have gone further, and have co-operated with the State (especially after the 1922 Rand Strike when the mineowners lost their battle for cheap black labour at the expense of the much more highly paid white labour[2]) in buttressing and perpetuating South Africa's racial socioeconomic system in order to control and monopolize the wage and work structure of the unskilled African labour force and so maximize their outputs and profits.[3]

This requirement of a plentiful and continuous supply of cheap black labour has meant that the British mineowners have consistently had one vital economic interest in common with Afrikanerdom (i.e. the Afrikaner farmer). As Lewin has suggested, this common economic interest would then explain the willingness of the English to abandon any thought of using their military victory in 1902 to impose the Cape's non-racial franchise policy on the rest of South Africa. It would also explain their failure, in their struggle with Afrikaner nationalism, to seek political allies amongst South Africa's non-white population (cf. Lewin, 1963). As a consequence of this situation, the English-speaking people have, in general, been mainly conciliatory in their dealings with Afrikanerdom; the predominantly English-

[2] The headquarters of the strike during its final stages were in the offices of the Communist Party. Roux comments: 'The Afrikaner strikers sang the "Red Flag" in English to the tune of the old republican "Volksleid", and the "Marxist Socialists", not to be outdone, refurbished an old May Day Banner so that its slogan read, "Workers of the World *fight and unite for a White South Africa*".' (Roux's emphasis.)

[3] The nub of the mineowners' policy is revealed in the Lansdowne Commission's Report of 1944. The Commission was appointed to investigate African mineworkers' wages, there having been no significant wage increase since 1914. The Commission noted that the Chamber of Mines' argument against wage increases based its case very largely on the argument that, in fixing the wage of mine labourers and in determining whether the wages so fixed are adequate, it is entitled to take cognizance of the full subsistence which a native is able to obtain from his holding in the Reserve. (cf. Horwitz, 1967, p. 341). Thus the mineowners' wage-policy was that an African man's family had to be supported by the rest of the family in the Reserve. In essence, the Reserve family was to subsidize the mineowners. This wage-scale policy was then adopted by secondary industry. As Horwitz remarks, 'What is good for the Chamber of Mines, is good for South Africa'.

speaking United Party's racial policy has remained consistently equivocal. That is, it has in the main merely followed the trail blazed by the Nationalists. Thus, by presenting the white electorate with nothing more than a modified and insipid form of Apartheid, the UP has moved in behind the Nationalists' extreme 'dominate or be dominated' racial 'definition of the situation', and so collaborated in and further exacerbated the narrow and increasingly rigid designations of the arena in which white South Africa's political dialogue can take place.

Omnipresent racialism

The contemporary omnipresence of racialism in South Africa is upheld through social and penal sanctions which intertwine to affect the socialization process whereby race differentiation is embedded in and defines the white man's 'social definition of reality'; his 'common sense view of the world'; his expectations of others, particularly the non-white; his future desires and hopes. The depth of this embeddedness of race consciousness in South Africa's socio-political structures and her very way of life must be comprehended if the fatuity of the reformist's optimistic belief in the 'withering away' of race discrimination and prejudice before the exigencies of 'economic rationality' is to be fully appreciated.

In the South African situation racial discrimination has become detached from its original historical conjunction with manual labour, conflict over land, and general economic deprivation and capitalist exploitation. Furthermore, and more crucially, racial discrimination in its mythical or ideological form has become detached from its original extreme proselytizers, the previous and present-day (Nationalist) political elite; that is, in so far as the white electorate firmly and intrinsically holds white superiority/non-white inferiority to be true, despite functional explanations to the contrary. Now inasmuch as racial ideology has become detached from its functional origins, so it has become a relatively autonomous, but real entity. *The upshot of which is that in its consequences it has unintended sequels for its initiators, and their successors.* This has, as will be seen, vitally important repercussions for any political analysis of South Africa and her future development.

The heightening of racial consciousness in South Africa, through the deliberate use of penal sanctions, has in the main taken place since the Nationalist Party came to power (1948). This is a consequence of the party's racial ideology; its endeavours to unite the white (English/Afrikaner) segment under its leadership, and to maintain and increase its domination over the non-white population. Kuper (1960) lists three particular techniques for the heightening of racial consciousness, and applies these to developments in South Africa since the Second World War.

Firstly, the weaving of racial classification into the perception of the individual. The consequence of this is that the individual, in his social perception of reality, is led to apply racial definitions over a very broad range of social situations. For example: the unambiguous method of racial classification introduced by the Nationalists with the Population Registration Act of 1950, which specifically classifies each person according to race; the Prohibition of Mixed Marriages Act of 1949; The Immorality Amendment Act of 1950. Thus within two years of their achieving power, the Nationalists had endeavoured to ensure by law the 'purity' of the 'pigmented aristocracy'.

Secondly, the extension of the range of situations in which racial classification is mandatory as a guide to conduct. In terms of the more prominent laws introduced by the Nationalists, the following social situations are based on racial criteria: marriage; 'illicit carnal intercourse'; proximity between neighbours and traders; inclusion on a common electoral role; school and university education; industrial reconciliation machinery for Africans; racial reservation of occupations; control of contact between races in clubs, hospitals, places of entertainment and public assemblies; occupation of premises for a substantial period of time. 'In consequence', writes Kuper (1960), 'the racial concept becomes increasingly weighted with social and cultural connotations.'

Thirdly, a system of punishment and rewards was introduced. (a) As Kuper points out, racial segregation in South Africa is highly discriminatory and is often immediately rewarding to those who impose it. In particular the increasingly vast bureaucracy which is needed in order to implement these discriminatory acts offers new occupational opportunities in State and local administration, with rewards of office stimulating conscientious devotion both to racialism and the Nationalist government. (b) For the non-whites, rewards and punishments reinforce the system, with penal sanctions which fall more heavily on their shoulders than on the whites. Finally, political activity is demarcated along racial lines. 'Political activity', writes Kuper, 'pressure towards conservatism or towards revolution is essentially racial and serves to heighten racial consciousness.'

Heightened racial consciousness does not necessarily lead to an increase in racial prejudice. But when it is channelled in this direction by unfavourable stereotypes of other races, and by policies and ideologies which create or intensify competition between the races, it is very likely to be itself intensified. Certainly in the case of South Africa's many racial laws, an image is compounded of unfavourable qualities. Thus the idea arises that other races are unfit as sexual partners, etc. 'These laws, policies and ideologies', writes Kuper (1960), 'presumably encourage conflict in racial contact, since there is an ideological expectation of conflict. Race consciousness is canalized in a sharply antagonistic form. . . .' And furthermore, 'as a result of systematic discrimination, the white man will find himself consistently in a position of superiority *and this routine experience may be expected to re-inforce sentiments of superiority expressed in the demand for its maintenance and perhaps its enhancement by further discrimination.'*

Consequently, in the context of the political situation in South Africa, as generations of her white politicians, particularly Nationalist politicians, have persistently defined and emphasized the situation in terms of race conflict, thereby heightening racial tension and antagonisms in the minds of the white electorate; so this electorate has in turn become even more race-conscious and as a result made consistent demands upon the politicians that *they uphold and consolidate white supremacy. The white electorate's racial prejudices thereby rebound back upon the politicians, who, in consequence, themselves become increasingly confined and circumscribed by their own racial ideology. In its unintended consequences the ideology of race has outrun its 'ideologues' and become an additional independent variable, as significant as the economic base, in the future development of South Africa.*

References

Horwitz, R. (1967), *The Political Economy of South Africa*, London.
Kuper, L. (1960), 'The heightening of racial tension', *Race*, vol. 2, no. 1, November.
Lewin, J. (1963), *Politics and Law in South Africa*, London.
Roux, E. (1964), *Time Longer than Rope: A History of the Struggle of the Black Man for Freedom in South Africa*, Madison.

6 *Robert Blauner,* Colonized and Immigrant Minorities

During the late 1960s a new movement emerged on the Pacific Coast. Beginning at San Francisco State College and spreading across the bay to Berkeley and other campuses, black, Chicano, Asian, and Native American student organizations formed alliances and pressed for ethnic studies curricula and for greater control over the programs that concerned them. Rejecting the implicit condescension in the label 'minority students' and the negative afterthought of 'nonwhite', these coalitions proclaimed themselves a 'Third World Movement'. (For accounts of this movement at San Francisco State, see McEvoy and Miller, 1969.) Later, in the East and Middle West, the third world umbrella was spread over other alliances, primarily those urging unity of Puerto Ricans and blacks. In radical circles the term has become the dominant metaphor referring to the nation's racially oppressed people.

As the term *third world* has been increasingly applied to people of color in the United States, a question has disturbed many observers. Is the third world idea essentially a rhetorical expression of the aspirations and political ideology of the young militants in the black, brown, red, and yellow power movements, or does the concept reflect actual sociological realities? Posed this way, the question may be drawn too sharply; neither possibility excludes the other. Life is complex, so we might expect some truth in both positions. Furthermore, social relationships are not static. The rhetoric and ideology of social movements, if they succeed in altering the ways in which groups define their situations, can significantly shape and change social reality. Ultimately, the validity of the third world perspective will be tested in social and political practice. The future is open.

Still, we cannot evade the question, to what extent—in its application to domestic race relations—is the third world idea grounded in firm historical and contemporary actualities? To assess this issue we need to examine the assumptions upon which the concept rests. There are three that seem to me central. The first assumption is that racial groups in America are, and have been, colonized peoples; therefore their social realities cannot be understood

Robert Blauner, *Racial Oppression in America*, Harper and Row, 1972, pp. 53–75.

in the framework of immigration and assimilation that is applied to European ethnic groups. The second assumption is that the racial minorities share a common situation of oppression, from which a potential political unity is inferred. The final assumption is that there is a historical connection between the third world abroad and the third world within. In placing American realities within the framework of international colonialism, similarities in patterns of racial domination and exploitation are stressed and a common political fate is implied—at least for the long run. I begin by looking at the first assumption since it sets the stage for the main task of this piece, a comparison and contrast between immigrant and third world experience. I return to the other points at the end of the essay.

The fundamental issue is historical. People of color have never been an integral part of the Anglo-American political community and culture because they did not enter the dominant society in the same way as did the European ethnics. The third world notion points to a *basic distinction between immigration and colonization as the two major processes through which new population groups are incorporated into a nation.* Immigrant groups enter a new territory or society voluntarily, though they may be pushed out of their old country by dire economic or political oppression. Colonized groups become part of a new society through force or violence; they are conquered, enslaved, or pressured into movement. Thus, the third world formulation is a bold attack on the myth that America is the land of the free, or, more specifically, a nation whose population has been built up through successive waves of immigration. The third world perspective returns us to the origins of the American experience, reminding us that this nation owes its very existence to colonialism, and that along with settlers and immigrants there have always been conquered Indians and black slaves, and later defeated Mexicans—that is, colonial subjects on the national soil. Such a reminder is not pleasant to a society that represses those aspects of its history that do not fit the collective self-image of democracy for all men.

The idea that third world people are colonial subjects is gaining in acceptance today; at the same time it is not at all convincing to those who do not recognize a fundamental similarity between American race relations and Europe's historic domination of Asia and Africa. (I discuss how U.S. colonialism differs from the traditional or classical versions toward the end of the essay.) Yet the experience of people of color in this country does include a number of circumstances that are universal to the colonial situation, and these are the very circumstances that differentiate third world realities from those of the European immigrants. The first condition, already touched upon, is that of a forced entry into the larger society or metropolitan domain. The second is subjection to various forms of unfree labor that greatly restrict the physical and social mobility of the group and its participation in the political arena. The third is a cultural policy of the colonizer that constrains, transforms, or destroys original values, orientations, and ways of life. These three points organize the comparison of colonized and immigrant minorities that follows.[1]

Group entry and freedom of movement

Colonialism and immigration are the two major means by which heterogeneous or plural societies, with ethnically diverse populations, develop. In the case of colonialism, metropolitan nations incorporate new territories or peoples through processes that are essentially involuntary, such as war, conquest, capture, and other forms of force or manipulation. Through immigration, new peoples or ethnic groups enter a host society more or less freely. These are ideal-types, the polar ends of a continuum; many historical cases fall in between. In the case of America's racial minorities, some groups clearly fit the criterion for colonial entry; others exemplify mixed types.

Native Americans, Chicanos, and blacks are the third world groups whose entry was unequivocally forced and whose subsequent histories best fit the colonial model. Critics of the colonial interpretation usually focus on the black experience, emphasizing how it has differed from those of traditional colonialism. Rather than being conquered and controlled in their native land, African people were captured, transported, and enslaved in the Southern states and other regions of the Western hemisphere. Whether oppression takes place at home in the oppressed's native land or in the heart of the colonizer's mother country, colonization remains colonization. However, the term *internal colonialism* is useful for emphasizing the differences in setting and in the consequences that arise from it.[2] The conquest and virtual elimination of the original Americans, a process that took three hundred years to complete, is an example of classical colonialism, no different in essential features from Europe's imperial control over Asia, Africa, and Latin America. The same is true of the conquest of the Mexican Southwest and the annexation of its Spanish-speaking population.

Other third world groups have undergone an experience that can be seen as part colonial and part immigrant. Puerto Rico has been a colony exploited by the mainland, while, at the same time, the islanders have had relative freedom to move back and forth and to work and settle in the States. Of the

---

[1] There is another aspect of colonization which I do not deal with in this essay: the experience of being managed and manipulated by outsiders in terms of ethnic status. This is derived from the fact that the lives of colonized people tend to be administered by representatives of the dominant political and legal order. Immigrant groups experienced a considerable degree of such control, but less intensely and for a shorter period of time. They achieved a relative community autonomy earlier and gained power in a wider range of institutions relevant to them. See Blauner (1972, chap. 3) for further discussion.

[2] In addition to its application to white-black relations in the United States—see for example, Carmichael and Hamilton (1967).

Asian-American groups, the situation of the Filipinos has been the most colonial. The islands were colonies of Spain and the United States, and the male population was recruited for agricultural serfdom both in Hawaii and in the States. In the more recent period, however, movement to the States has been largely voluntary.

In the case of the Chinese, we do not have sufficient historical evidence to be able to assess the balance between free and involuntary entry in the nineteenth century. The majority came to work in the mines and fields for an extended period of debt servitude; many individuals were 'shanghaied' or pressed into service; many others evidently signed up voluntarily for serflike labor (Barth, 1964). A similar pattern held for the Japanese who came toward the end of the century, except that the voluntary element in the Japanese entry appears to have been considerably more significant (Kitano, 1969). Thus, for the two largest Asian groups, we have an original entry into American society that might be termed semicolonial, followed in the twentieth century by immigration. Yet the exclusion of Asian immigrants and the restriction acts that followed were unique blows, which marked off the status of the Chinese and Japanese in America, limiting their numbers and potential power. For this reason it is misleading to equate the Asian experience with the European immigrant pattern. Despite the fact that some individuals and families have been able to immigrate freely, the status and size of these ethnic groups have been rigidly controlled.

There is a somewhat parallel ambiguity in the twentieth-century movement from Mexico, which has contributed a majority of the present Mexican–American group. Although the migration of individuals and families in search of work and better living conditions has been largely voluntary, classifying this process as immigration misses the point that the Southwest is historically and culturally a Mexican, Spanish-speaking region. Moreover, from the perspective of conquest that many Mexicans have retained, the movement has been to a land that is still seen as their own. Perhaps the entry of other Latin-Americans approaches more nearly the immigrant model; however, in their case, too, there is a colonial element, arising from the Yankee neo-colonial domination of much of South and Central America; for this reason, along with that of racism in the States, many young Latinos are third world oriented.

Thus the relation between third world groups and a colonial-type entry into American society is impressive, though not perfect or precise. Differences between people of color and Europeans are shown most clearly in the ways the groups first entered. The colonized became ethnic minorities *en bloc*, collectively, through conquest, slavery, annexation, or a racial labor policy. The European immigrant peoples became ethnic groups and minorities within the United States by the essentially voluntary movements of individuals and families. Even when, later on, some third world peoples were able to immigrate, the circumstances of the earlier entry affected their situation and the attitudes of the dominant culture toward them.

The essentially voluntary entry of the immigrants was a function of their status in the labor market. The European groups were responding to the industrial needs of a free capitalist market. Economic development in other societies with labor shortages—for example, Australia, Brazil, and Argentina —meant that many people could at least envision alternative destinations for their emigration. Though the Irish were colonized at home, and poverty, potato famine and other disasters made their exodus more of a flight than that of other Europeans, they still had some choice of where to flee (Handlin, 1959, chap. 2). Thus, people of Irish descent are found today in the West Indies, Oceania, and other former British colonies. Germans and Italians moved in large numbers to South America; Eastern Europeans immigrated to Canada as well as to the United States.

Because the Europeans moved on their own, they had a degree of autonomy that was denied those whose entry followed upon conquest, capture, or involuntary labor contracts. They expected to move freely within the society to the extent that they acquired the economic and cultural means. Though they faced great hardships and even prejudice and discrimination on a scale that must have been disillusioning, the Irish, Italians, Jews, and other groups had the advantage of European ancestry and white skins. When living in New York became too difficult, Jewish families moved on to Chicago. Irish trapped in Boston could get land and farm in the Midwest, or search for gold in California. It is obvious that parallel alternatives were not available to the early generations of Afro-Americans, Asians, and Mexican–Americans, because they were not part of the free labor force. Furthermore, limitations on physical movement followed from the purely racial aspect of their oppression (see Blauner, 1972, chap. 1).

Thus, the entrance of the European into the American order involved a degree of choice and self-direction that was for the most part denied people of color. Voluntary immigration made it more likely that individual Europeans and entire ethnic groups would identify with America and see the host culture as a a positive opportunity rather than an alien and dominating value system. It is my assessment that this element of choice, though it can be overestimated and romanticized, must have been crucial in influencing the different careers and perspectives of immigrants and colonized in America, because choice is a necessary condition for commitment to any group, from social club to national society.

Sociologists interpreting race relations in the United States have rarely faced the full implications of these differences. The *immigrant model* became the main focus of analysis, and the experiences of all groups were viewed through its lens. (A crucial treatment of the model of immigration and assimilation is in Handlin, 1951.) It suited the cultural mythology to see everyone in America as an original immigrant, a later immigrant, a quasi-immigrant or a potential immigrant. Though the black situation long posed problems for this framework, recent developments have made it possible for scholars and ordinary citizens alike to force Afro-American realities into this comfortable schema. Migration from rural South to urban North became an analog of European immigration, blacks became the latest newcomers to the cities, facing parallel problems of assimilation. In the no-nonsense language of Irving Kristol, 'The Negro Today Is Like the Immigrant of Yesterday'.[3]

The colonial labor principle in the United States

European immigrants and third world people have faced some similar conditions, of course. The overwhelming majority of both groups were poor, and their early generations worked primarily as unskilled laborers. The question of how, where, and why newcomers worked in the United States is central, for the differences in the labor systems that introduced people of color and immigrants to America may be the fundamental reason why their histories have followed disparate paths.

The labor forces that built up the Western hemisphere were structured on the principle of race and color. The European conquest of the Native Americans and the introduction of plantation slavery were crucial beginning points for the emergence of a worldwide colonial order. These 'New World' events established the pattern for labor practices in the colonial regimes of Asia, Africa, and Oceania during the centuries that followed. The key equation was the association of free labor with people of white European stock and the association of unfree labor with non-Western people of color, a correlation that did not develop all at once; it took time for it to become a more or less fixed pattern.

North American colonists made several attempts to force Indians into dependent labor relationships, including slavery (Macleod, 1928). But the native North American tribes, many of which were mobile hunters and warrior peoples, resisted agricultural peonage and directly fought the theft of their lands. In addition, the relative sparsity of Indian populations north of the Rio Grande limited their potential utility for colonial labor requirements. Therefore Native American peoples were either massacred or pushed out of the areas of European settlement and enterprise. South of the Rio Grande, where the majority of Native Americans lived in more fixed agricultural societies, they were too numerous to be killed off or pushed aside, though they suffered drastic losses through disease and massacre.[4] In most of Spanish

---

[3] *New York Times Magazine* (September 11, 1966), reprinted in Glazer (1970, pp. 139–57). Another influential study in this genre is Banfield (1970).

[4] For a discussion of these differences in ecological and material circumstances, see Harris (1964, chaps. 1–4).

America, the white man wanted both the land and the labor of the Indian. Agricultural peonage was established and entire communities were subjugated economically and politically. Either directly or indirectly, the Indian worked for the white man.

In the Caribbean region (which may be considered to include the American South, see Hoetink, 1967) neither Indian nor white labor was available in sufficient supply to meet the demands of large-scale plantation agriculture. African slaves were imported to the West Indies, Brazil, and the colonies that were to become the United States to labor in those industries that promised and produced the greatest profit: indigo, sugar, coffee, and cotton. Whereas many lower-class Britishers submitted to debt servitude in the 1600s, by 1700 slavery had crystallized into a condition thought of as natural and appropriate only to people of African descent. (For an historical account of this development, see Jordan, 1968, chap. 2.) White men, even if from lowly origins and serf-like pasts, were able to own land and property, and to sell their labor in the free market. Though there were always anomalous exceptions, such as free and even slave-owning Negroes, people of color within the Americas had become essentially a class of unfree laborers. Afro-Americans were overwhelmingly bondsmen; Native Americans were serfs and peons in most of the continent.

Colonial conquest and control has been the cutting edge of Western capitalism in its expansion and penetration throughout the world. Yet capitalism and free labor as Western institutions were not developed for people of color; they were reserved for white people and white societies. In the colonies European powers organized other systems of work that were noncapitalist and unfree: slavery, serfdom, peonage. Forced labor in a myriad of forms became the province of the colonized and 'native' peoples. European whites managed these forced labor systems and dominated the segments of the economy based on free labor. (See Carrasco, 1959, pp. 52–3; Kloosterboer, 1960.) This has been the general situation in the Western hemisphere (including the United States) for more than three out of the four centuries of European settlement. It was the pattern in the more classical colonial societies also. But from the point of view of labor, the colonial dynamic developed more completely within the United States. Only here emerged a correlation between color and work status that was almost perfect. In Asia and Africa, as well as in much of Central and South America, many if not most of the indigenous peoples remained formally free in their daily work, engaging in traditional subsistence economies rather than working in the plantations, fields, and mines established by European capital. The economies in these areas came within the orbit of imperial control, yet they helped maintain communities and group life and thus countered the uprooting tendencies and the cultural and psychic penetration of colonialism. Because such traditional forms of social existence were viable and preferred, labor could only be moved into the arenas of Western enterprise through some form of coercion. Although the association of color and labor status was not perfect in the classical colonial regimes, as a general rule the racial principle kept white Europeans from becoming slaves, coolies, or peons.

Emancipation in the United States was followed by a period of rapid industrialization in the last third of the nineteenth century. The Civil War and its temporary resolution of sectional division greatly stimulated the economy. With industrialization there was an historic opportunity to transform the nation's racial labor principle. Low as were the condition and income of the factory laborer, his status was that of a free worker. The manpower needs in the new factories and mines of the East and Middle West could have been met by the proletarianization of the freedmen along with some immigration from Europe. But the resurgent Southern ruling class blocked the political economic democratization movements of Reconstruction, and the mass of blacks became sharecroppers and tenant farmers, agricultural serfs little removed from formal slavery.[5] American captains of industry and the native white proletariat preferred to employ despised, unlettered European peasants rather than the emancipated Negro population of the South, or for that matter than the many poor white Southern farmers whose labor mobility was also blocked as the entire region became a semi-colony of the North.

The nineteenth century was the time of 'manifest destiny', the ideology that justified Anglo expansionism in its sweep to the Pacific. The Texan War of 1836 was followed by the full-scale imperialist conquest of 1846–1848 through which Mexico lost half its territory. By 1900 Anglo-Americans had assumed economic as well as political dominance over most of the Southwest. As white colonists and speculators gained control (often illegally) over the land and livelihood of the independent Hispano farming and ranching villages, a new pool of dependent labor was produced to work the fields and build the railroads of the region (see McWilliams, 1968, for a summary discussion). Leonard Pitt (1970, p. 296) sums up the seizure of California in terms applicable to the whole Southwest:

> In the final analysis the Californios were the victims of an imperial conquest. . . . The United States, which had long coveted California for its trade potential and strategic location, finally provoked a war to bring about the desired ownership. At the conclusion of fighting, it arranged to 'purchase' the territory outright, and

[5] This pattern was not unique to the United States. The emancipation of slaves in other societies has typically led to their confinement to other forms of unfree labor, usually sharecropping. In this context Kloosterboer (1960) cites the examples of the British West Indies, South Africa, the Dutch West Indies, the Dutch East Indies (Java), Portuguese Africa, Madagascar, the Belgian Congo, and Haiti. The great influx of European immigration to Brazil also followed the abolition of slavery, and the new white Brazilians similarly monopolized the occupational opportunities brought by the industrialization that might have otherwise benefited the black masses (Fernandes, 1969, pp. 283–6).

set about to colonize, by throwing open the gates to all comers. Yankee settlers then swept in by the tens of thousands, and in a matter of months and years overturned the old institutional framework, expropriated the land, imposed a new body of law, a new language, a new economy, and a new culture, and in the process exploited the labor of the local population whenever necessary. To certain members of the old ruling class these settlers awarded a token and symbolic prestige, at least temporarily; yet with that status went very little genuine authority. In the long run Americans simply pushed aside the earlier ruling élite as being irrelevant.

Later, the United States' economic hegemony over a semicolonial Mexico and the upheavals that followed the 1910 revolution brought additional mass migrations of brown workers to the croplands of the region. The Mexicans and Mexican–Americans who created the rich agricultural industries of the Southwest were as a rule bound to contractors, owners, and officials in a status little above peonage. Beginning in the 1850s, shipments of Chinese workmen—who had sold themselves or had been forced into debt servitude— were imported to build railroads and to mine gold and other metals. Later other colonized Asian populations, Filipinos and East Indians, were used as gang laborers for Western farm factories (see McWilliams, 1934; 1942; 1948). Among the third world groups that contributed to this labor stream, only the Japanese came from a nation that had successfully resisted Western domination. This may be one important reason why the Japanese entry into American life and much of the group's subsequent development show some striking parallels to the European immigrant pattern. But the racial labor principle confined this Asian people too; they were viewed as fit only for subservient field employment. When they began to buy land, set up businesses, and enter occupations 'reserved' for whites, the outcry led to immigration restriction and to exclusion acts (see Daniels and Kitano, 1970, pp. 45–66; Daniels, 1962, Miller, 1969).

A tenet central to Marxian theory is that work and systems of labor are crucial in shaping larger social forces and relations. The orthodox Marxist criticism of capitalism, however, often obscures the significance of patterns of labor status. Since, by definition, capitalism is a system of wage slavery and the proletariat are 'wage slaves', the varied degrees of freedom within industry and among the working class have not been given enough theoretical attention. Max Weber's treatment of capitalism, though based essentially on Marx's framework, is useful for its emphasis on the unique status of the free mobile proletariat in contrast to the status of those traditional forms of labor more bound to particular masters and work situations. Weber saw 'formally free' labor as an essential condition for modern capitalism (Weber, 1950, p. 277). Of course, freedom of labor is always a relative matter, and formal freedoms are often limited by informal constraint and the absence of choice. For this reason, the different labor situations of third world and of European newcomers to American capitalism cannot be seen as polar opposites. Many

European groups entered as contract laborers (Higham, 1969, pp. 45–52), and an ethnic stratification (as well as a racial one) prevailed in industry. Particular immigrant groups dominated certain industries and occupations: the Irish built the canal system that linked the East with the Great Lakes in the early nineteenth century; Italians were concentrated in roadbuilding and other construction; Slavs and East Europeans made up a large segment of the labor force in steel and heavy metals; the garment trades was for many years a Jewish enclave. Yet this ethnic stratification had different consequences than the racial labor principle had, since the white immigrants worked within the wage system whereas the third world groups tended to be clustered in precapitalist employment sectors.[6]

The differences in labor placement for third world and immigrant can be further broken down. Like European overseas colonialism, America has used African, Asian, Mexican and, to a lesser degree, Indian workers for the cheapest labor, concentrating people of color in the most unskilled jobs, the least advanced sectors of the economy, and the most industrially backward regions of the nation. In an historical sense, people of color provided much of the hard labor (and the technical skills) that built up the agricultural base and the mineral-transport-communication infrastructure necessary for industrialization and modernization, whereas the Europeans worked primarily within the industrialized, modern sectors.[7] The initial position of European ethnics, while low, was therefore strategic for movement up the economic and social pyramid. The placement of nonwhite groups, however, imposed barrier upon barrier on such mobility, freezing them for long periods of time in the least favorable segments of the economy.

Rural versus urban

European immigrants were clustered in the cities, whereas the colonized minorities were predominantly agricultural laborers in rural areas. In the United States, family farming and corporate agriculture have been primarily white industries. Some immigrants, notably German, Scandinavian, Italian, and Portuguese, have prospered through farming. But most immigrant groups did not contribute to the most exploited sector of our industrial economy,

---

[6] In a provocative paper which contains a comparison of black and European immigrant experience, Posey argues (in McEvoy and Miller, 1969, pp. 264–71) that Afro-Americans were never permitted to enter the nation's class system.

A contrast between the Mexican and European immigrant patterns of work and settlement, and their consequences for social mobility is found in Grebler, Moore, and Guzman (1970, chap. 5).

[7] I do not imply a perfect correlation between race and industrial type, only that third world workers have been strikingly overrepresented in the 'primary sector' of the economy. Unlike in classical colonialism, white labor has outnumbered colored labor in the United States, and therefore white workers have dominated even such industries as coal mining, non-ferrous metals, and midwestern agriculture.

that with the lowest status: agricultural labor. Curiously, the white rural proletariat of the South and West was chiefly native born.

Industry: exclusion from manufacturing

The rate of occupational mobility was by no means the same for all ethnics. Among the early immigrants, the stigmatized Irish occupied a quasi-colonial status, and their ascent into a predominantly middle-class position took at least a generation longer than that of the Germans. Among later immigrants, Jews, Greeks, and Armenians—urban people in Europe—have achieved higher social and economic status than Italians and Poles, most of whom were peasants in the old country.[8] But despite these differences, the immigrants as a whole had a key advantage over third world Americans. As unskilled laborers, they worked within manufacturing enterprises or close to centers of industry. Therefore they had a foot in the most dynamic centers of the economy and could, with time, rise to semiskilled and skilled positions.[9]

Except for a handful of industrial slaves and free Negroes, Afro-Americans did not gain substantial entry into manufacturing industry until World War I (see Starobin, 1970; Litwack, 1961; Baron, 1971), and the stereotype has long existed that Asians and Indians were not fit for factory work. For the most part then, third world groups have been relegated to labor in preindustrial sectors of the nonagricultural economy. Chinese and Mexicans, for example, were used extensively in mining and building railroads, industries that were essential to the early development of a national capitalist economy, but which were primarily prerequisites of industrial development rather than industries with any dynamic future.[10]

Geography: concentration in peripheral regions

Even geographically the Europeans were in more fortunate positions. The dynamic and modern centers of the nation have been the North-east and the Midwest, the predominant areas of white immigration. The third world groups were located away from these centers: Africans in the South, Mexicans

[8] Analyzing early twentieth-century data on European immigrant groups, Steinberg (1971) has found significant differences in occupational background, literacy, and other mobility-related factors. The Jews were consistently advantaged on these points, Catholic ethnic groups such as Poles and Italians disadvantaged.

[9] Even in the first generation, immigrants were never as thoroughly clustered in unskilled labor as blacks, Mexicans, and Chinese were in their early years. In 1855, when New York Irishmen dominated the fields of common labor and domestic service, there were sizable numbers (more than a thousand in each category) working as blacksmiths, carpenters, masons, painters, stonecutters, clerks, shoemakers, tailors, food dealers and cartmen (Ernst, 1965, pp. 214–17).

[10] Of course some Europeans did parallel labor in mining and transportation construction. But since they had the freedom of movement that was denied colored laborers, they could transfer the skills and experience gained to other pursuits.

in their own Southwest, Asians on the Pacific Coast, the Indians pushed relentlessly 'across the frontier' toward the margins of the society. Thus Irish, Italians, and Jews went directly to the Northern cities and its unskilled labor market, whereas Afro-Americans had to take two extra 'giant steps', rather than the immigrants' one, before their large-scale arrival in the same place in the present century: the emancipation from slavery and migration from the underdeveloped semicolonial Southern region. Another result of colonized entry and labor placement is that the racial groups had to go through major historical dislocations within this country before they could arrive at the point in the economy where the immigrants began! When finally they did arrive in Northern cities, that economy had changed to their disadvantage. Technological trends in industry had drastically reduced the number of unskilled jobs available for people with little formal education (Kerner Report, 1968).

Racial discrimination

To these 'structural' factors must be added the factor of racial discrimination. The argument that Jews, Italians, and Irish also faced prejudice in hiring misses the point. Herman Bloch's historical study (1969, pp. 34–46) of Afro-Americans in New York provides clear evidence that immigrant groups benefited from racism. When blacks began to consolidate in skilled jobs that yielded relatively decent wages and some security, Germans, Irish, and Italians came along to usurp occupation after occupation, forcing blacks out and down into the least skilled, marginal reaches of the economy.[11] Although the European immigrant was only struggling to better his lot, the irony is that his relative success helped to block the upward economic mobility of Northern blacks. Without such a combination of immigration and white racism, the Harlems and the South Chicagos might have become solid working-class and middle-class communities with the economic and social resources to absorb and aid the incoming masses of Southerners, much as European ethnic groups have been able to do for their newcomers. The mobility of Asians, Mexicans, and Indians has been contained by similar discrimination and expulsion from hard-won occupational bases.[12]

Our look at the labor situation of the colonized and the immigrant minorities calls into question the popular sociological idea that there is no funda-

[11] That discrimination in the labor market continues to make a strong contribution to income disparity between white and nonwhite is demonstrated in Thurow's careful study (1969).

[12] As far as I know no study exists that has attempted to analyze industrial and occupational competition among a variety of ethnic and racial groups. Such research would be very valuable. With respect to discrimination against Asians and Mexicans, Pitt (1970, chap. 3), for example, describes how white and European miners were largely successful in driving Chinese and Mexican independent prospectors out of the gold fields.

mental difference in condition and history between the nonwhite poor today and the ethnic poor of past generations. This dangerous myth is used by the children of the immigrants to rationalize racial oppression and to oppose the demands of third world people for special group recognition and economic policies—thus the folk beliefs that all Americans 'started at the bottom' and most have been able to 'work themselves up through their own efforts.' But the racial labor principle has meant, in effect, that 'the bottom' has by no means been the same for all groups. In addition, the cultural experiences of third world and immigrant groups have diverged in America, a matter I take up in the next section.

Culture and social organization

Labor status and the quality of entry had their most significant impact on the cultural dynamics of minority people. Every new group that entered America experienced cultural conflict, the degree depending on the newcomers' distance from the Western European, Anglo-Saxon Protestant norm. Since the cultures of people of color in America, as much as they differed from one another, were non-European and non-Western, their encounters with dominant institutions have resulted in a more intense conflict of ethos and world view than was the case for the various Western elements that fed into the American nation. The divergent situations of colonization and immigration were fateful in determining the ability of minorities to develop group integrity and autonomous community life in the face of WASP ethnocentrism and cultural hegemony.

Voluntary immigration and free labor status made it possible for European minorities to establish new social relationships and cultural forms after a period of adjustment to the American scene. One feature of the modern labor relationship is the separation of the place of work from the place of residence or community. European ethnics were exploited on the job, but in the urban ghettos where they lived they had the insulation and freedom to carry on many aspects of their old country cultures—to speak their languages, establish their religions and build institutions such as schools, newspapers, welfare societies, and political organizations. In fact, because they had been oppressed in Europe—by such imperial powers as England, Tsarist Russia, and the Hapsburg Monarchy—the Irish, Poles, Jews, and other East Europeans actually had more autonomy in the New World for their cultural and political development. In the case of the Italians, many of their immigrant institutions had no counterpart in Italy, and a sense of nationality, overriding parochial and regional identities, developed only in the United States (Nelli, 1970).

But there were pressures toward assimilation; the norm of 'Anglo-conformity' has been a dynamic of domination central to American life (Gordon, 1964). The early immigrants were primarily from Western Europe. Therefore, their institutions were close to the dominant pattern, and assimilation for them did not involve great conflict. Among later newcomers from Eastern and Southern Europe, however, the disparity in values and institutions made the goal of cultural pluralism attractive for a time; to many of the first generation, America's assimilation dynamic must have appeared oppressive. The majority of their children, on the other hand, apparently welcomed Americanization, for with the passage of time many, if not most, European ethnics have merged into the larger society, and the distinctive Euro-American communities have taken on more and more of the characteristics of the dominant culture.

The cultural experience of third world people in America has been different. The labor systems through which people of color became Americans tended to destroy or weaken their cultures and communal ties. Regrouping and new institutional forms developed, but in situations with extremely limited possibilities. The transformation of group life that is central to the colonial cultural dynamic took place most completely on the plantation. Slavery in the United States appears to have gone the farthest in eliminating African social and cultural forms; the plantation system provided the most restricted context for the development of new kinds of group integrity.[13]

In New York City, Jews were able to reconstruct their East European family system, with its distinctive sex roles and interlocking sets of religious rituals and customs. Some of these patterns broke down or changed in response, primarily, to economic conditions, but the changes took time and occurred within a community of fellow ethnics with considerable cultural autonomy. The family systems of West Africans, however, could not be reconstructed under plantation slavery, since in this labor system the 'community' of workers was subordinated to the imperatives of the production process. Africans of the same ethnic group could not gather together because their assignment to plantations and subsequent movements were controlled by slaveholders who endeavored to eliminate any basis for group solidarity. Even assimilation to American kinship forms was denied as an alternative, since masters freely broke up families when it suited their economic or other interests.[14] In the nonplantation context, the disruption of culture and sup-

---

[13] Beltran (1959, p. 70) makes the point that the plantation system was more significant than enforced migration in affecting African cultural development in the new world. 'This system, which had created institutionalized forms of land tenure, work patterns, specialization of labor, consumption and distribution of produce, destroyed African economic forms by forceably imposing Western forms. [. . .] Negro political life along with African social structure, was in a position of subordination.'

[14] I do not imply here that African culture was totally eliminated, nor that Afro-Americans have lived in a cultural vacuum. A distinctive black culture emerged during slavery. From the complex vicissitudes of their historical experience in the United States, Afro-American culture has continued its development and differentiation to the present day, providing an ethnic content to black peoplehood. For a full discussion, see Blauner (1972, chap. 4).

pression of the regrouping dynamic was less extreme. But systems of debt servitude and semifree agricultural labor had similar, if less drastic, effects. The first generations of Chinese in the United States were recruited for gang labor; they therefore entered without women and children. Had they been free immigrants, most of whom also were male initially, the group composition would have normalized in time with the arrival of wives and families. But as bonded laborers without even the legal rights of immigrants, the Chinese were powerless to fight the exclusion acts of the late nineteenth century, which left predominantly male communities in America's Chinatowns for many decades. In such a skewed social structure, leading features of Chinese culture could not be reconstructed. A similar male-predominant group emerged among mainland Filipinos. In the twentieth century the migrant work situation of Mexican–American farm laborers has operated against stable community life and the building of new institutional forms in politics and education. However, Mexican culture as a whole has retained considerable strength in the Southwest because Chicanos have remained close to their original territory, language, and religion.

Yet the colonial attack on culture is more than a matter of economic factors such as labor recruitment and special exploitation. The colonial situation differs from the class situation of capitalism precisely in the importance of culture as an instrument of domination.[15] Colonialism depends on conquest, control, and the imposition of new institutions and ways of thought. Culture and social organization are important as vessels of a people's autonomy and integrity; when cultures are whole and vigorous, conquest, penetration, and certain modes of control are more readily resisted.[16] Therefore, imperial regimes attempt, consciously or unwittingly, either to destroy the cultures of colonized people, or when it is more convenient, to exploit them for the purposes of more efficient control and economic profit. As Mina Caulfield (1972) has put it, imperialism exploits the cultures of the colonized as much as it does their labor. Among America's third world groups, Africans, Indians, and Mexicans are all conquered peoples whose cultures have been in various degrees destroyed, exploited, and controlled. One key function of racism, defined here as the assumption of the superiority of white Westerners and their cultures and the concomitant denial of the humanity of people of color, is that it 'legitimates' cultural oppression in the colonial situation.

The present-day inclination to equate racism against third world groups

[15] According to Stokely Carmichael (1971), capitalism exploits its own working classes, while racist systems colonize alien peoples of color. Here colonization refers to dehumanization, the tendency toward the destruction of culture and peoplehood, above and beyond exploitation.

[16] An historical study of Brazilian coffee plantations illustrates how African cultural institutions were the focal point for the slave's resistance to intensified exploitation (Stein, 1957, pt. 3).

with the ethnic prejudice and persecution that immigrant groups have experienced is mistaken. Compare, for example, intolerance and discrimination in the sphere of religion. European Jews who followed their orthodox religion were mocked and scorned, but they never lost the freedom to worship in their own way. Bigotry certainly contributed to the Americanization of contemporary Judaism, but the Jewish religious transformation has been a slow and predominantly voluntary adaptation to the group's social and economic mobility. In contrast, the U.S. policy against Native American religion in the nineteenth century was one of all-out attack; the goal was cultural genocide. Various tribal rituals and beliefs were legally proscribed and new religious movements were met by military force and physical extermination. The largest twentieth-century movement, the Native American Church, was outlawed for years because of its peyote ceremony (Collier, 1947, pp. 132–42) Other. third world groups experienced similar, if perhaps less concerted, attacks on their cultural institutions. In the decade following the conquest, California prohibited bullfighting and severely restricted other popular Mexican sports (Pitt, 1970, pp. 196–7). In the same state various aspects of Chinese culture, dress, pigtails, and traditional forms of recreation were outlawed. Although it was tolerated in Brazil and the Caribbean, the use of the drum, the instrument that was the central means of communication among African peoples, was successfully repressed in the North American slave states (Jahn, n.d., p. 217).

American capitalism has been partially successful in absorbing third world groups into its economic system and culture. Because of the colonial experience and the prevalence of racism, this integration has been much less complete than in the case of the ethnic groups. The white ethnics who entered the class system at its lowest point were exploited, but not colonized. Because their group realities were not systematically violated in the course of immigration, adaptation, and integration, the white newcomers could become Americans more or less at their own pace and on their own terms. They have moved up, though slowly in the case of some groups, into working-class and middle-class positions. Their cultural dynamic has moved from an initial stage of group consciousness and ethnic pluralism to a present strategy of individual mobility and assimilation. The immigrants have become part of the white majority, partaking of the racial privilege in a colonizing society; their assimilation into the dominant culture is now relatively complete, even though ethnic identity is by no means dead among them. In the postwar period it has asserted itself in a third-generation reaction to 'overassimilation' (see Herberg, 1955) and more recently as a response to third world movements. But the ethnic groups have basically accepted the overall culture's rules of 'making it' within the system, including the norms of racial oppression that benefit them directly or indirectly.

The situation and outlook of the racial minorities are more ambiguous. From the moment of their entry into the Anglo-American system, the third world peoples have been oppressed as groups, and their group realities have been under continuing attack. Unfree and semifree labor relations as well as the undermining of non-Western cultures have deprived the colonized of the autonomy to regroup their social forms according to their own needs and rhythms. During certain periods in the past, individual assimilation into the dominant society was seen as both a political and a personal solution to this dilemma. As an individual answer it has soured for many facing the continuing power of racism at all levels of the society. As a collective strategy, assimilation is compromised by the recognition that thus far only a minority have been able to improve their lot in this way, as well as by the feeling that it weakens group integrity and denies their cultural heritage. At the same time the vast majority of third world people in America 'want in'. Since the racial colonialism of the United States is embedded in a context of industrial capitalism, the colonized must look to the economy, division of labor, and politics of the larger society for their individual and group aspirations. Both integration into the division of labor and the class system of American capitalism as well as the 'separatist' culture building and nationalist politics of third world groups reflect the complex realities of a colonial capitalist society.[17]

The colonial interpretation of American race relations helps illuminate the present-day shift in emphasis toward cultural pluralism and ethnic nationalism on the part of an increasing segment of third world people. The building of social solidarity and group culture is an attempt to complete the long historical project that colonial domination made so critical and so problematic. It involves a de-emphasis on individual mobility and assimilation, since these approaches cannot speak to the condition of the most economically oppressed, nor fundamentally affect the realities of colonization. Such issues require group action and political struggle. Collective consciousness is growing among third world people, and their efforts to advance economically have a political character that challenges longstanding patterns of racial and cultural subordination.

Conclusion: the third world perspective

Let us return to the basic assumptions of the third world perspective and examine the idea that a common oppression has created the conditions for effective unity among the constituent racial groups. The third world ideology attempts to promote the consciousness of such common circumstances by emphasizing that the similarities in situation among America's people of

---

[17] These two poles of the pendulum, integration and nationalism, have long been recognized as central to the political dynamics of American blacks. As early as 1903 Du Bois (1903) analyzed the existential 'twoness' of the American Negro experience which lies behind this dilemma. However it is a general phenomenon applicable to all third world people in the United States, to the extent that their history has been a colonial one.

color are the essential matter, the differences less relevant. I would like to suggest some problems in this position.

Each third world people has undergone distinctive, indeed cataclysmic, experiences on the American continent that separate its history from the others, as well as from whites. Only Native Americans waged a 300-year war against white encroachment; only they were subject to genocide and removal. Only Chicanos were severed from an ongoing modern nation; only they remain concentrated in the area of their original land base, close to Mexico. Only blacks went through a 250-year period of slavery. The Chinese were the first people whose presence was interdicted by exclusion acts. The Japanese were the one group declared an internal enemy and rounded up in concentration camps. Though the notion of colonized minorities points to a similarity of situation, it should not imply that black, red, yellow, and brown Americans are all in the same bag. Colonization has taken different forms in the histories of the individual groups. Each people is strikingly heterogeneous, and the variables of time, place, and manner have affected the forms of colonialism, the character of racial domination, and the responses of the group.

Because the colonized groups have been concentrated in different regions, geographical isolation has heretofore limited the possibilities of cooperation.[18] When they have inhabited the same area, competition for jobs has fed ethnic antagonisms. Today, as relatively powerless groups, the racial minorities often find themselves fighting one another for the modicum of political power and material resources involved in antipoverty, model-cities, and educational reform projects. Differences in culture and political style exacerbate these conflicts.

The third world movement will have to deal with the situational differences that are obstacles to coalition and coordinated politics. One of these is the great variation in size between the populous black and Chicano groups and the much smaller Indian and Asian minorities. Numbers affect potential political power as well as an ethnic group's visibility and the possibilities of an assimilative strategy. Economic differentiation may be accelerating both between and within third world groups. The racial minorities are not all poor. The Japanese and, to a lesser extent, the Chinese have moved toward middle class status. The black middle class also is growing. The ultimate barrier to effective third world alliance is the pervasive racism of the society, which affects people of color as well as whites, furthering division between all groups in America. Colonialism brings into its orbit a variety of groups, which it oppresses and exploits in differing degrees and fashions; the result is a complex structure of racial and ethnic division.[19]

[18] The historical accounts also indicate a number of instances of solidarity. A serious study of the history of unity and disunity among third world groups in America is badly needed.

[19] The ethnic and racially 'plural society' is another characteristic colonial phenomenon See Furnivall (1956), and Smith (1965).

The final assumption of the third world idea remains to be considered. The new perspective represents more than a negation of the immigrant analogy. By its very language the concept assumes an essential connection between the colonized people within the United States and the peoples of Africa, Asia, and Latin America, with respect to whom the idea of *le tiers monde* originated. The communities of color in America share essential conditions with third world nations abroad: economic underdevelopment, a heritage of colonialism and neocolonialism, and a lack of real political autonomy and power.[20]

This insistence on viewing American race relations from an international perspective is an important corrective to the parochial and a historical outlook of our national consciousness. The economic, social, and political subordination of third world groups in America is a microcosm of the position of all peoples of color in the world order of stratification. This is neither an accident nor the result of some essential racial genius. Racial domination in the United States is part of a world historical drama in which the culture, economic system, and political power of the white West has spread throughout virtually the entire globe. The expansion of the West, particularly Europe's domination over non-Western people of color, was the major theme in the almost five hundred years that followed the onset of 'The Age of Discovery'. The European conquest of Native American peoples, leading to the white settlement of the Western hemisphere and the African slave trade, was one of the leading historical events that ushered in the age of colonialism.[21] Colonial subjugation and racial domination began much earlier and have lasted much longer in North America than in Asia and Africa, the continents usually thought of as colonial prototypes. The oppression of racial colonies within our national borders cannot be understood without considering worldwide patterns of white European hegemony.

The present movement goes further than simply drawing historical and contemporary parallels between the third world within and the third world external to the United States. The new ideology implies that the fate of colonized Americans is tied up with that of the colonial and former colonial peoples of the world. There is at least impressionistic evidence to support this idea. If one looks at the place of the various racial minorities in America's stratified economic and social order, one finds a rough correlation between relative internal status and the international position of the original fatherland. According to most indicators of income, education, and occupation, Native Americans are at the bottom. The Indians alone lack an inde-

[20] The connection has been cogently argued by Johnson (1971) and by Tabb (1970, chap. 2).

However, the international perspective on American racial problems is by no means new. W. E. B. Du Bois was one of its early exponents, and in more recent years Malcolm X placed domestic racism and strategies of liberation in a worldwide context. For a discussion of the internationalizing of Malcolm's politics, see Allen (1969, pp. 31–4).

[21] The other major event was instituting trade with India.

pendent nation, a center of power in the world community to which they might look for political aid and psychic identification. At the other pole, Japanese–Americans are the most successful nonwhite group by conventional criteria, and Japan has been the most economically developed and politically potent non-Western nation during most of the twentieth century. The transformation of African societies from colonial dependency to independent statehood, with new authority and prestige in the international arena, has had an undoubted impact on Afro-Americans in the United States; it has contributed both to civil rights movements and to a developing black consciouⁿness.[22]

What is not clear is whether an international strategy can in itself be the principle of third world liberation within this country. Since the oppression, the struggle, and the survival of the colonized groups have taken place within our society, it is to be expected that their people will orient their daily lives and their political aspirations to the domestic scene. The racial minorities have been able to wrest some material advantages from American capitalism and empire at the same time that they have been denied real citizenship in the society. Average levels of income, education, and health for the third world in the United States are far above their counterparts overseas; this gap will affect the possibility of internationalism. Besides which, group alliances that transcend national borders have been difficult to sustain in the modern era because of the power of nationalism.

Thus, the situation of the colonized minorities in the United States is by no means identical with that of Algerians, Kenyans, Indonesians, and other nations who suffered under white European rule. Though there are many parallels in cultural and political developments, the differences in land, economy, population composition, and power relations make it impossible to transport wholesale sociopolitical analyses or strategies of liberation from one context to another. The colonial analogy has gained great vogue recently among militant nationalists—partly because it is largely valid, partly because its rhetoric so aggressively condemns white America, past and present. Yet it may be that the comparison with English, French, and Dutch overseas rule lets our nation off too easily! In many ways the special versions of colonialism

[22] In the early 1970s Pan-Africanism seems to be gaining ground among black American militants and intellectuals. The most celebrated spokesman has been Stokely Carmichael who has virtually eschewed the struggle in the United States. The *Black Scholar* devoted its February and March (1971) issues to Pan-Africanism. Afro-American organizations have been challenging the South African involvements of U.S. business and government, as, for example, in the action of black employees against the Polaroid Corporation. Chicano groups have been taking an active political interest in Mexico and Latin America. On some university campuses Asian militants have taken the lead in protesting American imperialism and genocide in Southeast Asia. Whereas only recently black and brown nationalists tended to see antiwar protest as a white middle-class 'trip', the third world perspective has led to an aggressive condemnation of the war in Indochina and a sense of solidarity with the Vietnamese people.

practiced against Americans of color have been more pernicious in quality
and more profound in consequences than the European overseas varieties.

In traditional colonialism, the colonized 'natives' have usually been the
majority of the population, and their culture, while less prestigious than that
of the white Europeans, still pervaded the landscape. Members of the third
world within the United States are individually and collectively outnumbered
by whites, and Anglo-American cultural imperatives dominate the society—
although this has been less true historically in the Southwest where the
Mexican–American population has never been a true cultural minority
(McWilliams, 1948). The oppressed masses of Asia and Africa had the
relative 'advantage' of being colonized in their own land.[23] In the United
States, the more total cultural domination, the alienation of most third world
people from a land base, and the numerical minority factor have weakened
the group integrity of the colonized and their possibilities for cultural and
political self-determination.

Many critics of the third world perspective seize on these differences to
question the value of viewing America's racial dynamics within the colonial
framework. But all the differences demonstrate is that colonialisms vary
greatly in structure and that political power and group liberation are more
problematic in our society than in the overseas situation. The fact that we
have no historical models for decolonization in the American context does
not alter the objective realities. Decolonization is an insistent and irreversible
project of the third world groups, although its contents and forms are at
present unclear and will be worked out only in the course of an extended
period of political and social conflict.

References

Allen, R. L. (1969), *Black Awakening in Capitalist America*, New York.
Banfield, E. (1970), *The Unheavenly City*, Boston.
Baron, H. M. (1971), 'The demand for black labor: historical notes on the political
economy of racism', *Radical America*, 5, March–April, pp. 1–46.
Barth, G. (1964), *Bitter Strength, A History of the Chinese in the United States,
1850–1870*, Harvard.
Beltran, G. A. (1959), 'African influences in the development of regional cultures
in the New World', in Pan American Union, 'Plantation systems of the New
World', *Social Science Monographs*, 7.
Blauner, R. (1972), *Racial Oppression in America*, New York.

[23] Within the United States, Native Americans and Chicanos, in general, retain more
original culture than blacks and Asians, because they faced European power in their home-
lands, rather than being transported to the nation of the colonized. Of course the ecological
advantage of colonization at home tends to be undermined to the extent to which large
European settlements overwhelm numerically the original people, as happened in much of
Indo-America. And in much of the Americas a relative cultural integrity among Indian
peoples exists at the expense of economic impoverishment and backwardness.

Bloch, H. (1969), *The Circle of Discrimination*, New York.
Carmichael, S. (1971), 'Free Huey' in E. Minor (ed.), *Stokely Speaks*, New York.
Carmichael, S. and Hamilton, C. (1967), *Black Power*, New York.
Carrasco, P. (1959), cited in S. W. Mintz, 'The plantation as a socio-cultural type', in Pan American Union, 'Plantation systems of the New World', *Social Science Monographs*, 7.
Caulfield, M. D. (1972), 'Culture and imperialism: proposing a new dialectic', in D. Himes (ed.), *Reinventing Anthropology*, New York.
Collier, J. (1947), *The Indians of the Americas*, New York.
Daniels, R. (1962), *The Politics of Prejudice*, Berkeley.
Daniels, R. and Kitano, H. (1970), *American Racism*, Englewood Cliffs, N.J.
Du Bois, W. E. B. (1903), *The Souls of Black Folk*, Chicago.
Ernst, R. (1965), *Immigrant Life in New York City, 1825–1863*, Port Washington, N.Y.
Fernandes, F. (1969), 'The weight of the past', in J. H. Franklin (ed.), *Color and Race*, Boston.
Furnival, J. S. (1956), *Colonial Policy and Practice*, New York.
Glazer, N. (ed.) (1970), *Cities in Trouble*, New York.
Gordon, M. (1964), *Assimilation in American Life*, Oxford.
Grebler, L., Moore, J. W. and Guzman, R. C. (1970), *The Mexican American People*, Glencoe, Ill.
Handlin, O. (1951), *The Uprooted*, New York.
Handlin, O. (1959), *Boston's Immigrants*, Harvard.
Harris, M. (1964), *Patterns of Race in America*, New York.
Herberg, W. (1955), *Protestant—Catholic—Jew*, New York.
Higham, J. (1969), *Strangers in the Land*, New York.
Hoetink, H. (1967), *Two Variants of Race Relations in the Caribbean*, Oxford.
Jahn, J. (n.d.), *Muntu*, New York.
Johnson, D. L. (1971), 'On oppressed classes and the role of the social scientist in human liberation', in F. Cockroft and D. Johnson (eds.), *The Political Economy of Underdevelopment in Latin America*, New York.
Jordan, W. (1968), *White over Black*, Chapel Hill, N.C.
Kerner, (1968), *Report of the National Advisory Commission on Civil Disorders*, New York.
Kitano, H. H. L. (1969), *Japanese–Americans: The Evolution of a Subculture*, Englewood Cliffs, N.J.
Kloosterboer, W. (1960), *Involuntary Labour Since the Abolition of Slavery*, New York.
Litwack, L. (1961), *North of Slavery*, Chicago.
Macleod, W. C. (1928), *The American Indian Frontier*, London.
McEvoy, J. and Miller, A. (eds.) (1969), *Black Power and Student Rebellion*.
McWilliams, C. (1934), *Factories in the Fields*, Boston.
McWilliams, C. (1942), *Ill Fares the Land*, Boston.
McWilliams, C. (1948), *North from Mexico*, Philadelphia.
McWilliams, C. (1968), *The Mexicans in America, A Student's Guide to Localized History*, New York.

Miller, S. (1969), *The Unwelcome Immigrant: The American Image of the Chinese, 1785–1882*, Berkeley.

Nelli, H. S. (1970), *Italians in Chicago 1880–1930: A Study in Ethnic Mobility*, Oxford.

Pitt, L. (1970), *The Decline of Californias, A Social History of the Spanish-Speaking Californians, 1846–1890*, Berkeley.

Smith, M. G. (1965), *The Plural Society in the British West Indies*, Berkeley.

Starobin, R. (1970), *Industrial Slavery in the Old South*, Oxford.

Stein, S. (1957), *Vassouras*, Harvard.

Steinberg, S. (1971), 'The religious factor in higher education', Doctoral Dissertation, Department of Sociology, University of California.

Tabb, W. K. (1970), *The Political Economy of the Black Ghetto*, New York.

Thurow, L. (1969), *Poverty and Discrimination*, New York.

Weber, M. (1950), *General Economic History*, Glencoe, Ill.

7 *R. A. Schermerhorn,* Comparative Ethnic Relations

System analysis and power-conflict theory as dialectically related perspectives on ethnic relations

By this time [*sic*] the attentive reader is doubtless beginning to wonder what the relevance of these theoretical issues is to the study of ethnic group relations. While no easy answer to this question can be given, it is imperative to make the attempt. At this stage of the discussion I can suggest only the barest outline of the resolution this query can receive and leave it to the rest of the volume to round out the story.

In the first place a comparative study requires a view of ethnic groups in a macrosociological perspective, i.e., in their relation to total societies. In observing these relations it is fruitful to become aware of the two major theoretical interpretations of total societies given by the system analysts and the power-conflict theorists. In this all-too-brief review of the two perspectives I have tried to present them in ways that would be useful for the purposes of comparative study. Parsons and Levy are singled out as the most significant contemporary representatives of system analysis, and Lenski is designated as the chief exponent of power-conflict theory with Dahrendorf as a subordinate figure. Applying system analysis to comparative ethnic relations actually centers attention on the functions the ethnic group performs for the entire system, viewing the ethnic group itself as a subsystem gradually fitted into the entire society by a series of adaptive adjustments regulated by the norms and values of its institutions that eventually become internalized by members of the ethnic groups involved. On the other hand, from the standpoint of power-conflict theory one can view each ethnic group as being in an embattled position, fighting for its life, its identity, or its prestige, subject to perpetual constraints that threaten its survival, its freedom, or its life chances in a precarious world. All of the discussion so far has suggested that I am not fully commited to either view. Actually, neither perspective can exclude the other without unwarranted dogmatism. This holds true both at the global

---

R. A. Schermerhorn, *Comparative Ethnic Relations: A Framework for Theory and Research*, Random House, 1970, pp. 50–9.

level of total societies as well as in the more limited spheres of ethnic groups and their interactions with dominant groups. In the broader perspective Robin Williams' proposition states explicitly what most sociologists would now accept with very little argument, i.e., 'all interacting human populations show both coerced and voluntary conformity' (Williams, 1966, p. 718). In like manner another functionalist concludes that 'opposition, i.e., organised and regulated antagonism, is, of course, an essential feature of every social system' (Radcliffe-Brown, 1952, p. 181n).

But the problem is also an empirical one. It is important to search out, by inductive inquiry, observation and analysis, the meanings of such propositions as Williams and Radcliffe-Brown have advanced, then to apprehend their meaning by seeing the specific properties of the facts to which our two different theories apply. And perhaps no field of inquiry is better fitted to exemplify the dual relevance of such ostensibly clashing theories than the sphere of ethnic relations.

To illustrate: the expansion of European peoples to other parts of the globe from the fifteenth to the nineteenth centuries was a succession of conquests overpowering innumerable 'native' peoples by coercion. To a number of Western Hemisphere countries with such a historical past came millions of immigrants in the nineteenth and twentieth centuries; yet in this latter invasion, strife and violence were exceptional rather than the rule. To anticipate later discussion in the present volume: here are two contrasting social situations, conquest and migration, where quite opposite forms of social interaction ensue. Stanley Lieberson (1961) refers to the former as 'migrant superordination' and the latter as 'migrant subordination', asserting that warfare is common in the first case, while the absence of long-term conflict characterizes the second.

A simple way of resolving these situational differences is to divide and rule, i.e., apply the power-conflict theory in those instances where it is pertinent, and do the same for system analysis in another set of situations amenable to *its* form of explanation. This mode of operation may be called *mechanical allocation*. It has the general support in Dahrendorf's suggestion that the uprising of East German workers in 1953 has a suitable explanation in 'coercion theory', while the addition of a personnel manager's role to bureaucratic organization in modern industry is better interpreted by 'integration theory' (Dahrendorf, 1959, pp. 161–2). Theoreticians may smile at the apparent simplemindedness of this approach and yet mechanical allocation is definitely a step forward. By allocating disparate theories to alternate sectors of the research field, it is certainly preferable to a theoretical monopoly on one side or the other. Monopoly in this case would bring with it either one or the other of two fateful consequences: (1) procrustean dogmatism stretching a theory beyond its clearly relevant application by rigid retention of categories regardless of their fitness; or (2) selective attention to problems and situations that the theory explains quite creditably, and ignoring all others. It is reassuring to reflect that social scientists in the main have opted for the second error rather than the first; at least the second alternative leaves the way open to fill in the areas left incomplete, while the first will accept any distortion so long as it supports the *a priori* assumptions. Thus the lapse of *omission* is less damaging than the positive offense of *commission;* though Dahrendorf formally recognizes mechanical allocation as an advance on selective attention —criticizing Parsons for the latter—his own elaborate exposition of conflict theory eventually turns out to be fully as one-sided in its way as the Parsonian is in the opposite way.

The field of ethnic relations lends itself so readily to power-conflict analysis that it runs the same risk of selective attention. On the face of it, as already noted, the relationship between subordinate ethnic groups and dominant groups in any society is a power relationship that gives the superordinates the chance to use sanctions on those below them with little fear of successful retaliation. It is possible to set up a macrosociological theory which makes the sole independent variable a set of power relations; these can then be assumed to have explanatory validity in accounting for the modes of action on the part of subordinates and superordinates vis-à-vis each other. I have already amplified and enlarged such a view in an earlier article where the implications of this type of theory are developed in some detail (Schermer-horn, 1965). Only after repeated unsuccessful attempts to apply this interpretation universally to ethnic relations throughout the world have I been driven to the conclusion that the framework is insufficient. It would require another volume to spell out all the reasons for this in detail—a task for another quite different and separate analysis—but at least it is possible to indicate briefly here and now the central reason for shifting to a more dialectical view in which system analysis assumes correlative importance.

As much as any one influence, the writings of Max Gluckman on conflict have been crucially important. What comes through clearly from his analysis is that conflict interactions between groups of unequal power *engender* integrative bonds that have system characteristics. They are not something superadded but an inherent feature of the process of change. Gluckman's portrayal of colonial conquest in South Africa, for example, has so many overtones reminiscent of parallel movements throughout the world, that it furnishes a kind of paradigm for them. He shows quite clearly that mutuality even appears at times when social conflict would seem to destroy it. In initial stages, the encounter as he pictures it, is highly ambiguous with numerous attempts (and successes) at finding reciprocal interests.

For example, when the British penetrated South Africa at first, they found Shaka, a Zulu king, who had established an empire of conquest over many adjacent tribes. As British traders opened up commerce with the Zulus, some traders became regular visitors to Shaka's court and soon were favored personages there. As a mark of royal favor, Shaka made them his 'chiefs' at Port Natal and incorporated them into his political system. Soon the Boers entered from the west, and when Shaka's brothers fought over the succession, one brother formed a coalition with the Dutch to oust the other. Later the British and Dutch came into opposition, but when Zulu tribes massacred the Boer trekkers, the British formed an alliance with the Dutch against the Zulu. Then as the British continued to extend their domains by force, many tribes, formerly conquered by Shaka, rallied to the British and, quite unsought, claimed protection from the latter. Eventually the Swazi called upon the British to stop Zulu attacks on the former, and another coalition came into existence. Thus a historical period that was, from one point of view, a series of intermittent conflicts, was also, from the opposite point of view, a period in which mutual interests found frequent, if temporary, stable points of reference. Alliances and coalitions changed rapidly, each of them constituting a temporary social system bringing order with it for the time being; when that order was threatened, a new order was quickly formed to prevent utter chaos and anarchy.

Gluckman then states the significance of these processes in the shape of a principle: 'when the members of two societies come into relationship with one another, they quickly establish regularized relations, and the form of these relations may be shaped by internal conflicts in either society' (Gluckman, 1955, p. 143).[1] It is also true that the vicissitudes of these shifting temporary systems in South Africa proved unsatisfactory and partial, so they were finally superseded by the *pax Britannica*. While this was obviously established by the superior force of British arms, it was also facilitated by the fact that it 'seemed a blessing to many Zulu' and 'while that rule put an end to certain things which the Zulu valued, it satisfied other Zulu interests, both general and particular' (p. 145). The fluctuations of such temporary alliances were also a feature of British colonials in their relations with American Indians at an earlier date, complicated by the presence of the French in North America, as it was by the Dutch in South Africa (McLeod, 1928).

Such forms of order also appear after the intermittent hostilities of initial conquest. System unities bind men together in functional bonds even when the more permanent rule is harsh and oppressive. With the passage of time, institutional links then bring a web of interdependencies that even the most

---

[1] As Van den Berghe (1967) succinctly puts it, 'the whole complex history of Boer–British–African conflict in South Africa can . . . be reduced to a few simplifying generalizations such as that, when the Africans constituted a threat, the Boer and the British stopped fighting each other and ganged up on the Africans. Conversely, when the Africans were subjugated, Boer–British conflicts became reactivated. The situation is one of "two-tiered" conflict (white-non-white and Boer–British) in which two levels of conflict stand in rough inverse relation to each other' (personal communication). One must add, in view of our main point here, that conflicts at one level or tier precipitated coalitions and reciprocal bonds at the other level.

unprivileged hesitate to break. We have already noted such relationships in the money economy of South Africa and its accompanying industrial organization. Such institutional bonds contain conflicts in ways not fully explained by the constraints of police or military personnel.

Thailand offers another and quite different example of the way that conflict and system linkages go hand in hand. There the Chinese community is only about ten per cent of the total population; intermittent conflict between Thai and Chinese is endemic. Much of this stems from the fact that the Chinese are outsiders, on the one hand (immigrants or of immigrant descent), or that they have captured the lion's share of commerce in Thailand's economy, on the other hand. As political regimes change, varieties of legislation are introduced with the Chinese as targets—now restricting immigration, now sharply limiting the privileges of citizenship, now putting differential regulations on the granting of licenses to Chinese for commercial purposes. The intense rivalry for shares of the market that exists among entrepreneurs in both communities, exacerbated by the special privileges that Thai legislation grants to members of its own group, has eventually precipitated a mechanism to regulate the discord and keep it within bounds. This regulatory mechanism is covert, clandestine, and non-institutional. It embraces ties of mutual advantage between economic leaders of the Chinese group and political figures of upper or lower status among the Thais. In the top echelons, the more wealthy Chinese not only have close connections with Thai rulers and the nobility, but often bring the latter into business partnership. In this way the Thai upper classes could win financial gain without expending much effort while the Chinese managers win protection. In the lower echelons the initiative often comes from Thai police or minor government officials who offer 'protection' to Chinese for a fee whenever taxes are collected, licenses granted, or discriminatory regulations are to be enforced. This amounts to a kind of surplus tax on Chinese commerce with a faint touch of blackmail (Skinner, 1958).

The upshot of these arrangements is that instrumental ties linking members of both ethnic groups together at many status levels are informal bonds that hold an over-arching system together by exploiting the very conflict that would otherwise be highly explosive. 'To a very considerable extent Chinese blood and Chinese money are now so deeply embedded in the metabolism of leadership, bureaucracy and industry in Bangkok that the city could scarcely survive without it' (Hunter, 1966, p. 47).

Three tentative conclusions result from observations like these: (1) system analysis obtrudes itself even at points where conflict theory is genuinely pertinent; (2) certain types of ethnic relations draw on sets of assumptions from *both* theories as heuristic guidelines for interpretive purposes; (3) 'mechanical allocation' as described above is insufficient; it is a definitely limited principle that must be superseded by positing some kind of dialectical re-

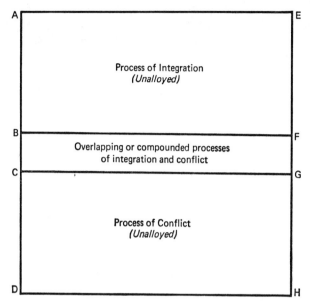

Figure 1. Rare linkage of integration and conflict

lationship even though the latter has *differential theoretical relevance* in one society as compared with another.

In the area of ethnic relations it is possible to bring out this duality by denying that integration is inevitably harmonious, or conflict necessarily disruptive. *There are times when integration can only occur in and through conflict, and conversely, other times when conflict is necessary to reach a new order of integration.* Whether relationships like these are modal or whether they are exceptional is a matter to be determined empirically; the probability surely is that on a comparative basis there will be widespread societal differentials on these parameters. It may turn out that the usual common-sense assumption is correct, i.e., modally, integration stands for a set of harmonious relations while conflict represents destructive ones—and the exceptions will be negligible. This conclusion is symbolized by Figure 1. However, the result could be quite the opposite with integration *usually* compounded with conflict and likewise conflict displaying integrative features. This possibility is shown in Figure 2. For purposes of the figure, integration will be regarded as a process whereby units or elements of a society are brought into a more active and coordinated compliance with the ongoing activities and objectives of the total society at any given period of time. On the other hand, conflict will be thought of as a process whereby units or elements of a society develop incompatible differences of objective, either with parallel units, authoritative units, or both, resulting in social clashes, disputes, tensions, or competitions at any given period of time. The two variables of integration and conflict are linked in ways to be determined by empirical observation; in general these ways are intermediate between the extremes portrayed in figures 1 and 2. Figure 1 and Figure 2 are constructs of two hypothesized extremes in the relations between integration and conflict. Sections ABFE and CDHG in both figures represent what are termed the unalloyed operations of integration or conflict as opposites in pure form. In this pure form they are hypothesized to stand in inverse relation to each other, such that the increase of either process necessarily entails a decrease of the other. BCGF in both figures represents a condition governed by an opposite hypothesis, i.e., one in which the two processes of integration and conflict no longer negate each other but combine in different ways and proportions.

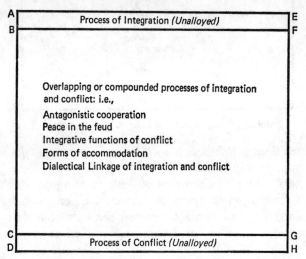

Figure 2. Modal linkage of integration and conflict

Thus each figure has two types of sectors, each governed by an opposite assumption. If the first assumption (the commonsense belief that conflict and integration are pure opposites with a negative relation to each other)—if this assumption governed all social phenomena we would have to redraw the figures and leave out the area BCGF, substituting a movable line in place of the area. This line could move upward as far as AE or downward as far as DH on the naive view that a society may be totally integrated and harmonious, or so ridden with conflict that it is wholly self-destructive. If the second assumption governs all social phenomena, conflict and integration are *always* processes of combination, never found separately; thus the area BCGF would expand until it was coextensive with ADHE. In general this was the view of C. H. Cooley who once remarked, 'The more one thinks of it, the more he will see that conflict and cooperation are not separable things, but phases of one process which always involves something of both' (Cooley, 1918, p. 19).

It seems more realistic to keep both of these assumptions but deny each of them unlimited relevance. This is precisely the function of a dialectical probe which regards an absolute dichotomy between integration and conflict as naivete, and a complete linkage at every point as hopelessly speculative in addition to being unprovable without perfect induction. The position accepted here is that both the common sense assumption and the assumption of *linked paired variables* have limited or circumscribed validity. And while we have labeled sector BCGF as dialectical linkage, this does not imply a synthesis in the manner of vulgar Hegelianism or vulgar Marxism—a synthesis that would cancel out the differences in an overriding unity, for sector BCGF represents an area in perpetual movement, either upward toward integration or downward toward conflict. Synthesis too often symbolizes permanent resolutions of opposing forces. It is this permanence which the social scientist must deny.

References

Cooley, C. H. (1918), *Social Process*, New York.

Dahrendorf, R. (1959), *Class and Class Conflict in Industrial Society*, Stanford.

Gluckman, M. (1955), *Custom and Conflict in Africa*, Oxford.

Hunter, G. (1966), *South-East Asia, Race, Culture and Nation,* New York.

Lieberson, S. (1961), 'A societal theory of race and ethnic relations', *A.S.R.*, vol. 26, pp. 902–10.

McLeod, W. C. (1928), *The American Indian Frontier*, New York.

Radcliffe–Brown, A. R. (1952), *Structure and Function in Primitive Society*, Glencoe, Ill.

Schermerhorn, R. A. (1965), 'Towards a general theory of minority groups', *Phylon*, vol. 25, pp. 238–46.

Skinner, G. W. (1958), *Leadership and Power in the Chinese Community of Thailand,* New York.

Van den Bergne, P. L. (1967), *Race and Racism*, New York.

Williams, R. M. Jr. (1966), 'Some further comments on chronic controversies', *A.J.S.*, vol. 71, pp. 717–21.

8 *Alfred Schutz,* The Stranger: An Essay in Social Psychology

The present paper intends to study in terms of a general theory of interpretation the typical situation in which a stranger finds himself in his attempt to interpret the cultural pattern of a social group which he approaches and to orient himself within it. For our present purposes the term 'stranger' shall mean an adult individual of our times and civilization who tries to be permanently accepted or at least tolerated by the group which he approaches. The outstanding example for the social situation under scrutiny is that of the immigrant, and the following analyses are, as a matter of convenience, worked out with this instance in view. But by no means is their validity restricted to this special case. The applicant for membership in a closed club, the prospective bridegroom who wants to be admitted to the girl's family, the farmer's son who enters college, the city-dweller who settles in a rural environment, the 'selectee' who joins the Army, the family of the war worker who moves into a boom town—all are strangers according to the definition just given, although in these cases the typical 'crisis' that the immigrant undergoes may assume milder forms or even be entirely absent. Intentionally excluded, however, from the present investigation are certain cases the inclusion of which would require some qualifications in our statements: (*a*) the visitor or guest who intends to establish a merely transitory contact with the group; (*b*) children or primitives; and (*c*) relationships between individuals and groups of different levels of civilization, as in the case of the Huron brought to Europe—a pattern dear to some moralists of the eighteenth century. Furthermore, it is not the purpose of this paper to deal with the processes of social assimilation and social adjustment which are treated in an abundant and, for the most part, excellent literature[1] but rather with the situation of approaching which precedes every possible social adjustment and which includes its prerequisites.

[1] Instead of mentioning individual outstanding contributions by American writers, such as W. G. Sumner, W. I. Thomas, Florian Znaniecki, R. E. Park, H. A. Miller, E. V. Stonequist, E. S. Bogardus, and Kimball Young, and by German authors, especially Georg Simmel and Robert Michels, we refer to the valuable monograph by Margaret Mary Wood (1934) and the bibliography quoted therein.

Alfred Schutz, 'The Stranger: an Essay in Social Psychology', *American Journal of Sociology*, vol. 49, no. 6, 1944, pp. 499–507.

As a convenient starting-point we shall investigate how the cultural pattern of group life presents itself to the common sense of a man who lives his everyday life within the group among his fellow-men. Following the customary terminology, we use the term 'cultural pattern of group life' for designating all the peculiar valuations, institutions, and systems of orientation and guidance (such as the folkways, mores, laws, habits, customs, etiquette, fashions) which, in the common opinion of sociologists of our time, characterize—if not constitute—any social group at a given moment in its history. This cultural pattern, like any phenomenon of the social world, has a different aspect for the sociologist and for the man who acts and thinks within it.[2] The sociologist (as sociologist, not as a man among fellow-men which he remains in his private life) is the disinterested scientific onlooker of the social world. He is disinterested in that he intentionally refrains from participating in the network of plans, means-and-ends relations, motives and chances hopes and fears, which the actor within the social world uses for interpreting his experiences of it; as a scientist he tries to observe, describe, and classify the social world as clearly as possible in well-ordered terms in accordance with the scientific ideals of coherence, consistency, and analytical consequence. The actor within the social world, however, experiences it primarily as a field of his actual and possible acts and only secondarily as an object of his thinking. In so far as he is interested in knowledge of his social world, he organizes this knowledge not in terms of a scientific system but in terms of relevance to his actions. He groups the world around himself (as the center) as a field of domination and is therefore especially interested in that segment which is within his actual or potential reach. He singles out those of its elements which may serve as means or ends for his 'use and enjoyment', (Dewey, 1938, ch. IV), for furthering his purposes, and for overcoming obstacles. His interest in these elements is of different degrees, and for this reason he does not aspire to become acquainted with all of them with equal thoroughness. What he wants is *graduated knowledge* of relevant elements, the degree of desired knowledge being correlated with their relevance. Put otherwise, the world seems to him at any given moment as stratified in different layers of relevance, each of them requiring a different degree of knowledge. To illustrate these strata of relevance we may—borrowing the term from cartography—speak of 'isohypses' or 'hypsographical contour lines of relevance', trying to suggest by this metaphor that we could show the distribution of the interests of an individual at a given moment with respect both to their intensity and to their scope by connecting elements of equal relevance to his acts, just as the cartographer connects points of equal height by contour lines in order to reproduce adequately the shape of a mountain. The graphical representation of these 'contour lines of relevance' would not show them as a single closed field but

---

[2] This insight seems to be the most important contribution of Max Weber's methodological writings to the problems of social science.

rather as numerous areas scattered over the map, each of different size and shape. Distinguishing with William James[3] two kinds of knowledge, namely, '*knowledge of acquaintance*' and '*knowledge about*', we may say that, within the field covered by the contour lines of relevance, there are centers of explicit knowledge *of* what is aimed at; they are surrounded by a halo knowledge *about* what seems to be sufficient; next comes a region in which it will do merely 'to put one's trust'; the adjoining foothills are the home of unwarranted hopes and assumptions; between these areas, however, lie zones of complete ignorance.

We do not want to overcharge this image. Its chief purpose has been to illustrate that the knowledge of the man who acts and thinks within the world of his daily life is not homogeneous; it is (1) incoherent, (2) only partially clear, and (3) not at all free from contradictions.

1. It is incoherent because the individual's interests which determine the relevance of the objects selected for further inquiry are themselves not integrated into a coherent system. They are only partially organized under plans of any kind, such as plans of life, plans of work and leisure, plans for every social role assumed. But the hierarchy of these plans changes with the situation and with the growth of the personality; interests are shifted continually and entail an uninterrupted transformation of the shape and density of the relevance lines. Not only the selection of the objects of curiosity but also the degree of knowledge aimed at changes.

2. Man in his daily life is only partially—and we dare say exceptionally—interested in the clarity of his knowledge, i.e., in full insight into the relations between the elements of his world and the general principles ruling those relations. He is satisfied that a well-functioning telephone service is available to him and, normally, does not ask how the apparatus functions in detail and what laws of physics make this functioning possible. He buys merchandise in the store, not knowing how it is produced, and pays with money, although he has only a vague idea what money really is. He takes it for granted that his fellow-man will understand his thought if expressed in plain language and will answer accordingly, without wondering how this miraculous performance may be explained. Furthermore, he does not search for the truth and does not quest for certainty. All he wants is information on likelihood and insight into the chances or risks which the situation at hand entails for the outcome of his actions. That the subway will run tomorrow as usual is for him almost of the same order of likelihood as that the sun will rise. If by reason of a special interest he needs more explicit knowledge on a topic, a benign modern civilization holds ready for him a chain of information desks and reference libraries.

[3] For the distinction of these two kinds of knowledge cf. William James (1890, I, pp 221–2).

3. His knowledge, finally, is not a consistent one. At the same time he may consider statements as equally valid which in fact are incompatible with one another. As a father, a citizen, an employee, and a member of his church he may have the most different and the least congruent opinions on moral, political, or economic matters. This inconsistency does not necessarily originate in a logical fallacy. Men's thought is just spread over subject matters located within different and differently relevant levels, and they are not aware of the modifications they would have to make in passing from one level to another. This and similar problems would have to be explored by a logic of everyday thinking, postulated but not attained by all the great logicians from Leibnitz to Husserl and Dewey. Up to now the science of logic has primarily dealt with the logic of science.

The system of knowledge thus acquired—incoherent, inconsistent, and only partially clear, as it is—takes on for the members of the in-group the appearance of a *sufficient* coherence, clarity, and consistency to give anybody a reasonable chance of understanding and of being understood. Any member born or reared within the group accepts the ready-made standardized scheme of the cultural pattern handed down to him by ancestors, teachers, and authorities as an unquestioned and unquestionable guide in all the situations which normally occur within the social world. The knowledge correlated to the cultural pattern carries its evidence in itself—or, rather, it is taken for granted in the absence of evidence to the contrary. It is a knowledge of trustworthy *recipes* for interpreting the social world and for handling things and men in order to obtain the best results in every situation with a minimum of effort by avoiding undesirable consequences. The recipe works, on the one hand, as a precept for actions and thus serves as a scheme of expression: whoever wants to obtain a certain result has to proceed as indicated by the recipe provided for this purpose. On the other hand, the recipe serves as a scheme of interpretation: whoever proceeds as indicated by a specific recipe is supposed to intend the correlated result. Thus it is the function of the cultural pattern to eliminate troublesome inquiries by offering ready-made directions for use, to replace truth hard to attain by comfortable truisms, and to substitute the self-explanatory for the questionable.

This 'thinking as usual', as we may call it, corresponds to Max Scheler's idea of the 'relatively natural conception of the world' *(relativ natürliche Weltanschauung)* (Scheler, 1926; cf. Becker and Dahlke, 1942); it includes the 'of-course' assumptions relevant to a particular social group which Robert S. Lynd describes in such a masterly way—together with their inherent contradictions and ambivalence—as the 'Middletown-spirit'. (Lynd, 1937, chap. XII; 1939, pp. 58–63). Thinking as usual may be maintained as long as some basic assumptions hold true, namely: (1) that life and especially social life will continue to be the same as it has been so far, that is to say, that the same problems requiring the same solutions will recur and that, therefore, our former experiences will suffice for mastering future situations; (2) that we may rely on the knowledge handed down to us by parents, teachers, governments, traditions, habits, etc., even if we do not understand their origin and their real meaning; (3) that in the ordinary course of affairs it is sufficient to know something *about* the general type or style of events we may encounter in our life-world in order to manage or control them; and (4) that neither the systems of recipes as schemes of interpretation and expression nor the underlying basic assumptions just mentioned are our private affair, but that they are likewise accepted and applied by our fellow-men.

If only one of these assumptions ceases to stand the test, thinking as usual becomes unworkable. Then a 'crisis' arises which, according to W. I. Thomas' famous definition, 'interrupts the flow of habit and gives rise to changed conditions of consciousness and practice'; or, as we may say, it overthrows precipitously the actual system of relevances. The cultural pattern no longer functions as a system of tested recipes at hand; it reveals that its applicability is restricted to a specific historical situation.

Yet the stranger, by reason of his personal crisis, does not share the above-mentioned basic assumptions. He becomes essentially the man who has to place in question nearly everything that seems to be unquestionable to the members of the approached group.

To him the cultural pattern of the approached group does not have the authority of a tested system of recipes, and this, if for no other reason, because he does not partake in the vivid historical tradition by which it has been formed. To be sure, from the stranger's point of view, too, the culture of the approached group has its peculiar history, and this history is even accessible to him. But it has never become an integral part of his biography, as did the history of his home group. Only the ways in which his fathers and grandfathers lived become for everyone elements of his own way of life. Graves and reminiscences can neither be transferred nor conquered. The stranger, therefore, approaches the other group as a newcomer in the true meaning of the term. At best he may be willing and able to share the present and the future with the approached group in vivid and immediate experience; under all circumstances, however, he remains excluded from such experiences of its past. Seen from the point of view of the approached group, he is a man without a history.

To the stranger the cultural pattern of his home group continues to be the outcome of an unbroken historical development and an element of his personal biography which for this very reason has been and still is the unquestioned scheme of reference for his 'relatively natural conception of the world.' As a matter of course, therefore, the stranger starts to interpret his new social environment in terms of his thinking as usual. Within the scheme of reference brought from his home group, however, he finds a ready-made idea of the pattern supposedly valid within the approached group—an idea which necessarily will soon prove inadequate.[4]

First, the idea of the cultural pattern of the approached group which the stranger finds within the interpretive scheme of his home group has originated in the attitude of a disinterested observer. The approaching stranger, however, is about to transform himself from an unconcerned onlooker into a would-be member of the approached group. The cultural pattern of the approached group, then, is no longer a subject matter of his thought but a segment of the world which has to be dominated by actions. Consequently, its position within the stranger's system of relevance changes decisively, and this means, as we have seen, that another type of knowledge is required for its interpretation. Jumping from the stalls to the stage, so to speak, the former onlooker becomes a member of the cast, enters as a partner into social relations with his co-actors, and participates henceforth in the action in progress.

Second, the new cultural pattern acquires an environmental character. Its remoteness changes into proximity; its vacant frames become occupied by vivid experiences; its anonymous contents turn into definite social situations; its ready-made typologies disintegrate. In other words, the level of environmental experience of social objects is incongruous with the level of mere beliefs about unapproached objects; by passing from the latter to the former, any concept originating in the level of departure becomes necessarily inadequate if applied to the new level without having been restated in its terms.

Third, the ready-made picture of the foreign group subsisting within the stranger's home-group proves its inadequacy for the approaching stranger for the mere reason that it has not been formed with the aim of provoking a response from or a reaction of the members of the foreign group. The knowledge which it offers serves merely as a handy scheme for interpreting the foreign group and not as a guide for interaction between the two groups. Its validity is primarily based on the consensus of those members of the home group who do not intend to establish a direct social relationship with members of the foreign group. (Those who intend to do so are in a situation analogous to that of the approaching stranger.) Consequently, the scheme of interpretation refers to the members of the foreign group merely as objects of this interpretation, but not beyond it, as addressees of possible acts emanating from the outcome of the interpretive procedure and not as subjects of anticipated reactions toward those acts. Hence, this kind of knowledge is, so to speak, insulated; it can be neither verified nor falsified by responses of the members of the foreign group. The latter, therefore, consider this knowledge

---

[4] As one account showing how the American cultural pattern depicts itself as an 'unquestionable' element within the scheme of interpretation of European intellectuals we refer to Martin Gumpert's (1941) humorous description cf. also books like Romains (1930) and Usonie (1939, pp. 245–66).

—by a kind of 'looking-glass' effect[5]—as both irresponsive and irresponsible and complain of its prejudices, bias, and misunderstandings. The approaching stranger, however, becomes aware of the fact that an important element of his 'thinking as usual', namely, his ideas of the foreign group, its cultural pattern, and its way of life, do not stand the test of vivid experience and social interaction.

The discovery that things in his new surroundings look quite different from what he expected them to be at home is frequently the first shock to the stranger's confidence in the validity of his habitual 'thinking as usual'. Not only the picture which the stranger has brought along of the cultural pattern of the approached group but the whole hitherto unquestioned scheme of interpretation current within the home group becomes invalidated. It cannot be used as a scheme of orientation within the new social surroundings. For the members of the approached group *their* cultural pattern fulfils the functions of such a scheme. But the approaching stranger can neither use it simply as it is nor establish a general formula of transformation between both cultural patterns permitting him, so to speak, to convert all the co-ordinates within one scheme of orientation into those valid within the other—and this for the following reasons.

First, any scheme of orientation presupposes that everyone who uses it looks at the surrounding world as grouped around himself who stands at its center. He who wants to use a map successfully has first of all to know his standpoint in two respects: its location on the ground and its representation on the map. Applied to the social world this means that only members of the in-group, having a definite status in its hierarchy and also being aware of it, can use its cultural pattern as a natural and trustworthy scheme of orientation. The stranger, however, has to face the fact that he lacks any status as a member of the social group he is about to join and is therefore unable to get a starting-point to take his bearings. He finds himself a border case outside the territory covered by the scheme of orientation current within the group. He is, therefore, no longer permitted to consider himself as the center of his social environment, and this fact causes again a dislocation of his contour lines of relevance.

Second, the cultural pattern and its recipes represent only for the members of the in-group a unit of coinciding schemes of interpretation as well as of expression. For the outsider, however, this seeming unity falls to pieces. The approaching stranger has to 'translate' its terms into terms of the cultural pattern of his home group, provided that, within the latter, interpretive equivalents exist at all. If they exist, the translated terms may be understood and remembered; they can be recognized by recurrence; they are at hand but not in hand. Yet, even then, it is obvious that the stranger cannot assume that his

[5] In using this term, we allude to Cooley's (1922, p. 184) well-known theory of the reflected or looking-glass self.

interpretation of the new cultural pattern coincides with that current with the members of the in-group. On the contrary, he has to reckon with fundamental discrepancies in seeing things and handling situations.

Only after having thus collected a certain knowledge of the interpretive function of the new cultural pattern may the stranger start to adopt it as the scheme of his own expression. The difference between the two stages of knowledge is familiar to any student of a foreign language and has received the full attention of psychologists dealing with the theory of learning. It is the difference between the passive understanding of a language and its active mastering as a means for realizing one's own acts and thoughts. As a matter of convenience we want to keep to this example in order to make clear some of the limits set to the stranger's attempt at conquering the foreign pattern as a scheme of expression, bearing in mind, however, that the following remarks could easily be adapted with appropriate modifications to other categories of the cultural pattern such as mores, laws, folkways, fashions, etc.

Language as a scheme of interpretation and expression does not merely consist of the linguistic symbols catalogued in the dictionary and of the syntactical rules enumerated in an ideal grammar. The former are translatable into other languages; the latter are understandable by referring them to corresponding or deviating rules of the unquestioned mother-tongue.[6] However, several other factors supervene.

1. Every word and every sentence is, to borrow again a term of William James, surrounded by 'fringes' connecting them, on the one hand, with past and future elements of the universe of discourse to which they pertain and surrounding them, on the other hand, with a halo of emotional values and irrational implications which themselves remain ineffable. The fringes are the stuff poetry is made of; they are capable of being set to music but they are not translatable.

2. There are in any language terms with several connotations. They, too, are noted in the dictionary. But, besides these standardized connotations, every element of the speech acquires its special secondary meaning derived from the context or the social environment within which it is used and, in addition, gets a special tinge from the actual occasion in which it is employed.

3. Idioms, technical terms, jargons, and dialects, whose use remains restricted to specific social groups, exist in every language, and their significance can be learned by an outsider too. But, in addition, every social group, be it ever so small (if not every individual), has its own private code, understandable only by those who have participated in the common past experiences in which it took rise or in the tradition connected with them.

4. As Vossler (1925, pp. 117ff.) has shown, the whole history of the lin-

---

[6] Therefore, the learning of a foreign language reveals to the student frequently for the first time the grammar rules of his mother-tongue which he has followed so far as 'the most natural thing in the world', namely, as recipes.

guistic group is mirrored in its way of saying things. All the other elements of group life enter into it—above all, its literature. The erudite stranger, for example, approaching an English-speaking country is heavily handicapped if he has not read the Bible and Shakespeare in the English language, even if he grew up with translations of those books in his mother-tongue.

All the above-mentioned features are accessible only to the members of the in-group. They all pertain to the scheme of expression. They are not teachable and cannot be learned in the same way as, for example, the vocabulary. In order to command a language freely as a scheme of expression, one must have written love letters in it; one has to know how to pray and curse in it and how to say things with every shade appropriate to the addressee and to the situation. Only members of the in-group have the scheme of expression as a genuine one in hand and command it freely within their thinking as usual.

Apply the result to the total of the cultural pattern of group life, we may say that the member of the in-group looks in one single glance through the normal social situations occurring to him and that he catches immediately the ready-made recipe appropriate to its solution. In those situations his acting shows all the marks of habituality, automatism, and half-consciousness. This is possible because the cultural pattern provides by its recipes typical solutions for typical problems available for typical actors. In other words, the chance of obtaining the desired standardized result by applying a standardized recipe is an objective one; that is open to everyone who conducts himself like the anonymous type required by the recipe. Therefore, the actor who follows a recipe does not have to check whether this objective chance coincides with a subjective chance, that is, a chance open to him, the individual, by reason of his personal circumstances and faculties which subsists independently of the question whether other people in similar situations could or could not act in the same way with the same likelihood. Even more, it can be stated that the objective chances for the efficiency of a recipe are the greater, the fewer deviations from the anonymous typified behavior occur, and this holds especially for recipes designed for social interaction. This kind of recipe, if it is to work, presupposes that any partner expects the other to act or to react typically, provided that the actor himself acts typically. He who wants to travel by railroad has to behave in that typical way which the type 'railroad agent' may reasonably expect as the typical conduct of the type 'passenger', and vice versa. Neither party examines the subjective chances involved. The scheme, being designed for everyone's use, need not be tested for its fitness for the peculiar individual who employs it.

For those who have grown up within the cultural pattern, not only the recipes and their efficiency chance but also the typical and anonymous attitudes required by them are an unquestioned 'matter of course' which gives them both security and assurance. In other words, these attitudes by their very anonymity and typicality are placed not within the actor's stratum of relevance which requires explicit knowledge *of* but in the region of mere acquaintance in which it will do to put one's trust. This interrelation between objective chance, typicality, anonymity, and relevance seems to be rather important.[7]

For the approaching stranger, however, the pattern of the approached group does not guarantee an objective chance for success but rather a pure subjective likelihood which has to be checked step by step, that is, he has to make sure that the solutions suggested by the new scheme will also produce the desired effect for him in his special position as outsider and newcomer who has not brought within his grasp the whole system of the cultural pattern but who is rather puzzled by its inconsistency, incoherence, and lack of clarity. He has, first of all, to use the term of W. I. Thomas, to *define* the situation. Therefore, he cannot stop at an approximate acquaintance with the new pattern, trusting in his vague knowledge *about* its general style and structure but needs an explicit knowledge *of* its elements, inquiring not only into their *that* but into their *why*. Consequently, the shape of his contour lines of relevance by necessity differs radically from those of a member of the in-group as to situations, recipes, means, ends, social partners, etc. Keeping in mind the above-mentioned interrelationship between relevance, on the one hand, and typicality and anonymity, on the other, it follows that he uses another yardstick for anonymity and typicality of social acts than the members of the in-group. For to the stranger the observed actors within the approached group are not—as for their co-actors—of a certain presupposed anonymity, namely, mere performers of typical functions, but individuals. On the other hand, he is inclined to take mere individual traits as typical ones. Thus he constructs a social world of pseudo-anonymity, pseudo-intimacy, and pseudo-typicality. Therefore, he cannot integrate the personal types constructed by him into a coherent picture of the approached group and cannot rely on his expectation of their response. And even less can the stranger himself adopt those typical and anonymous attitudes which a member of the in-group is entitled to expect from a partner in a typical situation. Hence the stranger's lack of feeling for distance, his oscillating between remoteness and intimacy, his hesitation and uncertainty, and his distrust in every matter which seems to be so simple and uncomplicated to those who rely on the efficiency of unquestioned recipes which have just to be followed but not understood.

---

[7] It could be referred to a general principle of the theory of relevance, but this would surpass the frame of the present paper. The only point for which there is space to contend is that all the obstacles which the stranger meets in his attempt at interpreting the approached group arise from the incongruence of the contour lines of the mutual relevance systems and, consequently, from the distortion the stranger's system undergoes within the new surrounding. But any social relationship, and especially any establishment of new social contacts, even between individuals, involves analogous phenomena, although they do not necessarily lead to a crisis.

In other words, the cultural pattern of the approached group is to the stranger not a shelter but a field of adventure, not a matter of course but a questionable topic of investigation, not an instrument for disentangling problematic situations but a problematic situation itself and one hard to master.

These facts explain two basic traits of the stranger's attitude toward the group to which nearly all sociological writers dealing with this topic have rendered special attention, namely, (1) the stranger's objectivity and (2) his doubtful loyalty.

1. The stranger's objectivity cannot be sufficiently explained by his critical attitude. To be sure, he is not bound to worship the 'idols of the tribe' and has a vivid feeling for the incoherence and inconsistency of the approached cultural pattern. But this attitude originates far less in his propensity to judge the newly approached group by the standards brought from home than in his need to acquire full knowledge *of* the elements of the approached cultural pattern and to examine for this purpose with care and precision what seems self-explanatory to the in-group. The deeper reason for his objectivity, however, lies in his own bitter experience of the limits of the 'thinking as usual', which has taught him that a man may lose his status, his rules of guidance, and even his history and that the normal way of life is always far less guaranteed than it seems. Therefore, the stranger discerns, frequently with a grievous clear-sightedness, the rising of a crisis which may menace the whole foundation of the 'relatively natural conception of the world', while all those symptoms pass unnoticed by the members of the in-group, who rely on the continuance of their customary way of life.

2. The doubtful loyalty of the stranger is unfortunately very frequently more than a prejudice on the part of the approached group. This is especially true in cases in which the stranger proves unwilling or unable to substitute the new cultural pattern entirely for that of the home group. Then the stranger remains what Park and Stonequist have aptly called a 'marginal man', a cultural hybrid on the verge of two different patterns of group life, not knowing to which of them he belongs. But very frequently the reproach of doubtful loyalty originates in the astonishment of the members of the in-group that the stranger does not accept the total of its cultural pattern as the natural and appropriate way of life and as the best of all possible solutions of any problem. The stranger is called ungrateful, since he refuses to acknowledge that the cultural pattern offered to him grants him shelter and protection. But these people do not understand that the stranger in the state of transition does not consider this pattern as a protecting shelter at all but as a labyrinth in which he has lost all sense of his bearings.

As stated before, we have intentionally restricted our topic to the specific attitude of the approaching stranger which precedes any social adjustment and refrained from investigating the process of social assimilation itself.

One single remark concerning the latter may be permitted. Strangeness and familiarity are not limited to the social field but are general categories of our interpretation of the world. If we encounter in our experience something previously unknown and which therefore stands out of the ordinary order of our knowledge, we begin a process of inquiry. We first define the new fact; we try to catch its meaning; we then transform step by step our general scheme of interpretation of the world in such a way that the strange fact and its meaning becomes compatible and consistent with all the other facts of our experience and their meanings. If we succeed in this endeavor, then that which formerly was a strange fact and a puzzling problem to our mind is transformed into an additional element of our warranted knowledge. We have enlarged and adjusted our stock of experiences.

What is commonly called the process of social adjustment which the new-comer has to undergo is but a special case of this general principle. The adaptation of the newcomer to the in-group which at first seemed to be strange and unfamiliar to him is a continuous process of inquiry into the cultural pattern of the approached group. If this process of inquiry succeeds, then this pattern and its elements will become to the newcomer a matter of course, an unquestionable way of life, a shelter, and a protection. But then the stranger is no stranger any more, and his specific problems have been solved.

References

Becker, H. and Dahlke, H. O. (1942), 'Max Scheler's sociology of knowledge', *Philosophy and Phenomenological Research*, vol. 2, pp. 310–22.
Cooley, C. (1922), *Human Nature and the Social Order*, New York.
Dewey, J. (1938), *Logic, the Theory of Inquiry*, New York.
Gumpert, M. (1941), *First Papers*, New York.
James, W. (1890), *Psychology*, New York.
Lynd, R. S. (1937), *Middletown in Transition*, New York.
Lynd, R. S. (1939), *Knowledge for What?*, Princeton.
Romains, J. (1930), *Visite chez les Américains*, Paris.
Scheler, M. (1926), 'Probleme einer Soziologie des Wissens', *Die Wissensformen und die Gesellschaft*, Leipzig.
Usonie, J. P. (1939), *Esquisse de la Civilisation Américaine*, Paris.
Vossler, K. (1925), *Geist und Kultur in der Sprache*, Heidelberg.
Wood, M. M. (1934), *The Stranger: A Study in Social Relationship*, New York.

9 *John Rex,* Race Relations and Sociological Theory

Racism

When the World War of 1939–45 came to an end, the United Nations and its various agencies made a systematic attempt to deal with what were regarded as being the roots of racism and racialism, or more specifically, the roots of problems like anti-semitic theories and practice in Nazi Germany. The easiest way in which these problems could be dealt with was by referring them to committees of intellectuals who concerned themselves with that aspect of the problem with which they, by their training, were best fitted to deal. The result has been that a great deal of the analytic work which has been done on the problems of race relations at this level has overemphasised the importance of the relatively systematic theories in terms of which hostile policies towards particular groups were justified.

To put such studies in perspective it might perhaps be useful to recall some of the basic analytic concepts used by Pareto (1935) in his analysis of social action. According to Pareto the theories which men offered as explaining their actions had to be taken as secondary manifestations of the same sentiments as led to the action to be explained. If one looked at these theories one would find that despite the tremendous variety of justifications of action which were offered there were certain constant 'residues' in all of them. The residues were the basic non-logical theories which would help us to understand what men were really about. Since, however, men were rationalising creatures they liked to give some kind of intellectual justification to their actions and so bolstered their basic non-logical reasons for acting with false arguments, appeals to authority and so on. These latter justifications Pareto called 'derivations'.

We do not agree wholly with Pareto's analysis. In particular, it seems misleading to suggest that the residues are simply the causal product of sentiments. As we see it, men act and interact in accordance with their interests or in conformity with norms which they accept for one reason or

John Rex, *Race Relations and Sociological Theory*, Weidenfeld and Nicolson and Schocken Books, 1970, pp. 136–47.

another. We cannot accept that there are basic psychological types of irrational behaviour at the root of all conduct. On the other hand we do accept, with Pareto, that the reasons which men give in order to account systematically for their behaviour are added after the behaviour is complete, and are not adequate to account for it. This means that we think it to be an important part of the analysis of social structures and interaction that we should explore the full variety of derivations which occur, when one group pursues hostile policies against another. If we do this, we shall avoid the misleading notion that these policies are the product of false theories and that if the theories are challenged the policies will cease.

An alternative approach to that which emphasises systematic racist theories is that which emphasises the study of attitudes. This is the approach of empiricist psychology to the study of race relations. It assumes that there are measurable tendencies to action by individuals, that one can find out to what extent particular tendencies exist in a population and what factors are correlated with the presence or absence of these tendencies.

Such an approach is a valuable corrective to that which over-emphasises highly articulate and systematic theory. It does emphasise action elements mobilised at the point of action. It is defective, however, in not seeking to understand and explain the tendencies to action called attitudes and hence represents them as static 'things'. What we wish to consider is the relationship between these mental elements, social action and interaction, and the social structure.

Our focus is on understanding society rather than personality, or to put the matter another way, our concept of personality is a sociological one. As Simpson and Yinger (1959) put it.

From our point of view personality is best conceived not as a collection of traits, not as a static system . . . but as a process . . . the process of carrying out functions of a shop steward in a union, superintendent of schools, or 'courteous customer' does not allow full individual variation to come into play. The rôles themselves have some compulsions that influence which of the various tendencies which the individual will express.

We might perhaps express a slight doubt about the use of the term 'role' in this context, in that the term does sometimes seem to refer to total and integrated social systems, whereas what we have in mind includes a variety of different types of socially governed action, ranging from the mobilisation of actors for collective action in order to achieve their interests to action which is completely governed by norms and rules. With this reservation, however, we can certainly accept Simpson and Yinger's formulation. The important point is that we are concerned, not merely with individual personality systems, but with the effect on individual conduct of social structures and social situations.

Our approach to the study of racist theory also has much in common with recent approaches to the sociology of knowledge, most notably that of Berger and Luckmann (1967) in their *Social Construction of Reality*. If, in general, their approach overemphasises the cognitive element in social interaction, so far as our present concern goes this is not relevant, for we are especially concerned here with the way in which ideas influence and are involved in interaction. At the same time Berger and Luckmann's book has the very great merit of recognising that 'knowledge' influences action not merely at highly abstract theoretical levels but in humble and humdrum ways at the level of social interaction in everyday life. This Schutzian perspective (Schutz, 1967) is especially important for us, in that we are concerned in the study of racism precisely with the role of ideas in everyday life.

The renewed emphasis on the sociology of knowledge as the precondition of all sociology, and of a cognitive element as the precondition of action, has occurred because writers in the phenomenological and symbolic interactionist traditions have recognised that it is only possible for one actor to 'orient his conduct to another' if it is possible for these two actors to share the same intersubjective world. Thus, long before actors in specialised roles can sit down and reason and argue about the world in abstract terms, other actors at the grass roots must have agreed to attribute common meanings to their experience. There is a sense, indeed, in which we must all 'prejudge' our experience, because, if we were not able to catch the fleeting moments of that experience in terms of 'typifications', 'ideal types' or stereotypes, we would not be able to share that experience with anybody else.

We create an intersubjective world of physical objects by agreeing to attach labels to our experience. In doing this, we make the claim that they are in some sense the same experiences that other people have had, and we also connect them with other experiences of our own, in that meanings do not stand by themselves but have definite relations to each other. Thus when I say that I see a cat, I am saying that I am having an experience which is similar to some of your experiences, and which has clear relationships of similarity and dissimilarity to other experiences, such as that which I describe as seeing a dog. In using language about the physical world, therefore, human beings must already be assumed to hold implicit shared theories about the world and how it works.

Such a mapping of the world and what is in it by a group of actors is not, however, simply a cognitive business. For at this level of 'theorising' no distinction is made between merely claiming that something exists and giving instructions as to how it should be treated, or saying whether it is good, beautiful or sacred. Thus one assumes that the process of teaching, whereby an Arunta boy in Central Australia was taught that a certain object was a 'churinga', was the starting point for a whole process of scientific, aesthetic, moral and religious education. He could really only learn what a 'churinga' was in a complete sense by understanding the whole set of concepts implicit in the totemic culture (Durkheim, 1954).

Our culture is, of course, distinguished by the fact that, so far as the objects of the physical world are concerned, we do try to distinguish the question, 'what is this object?', from all questions about its aesthetic and other qualities. Thus there is a set of agreed procedures called 'science' by which we arrive at a picture of the world which is held to be most relevant for a number of purposes. But, even in our culture, this is not always the most relevant picture. There is little point, for instance, in a scientific demonstration of the chemical properties of the substances used in religious sacraments, any more than there is in a geometric analysis and a description of a painting. For these purposes other procedures for reaching agreement than those of natural science are resorted to.

In everyday life, however, distinctions of this kind are not made and the structuring of interaction in a social way depends upon their not being made. There is no society, not even our own, with its highly scientistic culture, in which the teaching of language is not used to impose an initial normative order upon the pupil, long before he learns explicit moral rules. This is quite obvious in the case of the opportunistic way in which we impose taboos on our children by drumming into them that, say, eating coal is nasty. But it goes far beyond this. What we imagine is a purely factual world is shot through with moral meanings.

But, if this is true in the case of the shared intersubjective world of physical objects which our language creates for us, how much more is it true of the world of social objects. Here 'scientific' techniques for discriminating between the question 'what is this?' and the question 'how should I feel or act towards this?' are ill developed and, even if they were fully developed, it is unlikely that they would influence everyday action to anything like the same extent that the scientific picture of the physical world does. The goal of positivism from Comte to Lundberg (1939) has, of course, always been that this should be the case, and that not merely sociologists but the man in the street should think scientifically about the social world; but it is a goal which has clearly not been realised.

It is not clear, in any case, what exactly a 'scientific' way of looking at and labelling social objects or other human beings would be. Even the assertion 'this is a human being', set against the assertion 'this is a Jew' or 'this is a negro', may involve implicit reference to some moral or political code, which asserts that the differences between men are less important than their similarities, and that being human as such imposes certain moral claims. Thus we should not be surprised to find that there is no known society in which social actors are not categorised in terms much narrower than 'human being'.

The simplest form of categorisation is that which is given in a system of kinship terminology. This means any participant actor in a primitive society is able to attach to any other participant, not merely a personal name, but a position term, so that it is clear what rights and duties the other participant has, not merely *vis-á-vis ego,* but *vis-á-vis* every other individual. Within a system of this kind we may say that rights and roles are particularistically and ascriptively defined. They take the form 'X is your grandfather and therefore he has certain rights and duties in relation to you. Necessarily he must have certain other rights and duties to each category of your relatives. There will, however, also be certain groups whose relationship to *ego* cannot be defined in terms of kinship terminology. Some of these will be grouped in classificatory groups such as clans, and the position of an individual *vis-á-vis* an individual in another group will follow from the relationship which any individual in the one group is held to have with any member of the other. In this case rights and roles may be said to be defined in an ascriptive but classificatory way.

To say this is, of course, by no means to say that such an intergroup relationship has any of the elements which we noted as typifying a race relations situation. A social system based upon normative consensus, and involving no elements of conflict or coercion, may be built up in this way. Indeed it seems to be a very common kind of system in primitive tribes particularly those with clan totems. What differentiates such a system from that which we shall presently be discussing in composite societies, is that the classificatory and ascriptive allocation of rights and duties is a means of achieving a division of labour, through which overall group ends, as well as the ends of the various parties, can be attained. There is no question of the group which is singled out in this way becoming the target of hostile policies. Such may be the case so far as people who fall right outside of the tribe or its constituent clans are concerned, and at this point there may be parallels with race relations problems (as for example in the case of neighbouring tribes with a long tradition of enmity like the Kikuyu and the Masai in Kenya). But even with regard to outsiders to the tribe, the image of the other may be more negative than positive. He is an individual, who is beyond the range within which it is possible to define rights and duties, rather than simply as an enemy.

It should, perhaps, be noted that we have made a distinction so far between roles and rights being defined on an ascriptive and *particularistic* basis on the one hand, and an ascriptive and *classificatory* basis on the other. We thus revert to using the term which Morgan (1877) used in his discussion of kinship terminology, rather than the term 'universalism' which Parsons contrasts with particularism. We do so because, while we believe that it is worth while making a distinction between situations in which individuals are treated as members of groups and categories and situations in which they are treated as individuals, yet we think that the term 'universalism' is misleading. It may be that it has simply been linked so much with the concept of 'achievement-orientation' by Parsons, that some of the meaning of that concept has rubbed off on to universalism, but the term itself seems to suggest a society which is meritocratic and based upon the rule of law with no place for nepotism. For the limited type of non-particularism which we have in mind, therefore, the simple term classificatory seems more appropriate.

On the other hand, of course, we do not use this term in Morgan's sense. He was concerned to compare the systems of kinship terminology of the advanced societies having isolated conjugal families with those of primitive societies where kinship was the rule. But we are concerned with the contrast between one total system and another. From this point of view, all kinship systems are, relatively speaking, particularistic, and it seems that, beyond the particularistic categories of kinship terminologies, primitive people are bound to resort to classificatory categories of one kind or another. Examples of verbalised responses of this kind are frequent in the literature of race relations. In [an earlier] chapter we quoted the Spanish historian (Hanke, 1949) who referred to the American Indians as a naturally 'lazy and vicious, melancholic, cowardly and in general a lying shiftless people'. Similarly the first Governor of the Cape Colony referred to the Hottentots as 'stupid, dull, stinking people' (de Kiewet, 1946, p. 20). And one could quote statements like this from many colonial, immigrant and, indeed, class situations.

It could be argued that statements like these are the result of false beliefs of a more generalised kind and we would admit that such reactions do not result simply from immediate perceptions and experience. None the less it is important to recognise that, if there is any 'theoretical' element in such statements, it is of an elementary and implicit kind. A situation where the typifications which one group has of another are of this direct kind, is far removed from that in which the perception of the member of the other group is conditioned by widely believed pre-existing theories.

What we are saying then is that in relatively complex social systems individuals react to each other in classificatory and ascriptive ways, and that sometimes the other who is reacted to in this way is also the target for hostile attitudes and policies. This, of course, is particularly likely to be the case in situations, such as those discussed in our first four chapters, in which distinguishable groups find themselves in situations of conflict or competition with one another. The basic and, in one sense, the objective facts of the situation are that the two groups find themselves in a state of competition with one another. But subjectively this state of competition results in attitudes of enmity and the verbalisations to which they give rise. Instead of the somewhat intellectualised response 'this type of person is my competitor and in attempting to realise my goals I have to stop him attaining his' one finds the much simpler response 'those people are evil'. It is arguable that statements of this kind, and certainly the attitudes which underlie them before they are verbalised, are as much forms of aggression resulting from frustration in the objective situation as they are deductions from theory.

It is also worth noting here that, as racist theories have become more disreputable, ways have been found of giving *intellectualised* expression to attitudes of hostility which make little appeal to complex theories at all. Thus one finds in contemporary Britain that a commonly expressed attitude to coloured people is simply this: 'We have nothing against you. You may be as good as us. But we don't want you here. And since we, like you, have a right to our own separate existence there is nothing wrong or racialist or immoral about our saying this'. Thus a way is found of expressing intergroup hostility, which has nothing of the intellectual disreputableness of racist theory, and also avoids immediate emotive sounding statements of hostility.

This kind of intergroup hostility to which we are referring may, it is true, be found, wherever there is an element of competition in the relation between groups. Orwell (1939) has noted that he and his fellow public schoolboys in England in the thirties all believed that the working classes stank, and no doubt similar reactions could be discovered in other ethnically homogeneous societies. Such reactions do not contradict our thesis, for we have not said that they were confined to interracial situations. They are, however, far more likely when the groups concerned appear to each other as alien and foreign.

A particularly interesting recent phenomenon has been seen in the development, in the American negro revolution, of assertions which are the direct opposite of those common amongst the ruling white group. Thus, whereas throughout the history of American society the whites have not merely made their own assertions about the negro's negative qualities, but have even required that the negro himself believed them, today politically articulate negroes are deliberately attempting to instil into negro children positive evaluations of their own qualities and negative evaluations of the whites. Thus the children are taught that 'black is beautiful' and that all white people are 'pigs'. Many liberal whites are appalled by these assertions and express their regret at negro 'racialism', but they are the exact equivalent of the expressions of sentiment which have been taken for granted for centuries in white dominated society.

Before we continue by considering the way in which these elementary expressions of one group's reaction to another are rationalised and developed into more articulate systems of thought, we might profitably consider the theoretical structure of what we ourselves are saying, and its relation to certain classical positions in sociological theory. In particular we should note the relationship between what we are saying and Marx's conception of the economic base and ideological superstructure on the one hand and Pareto's conception of residues and sentiments on the other.

We saw earlier the importance of Pareto's notation of 'derivations' as the attempt which men make to rationalise their actions after the event and the contrast which had to be made between these derivations and the 'constant part' (the residues) which explained their action. We should now note the point which Parsons (1949, chap. 5) made so forcibly in his analysis of Pareto's thought, *viz.* that the residues are not simply sentiments or instincts, but essentially non-logical theories of action. Similarly we are trying here to distinguish between attempts to justify and rationalise action on a fairly high theoretical level and the simple and elementary evaluations which one group makes of another, but would not by any means wish to claim that these were in any sense primary instinctive reactions. What we are talking about are elementary verbal guides to action as contrasted with complex theories.

We do wish to assert, however, that such elementary reactions are not simply deductions from explicit theories on a higher level (though they may be strengthened by their relationship to such theories). We would therefore argue that they are in part caused by men's reactions to their enemies and competitors in some kind of basic struggle to survive or earn a living. Clearly Marx was right in insisting that, at this level, one was not dealing with some kind of psychological cause, as are other sociologists such as Oppenheimer, who see the business of conquest rather than economic exploitation as the basic process. But both economic competition and exploitation on the one hand, and military struggle on the other, do produce psychological reactions of aggression, and these reactions are verbalised in the form of elementary statements and stereotypes which we have been discussing. Thus both Pareto and the Marxists are emphasising part of the truth. What we have in inter-group relations is a succession of the following elements: (*a*) a process of conflict, competition or struggle for survival between groups, (*b*) psychological reactions of aggression and hostility on the part of members of one group against members of the other, (*c*) verbal expressions of this hostility asserting that the other group has undesirable qualities or demanding that in some way it should cease to exist. Beyond this there are a number of further stages which would seem to belong to the area of what Marxists call the super-structure and Pareto 'derivations'. What we wish to insist on is that, despite the verbalisations involved at this level, it has to be distinguished from the more explicit theorising level.

References

Berger, B. L. and Luckmann, T. (1967), *The Social Construction of Reality*, London.
Durkheim, C. E. (1954), *The Elementary Forms of Religious Life*, London.
Hanke, L. (1949), *The Spanish Struggle for Justice in the Conquest of America*, Philadelphia.
Kiewet, C. W., de (1946), *A History of South Africa*, Oxford.
Lundberg, G. (1939), *Foundations of Sociology*, New York.
Morgan, L. (1877), *Ancient Society*, New York.

Orwell, G. (1939), *The Road to Wigan Pier*, London.
Pareto, V. (1935), *Mind and Society*, New York.
Parsons, T. (1949), *The Structure of Social Action*, Glencoe, Ill.
Schutz, A. (1967), *The Problem of Social Reality*, The Hague.
Simpson, G. E. and Yinger, Y. M. (1959), 'Sociology of race and ethnic relations', in Merton, Broom and Cottrell (eds.), *Sociology Today*, New York.

Part two **Ethnic Stratification**

The order and conflict models of race relations are the creations and conceptualizations of sociologists and other social scientists who have attempted, through the application of these models (Horton, 1966) to describe and explain current race relations situations.[1] The attempt has been successful in one direction, in pointing out that race relations between dominant and subordinate groups have not always been the unforeseen results of unintended social action, but have been linked specifically to forms of economic organization, ideological legitimations and the deliberate orderings of institutional arrangements so as to perpetuate current forms and styles of relationships. The writers whose selections are included in Part 2 have used the 'sociological imagination' as Wright Mills (1970, p. 17) recommended it could be used: 'to understand the changes of many personal milieux...and look beyond them. ...To be aware of the idea of social structure and to use it with sensibility is to be capable of tracing such linkages among a great variety of milieux. To be able to do that is to possess the sociological imagination.'

The intention of this section is to suggest that the sociological imagination can be used by tracing linkages back from the current situation through using the concept of *stratification* as the continuous link between different types of social structure and race. The concept of ethnic stratification draws attention to that continuous link which exists between societies at different points in time; within different cultural contexts; and with different belief systems. Stratification based on ethnic differences therefore is the bed rock of modern race relations situations.

Four fundamental types of stratification with their associated belief systems are given in the examples of slavery, caste, race and pluralism which follow as inclusions in this volume. These selected forms of stratification draw attention to the subjective but dynamic and omnipresent effect of belief systems on race relations, and they also show that stratification theory underpins most discussions of race relations, either explicitly or implicitly.

Without question, the association of the condition of slavery with black

[1] Park (1939) defines race relations as 'all the relations which exist between members of different ethnic and genetic groups which are capable of provoking race conflict and race consciousness, or of determining the relative status of the social groups of which a community is composed'.

men has been linked in the conventional wisdoms of modern societies since the rise of slavery in the Southern States of America in the late seventeenth century. On this theme, see Woodward (1957), Phillips (1918), Tannenbaum (1948), Williams (1961) and Patterson (1967). The importance of Jordan's contribution (Extract 10) is that it shows that the question of slave status and its association with black men in the USA is a contentious issue in American historiography and intellectual history. Jordan is able to point up the contentious, but general issue in social science writing, of cause and effect and show at the same time that intellectual interest in an area of subject matter which appears dated, and assigned the comfortable status of 'historical fact', is related to current ideologies; in this example, modern race relations and the question of slave status in early colonial America. This inclusion is an excellent example of how difficult it is to uncover the roots of modern race relations situations simply by positing that that the status of slave was associated with that of black man, and owner status with white man. Although the evidence mustered by Jordan for this association is powerful and compelling, his own scepticism about the writings and interpretations of others is a useful guide to his own contribution.

Elkins' contribution (Extract 11) is included to show that slavery *per se* was not necessarily associated with the irrevocable status of life-time bondage. Although Elkins' book is really concerned with the total problem of applying concepts to different historical structures and so is as much a treatise on comparative methodology, for our purposes its importance lies in the attempt to distinguish the form and the consequences of slavery in the different societies —the Southern USA, Brazil and Spanish America. Basically, Elkins' argument is as follows: that whereas the Southern States of America represented an ideal type of unrestricted authority wielded by a planter class which was not controlled by any strong countervailing institutions, the situation in Spanish South America differed in that there the slave had an alternative status besides slavery, guaranteed to him by the most powerful of historical alliances—the Spanish Church and the Spanish Crown. In the Spanish colonies, therefore, rampant and unrestrained dynamic capitalism was curbed on the basis of the proposition that the slave 'was a man, that he had a soul as precious as any other man's, that he had a moral nature, that he was not only as susceptible to sin but also as eligible for grace as his master—that master and slaves were brothers in Christ.'

The Tannenbaum and Elkins' theses are controversial, and in Winthrop Jordan's 'White over Black' (section entitled Essay on Sources) the point is made (p. 605) that although 'there is great merit in these [Elkins'] points, Elkins' assumption that the Negro enslaved by Englishmen was infantilized by a closed system of slavery greatly distorts the facts, which he made little attempt to investigate'. This is a serious charge but it is also indicative of the issues that have been generated within this field; questions of race conscious-

ness and their different levels between societies; the materialist versus cul-
turalist school of thought on the question of the origin and persistence of
slavery and its relationship to modern race relations; and finally, the question
of whether an ascribed racial status can be overcome by modern social
policies in the face of race consciousness which is rooted in notions of
superior and inferior (owner/slave) status.

Genovese (Extract 12) attempts to pick his way between the strongly
materialist conception as applied to the dynamics of slavery and the process
of race, and the conditioning influence of culture that was to determine the
form that modern American race relations, historically linked to slavery, was
to take. With respect to Tannenbaum and therefore Elkins, Genovese argues
that 'the great weakness in [his] presentation is that it ignores the material
foundations of each particular slave society, and especially the class relations,
for an almost exclusive concern with tradition and cultural continuity'.

The materialist and idealist perspectives presented in this essay do not
simply provide a clue to how current race situations are explained or legitimated, they also provide a productive methodology which can permeate the
following discussion.

The two main characteristics of any group defined as a caste are, first that
their position within society has been religiously ordained, legitimated,
sanctioned and approved, and therefore by acting out a caste role the individual helps to stabilize the normative order and to strengthen the moral
community and secondly, that where those individuals from a lower caste
come into contact with a higher caste—whether by choice, intention or
accident—then inevitably the higher caste is polluted by such contact. Caste,
therefore, has both a structural and a cultural aspect; structural, in that
individuals are born into ascribed caste groups and the interaction which
follows from this event depends upon the position of the caste in the overall
stratification system; cultural, in that the norms which govern all interaction
are religiously sanctioned norms, peculiar to the one society where caste
pervades and controls the total social structure, as for example in India. Max
Weber (1947) describes these two aspects as follows: 'Caste is the fundamental
institution of Hinduism. . . . Caste is, and remains essentially, social rank, and
the central position of the Brahmans in Hinduism rests more upon the fact that
social rank is determined with reference to them than upon anything else'.

In 1936 W. Lloyd Warner (Extract 13) published an influential paper in
which he insisted that 'the social organization of the Deep South consists of
two different kinds of social stratification'; a caste system and a class structure. He describes 'a negro caste since slavery' in the Deep South, characterized by being situated on one side of the 'caste line', having all the features
of a caste situation.[2]

---

[2] Warner was still presenting this 'caste case' in 1945: 'The negro and other dark-skinned
groups are still ranked as colour-castes' (Warner and Srole, 1945, p. 296).

Warner suggests that this caste line is so inflexible with regard to exogamous marriage that black and white society exist side by side, separated by a cultural barrier while being stratified on their respective sides of the line in class terms. The dominant social caste then controls all the major social institutions, effectively excluding upper class negroes, whose caste position is automatically low.

A similar view is expressed in Berreman's (Extract 14) essay which argues that the phenomenon of caste has three analytically separate dimensions: stratification, pluralism and interaction. By stratification, Berreman refers to the traditional hierarchical ordering of society, the ideal type of which is to be found in India, and which results in 'differential evaluation, rewards and association'. Berreman's intention is to show that the Indian model can be used to analyse other societies, with the help of the concepts of pluralism and interaction. This is especially so with American society. Although pluralism is not rigorously defined its essential feature for Berreman is the fact that power is expressed in different ways in plural societies. This being so, he suggests that there are similarities between India and the United States.

If the defining characteristic of caste is power and the resulting social interaction is based on the distribution of power, then Berreman is correct and American society approximates to a caste society as Warner argued. However, to admit this is to ignore one very important feature of caste societies and the resultant caste status. As O. C. Cox (Extract 15) points out, 'caste is a total status'. For Cox there is no question that, in American society, 'caste is not a substitute title or name for "race". As applied to race, it [caste] is decidedly worthless'. Cox sees the use of caste as a description of American race relations as a 'comforting blanket assumption' obscuring the true situation.

Although not basing his position, as Cox does, on the specifically Marxist contention that the American race situation is a political-class struggle, Edmund Leach (Extract 16) gives further support to the Weberian interpretation of caste. For him 'it denotes a particular species of structural organization indissolubly linked with a Pan-Indian civilization'.

Banton's (Extract 17) argument that race serves as a role-sign supports the view that the white social structure allocates ascribed social roles which have been largely unquestioned by black populations. Racial status might be lost by 'passing' or violent challenges to the process of role ascription, but as Banton points out 'in many regions there is little opportunity for people to manipulate their claims to racial status.'

Racial classification 'determines the allocation of highly important political, economic and social rights such as voting, employment and housing, and such distinctions are reinforced in everyday conventions about the respect which inferiors must pay to superiors'. Furthermore, 'Racial roles, like sex roles, are usually ascribed at birth and cannot be varied. An individual in a racially divided society is usually forced to play his racial role whether he will or not, for the sanctions utilized by the dominant group are extremely powerful' (Banton, p. 59).

'Passing' as a member of a different racial group is one response to the invariability and inflexibility of racial role playing. St Clair Drake (Extract 18) suggests that in the USA 'passing' for blacks progresses from a nonchalant process to a serious final stage of crossing the colour line completely. He suggests that 'unintentional passing' by accident, might lead to a realization that passing for fun can be carried out successfully. This stage precedes a more serious stage of passing 'for convenience' and passing for 'economic necessity'. This process ends in what St Clair Drake terms 'sociological death'.

The intellectual decision to reject one moral community for another and in the process deliberately to reject family and the traditional safe ways of interaction, sums up in an ideal-typical way the structural pressures generated upon individuals by a society organized along stratification lines of race. The phenomenon of 'passing' cannot just be applied to American negroes. There have long existed conventional wisdoms among Jewish communities concerning those members of that religious affiliation who also 'pass' as non-Jews because they 'look' Anglo-Saxon.[3] 'Passing' then can be defined as a process generated by societies where the self-perceptions of individuals are made so insecure that to 'pass out' is the last risk taken.

It is sometimes argued that 'race' as a basis for social stratification is gradually undermined by economic developments in what Furnival has called a 'pluralistic society'.

In Burma, as in Java, probably the first thing that strikes the visitor is the medley of peoples—European, Chinese, Indian and native. It is in the strictest sense a medley, for they mix but do not combine. Each group holds by its own religion, its own culture and language, its ideas and ways. As individuals they meet, but only in the market place, in buying and selling. There is a plural society, with different sections of the community living side by side, but separately within the same political unit. Even in the economic sphere there is a division of labour on racial lines.

This definition (Extract 19) of pluralism is taken from an analysis of how a social structure alters under the impact of colonial dominance. In this example the Dutch dependency of Java had imposed upon it a western superstructure which was totally oriented towards economic goals and in which all social interaction was subordinated to those ends. In a case like this, the heterogeneity of the population ensures a 'mixing' for economic transations.

---

[3] One of Portnoy's fantasies involved him in estimating how he could 'pass' from Jewish to Gentile status; 'Secretly I have been practising writing Peterson all winter long, practising on sheets of paper that I subsequently tear from my notebook after school and burn so that they won't have to be explained to anybody in my house' (Roth, 1969, p. 164).

This form of social interaction arises where economic forces predominate over social forces. Plural societies therefore lack shared moral communities.

The contributions of Smith and Michael Lofchie (Extracts 19 and 20) are included for two reasons; firstly, Smith provides us with a more sophisticated analytical insight than Furnivall, on the question of whether pluralism was composed simply of a political and economic dimension. For Smith, the three levels of pluralism—cultural, social and structural—are suggestive of institutional diversity without the corresponding and concomitant collective segregation outlined by Furnivall as applying to Java. Secondly, Lofchie is able to apply the concept to pre-revolutionary Zanzibar and show that there is a congruence between the analytically and intellectually separate components which constitute pluralism and the ethnic, cultural and racial configuration of Zanzibar society before its recent political change. If Smith's theorizing is but a confirmation of the debate begun by Furnivall, then Lofchie's use of Zanzibar as a paradigm case to which this theoretical enterprise can be applied is an example of the complementarity of theory building and its research applications. The work of Smith and Lofchie in providing theoretical definitions of the phenomenon and applying these to societies at different stages in their political and economic development (the USA and Zanzibar) is an example of how the issue of race relations can call into question the total structure and working of modern societies, as well as the arrangements and bargains entered into by their majority and minority groups.

Glazer and Moynihan (Extract 21) make a contribution which, although academic in style and intention, verges on a political plea that pluralism in the USA is the only alternative left to the American race relations scene.[4] What worries Glazer and Moynihan in their review of race relations in the 1960s in American society is that the alternatives for ethnic groups then were polarized between assimilation and ethnic group status. The failure of these alternatives to be adopted is laid at the door of the intelligentsia and the black community. Instead, the alternatives are now ethnic group status and separatism. Glazer and Moynihan define the Northern model of race relations as the ethnic group status/plural society model, based upon toleration of differences; against this looms the Southern model of total division and separatism based on violence. The authors plead for the economic, cultural, social and political incorporation of negroes into the mainstream of American society. 'Pluralism' therefore has its use outside the strictly colonial situation as the last chance for the 'order model' of race relations to predominate over the 'conflict' reality which is thought to be looming on the horizon of modern

[4] The Black Power groups in the USA of course reject this view of the future. Pluralism is akin to slavery and only revolt has dignity: 'I don't want to raise any more black slaves. We have a determined enemy who will accept us only on a master-slave basis. When I revolt, slavery dies with me. I refuse to pass it down again. The terms of my existence are founded on that' (Jackson, 1971, p. 220).

race relations. Events in the United States since the publication of Glazer and Moynihan (Extract 21) shows that their pessimism was well founded.

This section of the book therefore ends with a modern view of race and ethnic relations which reminds us of the underlying theme of stratification which has given these inclusions an affinity and identity.

References

Bolt, C. (1971), *Victorian Attitudes to Race*, London.

Horton, J. (1966), 'Order and conflict theories of social problems as competing ideologies', *A.J.S.*, vol. 71, pp. 701–3, May.

Jackson, G. (1971), *Soledad Brother*, Harmondsworth.

Mills, C. W. (1970), *The Sociological Imagination*, Harmondsworth.

Park, R. E. (1939), 'The nature of race relations', in E. T. Thompson (ed.), *Race Relations and the Race Problem*, pp. 3–45, New York.

Patterson, O. (1967), *The Sociology of Slavery*, London.

Phillips, V. B. (1918), *American Negro Slavery*, New York.

Roth, P. (1969), *Portnoy's Complaint*, London.

Tannenbaum, F. (1947), *Slave and Citizen*, New York.

Warner, W. L. and Srole, L. (1945), *The Social Systems of American Ethnic Groups*, Yankee City Series, vol. III, Yale.

Weber, M. (1947), in H. Gerth and C. W. Mills (eds.), *From Max Weber*, London.

Williams, E. (1961), *Capitalism and Slavery*, New York.

Woodward, C. V. (1957), *The Strange Career of Jim Crow*, New York.

10 *Winthrop D. Jordan,* Modern Tensions and the Origins of American Slavery

Thanks to John Smith we know that Negroes first came to the British continental colonies in 1619.[1] What we do not know is exactly when Negroes were first enslaved there. This question has been debated by historians for the past seventy years, the critical point being whether Negroes were enslaved almost from their first importation or whether they were at first simply servants and only later reduced to the status of slaves. The long duration and vigor of the controversy suggest that more than a simple question of dating has been involved. In fact certain current tensions in American society have complicated the historical problem and greatly heightened its significance. Dating the origins of slavery has taken on a striking modern relevance.

During the nineteenth century historians assumed almost universally that the first Negroes came to Virginia as slaves. So close was their acquaintance with the problem of racial slavery that it did not occur to them that *Negroes* could ever have been anything but slaves. Philip A. Bruce, the first man to probe with some thoroughness into the early years of American slavery, adopted this view in 1896, although he emphasized that the original difference in treatment between white servants and Negroes was merely that Negroes served for life. Just six years later, however, came a challenge from a younger, professionally trained historian, James C. Ballagh. His *A History of Slavery in Virginia* (1902, pp. 28–35) appeared in the *Johns Hopkins University Studies in Historical and Political Science,* an aptly named series which was to usher in the new era of scholarly detachment in the writing of institutional history. Ballagh offered a new and different interpretation; he took the position that the first Negroes served merely as servants and that enslavement did not begin until around 1660, when statutes bearing on slavery were passed for the first time (Bruce, 1896, vol. 2, pp. 57–130).

There has since been agreement on dating the statutory establishment of slavery, and differences of opinion have centered on when enslavement began in actual practice. Fortunately there has also been general agreement on slavery's distinguishing characteristics: service for life and inheritance of

[1] About the last of August came in a dutch man of warre that sold us twenty Negars' Smith was quoting John Rolfe's account (Arber and Bradley, 1910, vol. II, p. 54).

Winthrop D. Jordan, 'Modern tensions and the origins of American slavery', *Journal of Southern History*, vol. XXVIII, February 1962, pp. 18–30.

like obligation by any offspring. Writing on the free Negro in Virginia for the Johns Hopkins series, John H. Russell (1913, pp. 23–39) in 1913 tackled the central question and showed that some Negroes were indeed servants but concluded that 'between 1640 and 1660 slavery was fast becoming an established fact. In this twenty years the colored population was divided, part being servants and part being slaves, and some who were servants defended themselves with increasing difficulty from the encroachments of slavery'. Ulrich B. Phillips (1918, 1929), though little interested in the matter, in 1918 accepted Russell's conclusion of early servitude and transition toward slavery after 1640. Helen T. Catterall (1926, pp. 54–63) took much the same position in 1926. On the other hand, in 1921 James M. Wright (1921, pp. 21–3), discussing the free Negro in Maryland, implied that Negroes were slaves almost from the beginning, and in 1940 Susie M. Ames (1940, pp. 100–6) reviewed several cases in Virginia which seemed to indicate that genuine slavery had existed well before Ballagh's date of 1660.

All this was a very small academic gale, well insulated from the outside world. Yet despite disagreement on dating enslavement, the earlier writers— Bruce, Ballagh, and Russell—shared a common assumption which, though at the time seemingly irrelevant to the main question, has since proved of considerable importance. They assumed that prejudice against the Negro was natural and almost innate in the white man. It would be surprising if they had felt otherwise in this period of segregation statutes, overseas imperialism, immigration restriction, and full-throated Anglo-Saxonism. By the 1920s however, with the easing of these tensions, the assumption of natural prejudice was dropped unnoticed. Yet only one historian explicitly contradicted that assumption: Ulrich Phillips (1918, p. viii) of Georgia, impressed with the geniality of both slavery and twentieth-century race relations, found no natural prejudice in the white man and expressed his 'conviction that Southern racial asperities are mainly superficial, and that the two great elements are fundamentally in accord'.

Only when tensions over race relations intensified once more did the older assumption of natural prejudice crop up again. After World War II American Negroes found themselves beneficiaries of New Deal politics and reforms, wartime need for manpower, world-wide repulsion at racist excesses in Nazi Germany, and growing successful colored anticolonialism. With new militancy Negroes mounted an attack on the citadel of separate but equal, and soon it became clear that America was in for a period of self-conscious reappraisal of its racial arrangements. Writing in this period of heightened tension a practiced and careful scholar, Wesley F. Craven (1949, pp. 217–19, 402–3), raised the old question of the Negro's original status, suggesting that Negroes had been enslaved at an early date. Craven also cautiously resuscitated the idea that white men may have had natural distaste for the Negro, an idea which fitted neatly with the suggestion of early enslavement. Original antipathy would mean rapid debasement.

R.A.E.R.—E

In the next year came a sophisticated counterstatement, which contradicted both Craven's dating and implicitly any suggestion of early prejudice. Oscar and Mary F. Handlin in 'Origins of the Southern Labor System (*William and Mary Quarterly*, 1950, pp. 119–222) offered a case for late enslavement, with servitude as the status of Negroes before about 1660. Originally the status of both Negroes and white servants was far short of freedom, the Handlins maintained, but Negroes failed to benefit from increased freedom for servants in mid-century and became less free rather than more. Embedded in this description of diverging status were broader implications: Late and gradual enslavement undercut the possibility of natural, deep-seated antipathy toward Negroes. On the contrary, if whites and Negroes could share the same status of half freedom for forty years in the seventeenth century, why could they not share full freedom in the twentieth?

The same implications were rendered more explicit by Kenneth M. Stampp (1956, pp. vii–viii, 3–33) in a major reassessment of Southern slavery published two years after the Supreme Court's 1954 school decision. Reading physiology with the eye of faith, Stampp frankly stated his assumption 'that innately Negroes *are*, after all, only white men with black skins, nothing more, nothing less'. Closely following the Handlins' article on the origins of slavery itself, he almost directly denied any pattern of early and inherent racial antipathy: '. . . Negro and white servants of the seventeenth century seemed to be remarkably unconcerned about their visible physical differences'. As for 'the trend toward special treatment' of the Negro, 'physical and cultural differences provided handy excuses to justify it (pp. 21–2).' Distaste for the Negro, then, was in the beginning scarcely more than an appurtenance of slavery.

These views squared nicely with the hopes of those even more directly concerned with the problem of contemporary race relations, sociologists and social psychologists. Liberal on the race question almost to a man, they tended to see slavery as the initial cause of the Negro's current degradation. The modern Negro was the unhappy victim of long association with base status. Sociologists, though uninterested in tired questions of historical evidence, could not easily assume a natural prejudice in the white man as the cause of slavery. Natural or innate prejudice would not only violate their basic assumptions concerning the dominance of culture but would undermine the power of their new Baconian science. For if prejudice was natural there would be little one could do to wipe it out. Prejudice must have followed enslavement, not vice versa, else any liberal program of action would be badly compromised. One prominent social scientist suggested in a UNESCO pamphlet that racial prejudice in the United States commenced with the cotton gin![2]

---

[2] Arnold Rose (1956, p. 224). For examples of the more general view see Detweiler (1932, p. 743), Montagu (1945, pp. 10–11, 19–20), Myrdal (1944, pp. 83–9, 97), and Keeskemeti (1954, pp. 364–6).

Just how closely the question of dating had become tied to the practical matter of action against racial prejudice was made apparent by the suggestions of still another historian. Carl N. Degler (1959a, 1959b) grappled with the dating problem in an article frankly entitled 'Slavery and the Genesis of American Race Prejudice'. The article appeared in 1959, a time when Southern resistance to school desegregation seemed more adamant than ever and the North's hands none too clean, a period of discouragement for those hoping to end racial discrimination. Prejudice against the Negro now appeared firm and deep-seated, less easily eradicated than had been supposed in, say, 1954. It was Degler's view that enslavement began early, as a result of white settlers' prejudice or antipathy toward the first Negroes. Thus not only were the sociologists contradicted but the dating problem was now overtly and consciously tied to the broader question of whether slavery caused prejudice or prejudice caused slavery. A new self-consciousness over the American racial dilemma had snatched an arid historical controversy from the hands of an unsuspecting earlier generation and had tossed it into the arena of current debate.

Ironically there might have been no historical controversy at all if every historian dealing with the subject had exercised greater care with facts and greater restraint in interpretation. Too often the debate entered the realm of inference and assumption. For the crucial early years after 1619 there is simply not enough evidence to indicate with any certainty whether Negroes were treated like white servants or not. No historian has found anything resembling proof one way or the other. The first Negroes were sold to the English settlers, yet so were other Englishmen. It can be said, however, that Negroes were set apart from white men by the word *Negroes*, and a distinct name is not attached to a group unless it is seen as different. The earliest Virginia census reports plainly distinguished Negroes from white men, sometimes giving Negroes no personal name; and in 1629 every commander of the several plantations was ordered to 'take a generall muster of all the inhabitants men woemen and Children as well *Englishe* as Negroes' (McIlwaine, 1924, p. 196). Difference, however, might or might not involve inferiority.

The first evidence as to the actual status of Negroes does not appear until about 1640. Then it becomes clear that *some* Negroes were serving for life and some children inheriting the same obligation. Here it is necessary to suggest with some candor that the Handlins' statement to the contrary rests on unsatisfactory documentation.[3] That some Negroes were held as slaves after about 1640 is no indication, however, that American slavery popped into the world fully developed at that time. Many historians, most cogently the Handlins, have shown slavery to have been a gradual development, a process

[3] The author develops this point in an extreme footnote, Jordan (1962, p. 23). The full references to the detailed argument which follows appear as footnotes in Jordan, pp. 24–9. Only those which develop significant points have been retained for our purposes.

not completed until the eighteenth century. The complete depreviation of civil and personal rights, the legal conversion of the Negro into a chattel, in short slavery as Americans came to know it, was not accomplished overnight. Yet these developments practically and logically depended on the practice of hereditary lifetime service, and it is certainly possible to find in the 1640s and 1650s traces of slavery's most essential feature. Latin-American Negroes did not lose all civil and personal rights, did not become mere chattels, yet we speak of 'slavery' in Latin America without hesitation (see Tannenbaum, 1947; Freyre, 1946).

The first definite trace appears in 1640 when the Virginia General Court pronounced sentence on three servants who had been retaken after running away to Maryland. Two of them, a Dutchman and a Scot, were ordered to serve their masters for one additional year and then the colony for three more, but 'the third being a negro named John Punch shall serve his said master or his assigns for the time of his natural life here or else where'. No white servant in America, so far as is known, ever received a like sentence. Later the same month a Negro was again singled out from a group of recaptured runaways: six of the seven were assigned additional time while the Negro was given none, presumably because he was already serving for life.[4] After 1640, too, county court records began to mention Negroes, in part because there were more of them than previously—about two per cent of the Virginia population in 1649. Sales for life, often including any future progeny, were recorded in unmistakable language. In 1646 Francis Pott sold a Negro woman and boy to Stephen Charlton 'to the use of him...forever'. Similarly, six years later William Whittington sold to John Pott 'one Negro girle named Jowan; aged about Ten yeares and with her Issue and produce duringe her (or either of them) for their Life tyme. And their Successors forever'; and a Maryland man in 1649 deeded two Negro men and a woman 'and all their issue both male and Female'. The executors of a York County estate in 1647 disposed of eight Negroes—four men, two women, and two children—to Captain John Chisman 'to have hold occupy posesse and inioy and every one of the afforementioned Negroes forever'. The will of Rowland Burnham of 'Rapahanocke', made in 1657, dispensed his considerable number of Negroes and white servants in language which clearly differentiated between the two by specifying that the whites were to serve for their 'full terme of tyme' and the Negroes 'for ever'. Nor did anything in the will indicate that this distinction was exceptional or novel.

In addition to these clear indications that some Negroes were owned for life, there were cases of Negroes held for terms far longer than the normal

---

[4] Smith (1947, p. 171), in the standard work on servitude in America says that 'there was never any such thing as perpetual slavery for any white man in any English colony'. There were instances in the seventeenth century of white men sold into 'slavery', but this was when the meaning of the term was still indefinite and often equated with servitude.

five or seven years. On the other hand, some Negroes served only the term usual for white servants, and others were completely free (Russell, 1913, pp. 24–41). One Negro freeman, Anthony Johnson, himself owned a Negro (Russell, 1916, pp. 234–7). Obviously the enslavement of some Negroes did not mean the immediate enslavement of all.

Further evidence of Negroes serving for life lies in the prices paid for them. In many instances the valuations placed on Negroes (in estate inventories and bills of sale) were far higher than for white servants, even those servants with full terms yet to serve. Since there was ordinarily no preference for Negroes as such, higher prices must have meant that Negroes were more highly valued because of their greater length of service. Negro women may have been especially prized, moreover, because their progeny could also be held perpetually. In 1645, for example, two Negro women and a boy were sold for 5500 pounds of tobacco. Two years earlier William Burdett's inventory listed eight servants (with the time each had still to serve) at valuations ranging from 400 to 1100 pounds, while a 'very anntient' Negro was valued at 3000 and an eight-year-old Negro girl at 2000 pounds, with no time-remaining indicated for either. In the late 1650s an inventory of Thomas Ludlow's large estate evaluated a white servant with six years to serve at less than an elderly Negro man and only one half of a Negro woman. The labor owned by James Stone in 1648 was evaluated as follows:

	lb tobo
Thomas Groves, 4 yeares to serve	1300
Francis Bomley for 6 yeares	1500
John Thackstone for 3 yeares	1300
Susan Davis for 3 yeares	1000
Emaniell a Negro man	2000
Roger Stone 3 yeares	1300
Mingo a Negro man	2000

Besides setting a higher value on the two Negroes, Stone's inventory, like Burdett's, failed to indicate the number of years they had still to serve. It would seem safe to assume that the time remaining was omitted in this and similar documents simply because the Negroes were regarded as serving for an unlimited time.

The situation in Maryland was apparently the same. In 1643 Governor Leonard Calvert agreed with John Skinner, 'mariner', to exchange certain estates for seventeen sound Negro 'slaves', fourteen men and three women between sixteen and twenty-six years old. The total value of these was placed at 24 000 pounds of tobacco, which would work out to 1000 pounds for the women and 1500 for the men, prices considerably higher than those paid for white servants at the time.

Wherever Negro women were involved, however, higher valuations may have reflected the fact that they could be used for field work while white women generally were not. This discrimination between Negro and white women, of course, fell short of actual enslavement. It meant merely that Negroes were set apart in a way clearly not to their advantage. Yet this is not the only evidence that Negroes were subjected to degrading distinctions not directly related to slavery. In several ways Negroes were singled out for special treatment which suggested a generalized debasing of Negroes as a group. Significantly, the first indications of debasement appeared at about the same time as the first indications of actual enslavement.

The distinction concerning field work is a case in point. It first appeared on the written record in 1643, when Virginia pointedly recognized it in her taxation policy. Previously tithable persons had been defined (1629) as 'all those that worke in the ground of what qualitie or condition soever'. Now the law stated that all adult men and *Negro* women were to be tithable, and this distinction was made twice again before 1660. Maryland followed a similar course, beginning in 1654.[5] John Hammond, in a 1656 tract defending the tobacco colonies, wrote that servant women were not put to work in the fields but in domestic employments, 'yet som wenches that are nasty, and beastly and not fit to be so imployed are put into the ground' (Force, 1836, vol. II). Since all Negro women were taxed as working in the fields, it would seem logical to conclude that Virginians found them 'nasty' and 'beastly'. The essentially racial nature of this discrimination was bared by a 1668 law at the time slavery was crystallizing on the statute books:

Whereas some doubts, have arisen whether negro women set free were still to be accompted tithable according to a former act, *It is declared by this grand assembly* that negro women, though permitted to enjoy their ffreedome yet ought not in all respects to be admitted to a full fruition of the exemptions and impunities of the English, and are still lyable to payment of taxes.[6]

Virginia law set Negroes apart in a second way by denying them the important right and obligation to bear arms. Few restraints could indicate more clearly the denial to Negroes of membership in the white community. This action, in a sense the first foreshadowing of the slave codes, came in 1640, at just the time when other indications first appear that Negroes were subject to special treatment.[7]

[5] Hening (1823, vol. I, pp. 144, 242, 292, 454). The Handlins erroneously placed the 'first sign of discrimination' in this matter at 1668 ('Origins', 217*n*). For Maryland, see *Maryland Archives*, vol. I, p. 342; vol. II, pp. 136, 399, 538–9; vol. XIII, pp. 538–9.
[6] Hening (1823, vol. II, p. 267). The distinction between white and colored women was neatly described at the turn of the century by Beverley (1947, pp. 271–2).
[7] Hening (1823, vol. I, p. 226), and for the same act in more detail see *William and Mary Quarterly*, ser. 2, vol. IV (July 1924), p. 147. The Handlins discounted this law: 'Until the 1660's the statutes on the Negroes were not at all unique. Nor did they add up to a decided trend'. ('Origins', 209.) The note added to this statement reads, 'That there was no trend is evident from the fluctuations in naming Negroes slaves or servants and in their right to bear

Finally, an even more compelling sense of the separateness of Negroes was revealed in early distress concerning sexual union between the races. In 1630 a Virginia court pronounced a now famous sentence: 'Hugh Davis to be soundly whipped, before an assembly of Negroes and others for abusing himself to the dishonor of God and shame of Christians, by defiling his body in lying with a negro'.[8] While there were other instances of punishment for interracial union in the ensuing years, fornication rather than miscegenation may well have been the primary offense, though in 1651 a Maryland man sued someone who he claimed had said 'that he had a black bastard in Virginia'. There may have been nothing racial about the 1640 case by which Robert Sweet was compelled 'to do penance in church according to laws of England, for getting a negroe woman with child and the woman whipt' (Hening, 1823, vol. I, p. 552; McIlwaine, 1924, p. 477). About 1650 a white man and a Negro woman were required to stand clad in white sheets before a congregation in Lower Norfolk County for having had relations, but this punishment was sometimes used in ordinary cases of fornication between two whites (Bruce, 1896, vol. II, p. 110).

It is certain, however, that in the early 1660s when slavery was gaining statutory recognition, the colonial assemblies legislated with feeling against miscegenation. Nor was this merely a matter of avoiding confusion of status, as was suggested by the Handlins. In 1662 Virginia declared that 'if any christian shall committ ffornication with a negro man or woman, hee or shee soe offending' should pay double the usual fine. Two years later Maryland prohibited interracial marriages:

forasmuch as divers freeborne English women forgettfull of their free Condicon and to the disgrace of our Nation doe intermarry with Negro Slaves by which alsoe divers suites may arise touching the Issue of such woemen and a great damage doth befall the Masters of such Negros for prevention whereof for deterring such freeborne women from such shamefull Matches . . . ,

---

arms'. See Hening (1823, vol. I, pp. 226, 258, 292, 540), Bruce (1910, vol. II, 5ff., 199ff). For similar fluctuations with regard to Indians, see Hening (1823, vol. I, pp. 391, 518). But since the terms 'servants' and 'slaves' did not have precise meaning, as the Handlins themselves asserted, fluctuations in naming Negroes one or the other can not be taken to mean that their status itself was fluctuating. Of the pages cited in Hening (1823, p. 258) is an act encouraging Dutch traders and contains nothing about Negroes, servants, slaves, or arms. Page 292 is an act providing that fifteen tithable persons should support one soldier; Negroes were among those tithable, but nothing was said of allowing them to arm. Page 540 refers to 'any negro slaves' and 'said negro', but mentions nothing about servants or arms. In the pages dealing with Indians, p. 391 provides that no one is to employ Indian servants with guns, and p. 518 that Indians (not 'Indian servants') are to be allowed to use their own guns; the two provisions are not contradictory. Bruce (1910, vol. II, 5ff.) indicates that Negroes were barred from arming in 1639 and offers no suggestion that there was any later fluctuation in this practice.

[8] Hening (1823, vol. I, p. 146). 'Christianity' appears instead of 'Christians' in McIlwaine (1924, p. 479).

strong language indeed if the problem had only been confusion of status. A Maryland act of 1681 described marriages of white women with Negroes as, among other things, 'always to the Satisfaccōn of theire Lascivious & Lustfull desires, & to the disgrace not only of the English butt allso of many other Christian Nations'. When Virginia finally prohibited all interracial liaisons in 1691, the assembly vigorously denounced miscegenation and its fruits as 'that abominable mixture and spurious issue'.[9]

One is confronted, then, with the fact that the first evidences of enslavement and of other forms of debasement appeared at about the same time. Such coincidence comports poorly with both views on the causation of prejudice and slavery. If slavery caused prejudice, then invidious distinctions concerning working in the fields, bearing arms, and sexual union should have appeared only after slavery's firm establishment. If prejudice caused slavery, then one would expect to find such lesser discriminations preceding the greater discrimination of outright enslavement.

Perhaps a third explanation of the relationship between slavery and prejudice may be offered, one that might fit the pattern of events as revealed by existing evidence. Both current views share a common starting point: They predicate two factors, prejudice and slavery, and demand a distinct order of causality. No matter how qualified by recognition that the effect may in turn react upon the cause, each approach inevitably tends to deny the validity of its opposite. But what if one were to regard both slavery and prejudice as species of a general debasement of the Negro? Both may have been equally cause and effect, constantly reacting upon each other, dynamically joining hands to hustle the Negro down the road to complete degradation. Mutual causation is, of course, a highly useful concept for describing social situations in the modern world (Homans, 1950). Indeed it has been widely applied in only slightly altered fashion to the current racial situation: Racial prejudice and the Negro's lowly position are widely accepted as constantly reinforcing each other.

[9] Hening (1823, vol. II, p. 170; vol. III, pp. 86–7), *Maryland Archives*, vol. I, pp. 533–4; vol. VII, p. 204. Opinion on this matter apparently was not unanimous, for a petition of several citizens to the Council in 1699 asked repeal of the intermarriage prohibition. McIlwaine (1918, vol. I, p. 262). The Handlins wrote ('Origins', 215), 'Mixed marriages of free men and servants were particularly frowned upon as complicating status and therefore limited by law'. Their citation for this, Hening (1823, vol. II, p. 114) and Jernegan (1931, pp. 55, 180) gives little backing to the statement. In Virginia secret marriage or bastardy between whites of different status got the same punishment as such between whites of the same status. A white servant might marry any white if his master consented. See Hening (1823, vol. I, pp. 252–3, 438–9; vol. II, pp. 114–15, 167; vol. III, pp. 71–5, 137–40). See also Ballagh (1895, p. 50). For Maryland, see *Maryland Archives*, vol. I, pp. 73, 373–4, 441–2; vol. II, pp. 396–7; vol. XIII, pp. 501–2. The Handlins also suggested that in the 1691 Virginia law, 'spurious' meant simply 'illegitimate', and they cited Calhoun (1917, vol. I, p. 42), which turns out to be one quotation from John Milton. However, 'spurious' was used in colonial laws with reference only to unions between white and black, and never in bastardy laws involving whites only. Mulattoes were often labeled 'spurious' offspring.

This way of looking at the facts might well fit better with what we know of slavery itself. Slavery was an organized pattern of human relationships. No matter what the law might say, it was of different character than cattle ownership. No matter how degrading, slavery involved human beings. No one seriously pretended otherwise. Slavery was not an isolated economic or institutional phenomenon; it was the practical facet of a general debasement without which slavery could have no rationality. (Prejudice, too, was a form of debasement, a kind of slavery in the mind.) Certainly the urgent need for labor in a virgin country guided the direction which debasement took, molded it, in fact, into an institutional framework. That economic practicalities shaped the external form of debasement should not tempt one to forget, however, that slavery was at bottom a social arrangement, a way of society's ordering its members in its own mind.

References

Ames, S. M. (1940), *Studies of the Virginia Eastern Shore in the Seventeenth Century*, Richmond.

Arber, E. and Bradley, A. G. (eds.) (1910), *Travels and Works of Captain John Smith*, Edinburgh.

Ballagh, J. C. (1895), *White Servitude in the Colony of Virginia*, Baltimore.

Ballagh, J. C. (1902), *A History of Slavery in Virginia*, Baltimore.

Beverley, R. (1947) in B. Wright (ed.), *The History and Present State of Virginia*, Chapel Hill, N.C.

Bruce, P. A. (1896), *Economic History of Virginia in the Seventeenth Century*, New York.

Bruce, P. A. (1910), *Institution History of Virginia in the Seventeenth Century*, 2 vols., New York.

Calhoun, A. W. (1917), *A Social History of the American Family from Colonial Times to the Present*, 3 vols., 1917–1919, Cleveland.

Catterall, H. T. (ed.) (1926), *Judicial Cases Concerning American Slavery and the Negro*, vol. 1, Washington.

Craven, W. F. (1949), *The Southern Colonies in the Seventeenth Century*, Baton Rouge.

Degler, C. N. (1959a), *Comparative Studies in Society and History*, vol. II, October, pp. 49–66.

Degler, C. N. (1959b), *Out of Our Past: The Forces that Shaped Modern America*, pp. 26–39, New York.

Detweiler, F. G. (1932), 'The rise of modern race antagonisms', *A.J.S.*, vol. XXXVII, March.

Force, P. (ed.) (1836), *Tracts [. . .]*, 4 vols., 1836–1846, vol. II, Washington.

Freyre, G. (1946), *The Masters and the Slaves: A Study in the Development of Brazilian Civilization*, New York.

Hening, W. W. (ed.) (1823), *The Statutes at Large; Being a Collection of All the Laws of Virginia*, 2nd ed., vols. 1–4, New York.

Homans, G. C. (1950), *The Human Group*, New York.

Jernegan, M. W. (1931), *Laboring and Dependent Classes in Colonial America, 1607–1783*, Chicago.

Jordan, W. D. (1962), 'Modern tensions and the origins of American slavery', *Journal of American History*, vol. XXXIII, February.

Kecskemeti, P. (1954), 'The psychological theory of prejudice: does it underrate the role of social history?', *Commentary*, vol. XVIII, October.

McIlwaine, H. R. (ed.) (1918), *Legislative Journals of the Council of Colonial Virginia*, 3 vols., 1918–1919, Richmond.

McIlwaine, H. R. (ed.) (1924), *Minutes of the Council and General Court of Colonial Virginia, 1622–1632, 1670–1676*, Richmond.

Montagu, M. F. A. (1945), *Man's Most Dangerous Myth: The Fallacy of Race*, New York.

Myrdal, G. (1944), *An American Dilemma: The Negro Problem and Modern Democracy*, New York.

Phillips, U. B. (1918), *American Negro Slavery*, New York.

Phillips, U. B. (1929), *Life and Labor in the Old South*, Boston.

Rose, A. (1956), 'The roots of prejudice' in UNESCO, *The Race Question in Modern Science*, New York.

Russell, J. H. (1913), *The Free Negro in Virginia, 1619–1865*, Baltimore.

Russell, J. H. (1916), 'Colored freemen as slave owners in Virginia', *Journal of Negro History*, vol. I, July.

Smith, A. E. (1947), *Colonists in Bondage: White Servitude and Convict Labor in America, 1607–1776*, Chapel Hill, N.C.

Stampp, K. M. (1956), *The Peculiar Institution: Slavery in the Ante-Bellum South*, New York.

Swem, E. G. (1934), *Virginia Historical Index*, vol. I, Roanoke Va.

Tannenbaum, F. (1947), *Slave and Citizen: The Negro in the Americas*, New York.

William and Mary Quarterly (1950), ser. 3, vol. VII, April.

Wright, J. M. (1921), *The Free Negro in Maryland, 1634–1860*, New York.

11 *S. Elkins,* Slavery

Neither in Brazil nor in Spanish America did slavery carry with it such precise and irrevocable categories of perpetual servitude, *'durante vita'* and 'for all generations', as in the United States. The presumption in these countries, should the status of a colored person be in doubt, was that he was free rather than a slave.[1] There were in fact innumerable ways whereby a slave's servitude could be brought to an end. The chief of these was the very considerable fact that he might buy his own freedom. The Negro in Cuba or Mexico had the right to have his price declared and could, if he wished, purchase himself in instalments. Slaves escaping to Cuba to embrace Catholicism were protected by a special royal order of 1733 which was twice reissued. A slave unduly punished might be set at liberty by the magistrate. In Brazil the slave who was the parent of ten children might legally demand his or her freedom (Johnston, 1910, p. 89). The medieval Spanish code had made a slave's service terminable under any number of contingencies—if he denounced cases of treason, murder, counterfeiting, or the rape of a virgin, or if he performed various other kinds of meritorious acts. Though all such practices did not find their way into the seventeenth- and eighteenth-century legal arrangements of Latin America, much of their spirit was perpetuated in the values, customs, and social expectations of that later period. It is important to appreciate the high social approval connected with the freeing of slaves. A great variety of happy family events—the birth of a son, the marriage of a daughter, anniversaries, national holidays—provided the occasion, and their ceremonial was frequently marked by the manumission of one or more virtuous servitors. It was considered a pious act to accept the responsibility of becoming godfather to a slave child, implying the moral obligation to arrange eventually for its freedom. Indeed, in Cuba and Brazil such freedom might be purchased for a nominal sum at the baptismal font.[2] All such manumissions had the strong approval of both

[1] 'In the Cuban market freedom was the only commodity which could be bought untaxed; every negro against whom no one had proved a claim of servitude was deemed free. . . .' Mathieson (1926, pp. 37–8).

[2] What I have said in this paragraph is virtually a paraphrase of the information which Mr Tannenbaum (1947, pp. 50, 53–4, 57–8) has collected and so skillfully summarized.

S. Elkins, *Slavery*, University of Chicago Press, 1959, pp. 72–80.

church and state and were registered gratis by the government (Johnston, 1910, p. 42).

In extending its moral authority over men of every condition, the church naturally insisted on bringing slave unions under the holy sacraments. Slaves were married in church and the banns published; marriage was a sacred rite and its sanctity protected in law. In the otherwise circumspect United States, the only category which the law could apply to conjugal relations between slaves—or to unions between master and slave—was concubinage. But concubinage, in Latin America, was condemned as licentious, adulterous, and immoral; safeguards against promiscuity were provided in the law,[3] and in Brazil the Jesuits labored mightily to regularize the libertinage of the master class by the sacrament of Christian marriage (Freyre, 1946, p. 85). Moreover, slaves owned by different masters were not to be hindered from marrying, nor could they be kept separate after marriage. If the estates were distant, the wife was to go with her husband, and a fair price was to be fixed by impartial persons for her sale to the husband's master (Johnston, 1910, pp. 44–5).[4] A slave might, without legal interference, marry a free person. The children of such a marriage, if the mother were free, were themselves free, inasmuch as children followed the condition of their mother (Tannenbaum, 1947, p. 56).

The master's disciplinary authority never had the completeness that it had in the United States, and nowhere did he enjoy powers of life and death over the slave's body. Under the Spanish code of 1789 slaves might be punished for failure to perform their duties, with prison, chains, or lashes, 'which last must not exceed the number of twenty-five, and those must be given them in such manner as not to cause any contusion or effusion of blood: which punishments cannot be imposed on slaves but by their masters or the stewards' (Johnston, 1910, p. 45). For actual crimes a slave was to be tried in an ordinary court of justice like any free person,[5] and, conversely, the

[3] 'The master of slaves must not allow the unlawful intercourse of the two sexes, but must encourage matrimony.' Spanish slave code of 1789, quoted in Johnston (1910, p. 44). Although slaves were allowed 'to divert themselves innocently' on holy days, the males were to be kept apart from the females.

[4] A diocesan synod of 1680 in Cuba issued weighty regulations on this subject which were supposed to supplement and have equal force with civil law. 'Constitution 5 established that "marriage should be free" and ordered that "no master prohibit his slaves from marriage, nor impede those who cohabit therein, because we have found that many masters with little fear of God and in grave danger of their consciences, proscribe their slaves from marrying or impede their cohabitation with their married partners, with feigned pretexts"; and also prohibited "that they go away to sell them outside the city, without that they take together husband and wife"' Ortiz (1916, p. 349). The church even made some concessions here to African tribal marriage agreements, to the extent that a slave with multiple wives might pick out the one he preferred and have his marriage with her solemnized under the sacraments.

[5] The sentence, however, was apparently to be executed by the master (Johnston, 1910, p. 45).

murder of a slave was to be prosecuted just as that of a free man would be.[6] Excessive punishments of slaves—causing 'contusion, effusion of blood, or mutilation of members'—by plantation stewards were themselves punishable. Although gross violations of the law occurred, the law here was anything but the dead letter it proved to be in our own southern states. In the important administration centers of both Brazil and the Spanish colonies there was an official protector of slaves, known variously as the syndic, procurador, or attorney-general, under whose jurisdiction came all matters relating to the treatment of slaves. His functions were nurtured by a well-articulated system of communications. The priests who made the regular rounds of the estates giving Christian instruction were required to obtain and render to him information from the slaves regarding their treatment, and investigation and the necessary steps would be taken accordingly. These priests were answerable to no one else for their activities. In addition, the magistrates were to appoint 'persons of good character' to visit the estates thrice yearly and conduct similar inquiries on similar matters. A further ingenious provision in the Spanish code caused all fines levied, for mistreatment and other excesses against slaves, to be divided up three ways: one-third went to the judge, one-third to the informer, and one-third to the 'Fines Chest'. Finally, the attorney-general and the justices themselves were made accountable to the crown for failure to carry out these ordinances. An implicit royal threat underlay all this; should the fines not have the desired effect and should the ordinances continue to be broken, 'I', His Majesty promised, 'will take my measures accordingly' (Johnston, 1910, pp. 45–6).[7]

As was implied in his right to purchase his own freedom, the slave in the Spanish and Portuguese colonies had the right to acquire and hold property. This meant something specific; in Brazil a master was obliged by law to give liberty to his slaves on all Sundays and holidays—which totalled eighty-five in the year—during which a slave might work for himself and accumulate money for his purchase price,[8] and the Spanish code of 1789 provided that slaves must be allowed two hours each day in which to be employed in 'occupations for their own advantage' (Johnston, p. 44). In many places slaves were encouraged to hire themselves out regularly (there were skilled artisans among them as well as ordinary laborers), an arrangement which was to the advantage of both the master and the slave himself, since the latter was allowed

---

[6] Ibid. The code does not make it clear whether the penalty would be the same against the slave's master as against another person. But in any case the murderer, master or other, was liable to prosecution.

[7] The liberal code of 1789 was not uniformly enforced at first; Ortiz (1916, pp. 363–4, 370), indeed, insists—contradicting the earlier historian, Saco—that it was widely evaded until well into the nineteenth century. The colonists, however, eventually had to succumb to pressure from the Spanish government, and by the 1840's the code had been written into local police regulations in Cuba.

[8] It was not even uncommon for ex-slaves who had thus acquired their freedom to become actual slaveholders on their own account (Johnston, 1910, p. 90).

to keep a percentage of the wage. Slaves even in rural areas might sell the produce of their gardens and retain the proceeds (Tannenbaum, 1947, pp. 58–61). For all practical purposes slavery here had become, as Mr. Tannenbaum puts it, a contractual arrangement: it could be wiped out by a fixed purchase price and leave no taint. 'There may have been no written contract between the two parties, but the state behaved, in effect, as if such a contract did exist, and used its powers to enforce it' (Tannenbaum, p. 55).[9] It was a contract in which the master owned a man's labor but not the man.

As for the privileges of religion, it was here not a question of the planting class 'permitting' the slave, under rigidly specified conditions, to take part in divine worship. It was rather a matter of the church's insisting—under its own conditions—that masters bring their slaves to church and teach them religion. Such a man as the Mississippi planter who directed that the gospel preached to his slaves should be 'in its original purity and simplicity' would have courted the full wrath of the Latin church. A Caribbean synod of 1622 whose *sanctiones* had the force of law, made lengthy provisions for the chastisement of masters who prevented their slaves from hearing Mass or receiving instruction on feast days. Here the power of the Faith was such that master and slave stood equally humbled before it. 'Every one who has slaves'. according to the first item in the Spanish code, 'is obliged to instruct them in the principles of the Roman Catholic religion and in the necessary truths in order that the slaves may be baptized within the (first) year of their residence in the Spanish dominions' (Johnston, 1910, p. 43). Certain assumptions were implied therein which made it impossible that the slave in this culture should ever quite be considered as mere property, either in law or in society's customary habits of mind. These assumptions, perpetuated and fostered by the church, made all the difference in his treatment by society and its institutions, not only while a slave, but also if and when he should cease to be one. They were, in effect, that he was a man, that he had a soul as precious as any other man's, that he had a moral nature, that he was not only as susceptible to sin but also as eligible for grace as his master—that master and slave were brothers in Christ.

The Spaniards and Portuguese had the widespread reputation by the eighteenth century—whatever may have been the reasons—for being among all nations the best masters of slaves. The standards for such a judgment cannot, of course, be made too simple. Were slaves 'physically maltreated' in those countries? They could, conceivably, have been treated worse than in

---

[9] A practical application of this contractual aspect of slavery was the institution of *coartación* which developed in Cuba in the eighteenth century. This was an arrangement whereby the slave might buy his freedom in instalments. He would first have his price declared (if he and his master disagreed, the local courts would determine it), whereupon he made his first payment. After that point, the price could not be changed, and he could at the same time change masters at will, the new master simply paying the balance of his price. See Aimes (1909, pp. 412–31).

our own nineteenth-century South without altering the comparison, for even in cruelty the relationship was between man and man.[10] Was there 'race prejudice'? No one could be more arrogantly proud of his racial purity than the Spaniard of Castile, and theoretically there were rigid caste lines, but the finest Creole families, the clergy, the army, the professions, were hopelessly 'defiled' by Negro blood;[11] the taboos were that vague in practice. Was there squalor, filth, widespread depression of the masses? Much more so than with us—but there it was the class system and economic 'underdevelopment', rather than the color barrier, that made the difference. In these countries the concept of 'beyond the pale' applied primarily to beings outside the Christian fold rather than to those beyond the color line.[12]

We are not, then, dealing with a society steeped, like our own, in traditions of political and economic democracy. We are concerned only with a special and peculiar kind of fluidity—that of their slave systems—and in this alone lay a world of difference. It was a fluidity that permitted a transition from slavery to freedom that was smooth, organic, and continuing. Manumitting slaves, carrying as it did such high social approval, was done often, and the spectacle of large numbers of freedmen was familiar to the social scene. Such opportunities as were open to any member of the depressed classes who had talent and diligence were open as well to the ex-slave and his descendants. Thus color itself was no grave disability against taking one's place in free society; indeed, Anglo-Saxon travelers in nineteenth-century Brazil were amazed at the thoroughgoing mixture of races there. 'I have passed black ladies in silks and jewelry', wrote Thomas Ewbank in the 1850's, 'with male slaves in livery behind them. . . . Several have white husbands. The first doctor

[10] Most writers and students do seem to think that the system was 'milder' in the Spanish colonies and in Brazil, but nobody has ever claimed that it was a life of ease and comfort [. . .] It could be pointed out that comparisons, when made, were made most frequently with the British colonies of the eighteenth century, especially the British West Indies. In the United States, on the other hand, by (say) 1850, slavery in a 'physical' sense was in general, probably, quite mild. However, even if it had been milder here than anywhere else in the Western Hemisphere, it would still be missing the point to make the comparison in terms of physical comfort. In one case we would be dealing with the cruelty of man to man, and, in the other, with the care, maintenance, and indulgence of men toward creatures who were legally and morally *not* men—not in the sense that Christendom had traditionally defined man's nature. It is for our purposes, in short, the *primary* relationship that matters. Masters and slaves in Brazil, according to João Ribeiro, 'were united into families, if not by law, at least by religion.' (Pierson, 1942, p. 81).

[11] Even the legendary corruption of the Spanish upper classes was apparently biracial in the New World. Beye Cisneros of Mexico City, during the course of the debates on the Spanish constitution of 1811, declared, 'I have known mulattoes who have become counts, marquises, *oidores*, canons, colonels, and knights of the military orders through intrigue, bribery, perjury, and falsification of public books and registers; and I have observed that those who have reached these positions and distinctions by reprehensible means, have been granted the corresponding honors without repugnance, despite their mixed blood. . . .' King (1953, p. 56).

[12] 'The thing that barred an immigrant in those days was heterodoxy; the blot of heresy upon the soul and not any racial brand upon the body' (Freyre, 1946, pp. 40–1).

of the city is a colored man; so is the President of the Province'. Free Negroes had the same rights before the law as whites, and it was possible for the most energetic of their numbers to take immediate part in public and professional life. Among the Negroes and mulattoes of Brazil and the Spanish colonies—aside from the swarming numbers of skilled craftsmen—were soldiers, officers, musicians, poets, priests, and judges. 'I am accustomed,' said a delegate to the Cortes of Cádiz in 1811, 'to seeing many engaged in all manner of careers' (King, 1953, p. 59).

All such rights and opportunities existed *before* the abolition of slavery; and thus we may note it as no paradox that emancipation, when it finally did take place, was brought about in all these Latin-American countries 'without violence, without blood-shed, and without civil war' (Tannenbaum, 1947, p. 106).

The above set of contrasts, in addition to what it may tell us about slavery itself, could also be of use for a more general problem, that of the conservative role of institutions in any social structure. The principle has been observed in one setting where two or more powerful interests were present to limit each other; it has been tested negatively in a setting where a single interest was free to develop without such limits. The latter case was productive of consequences which could hardly be called, in the classical sense of the term, 'conservative'.

References

Aimes, H. H. (1909), 'Coartación: a Spanish institution for the advancement of slaves into freedmen', *Yale Review*, vol. XVII, February.

Ewbank, T. (1856), *Life in Brazil*, New York.

Freyre, G. (1946), *The Masters and the Slaves*, New York.

Johnston, H. (1910), *The Negro in the New World*, London.

King, J. F. (1953), 'The colored castes and American representation in the Cortes of Cádiz', *Hispanic American Historical Review*, vol. XXXIII, February.

Mathieson, W. L. (1926), *British Slavery and its Abolition*, London.

Ortiz, F. (1916), *Los Negros Esclaves*, Havana.

Pierson, D. (1942), *Negroes in Brazil*, Chicago.

Tannenbaum, F. (1947), *Slave and Citizen*, New York.

12 *E. D. Genovese,* Materialism and Idealism in the History of Negro Slavery in the Americas

The study of Negro slavery in the United States is verging on a new and welcome development as historians begin to appreciate the need for a hemispheric perspective. In 1950, Allan Nevins entitled the appropriate chapter of his *Emergence of Lincoln* 'Slavery in a World Setting', and in 1959 Stanley M. Elkins rescued the work of Frank Tannenbaum from an undeserved obscurity. It was Tannenbaum's (1947) remarkable essay, *Slave and Citizen* that first demonstrated the sterility of treating Southern slavery in national isolation, although the point had been made previously. Oliveira Lima, as early as 1914, had discussed the profound differences between Brazilian and North American race relations and historical experiences with slavery, and Gilberto Freyre (1922, pp. 597–628) has been offering suggestive comparisons since the 1920s. Without claiming for Tannenbaum an originality beyond reasonable limits, we may credit him with having been the first to show that only a hemispheric treatment could enable us to understand the relationship between slavery and race relations and the social and political dynamics of the transition from slavery to freedom. Simultaneously, the questions Tannenbaum posed and the method he suggested wiped out the line between history and the social sciences; Elkins' controversial book illustrates how quickly the discussion [of slavery] must pass into considerations of psychology and anthropology. The improved prospects for comparative analysis derive in part from the advances being made by Spanish American and especially Brazilian historians, sociologists, and anthropologists and in part, as Magnus Mörner (1966, pp. 17–44) suggests, from the excellent work done recently on slavery in the Iberian peninsula itself.

Under the circumstances it is appropriate that the first sweeping assault on Tannenbaum's thesis should come from Marvin Harris (1964) an anthropologist, and equally appropriate that the assault implicitly should accept Tannenbaum's main point—that slavery and race relations must be studied hemispherically.[1] The argument has been joined on two levels: on such

[1] Since Harris published, Davis (1966) has brought out his remarkable study which takes up a critical stance toward Tannenbaum. His criticisms, which will be noted briefly below, are tangential to the main task of his book. Harris' book is, so far, the only attempt to replace the full burden of Tannenbaum's argument.

E. D. Genovese, 'Materialism and idealism in the history of Negro slavery in the Americas', *Journal of Social History*, vol. IV, no. 4, 1971, pp. 333–56.

specific questions as the significance of different slave codes, the degree of paternalism in the social system, and the daily treatment of slaves; and on such general questions of method and philosophy as reflect the age-old struggle between idealist and materialist viewpoints. The specific questions will hopefully be settled in due time by empirical research; the second are likely to stay with us. Since empirical research will necessarily be conditioned by contending viewpoints we must make every effort to clarify the methodological and philosophical issues or risk wasting a great deal of time and effort talking past each other and chasing solutions to spurious problems. The value of Harris' book, apart from specific contributions to our knowledge, is that it extends the discussion in a fruitful way. Presumably, its deficiencies of style will not deny it a hearing. Unlike Harris' *The Nature of Cultural Things,* which comes close to being unreadable, *Patterns of Race in the Americas* (1964), despite lapses into unnecessary jargon and some regrettable rhetoric, is straightforward and vigorous. Unfortunately, it is marred by savage polemical excursions. Harris appears to be a man of strong and, to me, admirable social views, but I fear that he is among those who confuse ideological zeal with bad manners. As a result, his harsh attacks on opposing scholars, some of whom are deservedly respected for their fairness and generosity to others, often result in unjust and arbitrary appraisals of their work and, in any case, leave the reader with a bad taste.

I propose to discuss Harris' demand for a materialist alternative to the idealist framework of Tannenbaum, Freyre, and Elkins and to avoid, so far as possible, discussions of specific differences about data. Those differences may be left to specialists and will not be resolved without much more work by scholars in several disciplines. I propose, too, to ignore Harris' illuminating work on the highland Indian societies. Since the book has much to offer on these and other themes it should be understood that no balanced review is intended here. Even if the book suffers from as grave weaknesses of method and assumption as I believe, it would retain considerable value on other levels and may properly be evaluated more fully elsewhere.

Tannenbaum (1947, p. 65) divides the slave systems of the Western Hemisphere into three groups—Anglo-Saxon, Iberian, and French. The Anglo-Saxon group lacked an 'effective slave tradition', a slave law, and religious institutions concerned with the Negro; the Iberian had a slave tradition and law and a religious institution imbued with the 'belief that the spiritual personality of the slave transcended his slave status'; the French shared the religious principles of the Iberian but lacked a slave tradition and law. Tannenbaum, to his cost, ignores the French case and does not, for example discuss the *Code Noir*. Were he to do so, he might reflect further on the significance of the Iberian codes, for the *Code Noir* was notoriously a dead letter in Saint-Domingue.

The burden of Tannenbaum's argument rests on his estimate of the strength of the Catholic Church in relation to the landowners and on the extent to which the law could be or was enforced. He undoubtedly takes too sanguine a view of Brazilian slavery and simultaneously greatly underestimates the force of community pressure and paternalism in reducing the harshness of the Southern slave codes. He risks broad generalizations and necessarily sacrifices much in the process; many of his generalizations, with qualifications, nonetheless obtain. The essential point is not that Brazilian slaves received kinder treatment but that they had greater access to freedom and once free could find a secure place in the developing national culture. Tannenbaum, accepting the authority of Gilberto Freyre, does suggest a correlation between class mobility, the absence or weakness of racism, and kind treatment, but he does so tentatively, and it forms no essential part of his argument.

Tannenbaum demonstrates that the current status of the Negro in the several societies of the New World has roots in the attitude toward the Negro as a slave, which reflected the total religious, legal, and moral history of the enslaving whites. From this assertion he proceeds to a number of theses of varying value. When, for example, he relates the acceptance of the 'moral personality' of the Negro to the peaceful quality of abolition, we may well wonder about Haiti, or about Brazil, where the peaceful abolition followed decades of bloody slave insurrections and social disorders (Graham, 1966 pp. 123–37), or about the British islands, where peaceful abolition followed a denial of that moral personality. We may, accordingly, take the book apart; it was intended to open, not close, the discussion of an enormously complicated subject. The essentials of the viewpoint remain in force: (1) Slavery was a moral as well as a legal relationship; (2) where tradition, law, and religion combined to recognize the moral personality of the slave, the road to freedom remained open, and the absorption of the freedmen into the national culture was provided for; (3) the recognition of moral personality flowed from the emergent slave-holders' legal and religious past, the extent and nature of their contact with darker peoples, and their traditional view of man and God —of their total historical experience and its attendant world view. Tannenbaum draws the lines much too tightly. As David Brion Davis (1966) shows, the duality of the slave as man and thing always created problems for enslavers, who rarely if ever were able to deny the slave a moral personality. We may nonetheless note a wide range of behavior and attitude within such recognition, and Tannenbaum's problem therefore remains with us.

The great weakness in Tannenbaum's presentation is that it ignores the material foundations of each particular slave society, and especially the class relations, for an almost exclusive concern with tradition and cultural continuity. Tannenbaum thereby avoids essential questions. How, for example, did the material conditions of life in the slave countries affect their cultural inheritance? Tannenbaum implies the necessary victory of the inheritance over contrary tendencies arising from immediate material conditions. Thus, Harris can label his viewpoint idealist and insist, as a materialist, that material conditions determine social relations and necessarily prevail over counter-tendencies in the historical tradition. The special usefulness of Harris' book lies in the presentation of an alternative, materialist interpretation and the concomitant attention paid to many problems that Tannenbaum avoids or obscures. Unfortunately, his materialism, like that of such earlier writers as Eric Williams, is generally mechanical and soon reveals itself as a sophisticated variant of economic determinism. It is, in short, ahistorical.

Harris (1964, p. 64) vigorously attacks Freyre for asserting that Brazil has been a virtual 'racial paradise', but his discussion actually reinforces Freyre's argument. Harris, like Charles Wagley (1963, p. 132) insists on a close relationship between class and race and insists that Brazilian Negroes have always faced intense discrimination because of their lower-class status. Brazil's racial paradise is occupied only by 'fictional creatures'; the real Negroes of Bahia and elsewhere suffer immensely as members of the lower classes in a country in which the rule of thumb alleges a correlation between class and race.

Harris slips into a position that Wagley largely avoids. Wagley (1963, p. 238), too, attacks Freyre by drawing attention to the class dimensions of race relations. He denies the absence of racism and refers to the 'widely documented color prejudice in almost every part of the nation'. Yet, Wagley properly adds that despite prejudice and discrimination Brazilian racial democracy is no myth. Brazilians happily do not usually put their racial chatter into practice; continuing miscegenation undermines racial lines; and the doctrine that 'money whitens the skin' prevails. In these terms, so different from those which might be applied to the United States, we may see Brazilian racial democracy as reality relative to other societies or as myth relative to national standards and pretensions and fully appreciate the force of Octavio Ianni's (1966, p. 15) reference to 'the intolerable contradiction between the myth of racial democracy and the actual discrimination against Negroes and mulattoes'.

The admirable work of C. R. Boxer (1952) at first glance supports Harris against Freyre, but that glance proves deceptive. Boxer (1952, p. 235) dismisses as 'twaddle' the notion that no color bar exists in the Portuguese-speaking world and brings us back to earth from Freyre's flights of romantic fancy, but he does not overthrow the essentials of his argument. What Boxer (1963) does show is how painful a struggle has had to be waged and how much racism has persisted. The strides toward racial democracy that he describes in *Race Relations in the Portuguese Colonial Empire, Portuguese Society in the Tropics, The Golden Age of Brazil,* and elsewhere remain impressive when considered against Anglo-Saxon models. The question is what accounts for the greater 'plasticity' (to use Freyre's word) of the Portuguese. The economic and demographic features of colonization, stressed almost exclusively by Harris, played a great role, but the careful research of so skeptical and cautious a historian as Boxer shows the force of legal, moral, religious, and national traditions. Viewed polemically, Boxer's work destroys the propagandistic nonsense of Dr. Salazar's court historians but only qualifies the main lines of argument in Freyre and Tannenbaum.

In asserting a racial paradise all Freyre (1940, p. 41) could possibly mean is that considerable racial mobility exists and that discrimination is held within tolerable bounds. The criticisms of Wagley, Harris, Boxer, and others demonstrate the existence of an acute class question with a racial dimension; they do not refute Freyre's main claim that society is not racially rent by the standards of the Anglo-Saxon countries. Freyre is undoubtedly open to criticism, for he slides impermissably from race to class. He insists that miscegenation 'never permitted the endurance in absolute antagonisms of that separation of men into masters and slaves imposed by the system of production. Nor the exaggerated development of a mystique of white supremacy nor of nobility'. When he writes that miscegenation negated the class antagonism of master and slave, he talks nonsense; but when he writes that it inhibited— he does not say prevented—a mystique of white supremacy, he is surely correct.

Freyre, possibly in response to criticism of his earlier exaggerations, tries to qualify his lyrical praise of Luso-Brazilian racial attitudes and practices. Sometimes, although by no means consistently even in his most recent work (1936b, p. 8), his evaluations are so well balanced as virtually to accept the criticisms and qualifications offered on all sides:

Not that there is no race or color prejudice mixed with class prejudice in Brazil. There is. . . . But no one in Brazil would think of laws against interracial marriage. No one would think of barring colored people from theatres or residential sections of a town.[2]

The main point for Freyre (1963b, p. 82) is not that race prejudice has been absent but that 'few Brazilian aristocrats were as strict about racial impurity as the majority of the Anglo-Saxon aristocrats of the Old South were'; and that the Brazilian Negro 'has been able to express himself as a Brazilian and has not been forced to behave as an ethnic and cultural intruder' (p. 144). Harris (1964, p. 64) writes: 'Races do not exist for Brazilians. But classes do exist both for the observer and *for* the Brazilians.' These words surrender the argument.

Law, Church, and cultural tradition are not viewed by Tannenbaum, or even Freyre, as unambiguous forces for racial equality; they appreciate the

---

[2] At that, he underestimates the extent of prejudice and discrimination. See, e.g., the important sociological studies of Cardoso and Ianni (1960) and Bastide and Fernandes.

internal conflicts and are concerned with the different outcomes of these conflicts in different cultures. 'The colonial governments, the Spaniards, and the *criollos* treated the mestizo as an inferior human being' (Tannenbaum, 1965, p. 43). Much race prejudice, Tannenbaum adds, existed and exists against Indians and Negroes throughout Latin America. He notes too, in a striking comment on class and race, that United States Negroes can and do advance themselves personally in the economic, social, and political arenas with greater ease than do Latin American Negroes, for whom class rigidities and the economic backwardness of society present severe limitations. The distance between rich and poor, cultured and uncultured in Latin America 'is obviously not racial, not biological, nor based on color of skin or place of origin, but it is perhaps even more effective as a dividing line, and perhaps more permanent. It is an ingrained part of the total scheme of things' (p. 52).

Harris rejects on principle the idea that Portuguese tradition, law, and religion could overcome the counterpressures inherent in Brazilian slavery. He makes some strange assumptions in his often admirable discussion of political relations of Church, state, and landowner in highland and lowland America. He properly portrays each as a separate entity, struggling for control of material resources, but he portrays them as only that. Apart from a grudging phrase here and there (and we find a touch of sarcasm even there), he leaves no room for landowners who on many matters would follow the advice and teaching of the Church simply out of religious commitment, nor for a state apparatus deeply infused with Catholic ethics, nor for a Church with a genuine sense of responsibility for the salvation of souls. Instead, he offers us three collective forms of economic man. Harris repeatedly dismisses as romantic nonsense and the like arguments appealing to Catholic sensibility or inherited values. He misses much of Tannenbaum's implicit schema of a society resting on a balance of power between state, church, and family-based economic interests, and he misses Elkins' acute restatement of Tannenbaum's schema as descriptive of precapitalist society in which minimal room is provided for unrestrained economic impulse.

The burden of Harris' criticism lies in his badly named chapter, 'The Myth of the Friendly Master'. He begins by asserting, 'Differences in race relations within Latin America are at root a matter of the labor systems in which the respective subordinate and superordinate groups become enmeshed....A number of cultural traits and institutions which were permitted to survive or were deliberately encouraged under one system were discouraged or suppressed in the other...(p. 65). He contrasts his view with those of Tannenbaum and Freyre: 'It is their contention that the laws, values, religious precepts, and personalities of the English colonists differed from those of the Iberian colonists. These initial psychological and ideological differences were sufficient to overcome whatever tendency the plantation system may have exerted toward parallel rather than divergent evolution' (pp. 65–6). Tannenbaum and Freyre may be read this way but need not be; Harris has reduced their position to its most idealist and superficial expression. Harris is not alone among social scientists of deserved reputation in caricaturing their ideas. K. Oberg (1966, p. 62), for example, hails *Patterns of Race in the Americas* for having demolished the supposedly prevalent notion that these patterns could be traced to 'the Iberian soul or the inherent racism of the Anglo-Saxon. For polemical purposes this reading scores points, but it does not get us very far. Tannenbaum and Freyre may be—and in my opinion ought to be—read another way, for each in effect describes the historical formation of slave-holding classes.

It is easy but unenlightening to dismiss discussions of psychology and ideology as if they were mere prejudices of romantics when laid against material interests. Harris (1959), like every sensible man, rejects 'simplistic economic determinism' and single-factor explanations, but on close inspection he rejects the simplistic rather than the economic determinism. 'From the standpoint of an evolutionary science of culture', he writes, 'it matters not at all if one starts first with changes in the technoenvironmental complex or first with changes in the institutional matrix; what matters is whether or not there is a correlation' (pp. 188, 194). For him, however, the correlation reduces itself to an ideological reflection of the material reality. What Harris' materialism, in contradistinction to Marxian materialism, fails to realize is that once an ideology arises it alters profoundly the material reality and in fact becomes a partially autonomous feature of that reality. As Antonio Gramsci (1949, p. 49) says about Marx's more sophisticated and useful comments on the role of ideas in history: 'The analysis of these statements, I believe, reinforces the notion of "historical bloc", in which the material forces are the content and ideologies the form—merely an analytical distinction since material forces would be historically inconceivable without form and since ideologies would have to be considered individual dabbling without material forces'. Thus understanding of ideology and economics as reciprocally influential manifestations of particular forms of class rule may be contrasted with Harris' mechanistic and economistic view. He replies (1966, p. 64) to a friendly critic who seeks to defend him against the charge of economic determinism by embracing it proudly: 'I share with all economic determinists the conviction that in the long run and in most cases, ideology is swung into line by material conditions—by the evolution of technoenvironmental and production relationships'. Psychology and ideology are, however, as much a part of class formation as economic interest. Harris implies that ideology simply reflects material interests, which fluctuate sharply, but the ideology of a ruling class ought to be understood as its world view—the sum of its interests and sensibilities, past and present. An essential function of the ideology of a ruling class is to present to itself and to those it rules a coherent world view that is sufficiently flexible, comprehensive, and mediatory to convince the subordinate classes of the justice of its hegemony. If this ideology were no more than a reflection of immediate economic interests, it would be worse than useless, for the hypocrisy of the class, as well as its greed, would quickly become apparent to the most abject of its subjects.[3]

Harris admits that the Portuguese in Portugal exhibited little race prejudice but adds, 'This datum can only be significant to those who believe that discrimination is caused by prejudice, when the true relationship is quite the opposite' (1964, p. 67). He argues, especially for Brazil, along the lines that the Marxists, Eric Williams (1961), and C.L.R. James (1963) have argued for the Caribbean and that American Marxists and non-Marxists like Herbert Aptheker (1943) and the Handlins (1950, pp. 199–222) have argued for the United States. Unhappily, Harris (1964, p. 68) asserts what needs to be proven, and the assertion exposes the fundamental weakness in his ideological armor: He insists on principle that the relationship must be one way and makes the case for materialism rest on this dogma. 'If, as asserted, the Iberians initially lacked any color prejudice, what light does this shed upon the Brazilian and other lowland interracial systems?' According to this view, the past plays no vital role in the present except for transmitted technology. If the case for materialism rests on a denial of the totality of human history and on the resurrection of an economic determinism brought to a higher level of sophistication, materialism has poor prospects.

It is easy to dismiss as idealism or subjectivity the view that prejudice existed prior to discrimination, but the tenacious defense of this position by such sober and diverse scholars as Carl Degler (1959, pp. 49–66), Juan Comas (1961, pp. 271–99), Arnold A. Sio (1965, pp. 289–308), and David Brion Davis ought to give us pause. Davis recounts the various origins of anti-Negro prejudice in Europe. 'The fact that Africans had traditionally been associated with Noah's curse of Canaan', he notes for example, 'may have disposed some Europeans to regard them as fit for bondage (Davis, 1966, p. 281). Winthrop D. Jordan has made a simple point to present us with a complex reality. He has persuasively traced the origins of anti-Negro prejudice in New England to the prior existence of slavery, discrimination, and racism in Barbados (Jordan, 1962, pp. 243–50). Thus, we may obediently agree on the materialist formulation exploitation .. discrimination .. prejudice and find themselves nowhere except on the further ahistorical assumption that ideas, once called into being, have no life of their own.[4] As M. I. Finley (1967, p. 10) observes:

[3] The most suggestive discussions of the problem from a Marxian point of view are to be found in Gramsci's *Opere*, but see also Cammett's (1967) excellent introduction to Gramsci's life and thought.

[4] In another essay Jordan (1962, pp. 18–30) gropes for a formulation that would subsume both prejudice and discrimination instead of relating them to each other causally. His answer is neither clear nor convincing, but he has presented the problem in a sensitive and illuminating way.

... For most of human history labor for others has been involuntary. ... Slavery in that context must have different overtones from slavery in a context of free labor. The way slavery declined in the Roman Empire ... illustrates that. Neither moral values nor economic interests nor the social order were threatened by the transformation of slaves and free peasants together into tied serfs. They were—or at least many powerful elements in society thought they were—by proposals to convert slaves into free men.

What sets the slave apart from all other forms of involuntary labor is that, in the strictest sense, he is an outsider. He is brought into a new society violently and traumatically; he is cut off from all traditional human ties of kin and nation and even his own religion; he is prevented from creating new ties, except to his masters, and in consequence his descendants are as much outsiders, as unrooted, as he was. ...

Dr. [Eric] Williams holds that 'slavery was not born of racism, rather racism was the consequence of slavery'. One wishes profoundly that one could believe that. However, the slave-outsider formula argues the other way, as does the fact that as early as the 1660's Southern colonies decreed that henceforth all Negroes who were imported should be slaves, but whites should be indentured servants and not slaves. The connection between slavery and racism has been a dialectical one, in which each element reinforced the other.

The most balanced and suggestive statement on the Portuguese remains Boxer's (1963, p. 56): 'One race cannot systematically enslave members of another on a large scale for over three centuries without acquiring a conscious or unconscious feeling of racial superiority'. The good sense of this observation enables us to grasp the necessarily racist influence of Negro slavery on European cultures without destroying our ability to distinguish between levels of influence and without compelling us to turn our backs on either historical-traditional or ecological processes.[5] The work of the distinguished Brazilian Marxian scholar, Caio Prado Junior (n.d., pp. 103–4), may be cited as an illustration of the way in which the force of the historical inheritance can be taken into account in a materialist analysis. For Prado the historical conditioning stressed by Freyre and Tannenbaum played its part precisely because the material basis of life and especially the class relationships provided room for it to breathe, but, given this room, it seriously affected that basis and those relationships.

Harris's failure to grasp the historical and class nature of Tannenbaum's argument appears most strikingly in his reference to English law. Tannenbaum notes that England had long lacked slavery and a slave code and therefore had no legal tradition to humanize the practice of colonial slavery. 'Why this legal lacuna should have been significant for the course run by slavery in the United States is quite obscure' (Harris, 1964, p. 70). There is nothing

[5] Regrettably, even Boxer slights the historical dimension. It is noteworthy that he begins his survey, *Race Relations*, with the conquest of Ceuta in 1415 and leaves aside the racial conditioning of Portuguese life that preceded it. For an excellent statement of the intersection of tradition and economic milieu in the formation of Brazilian attitudes see Roger Bastide (1957, pp. 495–512).

obscure about it, and Harris could find the answer in Elkins' discussion of a slave system's rise amidst an 'uncontrolled capitalism'. Here again, idealists or no, Tannenbaum and Elkins have greatly deepened our understanding of the processes by which specific slave-holding classes were formed, and those processes are, or ought to be, the central concern of a materialist interpretation of history.

'At one point, and one point only', Harris writes, 'is there a demonstrable correlation between the laws and behavior, the ideal and the actual, in Tannenbaum's theory: the Spanish and Portuguese codes ideally drew no distinction between the ex-slave and the citizen, and the actual behavior followed suit' (p. 79). This one point kills Harris' argument since Tannenbaum set out to explain the absorption of former slaves into the national culture in Brazil and the extreme difficulties in the United States. Harris has much to offer to complement the work of Freyre and Tannenbaum; in particular, he is strong on the economic and material exigencies of colonial Brazil and their influence in promoting race patterns. Instead of seeing a two-fold process within which colonial conditions reinforced tradition and allowed it to expand and within which tradition altered, however secondarily, material conditions, he insists dogmatically on either/or. 'One can be certain that if it had been materially disadvantageous to the Latin colonists, it would never have been tolerated—Romans, *Siete Partidas*, and the Catholic Church notwithstanding' (p. 81). Harris may be certain; others may be permitted some doubt. Had such a divergence occurred, the outcome would have been determined by the strength of the contending forces, with Church and state opposing slave-holders and with the conscience and consciousness of the slave-holders split among various commitments. Harris' crystal ball gazing constitutes not materialism but fatalism, not history but a secular equivalent of theology.

Harris misunderstands and misrepresents Tannenbaum as arguing that Negro slaves were better treated in Brazil than in the United States. Tannenbaum does express such an opinion, but he merely accepts Freyre's probably erroneous judgment; it forms no essential part of his thesis. Tannenbaum could live comfortably with evidence that Brazilian slaves were treated more harshly than American, for his case rests on the degree of class and race mobility. Harris, by identifying Tannenbaum with Freyre here and by merging two separate theses in Freyre, confuses the issues. Elkins (1959, p. 75) argues quite sensibly that Hispanic slaves could have been more severely mistreated than American 'without altering the comparison'. Harris replies, in one of his most inexcusable polemical outbursts, with sarcasm and personal abuse; he does not reply to the argument.

Harris' discussion of demographic and economic forces in the formation of a mulatto population and a class of free blacks is a solid contribution, notwithstanding some statistical juggling, but the methodological difficulties reappear. He insists that Brazilian slave-holders 'had no choice but to create a class of half-castes' to function as soldiers, cattlemen, food-growers, and intermediaries of various kinds (Harris, 1964, p. 86). Unlike the United States, he notes, Brazil lacked a white population large enough to serve as a middle class and to provide a political and military establishment. Brazilian slave-holders consequently smiled on the elevation of the mulattoes. Winthrop D. Jordan (1962b, pp. 183–200) also questions the emphasis on national characteristics by pointing out that in the British West Indies, where conditions similar to those in Brazil existed, Anglo-Saxon hostility toward miscegenation was much softened and a much greater respect for the mulatto emerged. Yet, the juxtaposition of the British West Indies, the United States, and Brazil favors a qualified version of Tannenbaum's argument, for what emerged in the islands was not the Brazilian pattern but a compromise: a three-caste system in which 'coloreds' were set apart from both whites and blacks. The material conditions of life had indeed prevailed over the purely ideological-institutional inheritance, as materialists would expect, but that inheritance significantly shaped and limited the force of those conditions.

Harris cites the work of Fernando Ortiz to show that law and tradition fared badly in Cuba against economic pressure. Here again, however, he assumes a fatalistic stance. Sidney W. Mintz (1959, pp. 273–83) also cited the Cuban case as especially instructive, but he does so with greater perception and caution: Cuba, he writes, shows what happens to 'those rosy institutional arrangements which protected the slave, once slavery became part of the industrial plantation system.... Institutional restrictions may have hampered the maturation of slave-based agricultural capitalism in Cuba; but...could not prevent it. In the mid-nineteenth century, Cuban slavery dehumanized the slaves as viciously as had Jamaican or North American slavery'. Mintz notes that Tannenbaum and Elkins 'circumvent critical evidence on the interplay of economic and ideological forces'. Elsewhere he writes that the way men were treated in colonial Caribbean societies was 'determined much more by the level of economic development than by the ideologies of the different metropolitan powers'. The words 'much more than' leave considerable room for the autonomous force of ideology. If Harris were to restrict himself within the limits of Mintz' critique, he might help develop the work of Freyre, Tannenbaum, and Elkins along materialist lines; instead he declares ideological war. Mintz' remarks on the intersection of ideology and economics constitute the beginning of a new departure, although I should prefer to assume both within a synthetic analysis of social classes that avoids compartmentalizing their constituent human beings. Social classes have historically formed traditions, values, and sentiments, as well as particular and general economic interest. Harris, like Mintz, Eric Williams, and others, refers to the components of the slave-holders' world view and the possible divergence between economic interests and traditional commitments. The solution of these problems awaits empirical research. A materialist interpretation must account for the full range of possibilities, but it can do so only if it eschews economic determinism and a narrow ecology for a concern with the historical formation of class interests and antagonisms under specific geographic and technological conditions.

Harris makes much of the philosophical idealism of Freyre, Tannenbaum, and Elkins but does not analyze it. Since Freyre has written at some length on his method and viewpoint Harris ought to examine them specifically instead of contenting himself with the application of labels. That Freyre, Tannenbaum, and Elkins may be safely classed as idealists I do not deny, but their superb work ought to warn their philosophical opponents that the subject matter resists simplistic materialist schemata. A review of Freyre's methodological comments will lay bare not only the weakness of idealist interpretations, but also the elusiveness of the reality which makes such interpretations possible and even enormously helpful.

Freyre's critique (1956, p. xxvii) of historical materialism is especially suggestive, for he rejects it without hostility and indeed with considerable appreciation. 'However little inclined we may be to historical materialism', he writes, 'which is so often exaggerated in its generalizations—chiefly in the works by sectarians and fanatics—we must admit the considerable influence, even though not always a preponderant one, exerted by the technique of economic production upon the structure of societies and upon the features of their moral physiognomies. It is an influence subject to the reaction of other influences, yet powerful as no other....' Freyre's words strike sharply at economic determinism, which has roots in Marxism, where it clutters up rich fields, and strike at certain schools of ecology, but they are generally consistent with a properly understood dialectical materialism. What is primarily missing in Freyre's organic view of society is a suitable concern for class antagonisms as the historical motor force, but that is precisely what is missing from Harris' materialism.

Freyre's (1963a, p. 305) objections to historical materialism rest largely on his narrow economic reading of Marxian theory. In *The Mansions and the Shanties* he refers to an essay by Lefebvre des Nöettes in which it is asserted that moral suasion proved helpless against slavery until technological developments gave it room to expand. Freyre asks, 'Does this mean the absolute dependence of moral progress on material progress, as narrowly sectarian "historical materialists" claim . . . ? (p. 305).' He answers negatively, citing the United States as proof that slavery and technological progress could coexist. I doubt that the United States would offer him much evidence to refute even vulgar-Marxism on this point, but we need not discuss the specific questions now. The main point is that he sees Marxism as an economic and technological determinism; in effect, he describes it in terms much more appropriate to certain schools of ecology. If it is Marxism, then certainly it is the kind that once drove Marx to protest, *'Je ne suis pas un marxiste'*. The class element has somehow disappeared, but without it historical materialism is a senseless abstraction.

If historical materialism is not a theory of class determinism, it is nothing, but to be a theory of class determinism it must accept two limitations. Certain social classes can only rise to political power and social hegemony under specific technological conditions. The relationship of these classes, from this point of view, determines the contours of the historical epoch. It follows, then, that changes in the political relationship of classes constitute the essence of social transformations; but this notion comes close to tautology, for social transformations are defined precisely by changes in class relationships. What rescues the notion from tautology is the expectation that these changes in class relationships determine—at least in outline—the major psychological, ideological, and political patterns, as well as economic and technological possibilities; that changes in class structure constitute the most meaningful of all social changes. To argue that they constitute the only meaningful changes is to reduce historical materialism to nonsense and to surrender its dialectical essence.

Freyre's (1956, p. 262) idealism appears most crudely in his discussion of Portuguese colonization. He refers to the 'task' of colonization as being 'disproportionate to the normal resources of the population, thereby obliging the people to maintain themselves in a constant state of superexcitation, in the interests of large-scale procreation'. Lapses into teleology and mysticism abound in his writings, and one could, if one wished, put them side by side to prove him quaint or foolish. He who wastes time doing so will be the loser, for Freyre's thought is too rich for us to focus on its weak side. To see where Freyre is going we need to analyze his notion of the 'creative image'.

In writing of Brazilian patriarchal society and of the intersection of Indian, Negro, and European cultures Freyre (1956) 'was trying to accomplish a pale equivalent of what Picasso has masterfully accomplished in plastic art: the merging of the analytic and the organic approaches to man: what one of his critics has called "a creative image"'' (p. xxi). Freyre seeks to use methods and data of the physical, biological, and social sciences to assist in what is essentially an artistic project, for only through artistic image can the wholeness of man and his world be glimpsed. He admits the large role assigned to intuition in his work. In a passage, which seems to me to reflect a strong Sombartian influence, he writes, 'The truth really seems to be that only "within" the living whole of human development can the relations between what is arbitrarily considered rationality and irrationality in human behavior, or between different human cultures, be fully understood' (p. xxii). Properly disciplined, this concern with getting 'within' a society should mean a concern with its spirit—its dominant ideology, system of values, and psychological patterns. Freyre's effort can and should be assimilated into a historical view of social classes, for it is essentially an attempt to grasp the wholeness of a society's world view, including its self-image. Only two steps are required to place Freyre's viewpoint on materialist ground. The first takes us to the realization that society's world view must necessarily be essentially the view of its ruling class; the second to the realization that, in order to rule, a ruling class must be sufficiently wise and flexible to incorporate much from the manners and sentiments of the classes being ruled.

Freyre is therefore not toying with us when he writes that he endeavors to be 'almost entirely objective' but that at certain points he introduces an 'objective-introspective' method. His purpose is to be able to feel life as lived by his long-dead subjects in all its 'sensual fullness of outline' (p. lviii). This attempt at psychological reconstruction, he wisely observes, depends less on 'the strictly psychological approach of academic psychologists than that of novelists who have found it necessary to add a psychological time to the conventional chronological one, in novels otherwise historical in their substance...' (p. lxix).[6] In this spirit he constructs, for example, a historical-psychological model of Indian and African personality traits, as absorbed into Brazilian cultures (1956, p. 284–5). So far as possible, he strives to discover the roots of these divergent patterns in social and technical modes of life. The problem lies in the elusiveness of a full explanation. The mechanisms and the extent of the inheritance of acquired group characteristics continue to elude us and may to some degree always do so. Recognition of this elusiveness and of how few definite, scientifically demonstrated conclusions we can borrow from psychologists or from other social and biological scientists throws Freyre and the rest of us back on our own fragile ability as social historians to reach for everything at once. Poetry, for us as well as for the ancient Greeks, remains truer than history. As Freyre (1963a, p. xxix) reminds us:

The human being can only be understood—insofar as he can be understood—in his total human aspect; and understanding involves the sacrifice of a greater or lesser degree of objectivity. For in dealing with the human past, room must be allowed for doubt, and even for mystery. The history of an institution, when undertaken or attempted in keeping with a sociological criterion which includes the psychological inevitably carries us into zones of mystery where it would be ridiculous for us to feel satisfied with Marxist interpretations or Behaviorist or Paretist explanations, or with mere description similar to those of natural history.

Freyre's willingness to speak approvingly of intuition, 'mystery', and the sacrifice of objectivity opens him to attack and even ridicule from those who are content to ignore the challenge. Yet Freyre's intuition, like the passionate

---

[6] Perhaps the most straightforward illustration of Freyre's method is, appropriately, *Mother and Son* which he describes as a seminovel and in which fictional situations are meant to represent historical and social reality, apparently on the principle of *se non e vero, e ben' trovato*. As the narrator writes of a character about whom he planned to write and who suddenly appears before him in real life (p. 4): 'I must be aware that she had existed before I had imagined her; if she had not, I would not have tried to conjure her up'.

opposition to racial and social injustice that informs all of Harris' work, has its place. As Gramsci observes, 'Only passion sharpens the intellect and co-operates to render intuition clearer' (Cammett, 1967, p. 197). Freyre, sensing the elusiveness of historical truth and the dangers of strict rationalism, has raised serious objections to materialist theory, and only superficial mechanists could fail to realize as much. Since a full reply would entail an effort beyond the editor's and reader's patience, I should like to restrict myself to a few observations.

The strength of Marxian materialism, relative to other materialisms, is its dialectic, which gives it, or ought to give it, the flexibility and wholeness Freyre demands. The principle of interrelatedness is fundamental to Hegelian and Marxian dialectics and cannot be sacrificed to convenient notions of simple causation. If dialectical materialism is taken seriously, it must assert historical continuity as well as discontinuity. Every historical event necessarily embraces the totality of its components, each of which brings to that event the product of its total historical development. For this reason alone, a failure to respect the force of a people's tradition and historically developed sensibility will always prove fatal to materialist thought and betray it into mechanism. The task of those who would confront Freyre's idealism with a convincing materialism is to account for the complexity of societies in their historical uniqueness and for the special manifestations of the human spirit embodied in each such society.

Freyre's (1962, p. xxiv) recourse to an idealist stance results from an irresponsible attitude toward the complex reality he seeks to explain. In his methodological preface to his study of postmonarchical Brazil, he identifies his subject as a society entering the modern world with a persistent tradition of patriarchalism; and he identifies his method as less the historical than the anthropological and psychological.[7] Life, he insists, is a process of development of values and lends itself only partially to scientific analysis. Perhaps so, but as Marx, Freud, and Weber, among others, have argued, it is both necessary and possible to deal rationally with the irrational and to develop, at least in approximation, a disciplined approach to a reality so rich that we shall certainly never fully grasp it. The most attractive inheritance of Marxism from the Hegelian dialectic is the simultaneous assertion of progress toward essential knowledge and yet the ultimate elusiveness of the whole; it is this inheritance that makes Marxian philosophy, when it is not trampled on by political imbeciles, enthusiastically embrace the experimental sciences without fear of losing its dogmatic virginity. Freyre's weakness lies in his unwillingness to try to discipline his many-sided viewpoint. I do not suggest that he ought to tell us which 'factor' in the social organism he analyses is 'primary'—I

---

[7] I deliberately pass over Freyre's extension of his psychological method in his theory of Luso-Tropicalism. This extension raises a different set of problems, beyond the scope of this paper. See Freyre (1961, p. 9).

cannot imagine what a 'historical factor' is, and the assignment of primacy would do violence to the spirit of his work. I do suggest that we need some clue to the motor force of social change. Freyre fails us here, hence the sharpness of Harris' critique.[8]

Freyre's (1956, pp. 64–5) failure—like Harris'—emerges most clearly from his friendly reply to an author who 'would place responsibility for the principal defects in our social, economic, and moral development upon slavery... where I am inclined to put the blame upon monoculture and the latifundia....' The difference, Freyre argues, is one of emphasis, and each emphasis does fall on the material conditions of life. Ironically, Harris' position is close to Freyre's, although more rigid, for Freyre himself often slides into a narrow mechanism when he discusses specific historical problems rather than theoretical and methodological ones. He does not, for example, pay nearly enough attention to the feudal-Catholic tradition in his discussions of morality, sexual relations, sadism in pedagogy, and some other matters (cf. 1956, pp. 368, 401, 416–17). The advantage of emphasizing slavery rather than monoculture lies not in the superior virtue of one 'factor' over the other, but in the focus on human relationships. The special quality of master-slave relationships in Brazilian slavery lies in their being a special case in a broad pattern of quasifeudal, paternalistic relationships brought from Portugal and reinvigorated on the virgin soil of Bahia and Pernambuco. Freyre himself contributes much toward such an analysis in at least two ways: by treating the slave plantation as an integrated community and by seeing that community as a projection of the traditional family unit. Tannenbaum's (1946, p. 248) early formulation of the problem remains one of the best:

It is better to speak of a slave society rather than of slavery, for the effects of the labor system—slave or free—permeate the entire social structure and influence all of its ways. If we are to speak of slavery, we must do it in its larger setting as a way of life for both master and slave, for both the economy and the culture, for both the family and the community.

What needs to be explored is the relationship between this peculiar class structure and the prevalent psychological and ideological patterns in society.

---

[8] There is also, apparently, a political and ideological component to this sharpness. Freyre's writings on Angola and Mozambique have come close to apologetics for Dr Salazar's imperialist policies. Harris sees a direct line between Freyre's point of view on Brazilian colonization and his recent political pronouncements. As one who has seen the ravages of Portuguese imperialism first hand and who has done good work in exposing them, Harris is incensed. I agree that there is a direct line between the two sets of views, but I also think that Freyre's polite criticisms of Portuguese racial policies as 'un-Portuguese' ought to be given due weight. His views of past and present can be related to a general ideological commitment that looks to me—he would probably deny it—like a sophisticated greater-Brazilian nationalism. In any case, we dare not permit criticisms of Freyre's politics to blind us to the value of his contributions to history and sociology. His formulations on Brazilian history and culture must be examined strictly on their merits.

A parallel weakness in Freyre's attempt at synthetic analysis may be found in his discussion of the economic ills of monoculture. These surely were not absolute; if they crippled society at a certain point, they did so because they badly compromised the ruling class and hampered its ability to rule with that even-handedness without which the successful exercise of social hegemony would be impossible. Whether slavery or monoculture caused soil exhaustion is not an especially useful question, for they were functionally related. More to the point, they represented social and economic aspects of a specific form of class rule. In economic experience, as in the psychology of the leading strata, the relationship of master to slave proved decisive: it set limits to labour productivity, the flexibility of organization, the growth of the home market, and the accumulation of capital; it determined, in essential respects, the sensibilities of those who could and did place their imprint on society.[9]

Of the planters Freyre writes that they 'represented, in the formation of Brazilian society, the most typical of Portuguese tendencies: namely, settledness, in the sense of patriarchal stability. A stability based upon sugar (the plantation) and the Negro (the slave hut)....I would merely set alongside the purely material or Marxist aspect of things or, better, tendencies the psychologic aspect. Or the psychophysiologic' (1956, p. xl). Harris has not yet answered this challenge satisfactorily. We need not choose between Freyre's eclecticism and Harris' version of materialism. The historical task, to which a properly understood materialism seems to me to offer the best solution, is two-fold: to relate satisfactorily the psychological, 'material', and other aspects of a society to each other in such a way as to present reality as an intergrated social process; and to avoid a sterile functionalism by uncovering the fundamental pattern of human relationships conditioning both material and spiritual life. To fulfill this task we need to examine historical continuity, with its cumulative traditions and ways of thought, as well as ecology, more narrowly understood.

Freyre's idealism may, as Harris alleges, weaken his work, but neither Freyre nor any of us could be expected to do better by rejecting a concern for the whole man in a social setting that links past to present. At his best Freyre is marvellously dialectical, as in his pregnant remarks on the Brazilian adaptation of the Portuguese language (p. 348), or in his discussion of the psychology of the Portuguese colonizer, which he relates to the 'intimate unity' of Portuguese culture as 'a consequence of the processes and of the conditions of Portuguese colonization' (Freyre, 1940, p. 39; 1963, p. 54).

The sad part of Harris' book (1964, p. 99), which is so impressive in many of its particular analyses, is the implicit conflict between his denigration of

---

[9] The most suggestive starting point for a psychology of slave-holding may be found in Hegel (1910, 183ff). I have tried to sketch, in a preliminary way, the slave-holding experience in the United States (Genovese, 1965, pp. 31–34).

ideas, ideals, and values and his passionate plea for racial and social justice. How ironical that he should end his book with an exhortation—to whom to do what is not clear:

The backwardness of vast multitudes of the New World peasantry, illiterate, unskilled, cut off from the twentieth century and its brilliant technological advances did not simply happen by itself. These millions, about whose welfare we have suddenly been obliged to concern ourselves, were trained to their role in world history by four centuries of physical and mental conditioning. They were deliberately bottled up. Now we must either pull the cork or watch the bottle explode.

In the context of his book these words are puzzling and might easily be dismissed, were it not for the obvious personal sincerity and social urgency they suggest. One is tempted to reply to Harris in the words Tannenbaum (1946, p. 252) used many years ago to reply to Eric Williams:

It is hard to be a child of the Renaissance and a high priest of economic interpretation. If slavery was merely economic, and if economic forces are the only conditioning factor in shaping human institutions, then why all the indignation and the sarcasm? Why the appeal to moral forces, to justice, and to humanity?

Harris, by attempting to construct a materialism that bypasses the ideological and psychological elements in the formation of social classes, passes over into a variant of vulgar Marxism. In so doing, he ranges himself much further from a consistent and useful materialism than do the idealists themselves, for he turns away from everything living in modern materialism—its dialectics and sense of historical process—and offers us the dead bones of a soulless mechanism.

References

Aptheker, H. (1943), *American Negro Slave Revolts*, New York.
Bastide, R. (1957), 'Race relations in Brazil', *International Social Science Bulletin*, vol. IX, no. 4.
Bastide, R. and Fernandes, F. (1959), *Brancos e Negros em São Paulo*, 2nd ed., São Paulo.
Boxer, C. R. (1952), *Salvador de Sá and the Struggle for Brazil and Angola 1602–1686*, London.
Boxer, C. R. (1963), *Race Relations in the Portuguese Colonial Empire*, Oxford.
Cammett, J. M. (1967), *Antonio Gramsci and the Origins of Italian Communism*, Stanford.
Cardoso, F. H. and Ianni, O. (1960), *Côr e mobilidade social em Florianopólis*, São Paulo.
Comas, J. (1961), 'Recent research on racial relations—Latin America', *International Social Science Journal*, vol. XIII, no. 2.
Davis, D. B. (1966), *The Problem of Slavery in Western Culture*, New York.

Degler, C. (1959), 'Slavery and the genesis of American race prejudice', *Comparative Studies in Society and History*, vol. II, October.

Elkins, S. M. (1959), *Slavery: A Problem in American Institutional and Intellectual Life*, Chicago.

Finley, M. I. (1967), review of Davis, 'The problem of slavery', in *New York Review of Books*, vol. VIII, January.

Freyre, G. (1922), 'Social life in Brazil in the middle of the nineteenth century', *Hispanic American Historical Review*, vol. V, November.

Freyre, G. (1940), *O Mundo que o portugues criou E Una Cultura ameacada*, Lisbon.

Freyre, G. (1956), *The Masters and the Slaves: A Study in the Development of Brazilian Civilization*, New York.

Freyre, G. (1961), *The Portuguese and the Tropics*, Lisbon.

Freyre, G. (1962), *Ordem e progresso* [. . .], 2 vols., Rio de Janeiro.

Freyre, G. (1963a), *The Mansions and the Shanties: The Making of Modern Brazil*, New York.

Freyre, G. (1963b), *New World in the Tropics, the Culture of Modern Brazil*, New York.

Genovese, E. D. (1965), *The Political Economy of Slavery*, New York.

Graham, R. (1966), 'Causes of the abolition of slavery in Brazil', *Hispanic American Historical Review*, vol. XLVI, May.

Gramsci, A. (1949), *Il Materialismo storico e la filosofia di Benedetto Croce*, Turin.

Handlin, O. and Handlin, M. F. (1950), 'Origins of the southern labor system', *William and Mary Quarterly*, 3rd ser., vol. VII.

Harris, M. (1959), 'The economy has no surplus', *American Anthropologist*, vol. LXI, April.

Harris, M. (1964), *Patterns of Race in the Americas*, New York.

Harris, M. (1966), 'Reply to K. Oberg', *Current Anthropology*, vol. VII, February.

Hegel, G. W. F. (1910), *The Phenomenology of Mind*, 2 vols., vol. I, London.

Ianni, O. (1966), *Raças e classes sociais no Brasil*, Rio de Janeiro.

James, C. L. R. (1963), *The Black Jacobins: Toussant L'Ouverture and the San Domingo Revolution*, 2nd ed.

Jordan, W. D. (1961), 'The influence of the West Indies on the origins of New England slavery', *William and Mary Quarterly*, 3rd ser., vol. XVIII, April, pp. 243–50.

Jordan, W. D. (1962a), 'Modern tensions and the origins of American slavery', *Journal of American History*, vol. XXVIII, Feb.

Jordan, W. D. (1962b), 'American chiaroscuro: the status and definition of mulattoes in the British colonies', *William and Mary Quaterly*, 3rd ser., vol. XIX, April.

Lima, O. (1914), *The Evolution of Brazil Compared with that of Spanish and Anglo-Saxon America*, Stanford.

Mintz, S. W. (1959), 'Labor and sugar in Puerto Rico and in Jamaica 1800–1850', *Comparative Studies in Society and History*, vol. I, March.

Mörner, M. (1966), 'The history of race relations in Latin America', *Latin American Research Review*, vol. I, Summer, pp. 17–44.

Nevins, A. (1950), *The Emergence of Lincoln*, New York.

Oberg, K. (1966), 'The cultural ecology of India's sacred cattle', *Current Anthropology*, vol. VIII, February.

Prado, C. Jr. (n.d.), *Formacao de Brasil contemporaneo: Colonia*, 7th ed. São Paulo.
Sio, A. (1965), 'Interpretations of slavery: the slave status in the Americas', *Comparative Studies in Society and History*, vol. VII, April.
Tannenbaum, F. (1946), 'A note on the economic interpretation of history', *Political Science Quarterly*, vol. LXI, June.
Tannenbaum, F. (1947), *Slave and Citizen*, New York.
Tannenbaum, F. (1965), *Ten Keys to Latin America*, New York.
Wagley, C. (1963), *An Introduction to Brazil*, New York.
Williams, E. (1961), *Capitalism and Slavery*, New York.

13 *W. Lloyd Warner,* American Caste and Class

The social organization of the Deep South consists of two different kinds of social stratification. There is not only a caste system, but there is also a class structure. Ordinarily the social scientist thinks of these two different kinds of vertical structure as antithetical to each other. It is rare that the comparative sociologist finds a class structure being maintained together with a caste structure.

Caste as used here describes a theoretical arrangement of the people of the given group in an order in which the privileges, duties, obligations, opportunities, etc., are unequally distributed between the groups which are considered to be higher and lower. There are social sanctions which tend to maintain this unequal distribution. Such a definition also describes class. A caste organization, however, can be further defined as one where marriage between two or more groups is not sanctioned and where there is no opportunity for members of the lower groups to rise into the upper groups or of the members of the upper to fall into the lower ones. In class, on the other hand, there is a certain proportion of interclass marriage between lower and higher groups, and there are, in the very nature of the class organization, mechanisms established by which people move up and down the vertical extensions of the society. Obviously, two such structures are antithetical to each other, the one inflexibly prohibiting movement between the two groups and intergroup marriage, and the other sanctioning intergroup movement and at least certain kinds of marriage between higher and lower classes. Nevertheless, they have accommodated themselves to each other in the southern community we examined.

Perhaps the best way to present the configurations of the two kinds of vertical structure is by means of Figure 3. The diagonal lines separate the lower Negro caste (*N*) from the upper white caste (*W*), and the two broken lines in each segment separate the three general classes (upper, middle, and lower) in each caste from each other. The two double-headed vertical arrows

W. Lloyd Warner, 'American caste and class', *American Journal of Sociology*, vol. 42, 1936, pp. 234–7.

indicate that movement up and down the class ladders in each caste can and does take place and is socially sanctioned, but that there is no movement or marriage between the two segments. The diagonal arrangement of the parallel lines which separate the two castes expresses the essential skewness created by the conflict of caste and class in the South. The gradual elaboration of the economic, educational, and general social activities of the Negro caste since slavery (and to some extent even before) has created new groups which have been vertically arranged by the society until certain fairly well-marked class groups have developed within the Negro caste. As the vertical distance of

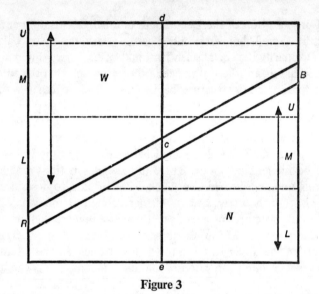

Figure 3

the Negro group has been extended during the years, the top Negro layer has been pushed higher and higher. This has swung the caste line on its axis (*c*), so that the top Negro group is higher in class than the lower white groups and is so recognized. (This recognition is expressed in circumlocutions and by unconscious actions, but is at times also consciously and openly stated by the members of both the white and the Negro groups.) If this process continues, as it seems to be doing at the present time, it is possible, and indeed probable, that the lines *AB* might move on the axis *c* until they approximate the hypothetical line *de*. (Theoretically, of course, this process could go farther, but it seems unlikely.) This tendency to bring the two groups out of vertical opposition and organization into a horizontal arrangement is being reflected at the present time in such movements as 'parallelism', as expounded by Dr DuBois. Such terms as 'parellelism' are kinds of collective representations which have come into existence and approximately express the social facts of the changing social structure; at the same time, of course, allowing the sentiments of some of the people who live in the structure also to find expression. Should the line *AB* reach the position *ed*, the class situation in either group would not be fundamentally disturbed, except that the top Negro group would be equivalent with the top white, while the lower classes in each of the parallel groups would also be equivalent. Even the present approximation of this gives the top Negro group certain advantages over his lower-class fellows which he is anxious to maintain.

On the other hand, the social skewness created by the present class-caste conflict which results in the process of changing the social location of the caste line has placed the upper-class Negro in a decidedly difficult situation. The Negro who has moved or been born into the uppermost group (see Figure 3) of his caste is superior to the lower whites in class, but inferior in caste. In his own personality he feels the conflict of the two opposing structures, and in the thinking and feeling of the members of both groups there is to be found this same conflict about his position. He is known to be superior to the 'poor white' (he is a doctor, say), but he is still a 'nigger' or 'Negro', according to the social context in which the words are used. Metaphorically speaking, although he is at the top of the Negro class hierarchy, he is constantly butting his head against the caste line. He knows himself to be superior to the poor white, yet to the poor white the upper-class Negro is still a 'nigger', which is a way of saying the Negro is in a lower caste than himself. Furthermore, if it ever came to an issue, the supraordinate white class would maintain the solidarity of the white group by repudiating any claims by any Negro of superiority to the lower-class whites. This would be true even though the admission might be made privately that the Negro was superior to certain of the lower-class whites.

The present and past political behavior of the South has to be understood, it seems to me, in terms of the maintenance of the caste lines, and as an effort to prevent the continued elaboration and segmentation of the class groups within the lower caste. The unequal distribution of school funds and privileges are an excellent example of how the system tends to maintain itself through the changing generations.[1] The operation of the courts and the activities of the police also reflect the same conscious or unconscious maintenance of control by the supraordinate white caste. For that matter, all social institutions in the South, including the family, school, association, clique, and church, are formed to fit the dominant caste social situation of the dominant social caste.

An interesting hypothesis may be built out of the skewed social position of the upper-class Negro. It seems possible that the instability of many of the individuals in this group (as compared, let us say, with the Negroes of the lower positions) may be due to the instability and skewness of the social

---

[1] The concepts of class and caste used here are briefly described in relation to the school system in Warner (1936).

situation in which they live. They are always 'off balance' and are constantly attempting to achieve an equilibrium which their society, except under extraordinary circumstances, does not provide for them.

Reference

Warner, W. L. (1936), *Journal of Educational Sociology*, May.

14 *Gerald D. Berreman,* Stratification, Pluralism and Interaction: A Comparative Analysis of Caste

The purpose of this paper is to analyse caste comparatively, which means cross-culturally. As a social scientist and specifically as a social anthropologist, I cannot justify doing less if I am to study caste at all (Berreman, 1960; 1962; 1966). The reasons for this derive from a belief that social science is necessarily and inherently comparative. Unless we compare, we cannot talk of caste in South Asia outside Hindu India (as Barth (1960), for example, does when he describes caste in Swat), and in fact we cannot study caste in different parts of Hindu India or among different groups in the same part of India. As Hutton (1946), pointed out caste within India is an extremely variable phenomenon—so variable that he did not venture to define it. In the comparative approach I follow Nadel (1954, p. 17) who, describing caste in Africa, said '. . . I am comparing *types* of society and wish to show that the same "type" (namely, caste-stratified society) can occur in widely different cultures and areas of the world, given certain common conditions or processes'. Rather than follow him all the way, however, I shall give heed to Spiro's recent admonition that to use single variables 'not only for the classification of single institutions, but also for the classification of whole societies, most certainly begs a very large question', namely, whether societies with one institution in common (in this case a caste system) are sufficiently similar in other respects that the entire societies can properly be classified together (1965, pp. 1097–8). I shall refer to instances of 'caste stratification' and to 'caste systems' rather than to 'caste societies'.

I want to analyse what caste systems are, how they work, and what they do to people. That is, I shall look at caste as a structural principle and as a social and cultural fact, and I shall look at the social, cultural, and psychological concomitants of caste systems.

The fact of relationship between caste as a structural principle and certain kinds of social relations and psychological mechanisms was suggested to me first by my own experience in two very different caste societies within a

Gerald D. Berreman, 'Stratification, pluralism and interaction', in A. V. S. de Reuck and J. Knight (eds.), *Caste and Race: Comparative Approaches*, Ciba Foundation, 1967.

period of a few years. I lived in Montgomery, Alabama, during 1953–55 and in North India during 1957–58. I was struck, when I went to India, with the similarity between the social relations and psychological mechanisms of Indians and of Southerners in the United States. They were too pervasive to be dismissed as coincidental and they obviously could not be attributed to a common historical source. I sought their explanation, therefore, in common human responses to similar social conditions (Berreman, 1960).

Subsequently I have inquired into several other societies, and have concluded that caste organization is found, in varying degrees, in a number of societies, and that it has many common consequences for those who live it' (Berreman, 1966).

Caste systems defined and characterized

When viewed comparatively and structurally, caste systems have been customarily described as systems of stratification—unusually rigid, birth-ascribed, permitting of no individual mobility, but nevertheless examples of ranked aggregates of people (Bailey, 1963, pp. 111–14). To the extent that theories have been employed, concepts applied, or hypotheses ventured, they have been derived primarily from the study of stratification. These have not proved inappropriate to the data, but they have been insufficient. As a colleague has remarked, there is a notable sterility—a striking lifelessness—manifest in the application of concepts of stratification to the Indian caste system, and to other caste systems as well. This is a failing not found in studies which define caste primarily in cultural terms. But the virtues of such studies are accompanied by an important limitation: failure to say anything very relevant to man and society outside India, or outside the particular region and the specific groups within that region which have been described.

I wish to suggest here a more comprehensive approach which makes for cross-cultural comparability without sacrificing cultural content. Such an approach uses concepts derived from three bodies of descriptive and analytical literature: studies of stratification, studies of cultural pluralism, and studies of social interaction. It is my contention that caste systems are indeed rigid systems of social stratification, but that they are also systems of socio-cultural pluralism and that both of these facts are to be understood largely in terms of distinctive patterns of social interaction. By viewing caste systems in this way we lend greater validity and hence greater utility, as well as increased credibility, to comparative studies of these phenomena. We can analyse a broader range of caste systems, caste-like systems and related phenomena than is possible with concepts derived only from stratification theory. We can analyse processes of change in caste systems and changes to or from caste systems. We can describe more satisfactorily the continuum from non-caste to caste organization and the dimensions which define that continuum. In short, to view caste in true perspective, we must use the three dimensions: stratification, pluralism and interaction.

Cross-cultural definitions of caste are necessarily highly abstract, for the term may be expected to apply to situations as different as India and the United States, and to groups as diverse as the Burakumin of Japan and the blacksmiths of East Africa. But a definition of caste must also be abstract even if it is to be applied within South Asia to both Swat and Ceylon and, in India, to Brahmans, Nayars and sweepers. Accordingly, my own definition of a caste system is abstract: *a caste system occurs where a society is made up of birth-ascribed groups which are hierarchically ordered and culturally distinct. The hierarchy entails differential evaluation, rewards, and association.*

In society

That a caste system is in a society implies that it is in fact a system. The groups comprising it are differentiated, interacting, and interdependent parts of a larger society. Often, and perhaps universally, they are economically interdependent and/or occupationally specialized. Their members view themselves and are viewed by others as being relatively homogeneous elements in a system of differentiated component groups rather than, as in the case of tribes in India, being relatively independent (and mutually unranked) systems in themselves.

Comprised of groups

That a caste system is comprised of groups implies that each rank in the hierarchy is shared by socially distinct aggregates of people. These people recognize that they comprise discrete, bounded, ranked entities. The size and degree of corporateness of such groups varies widely. The members usually share a group name; always they interact with one another in characteristic ways; always there are symbols of group membership ranging from skin colour to cultural features such as language, occupation, dress, place of residence, and the like. Only members of the group are one's peers. Where group affiliation is relevant, individual attributes are irrelevant.

Birth-ascription

That membership in castes is determined by birth means that an individual is assigned his lifelong and unalterable status according to his parentage—a status which he shares with others of similar birth who are therefore assigned to the same group (caste). A common means of guaranteeing this status is by prescribing endogamous marriage in the caste, and assigning to the child the caste affiliation of its parents. But this method is by no means universal even in India, for caste, like kin-group affiliation, can be assigned unilineally or according to other, more complex, rules based on birth (Berreman, 1966).

Hierarchy

That a caste system is a hierarchy implies that it is a system of differential evaluation, differential power and rewards, and differential association; in short, a system of institutionalized inequality. This is a sufficiently complex and crucial aspect of the definition to warrant elaboration.

Differential evaluation. Castes are ranked, ultimately, in terms of differential 'intrinsic worth' ascribed to those who comprise them. This may be expressed in many different idioms: idioms such as purity (as in India), honour (as in Swat), or genetically determined capabilities (as in the United States)—but always those who are high regard themselves as more worthy than those who are low. Those who are low universally question, if not the criteria of rank, then the judgment which relegates them to the low end of the hierarchy (Berreman 1960). They may take the alleged criteria more literally than do others, or confuse the idiom in which rank is expressed for the criteria by which it is conferred. Thus, they may adopt the attributes and behaviour of those above them on the assumption that these are the bases for status, only to find that (in the short run at least) it is the fact that they were born low rather than that they are dirty, or polluted which makes them unworthy and hence low.

Caste systems rank birth-ascribed group membership rather than attributes (cf. Smith, 1960, p. 769; Bohannan, 1963, p. 168). Class systems, by contrast, define the rank of their members according to their individual attributes and behaviour. *In a caste system an individual displays the attributes of his caste because he is a member of it. In a class system, an individual is a member of his class because he displays its attributes.* Individual mobility is by definition impossible in a caste system, and possible (although in some systems statistically very unlikely) in a class system.

Differential rewards. Differential evaluation is accompanied by differential power and other differential rewards contingent upon caste membership: access to goods, services and other valued things. The ability to influence the behaviour of others, the source of one's livelihood, the kind and amount of food, shelter, and medical care, of education, justice, esteem, and pleasure— all of these things which an individual will receive during his life—and the very length of life itself, are determined in large measure by caste status. I have elsewhere (Berreman 1960) compared some of the specific rewards and costs of caste status in the Indian village that I studied with those in a Southern town of the United States reported by Dollard (1957).

Differential association (interaction). A caste hierarchy is to a large extent an interactional hierarchy (Berreman, 1965; cf. Marriott, 1959). Social interaction is inherently symbolic—that is, it has meaning. Rank is expressed and validated in interaction between persons, it is manifest in patterns of interpersonal behaviour and in patterns of differential association. Who may be one's friend, one's wife, one's neighbour, one's master, one's servant, one's client, one's competitor, is largely a matter of caste. Every relevant other is a superior, a peer or an inferior, depending upon caste. Only within the caste is status equality found. Between castes any kind of interaction which defies or jeopardizes the rules of hierarchy is taboo even when such behaviour does not directly challenge the official bases (the criteria) of the rank system. Thus, there is always a more or less elaborate etiquette of inter-caste relations which is stringently enforced from within and above. Deference is a group matter, not merely an individual one, for it demonstrates and validates the system of ranked groups. The hierarchical nature of interaction between castes is such as to bestow responsibilities and prerogatives implying different degrees of responsibility, maturity and even humanity to different castes (Berreman, 1962; Maquet, 1961).

It is becoming increasingly evident that castes cannot be defined adequately, at least in any operational sense, without reference to interaction patterns. Bailey (1963, p. 109), Karve (1961), and Leach (1960) have defined castes in India as the most extensive kin groups, for they are the maximal limit of the marriage network. Caste membership, like caste ranking, could be empirically determined by observations (or reports) of interaction (cf. Mahar, 1959), since that is the way in which membership is expressed. An interactional definition of a caste system might be: *a system of birth-ascribed groups each of which comprises for its members the maximum limit of status-equal interaction, and between all of which interaction is consistently hierarchical.* A caste might be defined as a network of status-equal interactions in a society characterized by a network of hierarchical interactions among birth-ascribed groups. The interactions referred to could range from informal social encounters to marriage, and could include a wide variety of interactional networks including occupational, economic, political, ritual, friendship, and so on. It is an interesting fact that although castes in India are widely recognized to be networks, no specific caste has been definitively studied or even delimited from this point of view.

Underlying hierarchical interaction between castes is the existence of what Barth has termed 'status summation' (1960, p. 144ff.). The multiple roles played by individual members of a caste. are mutually equivalent in the relative status they confer vis-à-vis members of other castes. They tend to coalesce into a single status. People are thus enabled as well as enjoined to interact with members of other castes in an unambiguous, consistent, and hierarchical manner.

Because intensive and status-equal interaction is limited to the caste, a common and distinctive caste culture is assured. This is a function of the density and quality of communication within the group (Berreman, 1960; Gumperz, 1958) for culture is learned, shared, and transmitted. More is inevitably held in common between those in meaningful and intense communication (that is to say, between caste members) than between such people and outsiders. Circularly, because of shared culture, communication is easier and hence more intense within the caste than outside it.

Castes are discrete social and cultural entities; caste hierarchies are discontinuous, echelon hierarchies. This is a key factor in understanding the dynamics of caste systems. They are maintained by defining and maintaining boundaries between castes; they are threatened when boundaries are compromised. Even when interaction between castes is maximal and cultural differences are minimal, the ideal of mutual isolation and distinctiveness is maintained and advertised among those who value the system. Similarly, even when mobility within, or subversion of, the system is rampant, a myth of stability is stolidly maintained among those who benefit from the system (cf. Van den Berghe, 1964, pp. 250-1).

References

Bailey, F. G. (1963), 'Closed social stratification in India', *Archives of European Sociology*, vol. 4, pp. 107–24.

Barth, F. (1960), 'The system of social stratification in Swat, North Pakistan', in E. R. Leach (ed.), *Aspects of Caste in South India, Ceylon, and North-West Pakistan,* pp. 113–46 (Cambridge Papers in Social Anthropology, no. 2), London.

Berreman, G. D. (1960), 'Caste in India and the United States', *A.J.S.*, vol. 66, pp. 120–7.

Berreman, G. D. (1960), 'Cultural variability and drift in the Himalayan hills', *American Anthropologist*, vol. 62, pp. 774–94.

Berreman, G. D. (1962), 'Behind many masks: ethnography and impression management in a Himalayan village', Monograph no. 4, The Society for Applied Anthropology, New York.

Berreman, G. D. (1962), 'Caste, racism, and stratification', *Contributions to Indian Sociology*, vol. 6, pp. 122–5.

Berreman, G. D. (1965), 'The study of caste ranking in India', *Southwestern Journal of Anthropology*, vol. 21, pp. 115–29.

Berreman, G. D. (1966), 'Caste in cross-cultural perspective' in G. De Vos and W. H. Berkeley (eds.), *Japan's Invisible Race: Caste in Culture and Personality*, pp. 251–92, Berkeley.

Bohannan, P. (1963), *Social Anthropology*, New York.

Dollard, J. (1957), *Caste and Class in a Southern Town*, New York.

Gumperz, J. J. (1958), 'Dialect differences and social stratification in a North Indian village', *American Anthropologist*, vol. 60, pp. 668–82.

Hutton, J. H. (1946), *Caste in India*, London.

Karve, I. (1961), *Hindu Society: An Interpretation*, Deccan College Postgraduate and Research Institute, Poona.

Leach, E. R. (1960), 'Introduction: what should we mean by caste?' in E. R. Leach (ed.) *Aspects of Caste in South India, Ceylon and North-West Pakistan*, pp. 1–10 (Cambridge Papers in Social Anthropology, no. 2), London.

Mahar, P. M. (1959), 'A multiple scaling technique for caste ranking', *Man in India*, vol. 39, pp. 127–47.

Maquet, J. (1961), *The Premise of Inequality in Ruanda*, Oxford.

Marriott, McK. (1959), 'Interactional and attributional theories of caste ranking', *Man in India*, vol. 39, pp. 92–107.

Nadel, S. F. (1954), 'Caste and government in primitive society', *Journal of the Anthropological Society of Bombay*, vol. 8, pp. 9–22.

Smith, M. G. (1960), 'Social and cultural pluralism', *Social and Cultural Pluralism in the Carribean*, pp. 763–85 (*Annals of the New York Academy of Sciences*, vol. 83, art. 5).

Spiro, M. E. (1965), 'A typology of social structure and the patterning of social institutions: a cross-cultural study', *American Anthropologist*, vol. 67, pp. 1097–119.

Van den Berghe, P. L. (1964), *Caneville: The Social Structure of a South African Town*, Middletown, Connecticut.

15 *Oliver Cromwell Cox,* Caste, Class and Race

There are few characteristics of the caste system which are so generally recognized as heredity, and yet the function of heredity in the system has been commonly misunderstood. Almost without exception those authorities who have identified caste and race relations have been prone to mistake the meaning of heredity among castes. Consider, in illustration, the following typical conclusion:

In essence the caste idea seems to be a barrier to legitimate descent. A union of members of the two castes may not have a legitimate child. All such children are members of the lower caste and cannot be legitimated into the upper caste by the fact that they have an upper caste father or mother (Dollard, 1937, p. 63).

The orientation here, as usual, is biological and evidently deduced from an observation of the obdurate dichotomized type of interracial adjustment in the South. Thus an insidious truism concerning American race relations has served to skew fundamentally thinking about caste. It runs somewhat as follows: 'No colored child can become white; in some colored-white societies whites have decided to ostracize all peoples of color; hence no intermarriage can result in offspring of equal status with whites. Since heredity is the "essence" of caste, it must follow that socially bipartite race systems are caste systems'. To those who think that castes are anti-color devices, this reasoning seems irrefragable. It may be shown, however that this very idea of heredity helps us further to distinguish between caste and race relations. [. . .]

Racial differences

In race relations it is almost always sufficient merely to look at a man to identify him; in caste relations his status must be inquired into. A man's child by a woman of lower caste, according to the pleasure of his caste, may be initiated and accepted into his caste. In the case of a racially dichotomized society it is not possible to legitimize the children of mixed marriages by their unreserved inclusion into the dominant race. This is so because nothing

Oliver Cromwell Cox, *Caste, Class and Race*, Doubleday, 1948, pp. 454–61.

short of making the colored child of an interracial marriage white will be sufficient. The 1901 *Census of India* explains further certain possibilities of inheritance based upon deficiencies of the sex ratio. Thus:

Where females are in marked defect, a relaxation of the restrictions on marriage inevitably follows. Sometimes it takes the form of expressly permitting males of a higher caste to marry females of a lower one. Thus in the Panjab, Khatris will marry Arora women and the Aroras in their turn take as their wives women of lower castes. But, more often, it leads to laxity in inquiring into the status and antecedents of the proposed bride, and to a willingness to accept the statements that may be made regarding her by her guardians or vendors. In this way there is in some parts a regular traffic in young females. Girls are often enticed from their homes in the Panjab and sold either in some other part of that province or in Sind. The purchasers of women in the Panjab are mainly Jats, Aroras, and Kirars, but the practice is also known among the Kombohs and Khatris.

A race inherits, then, physical marks, real or imputed; the caste inherits intangible cultural or personality attributes. It is true that a person's caste ordinarily comes to him as a cultural heritage, but we may emphasize that descent within the meaning of the Brahmanical system does not have the same application as can be given it in discussions of race relationships in, say, the Southern states of the United States. To use the term at all in describing race relationships in the South, we must mean racial identity, for a person of Negro blood born in England or France or the West Indies, who happens to be in the South, must expect to assume the racial status of all other Negroes. It should be gross, indeed, to hold that all Negroes in the world belong to the same caste by descent.

If we look beyond the misguiding truth that a colored child cannot become white, then we may examine the meaning of legitimacy in racially dichoto-mized societies. In the first place, it appears that the mixed-blood offspring may be legitimate according to statutory law. Consequently, although mixed-blood children may not be accepted as white in any part of the United States, in all states where mixed marriages are not declared illegal the child may inherit property as though his parents were of one race. In one state, Indiana, the child is legitimate, even though there is an intermarriage prohibition law. In the eyes of the law, then, the mixed-blood child may be legitimate. We know of no case in Hindu law where a child who is able to inherit without discrimination the estate of his father remains debarred from inheriting his father's caste.

In the second place, the child may be unreservedly accepted by both mother and father as a natural member of their family. In Haiti, before the revolution, white planters married colored women, and their children ordinarily inherited normal parental affections. These children, however, were not regarded by the white public as its equal. The criterion of acceptance depended not upon superiority of caste but upon superiority of race; in other words, their color alone determined their acceptability. If the colored woman happened to be light enough in complexion, the children were likely to be considered white as a matter of course. And finally the child may be legally defined as a member of its colored-parent group, as in the United States; or it may enter a new group, such as the Cape Coloreds of South Africa or the Eurasians of India. However, by the very definition and purpose of a dichotomized racial situation, the children of mixed marriages, can never be given social opportunities identical with the dominant whites. To be legitimized in the white group, of course, can mean only that the mixed-blood child has equal economic, juridical, and social opportunities with the whites.

All Hindus inherit not only a caste status with respect to other caste-men, but also the physical marks of Hindus. Because of the latter heritage they may be considered social subordinates of white men. But the latter assumption develops a power relationship of white dominance and not a caste position of inferiority. The Hindu's racial heritage identifies him with all other Hindus, while his caste heritage differentiates him from all other-caste Hindus. All caste members must of necessity inherit some racial affiliation, but obviously racial affiliation does not presuppose caste membership.

When reference is being made to relationships between races, it becomes rather cumbersome to think of the legitimizing of children as a determining factor. If the colored parent is accepted among the whites, then the child will also be accepted; but if the parents are not accepted, the children may be. In America both parties to a mixed Negro-white marriage can belong legitimately to neither group; yet, according to the lightness of color of the colored partner, their children may become a part of either the white or the Negro group.

[. . .] Now let us consider the possibilities of outcasting among races. It has been frequently said, in support of the race-caste hypothesis, that in the United States white persons are outcasted for marrying colored persons and vice versa. We propose to examine the accuracy of this conclusion. When we speak of a white or Negro person's losing caste for breach of caste rules, what really do we mean has been lost? In this society only the state can punish, and outcasting is no constituted form of punishment. It is not even recognized by the state. Outcasting must mean, then, that the white or Negro race shuns one or a group of its members, though the latter may stand unblemished before the law. It seems too indefinite, however, to hold that a race can shun a person, for a race is ordinarily too socially heterogeneous. Only some persons of certain social-class levels may laugh at or ridicule the individual for breach of social-class convention. In fact, the likelihood is that social-class demotion may be mistaken for outcasting.

For the breach of many types of social sanctions, or even misfortunes, such as loss of employment, going to prison, intermarriage with Indians, Jews, or Negroes, white persons may suffer more or less serious loss of class status, yet they can never 'lose caste' in the sense of becoming anything other than white persons. Far less is it possible to conceive of the 'white caste' as a whole, or any significant part of it, as falling or rising into some other caste. This seems to be a vital distinction between caste and race relations.[1]

Moreover, neither a Negro nor a white person can be outcasted in the sense that a Hindu caste-man can be, for the simple reason that neither belongs to a caste as the Hindu does. Death alone can remove an individual from his race.[2] Although the latter fact seems clearly evident, much confusion has resulted from letting it out of view. A man could be expelled from his caste and forgotten; he cannot be expelled from his race. A white man in the United States who has committed the cardinal sin against his race, let us say by intermarrying, will continue to represent his race. In spite of sentiment against him, he remains a major concern of interracial policy makers.

Therefore, the racially articulate whites are interested, as all the interracial laws indicate, in disrupting his mixed marriage and not in outcasting him. In fact, the instrumentality of outcasting is not available in the American social order. In the caste system the outcaste is dead so far as his former caste is concerned, but a race cannot thus easily give up its members. Should the white woman or man find sanctuary among colored persons, he will remain even as threatening to white dominance as if there were no white sentiment against him.

The crux of the matter lies in the fact that no race by vote or sporadic agreement can determine who shall be included within its ranks. Sociologically speaking, races are defined by intergroup conflict and not by internal selection. A caste, however, is the sole arbiter of questions concerning its membership. It may exclude or include persons at will, and birth presents no bar to this prerogative. The destiny of a caste is consciously in the hands of its members.

[. . .] To be sure, no one need be overmeticulous about an offhand use of the term 'caste' in discussions of race relations. In formal sociological writings, however, its indiscriminate use may be insidiously misleading. Indeed, attempts to give the vulgar use of this term scientific precision have probably divested it of much of its former odium. In the sociology books it has been objectified and desiccated so that race relations in the Southern states, for instance, are sometimes made to appear as one of the natural forms of social

---

[1] In India it seems quite possible for entire castes to change their status and identity. 'The Sahnsars of Hushyarpur were admittedly Rajputs till only a few generations ago, when they took to growing vegetables, and now rank with Arains. Some of the Tarkhars, Lohars, and Nais of Siras are known to have been Jats or Rajputs who within quite recent times have taken to the hereditary occupation of these castes; and some of the Chubans of Karnal, whose fathers were born Rajputs, have taken to weaving and become Shekhs', Ibbetson (1916, p. 8).

[2] The caste system presumes life membership in the caste, but the biological fact of race ensures inevitable affiliation.

organization. The idea of a 'type of society' obscures the actual pathological racial antagonism, leaving some diffused impression that it is socially right, even as the caste system in India is right.[3]

The terms 'race prejudice' and 'racial discrimination' have already been defined in the world view of Western society as social sins per se. However, such subjects as race prejudice and discrimination call for delicate handling in the textbooks. Consequently many writers will find it more incommodious to discuss and explain these phenomena than to couch the situation in the euphonious terminology of 'American caste'.

If we have caste among blacks and blacks in Haiti (Lobb, 1940, pp. 23–34), among peoples of color of India, and among whites and whites in England,[4] then there may be all the more reason and justification for having caste between whites and blacks in the South. The implication of the 'naturalness' of caste provides a comforting blanket assumption.

Reference

Dollard, J. (1937), *Caste and Class in a Southern Town*, New York.
Ibbetson, D. (1916), *Panjab Castes*, Lahore.
Johnson, G. B. (1939), 'Patterns of race conflict', in E. T. Thompson (ed.), *Race Relations and the Race Problems*, New York.
Lobb, J. (1940), 'Caste in Haiti', *A.J.S.*, vol. XLVI, July.

[3] Observe, in illustration, with what nicety of reasoning Johnson (1939, p. 146) gets around his problem: 'There has lately been much agitation for the suppression of lynching by Federal law. Some people, with characteristic faith in the magic of legislation, imagine that Federal law can stop lynching. Any custom which is as deeply rooted in caste consciousness as lynching is, will not be eradicated easily'.

[4] *The University of Chicago Round Table*, December 8, 1940, p. 20.

16 *E. R. Leach,* What Should We Mean by Caste?

In the writings of anthropologists and sociologists the word 'caste' is used in two different senses. As an ethnographic category it refers exclusively to a system of social organization peculiar to Hindu India, but as a sociological category it may denote almost any kind of class structure of exceptional rigidity. Such double usage is unfortunate; the tendency to stress the 'status-group' component of caste prejudges the whole question as to what is the essential sociological nature of the Indian phenomenon. Conversely the merging of class and caste concepts is liable to lead to a highly distorted image of the nature of 'colour-bar' and other manifestations of rigid social differentiation (Cox ,1948). [. . .]

[This issue] raises directly the question as to whether caste is best considered as a cultural or as a structural phenomenon. This is an issue on which the authorities seem notably confused. Weber, for example, states categorically that 'Caste . . . is the fundamental institution of Hinduism'. He implies thereby that caste is a specifically *cultural* concept, but then he proceeds at once to the remark that 'there are also castes among the Mohammedans of India . . . castes are also found among the Buddhists' (Gerth and Mills, 1947, p. 396). This contradiction leads logically enough to an inquiry into the nature of caste, but here Weber's standpoint keeps shifting. On the one hand we are given various illustrative details of typical Hindu caste behaviour (i.e. cultural evidence) but this is backed up with a highly generalized discussion of the nature of 'closed status groups', race relations in the United States, and the behaviour of the European nobility (i.e. structural evidence). Weber thus evades the whole question as to what there is about caste which is specifically Hindu. Having started by implying that caste is peculiarly a Pan-Indian phenomenon, he proceeds immediately to the discussion of caste analogues in non-Indian contexts. Clearly he is using the word caste in an ambiguous way but he does not justify this procedure.

The same criticism may be levelled against those 'diffusionist' writers who manage to find historical examples of caste behaviour all the way from Ancient Egypt to modern Fiji (e.g. Hocart, 1950; Hutton, 1946, chaps. ix–xi). They

E. R. Leach, 'What should we mean by caste?', in E. R. Leach (ed.), *Aspects of Caste in South India*, Cambridge University Press, 1969, extracts from pp. 1–10.

start by assuming that caste is definable as a list of ethnographic traits characteristic of Hindu India and then slide imperceptibly into the assumption that
caste refers to certain features of social structure. Such ambiguity is no
doubt difficult to avoid, but we need to be clear that it exists.

Definitions of Indian caste have usually taken the form of a list of cultural
traits which are supposed to form a syndrome. The authorities, while ad-
mitting a great range of detailed variation, have mostly maintained that there
is a certain minimal set of primary characteristics which together embody the
real essence of caste everywhere; Hutton, for example, holds that normally
caste conforms to the following criteria:

1. A caste is endogamous.
2. There are restrictions on commensality between members of different
castes.
3. There is a hierarchical grading of castes, the best-recognized position
being that of the Brahman at the top.
4. In various kinds of context, especially those concerned with food, sex
and ritual, a member of a 'high' caste is liable to be 'polluted' by either
direct or indirect contact with a member of a 'low' caste.
5. Castes are very commonly associated with traditional occupations.
6. A man's caste status is finally determined by the circumstances of his
birth, unless he comes to be expelled from his caste for some ritual offence.
7. The system as a whole is always focused around the prestige accorded
the Brahmans (Hutton, 1946, 49 and chap. vi). [. . .]

Caste, in my view, denotes a particular species of structural organization
indissolubly linked with what Dumont rightly insists is a Pan-Indian civilization (Dumont, 1957 b). Consequently I believe that those who apply the
term to contexts wholly remote from the Indian world invariably go astray.
The specific character of caste systems lies in the peculiar nature of the systemic organization itself. Let me elaborate this tautology.

Most conventional Indian ethnographies are written in a way which suggests
that individual castes can usefully be considered in isolation. This is deceptive.
In fact, a caste does not exist by itself. A caste can only be recognized in
contrast to other castes with which its members are closely involved in a network of economic, political and ritual relationships. Furthermore, it is precisely with these intercaste relationships that we are concerned when we
discuss caste as a social phenomenon. The caste society as a whole is, in
Durkheim's sense, an organic system with each particular caste and subcaste
filling a distinctive functional role. It is a system of labour division from which
the element of competition among the workers has been largely excluded.
The more conventional sociological analysis which finds an analogy between
castes, status groups, and economic classes puts all the stress upon hierarchy
and upon the exclusiveness of caste separation. Far more fundamental is the

economic interdependence which stems from the patterning of the division of labour which is of a quite special type.

It is a characteristic of *class*-organized societies that rights of ownership are the prerogative of minority groups which form privileged elites. The capacity of the upper-class minority to 'exploit' the services of the lower-class majority is critically dependent upon the fact that the members of the underprivileged group must compete among themselves for the favours of the elite. It is the specific nature of a *caste* society that this position is reversed. Economic roles are allocated by right to closed minority groups of low social status: members of the high-status 'dominant caste', to whom the low-status groups are bound, generally form a numerical majority and must compete among themselves for the services of individual members of the lower 'castes'.

In a class system, social status and economic security go together—the higher the greater; in contrast, in a caste society, status and security are polarized. It is open to every man to become a *sannyasi* and receive the adulations of his society but only at the cost of forgoing all his social rights. Under Ceylon conditions any 'Washerman' or 'Drummer' or 'Blacksmith' or other 'low-caste' individual who wishes to go to the trouble can repudiate his caste but only at the cost of losing those economic rights which accrue automatically to members of 'low-status' groups. In a class society the 'people at the bottom' are those who have been forced there by the ruthless processes of economic competition; their counterparts in a caste society are members of some closely organized kinship group who regard it as their privileged right to carry out a task from which all other members of the total society are rigorously excluded. This is just as true of Swat as of Tanjore.

The point will be clearer perhaps if we consider its negation.

In India today, a major section of the population consists of landless labourers who stand at the bottom of the social hierarchy. These people are the victims of extreme economic insecurity and are often in violent political revolt against the formal strictures of the caste system. But their economic sufferings are not *due to* their position in the caste system. The low castes suffer economically not because they are low *castes* but because present conditions have turned them into an unemployed working-*class*. What has put them in this position is not their caste but the recent rapid increase in population, coupled with the fact that the caste rules which formerly compelled the high-status landlords to support their low-status servitors have been progressively destroyed by arbitrary acts of 'liberal' legislation extending over the past 150 years.

Everywhere in India and Ceylon today whole caste groups are tending to emerge as political factions but it is misleading to think of such behaviour as a characteristic of caste as such. If a whole caste group plays the role of a political faction by competing with other such factions for some common economic or political goal it thereby acts in defiance of caste tradition. But such change of role may not be clear either to the actors or to the anthropological observer. [. . .]

For me, caste *as distinct from either social class or caste grade* manifests itself in the external relations between caste groupings. These relations stem from the fact that *every* caste, not merely the upper elite, has its special 'privileges'. Furthermore, these external relations have a very special quality since, ideally, they exclude kinship links of all kinds. In this respect all caste systems are similar; where they differ is in the degree to which the boundaries of caste groupings coincide with boundaries of territorial grouping—this last being a variable which I shall not here discuss.

For an anthropologist interested in the comparison of kinship structures there is nothing that is peculiar to Indian caste. Internally, a caste presents itself to its members as a network of kin relationships, but this network is of no specific type. The kinship systems of caste-ordered societies vary, but all types are readily duplicated in other societies historically unconnected with the Indian world. As Morgan discovered, the formal kinship organization of the Tamils is not unlike that of the League of the Iroquois!

The kinship peculiarity of caste systems does not lie in the internal structuring of kinship, but in the total absence of kinship as a factor in extra-caste systemic organization. The cultural rules of caste behaviour establish a dichotomy in the total field of social relationships—political, economic and ritual relations are external, kinship relations are exclusively internal. [. . .]

In the ideal type, recognition of kinship automatically implies recognition of common caste and recognition of equal social status. Hence, since caste is immutable, social status must be immutable also. Contrariwise, any difference of specialized economic or ritual function automatically implies difference of caste and social status and this difference also is immutable. I am not satisfied that any actual society ever possessed quite this kind of rigidity; the situation described for our 'marginal' cases is much more plausible. Here the opposition between caste and kinship does not in every case unambiguously distinguish social equals from social unequals; instead the system presents itself to the individual as an unstable set of conflicting obligations which call for personal decision. [. . .]

I have already made a general distinction between caste systems and class systems on the basis of their structural organization, but the case of an aristocracy deserves special attention. There are some respects in which the characteristics of a 'hereditary aristocracy' appear deceptively close to those of a 'dominant caste'.

Like castes, aristocracies everywhere show a marked tendency towards rigorous endogamy. As with caste, the sanctions which support this rule often include a valuation which makes sexual and commensal relations with the lower classes 'polluting'. We can see this in various contemporary 'colour-bar' societies, but the principle is very general. It applied to the ruling class in nineteenth-century England and even to the *aristoi* of Plato's Republic.

Again, it is true of such hereditary aristocracies that they tend, like castes, to maintain a rigid dichotomy between kinship relations and economic relations. In nineteenth-century England, the aristocracy considered it proper to intermarry with the 'professions' but never with those engaged in 'trade'.[1] Anyone with whom an aristocrat had direct financial dealings was automatically contaminated as lower-class no matter what his financial status.

Nevertheless I must insist that the difference between an aristocracy and a dominant caste is fundamental. Aristocratic behaviour is essentially confined to a small ruling clique; it is behaviour which serves to distinguish and separate the rulers from the ruled. In contrast, in a caste system, caste behaviour is something which pervades the whole society. All castes within a given cultural area are based on common fundamental institutions (Dumont, 1957 a, p. iii). Essentially the same rules apply to those at the bottom as to those at the top. Caste therefore does not simply isolate an elite; instead it defines the structural role of every sector in a total organic system. Whereas a ruling aristocracy is invariably a numerical minority, a dominant caste may be, and usually is, a majority element in the total population.

It follows that the kind of dominance asserted by individual members of an aristocracy upon individual members of the lower classes is entirely different in quality from intercaste hierarchy, even though both types of relationship are concerned with economic service and even though, in both cases, one of the parties involved is necessarily of 'higher social status' than the other.

I have commented at length upon the special qualities of intercaste relationship because the various contributors, in their treatment of this topic, seem to me particularly illuminating. They have led me to the conclusion that there is something fundamentally wrong about Kroeber's well-known definition: 'A Caste may be defined as an endogamous and hereditary subdivision of an ethnic unit occupying a position of superior or inferior rank or social esteem in comparison with other subdivisions' (Kroeber, 1931). It is wrong because it puts the emphasis in the wrong place—upon endogamy and rank, and because it slurs the really crucial fact that caste is a system of interrelationship and that every caste in a caste system has its special privileges.

[1] 'Professions' were clergy of the Church of England, naval and military officers, barristers-in-law. In the English legal system a barrister has no direct financial dealings with his client. The practice of endogamy was less strict than the theory; wealthy brewers and bankers especially were deemed to be respectable.

References

Cox, O. C. (1948), *Caste, Class and Race*, New York.

Dumont, L. (1957a), *Une Sous-Caste de l'Inde du Sud: Organisation Sociale et Religion des Pramalai Kallar*, Paris.

Dumont, L. (1957b), 'For a sociology of India', in Dumont and Pocock, *Contributions to Indian Sociology*, no. 1.

Gerth, H. H. and Mills, C. W. (1947), *From Max Weber: Essays in Sociology*, London.

Hocart, A. M. (1950), *Caste: A comparative Study*, London.

Hutton, J. H. (1946), *Caste in India*, London.

Kroeber, A. L. (1931), 'Caste' in *Encyclopaedia of the Social Sciences*, London.

17 *Michael Banton,* Race Relations

Roles and role signs[1]

When racial differences are used as a way of dividing up a population and different sets of rights and obligations (roles) are ascribed to the divisions, then these outward differences serve as signs telling others the sorts of privileges and facilities to which the person in question is conventionally entitled. They may be stimuli as well as signs, evoking particular feelings, just as items associated with age or sex categories, such as white hair, babies' rompers, or women's underclothing, may evoke particular reactions; but for sociological analysis it is the sign function of racial characteristics that is usually the more important. It is also advisable to emphasize that many features of individuals, their behaviour and possessions, have sign values which are often, though not always, incidental to the purpose of the things in question. A man may buy a big motor car not for show but because he has a big family; but, whatever the reasons for his buying it, ownership of a large car will be interpreted as denoting greater wealth than ownership of a small car. Just as the sign value of material possessions changes from place to place, so does the social significance of racial variation. Racial signs tend to be important when they can be used to classify unequivocally a high proportion of the population, marking off social categories whose members have frequent dealings with one another. If members of the categories lead separate lives, then there are fewer occasions on which people have to look for racial difference in order to inform themselves about social differences, and consequently race does not then have any high sign value. Racial characteristics do not serve as role signs in places where everyone is classed as belonging to one race, or in circumstances where the contact between two races has been too fleeting for ideas to develop about the relative rights and obligations of members of the two categories. Race is a role sign only in multiracial societies or in situations of racial contact in which expectations of behaviour have crystallized into patterns of some sort.

How race is employed as a sign may vary from one culture to another. In Europe and North America, complexion tends to be the primary basis of distinction, but in a community in the Amazon basin, where there was con-

---

Michael Banton, *Race Relations*, Tavistock and Basic Books, 1967, pp. 57–62.

siderable Indian as well as Negro mixture, an anthropologist found that
people regarded the thickness of lips, the height of the cheek bones, and even
skin colour as unreliable criteria, preferring to give more attention to a person's hair as his deciding trait (Wagley, 1952, p. 122). In Brazil, circumstances more frequently arise in which the sign value of racial traits is can-
celled by the value of other traits. The story is told of a tram conductor who
sent all the men wearing collars into the first-class compartment, whether
they were white, yellow, brown, or black. He relegated all the men without
collars to the second class. Thus a black boy with a collar but no boots or
shoes was sent into the first class, and 'a handsome English lad in a low-cut
jersey' into the second-class compartment. An English writer adds to this
account by relating how, in the West Indies, his failure to wear a collar
brought him not only a diminution of status but even suspicion, since on one
occasion he was detained by the police for questioning, and his movements in the interior were notified to the various police stations in advance
(Dingwall, 1946, pp. 184–5).

But in many regions there is little opportunity for people to manipulate
their claims to racial status. The kind of classification effected is neither trivial
nor like the abstract ordering of a statistical table; it determines the allocation of highly important political, economic, and social rights such as voting,
employment, and housing, and such distinctions are reinforced in everyday
conventions about the respect which inferiors must pay to superiors. In most
societies an individual can choose his occupational role; he cannot choose his
sex role, and only to a limited extent can he manipulate his age role. Racial
roles, like sex roles, are usually ascribed at birth and cannot be varied. An
individual in a racially divided society is usually forced to play his racial role
whether he will or not, for the sanctions utilized by the dominant group
are extremely powerful. A Southern writer has told how he had his head
shaven and his skin artificially darkened before making a journey through
Mississippi, Alabama, and Georgia (Griffin, 1961). Had he sickened of his
experiment and wished to give up the deception, what could he have done?
It would have been little use explaining that he wanted to sit in the front of
the bus because he was really white. He would soon have been kicked off.
Had he stopped to talk to the average white farmer he would have been
under pressure to behave in a mildly deferential manner, by doffing his hat,
saying 'Sir' frequently, or laughing at any jokes made at his expense, and so
on. Had his failure to conform in this respect given offence, he might well
have been beaten. Once he had blackened his skin, Griffin *had* to play the
Negro role until the colouring had weakened sufficiently for him to try be-
having, in carefully selected circumstances, in a less subordinate manner.
In the Southern states, deferential behaviour has been required (with minor
exceptions) of all Negroes, including fair-skinned men and women who
might not elsewhere have been thought of as Negro, but who in their own

localities were known to be of partly Negro descent and were therefore classed as Negro. They, too, were obliged to play the social role of the Negro so long as they remained in their districts. Nor are the persons in the lower category the only ones who, in such a system, have to conform to conventional expectations; as later chapters will show, the deviations of people in the upper category also evoke sanctions.

The operation of race as a role sign can be illustrated most easily by reference to the well-known pattern that has prevailed in the Southern region of the United States, but this pattern is only one among several different kinds to be outlined later in this chapter. Race may serve as a role sign even though the role is relevant to behaviour in only a minority of situations. The sign function remains the same, but the kind of role is different. However, reference to race relations in the Southern states does bring out more clearly a point of some importance. Social roles usually have a core of elements of behaviour which are necessary to them and an outer range of elements which are conventional but not strictly essential—professors are often expected to be absent-minded, opera singers temperamental, and so on. Because new situations are legion and cannot be legislated for completely, roles often grow by having new elements added on which are logically separable from the others. Then, because some roles need to be signalized, they require additional patterns of behaviour which reinforce the role. Racial roles become important, as in the Southern states, when they combine many and varied patterns of expected behaviour which, in another social order, could be split up or combined differently.

Some studies of colour awareness and colour blindness bear upon this point, for social factors influence the perception of skin-colour differences. The processes by which children are taught that certain qualities are masculine or feminine, or that people of a particular appearance are socially inferior, may not feature in any school curriculum; parents and teachers may not be aware that they transmit such ideas, but they do so none the less effectively because the process is unacknowledged. In a city in the North-east of the United States, intensive study was made of the ideas and behaviour of 103 four-year-old children, roughly half of them white and half coloured. Fifteen per cent of both groups displayed low awareness of racial differences: only erratically were they interested in their own colour; they seldom used racial terms in describing people or tried to generalize on this basis. Sixty-one per cent of the white and 45 per cent of the Negro children showed medium awareness. Twenty-four per cent of the white and 40 per cent of the Negro children revealed high awareness; they already had a clear perception of skin colour as a social attribute and paid consistent attention to it; they used numerous race terms accurately; they thought in terms of racial categories and sensed patterns of racial discrimination (Goodman, 1964, pp. 76–7). Studies of three-year-old Negro children in both Northern and

Southern communities have concluded that more than three children in every four were conscious of the difference between 'white' and 'coloured' (Goodman, 1964, p. 253).

Some comparable information about the genesis of attitudes to Negroes in Britain is becoming available from a study of 172 white children in three north London areas. On doll-choice tests about social situations, 31 per cent of the children were rated consistently unfavourable to the Negro; the age-group proportions of these rose from 22 per cent at age three to 65 per cent at age six. In another test, 25 per cent chose very distant or distant houses for Negro children. The choice patterns, deliberation, and spontaneous comments of many children indicated an awareness of physical attributes and of the inferior social status of the Negro. The mothers of the consistently unfavourable children tended to be very hostile to Negroes, but no general relationship between ethnic attitudes of mothers and their children was found. The mood of the district was important for, as between two areas with fairly large Negro populations, the one more pervaded by tensions and adult hostility to the Negro out-group displayed the greater hostility in its white children (Jahoda, Veness and Pushkin, 1966, pp. 65–7). In some parts of Britain, children show decided colour blindness. A true story is told of a little boy who one day returned home from school and asked his mother whether he could have a friend to tea. It was a mixed racial school in East London and his mother asked him whether his friend was a black boy. 'I don't know, Mummie,' he replied, 'but I'll look tomorrow' (Polack, 1965; cf. Silberman and Spice, 1950). However, such reactions seem not to be typical of the districts in which coloured immigrants settle.

Another English experiment showed that the mildly antipathetic attitudes of children aged twelve to fourteen, based mainly upon the characterizations of the cinema screen, could be decisively modified by favourable personal contact with African schoolteachers. Racial categories were not so firmly embedded in the wider social structure that attitudes could not be transformed in a space of two weeks (James and Tenen, 1951).

Among the more important social factors influencing the perception of racial traits are ideas about roles. Gunnar Myrdal maintained that Southerners in the United States were so accustomed to seeing Negroes in certain roles that they recognized them as much by their bearing and way of doing things as by their colour. He gave examples from his observations in 1939 to show that a man with unmistakable Negro features who walked, talked, and behaved like an ordinary white man (e.g. walking into a hotel with his hat on and carrying himself with assurance and ease) was, in relatively impersonal contexts, treated as a white man. On the other hand, a white woman associating with Negroes was considered to be a fair-skinned Negro because Southern men could not believe that a real white woman would want to go about with Negroes (Myrdal, 1944, pp. 683–4). Another study shows how, in these relatively impersonal relationships, people may be less concerned about the skin colour of the party playing the other role than about whether he plays it properly. The experiment was conducted in a large department store in New York City. A Negro and a white clerk (shop assistant) served side by side. The customers were followed into the street, and, without knowing that they had been under observation, were interviewed. When asked if they had ever seen any Negroes employed as sales personnel at the store where they had just been, one in four replied 'No'. Five of the 114 shoppers interviewed stated that they would refuse to buy in any store employing Negro sales clerks—although they had just patronized such an establishment, and two of them had been served by a Negro clerk! Among the more prejudiced individuals who recalled having been served by a Negro, there were some who rationalized what had happened. A woman who had just bought three pairs of stockings from the Negro clerk said that Negroes ought not to be employed in the more intimate relations involved in the sale of food. Had the persons interviewed been served in the food department, some would have insisted that Negroes should not be employed in the clothing department (Saenger and Gilbert, 1950). Once something is represented as customary, some of the opposition to it disappears. Recent research has shown that emotive attitudes often influence perception to a considerable extent (Tajfel, 1967).

References

Dingwall, E. J. (1946), *Racial Pride and Prejudice*, London.

Goodman, M. E. (1964), *Race Awareness in Young Children*, rev. ed., New York.

Griffin, J. H. (1961), *Black Like Me*, London.

Jahoda, G., Veness, T. and Pushkin, I. (1966), 'Awareness of ethnic differences in young children: proposals for a British study', *Race*, vol. 8, pp. 63–74.

James, H. E. O. and Tenen, C. (1951), 'How adolescents think of people', *British Journal of Psychology*.

Myrdal, G. (1944), *An American Dilemma: the Negro Problem and Modern Democracy*, New York.

Polack, A. I. (1965), 'Education: children and adults', in R. Hooper (ed.), *Colour in Britain*, London.

Saenger, C. and Gilbert, E. (1950), 'Customer reactions to the integration of Negro sales personnel', *International Journal of Opinion and Attitude Research*, vol. 4, pp. 57–76.

Silberman, L. and Spice, B. (1950), *Colour and Class in Six Liverpool Schools*, Liverpool.

Tajfel, H. (1967), 'Social and cultural factors in perception', in G. Lindzey and E. Aronsen (eds.), *Handbook of Social Psychology*, 2nd ed., Reading, Mass.

Wagley, C. (1952), *Race and Class in Rural Brazil*, Paris.

18 *St Clair Drake and H. Cayton,* Black Metropolis

A rose by any other name

'Passing' is one of the most prevalent practices that has arisen out of the American pattern of race relations. It grows from the fact that one known drop of 'colored' blood is sufficient to make an otherwise completely white person a Negro. As there are thousands of Negroes whom neither colored nor white people can distinguish from full-blooded whites, it is understandable that in the anonymity of the city many Negroes 'pass for white' daily, both intentionally and unintentionally. But, should white people become aware of their remote colored ancestors they would, in all probability, treat them as Negroes.[1]

There are few figures on the amount of passing which takes place in the United States. Estimates of the number of people who permanently leave the Negro group and are assimilated into white society each year vary from 25 000 to 300 000. These are only estimates, and no conclusive body of statistical data is or ever could be available, especially on those who pass only temporarily or occasionally. There is not, however, a single Negro family known to the authors, that has not been aware of instances sometimes of scores of instances, in which friends, acquaintances, or relatives have crossed the color-line and become white—'gone over to the other side', as Negroes phrase it.

There are various degrees of passing, accompanied by different degrees of estrangement from the Negro group and emotional identification with the white community. Thousands of Negroes pass unintentionally daily. In a large city such as Midwest, Metropolis light-skinned Negroes who go into restaurants, who seek choice seats at a theater, or who are hired in certain

[1] The authors have interviews which suggest that some white people in the North are willing to overlook a small infusion of Negro blood provided the person who is passing has no social ties with Negroes. Several persons when questioned on this matter said that they knew of white people who were suspected of having Negro blood and that it was a joking matter. In one case everybody, including the suspect, saved face by saying it was perhaps *Indian* blood.

St Clair Drake and H. Cayton, *Black Metropolis*, Harcourt Brace Jovanovich, 1946, pp. 159–63.

jobs are mistaken for white without their being aware of it. A very light woman recently went to an exclusive photographer to have her picture taken. She returned at a later date with her daughter, who was obviously a Negro. The photographer refused to take the daughter's picture and told the mother that he did not care for colored patronage. Only then did she realize that she had been unconsciously passing for white.

Often, when caught in a situation in which he or she is taken for white, a Negro will carry through the bluff even when challenged, in order to avoid embarrassment. A young lady who did not approve of passing related the following incident:

'Speaking of passing—a strange thing happened to me this summer. When I went down to visit my father in Kentucky, I had to change trains at a station on the other side of the Mason-Dixon line. The porter took my bags and escorted me to the coach. I wasn't paying any attention to him. I just took it for granted that he was taking me to the correct coach. When I stepped into the coach, I immediately knew that he had made a mistake. All of these white people were seated and there I was! I said, 'Listen, porter—' and that's all the further I got. He said, "That's all right, miss, the conductor will call your stop." He passed my bags overhead and tipped his hat and walked away. So I sat down and was so ill at ease.

'I noticed several of the white people glancing at me and then after the second look, they looked off. I had had my hair freshly done, and when it is fresh it looks dark brown and wavy, and I did look decent because I was wearing my best. I took a magazine and began reading. After a bit, the conductor came up and after removing his hat and apologetically clearing his throat said, "I know this is highly irregular, miss, but—uh—pardon me—may I ask you what nationality you are? Uh—are you Jewish?" I could have kissed the conductor for giving me that lead, because as soon as he started talking, I knew what he was going to say. I knew that if I said I was a Negro and tried to explain that I wasn't trying to pass, he wouldn't believe it. Also, to have to go back into the Negro coach with the conductor leading the way would be quite embarrassing to me. The Negroes would think I was trying to pass and got caught. So I decided to play up to the situation. "After all", I said, "this is highly ridiculous. Yes, I am a Jewess, and I consider this a grand insult". I wore my haughtiest expression, and I was scared to death. By this time several of the white people had turned around and were listening to us.

'The conductor flushed and was very much embarrassed. I just know how he must have felt. He apologized again and then walked away. I was scared. I didn't enjoy the ride at all, and but for the company of a little eight-year-old white child, I talked to no one. It was lucky for me that I hadn't told Father I was coming. Suppose he had been at the station to meet me—then I would have been in a mess. I told Daddy about it and he just laughed. He thought it was a joke! And that's why I couldn't be bothered with trying to pass. I'd rather be colored and not be bothered. That's why I hate the South'.

As the above incident suggests, passing in the South can often lead to serious trouble—it violates both customs and law. There are numerous stories about the dashing young man who comes to a southern town, cuts quite a figure, perhaps becomes engaged to a socially prominent local girl, and then suddenly and mysteriously disappears, never to be spoken of again. It is discovered by accident in such instances, so the tales go, that the man, though he appeared to be white, had Negro blood. In the North, however, where the population is not so sensitized, and in the crowded and impersonal atmosphere of the big cities, little thought is given to the possibility that someone might be passing, and no punitive action is taken by the society even when a person who is passing is discovered. In Midwest Metropolis, many Negroes pass merely for convenience. A light-complexioned girl remarked to one of the authors, 'Whenever I am downtown alone I always go to one of the better restaurants. They think I am white, I guess; I never ask them. I wouldn't think of going with my husband, who is dark, for they might refuse us and we would be humiliated. Of course I never speak about this to him, as he is so sensitive about his color'. It is common practice for very light women to patronize white beauty parlors where, according to them, they can get better service cheaper and without waiting. Often, too, a light person will purchase theater tickets for darker persons so that the latter will not be Jim-Crowed with other Negroes in the theater, or refused seats on the main floor.

From the initial state of passing unintentionally or passing for convenience, there often develops, in more adventurous persons, a practice of passing for fun. This behavior, too, can be engaged in without any feeling of guilt or disloyalty to the race; it is looked upon as having fun at the white folks' expense. Couples, and sometimes parties, will go to white cabarets and exclusive dancing places, just to see what they are like and to get a thrill. Even in these cases, however, the persons involved are rather careful about relating these escapades to their friends for fear of censure from the darker persons. 'I wouldn't tell everyone this, but you get around and would understand', said a light-complexioned girl. 'The other night I was out with Harry—you know he can pass for white—and after we had seen a show in the Loop he said, "Let's go over to the Pump Room". We did and had a glorious time and it wasn't any more expensive than the Rhumboogie. No, I wasn't in the least nervous. How could they tell we were colored? There were no colored waiters who might have recognized us. After this I am going to places like that any time I am out with him.' Light-complexioned people who go out with white persons of the opposite sex frequently prefer to go to white places, for there is less fear of detection on the part of the Negro community, which in the case of a woman is a matter of some concern.

A fourth type of passing arises out of economic necessity or advantage. Negro girls have had difficulty in obtaining employment in white-collar jobs. Positions as stenographers, telephone operators, receptionists, and clerks are usually closed to anyone who is known to be colored. As there are many Negro girls of superior ability and training who wish such jobs, it is not unusual for some of them to pass, if they can, in order to obtain such work. There is no way of knowing how frequently such passing occurs, but there are few upper- or middle-class Negroes who do not claim knowledge of persons who have passed for economic reasons. Men in this category usually pass to obtain technical positions, and there are verifiable instances where eminent positions as scientists, physicians, and public administrators are held by these 'white Negroes'.

Usually the individual returns to the Negro community for all of his social contacts and uses his light skin color simply as a method of circumventing economic discrimination. Friendships with whites are generally avoided, as they would lead to complications. One girl reported:

'My mother is very fair and passes for white on most of the jobs she has had, but she doesn't like to do it. It always brings about so much trouble. She makes friends and soon they want her to come to see them and they want to come to see her. One friend that she had had for over a year used to invite Mother to her apartment. This woman knew Mother had two children, and she would say, "You'll just have to bring those children over so I can see them." We would have fun talking about it. Well, she finally had to quit; the girl was becoming too chummy'.

The final stage of passing—crossing over completely to the other side of the color-line—involves passing in order to associate socially with white people. For a Negro to pass socially means sociological death and rebirth. It is extremely difficult, as one loses in the process his educational standing (if he has gone to a Negro school), intimate friends, family; and work references. People well established in the Negro world and older people seldom pass socially and completely. There is too much to lose and too little to be gained.

19 *M. G. Smith,* Pluralism in Africa

Pluralism is a condition in which members of a common society are internally distinguished by fundamental differences in their institutional practice. Where present, such differences are not distributed at random; they normally cluster, and by their clusters they simultaneously identify institutionally distinct aggregates or groups, and establish deep social divisions between them. The prevalence of such systematic disassociation between the members of institutionally distinct collectivities within a single society constitutes pluralism. Thus pluralism simultaneously connotes a social structure characterized by fundamental discontinuities and cleavages, and a cultural complex based on systematic institutional diversity. [...]

We can now begin to examine the relations between institutional divergences of differing degree and type and pluralism or heterogeneity. Our basic question concerns the minimal combinations of institutional or political difference which are necessary and sufficient to incorporate collectivities as separate sections of a wider society. More precisely, we must also try to show how these differing combinations of institutional or political differentiations come to take such effect. These questions are equally central to our understanding of the social processes and structures of plural and heterogeneous societies.

It is true that differences in the basic institutional systems of two collectivities constitute pluralism and establish plural societies where the minority, by reason of its superior resources and organization, dominates the majority, whose institutional organization and resources reduce their capacity for resistance. The ensuing domination may be based on conquest, negotiation, enslavement, indenture, or ideological ascendancy, separately or together. It may be instituted as serfdom, helotage, peonage, slavery, or colonialism, or through restrictive political franchise. In some cases the structure of domination takes the form of caste, although, as we shall see, such 'caste' differs profoundly from the Indian institution. In all contexts of pluralism, the dominant section distinguishes itself from the dominated, both

M. G. Smith in L. Kuper and M. G. Smith (eds.), *Pluralism in Africa*, Oxford University Press, 1969; pp. 27, 37–8, 46–53, 444–9.

politically and by means of their institutional differentiae; and where these social and cultural differences coincide with differences of 'race', corporate exclusions and oppositions are frequently expressed in racial terms. Indeed, 'racial' coefficients of institutional and political division are often invoked as stereotypes despite their objective absence or their marginal biological significance. The social validity of these racialist classifications and interpretations of social cleavage is obviously unaffected by their scientific status. Where institutionalized, such racial categories are generally local developments of modes of thought that formed part of the traditional culture of the dominant ethnic group. [...]

We can learn most about the specific combinations of conditions which constitute or prevail under pluralism by examining further the varying combinations of institutional and structural diversity in American society.

Among American whites, Jews, distinguished by religion and descent form an internally divided, relatively endogamous group. Adherents of the Orthodox and Catholic faiths are likewise religiously differentiated and internally divided into a number of relatively closed ethnic groups, each distinguished also by its own specific religious organizations, by deep-set tendencies toward endogamy, by ethnic traditions, and sometimes by alternate languages. Protestants, subdivided by denomination and sect and also by ethnic group, probably have the lowest general tendencies toward ethnic and religious endogamy of all major divisions in the white American population. We have to ask in what ways do these parallel Jewish, Orthodox, Protestant, and Catholic differentiations differ, if at all, from the conditions of pluralism.

White Americans of Jewish, Orthodox, Catholic, or Protestant faith may participate freely and equally in common economic, educational, and political institutions; they are legally free to marry or to worship as they please; and in consequence, such closures as these ethnic and religious collectivities separately exhibit are optional and not societally prescribed. Given the institutional continuities in religious and familial institutions shared among these collectivities, individual mobility and assimilation are greatly facilitated so that uniform disassociations are restricted to such specific spheres as ethnicity or cult, where individual affiliations are also optional. Thus, neither the Orthodox nor the Jews nor the Catholics nor any of the various ethnic segments in 'White America' are permanently or effectively closed. Indeed, within each group the members are extensively differentiated by various and often contraposed alignments with individuals and groups of differing kinds outside the collectivity concerned. In effect the secular organization of United States society treats religion as one of several institutional spheres in which personal affiliations are optional, expectably diverse, and formally indifferent to the central organization of the common public domain. In consequence, intra- or interethnic and denominational marriages or associations have limited significance in themselves for the wider society, or for the placement of individuals within it. The social identities and capacities of white Americans are not determined by their religious or ethnic affiliations; and, despite their undeniable significance to the individuals and religious or ethnic collectivities concerned, institutional identifications as Catholic, Orthodox, Jewish, or Protestant, or as Irish, Swedish or Italian, are formally and substantively equivalent alternatives accommodated indifferently to the secular organization of the inclusive aggregate. By themselves, such ethnic and religious affiliations entail no direct or systematic differentiations or inequalities in the public sphere, in the educational, economic, social, and political systems, although they provide effective bases for the organization of corporate groups in pursuit of common interests.

These patterns of social heterogeneity among white Americans presuppose equally effective and uniform segregations of the several institutional spheres —kinship, cult, polity, economy, and education—so that differentiations among the population in kinship or cult do not necessarily entail corresponding differentiations or incapacities in other spheres. Thus, given the formal equivalence in familial institutions and the uniform segregation of religious organizations required by law as a necessary condition of secular equality, collective or individual differences in family and/or culture neither entail, presume, nor systematically correspond with parallel differences in other fields of individual or collective activity. Only by rigorous prescriptive closure such as Amish or Hutterites maintain can religious enclaves achieve a truly autarchic corporate differentiation in this society. In consequence, the structural significance of these ethnic or religious divergences and corporate affiliations for the total society and for the placement of individuals within it remains limited, conditional, and variable. In effect, such differentiated collectivities are equally consistent with the free participation of their members in the common heterogeneous society and can neither disqualify nor differentiate individuals by status or by capacity in the public sector, being themselves by the law and conditions of the secular society together incapable of subsuming and prescriptively regulating the major institutional interests and needs of their members. Thus, these institutional differentiations and collectivities are segregated as equivalent alternatives at the structurally secondary levels of national organization and personal affiliation. They fall primarily within the private domain of the wider collectivity.

It is revealing to compare these white American patterns with others found among Negroes in the United States. Such a comparison shows how corporate divisions, once instituted as structural and institutional disjunctions in the public domain, are internally and externally reinforced and may perpetuate primary cleavages, irrespective of later institutional continuities across their boundaries and discontinuities within them.

Franklin Frazier (1940) shows how the Negro's social situation in the

United States has tended to institutionalize deformities in all sectors of its private domain, kinship, mating, family, paternity, and domestic organization alike. He shows also that, especially in northern cities, where conditions permit limited Negro professionalization and property accumulations, although Negro family and other social forms have tended to approximate the models institutionalized among American whites, the public domain of Negro society remains equally separate and distinctive (Frazier, 1949; 1962). Comparable contrasts in the religious, social, and family life of whites and Negroes in the Deep South are familiar to all (Dollard, 1957; Powdermaker, 1939). In the North, Negroes and whites are segregated residentially, occupationally, and socially by informal caste or color-caste. The two racial divisions operate parallel but separate and distinctive organizations, and the Negro community characteristically remains economically depressed and dependent on the wealthier, more numerous, and more powerful whites. Thus, economic differentials and spatial and social boundaries interact to reinforce one another.

In the Deep South, despite recent tokenism in churches, courts, registration booths, and schools, caste divisions are basic, formal, and deeply entrenched as the fundamental conditions of Southern corporate structure. The requisite Negro subjugation is facilitated and maintained by their corporate exclusion as a residual category from the public domain of Southern white society. White control is pursued by various devices such as differential justice, denial of political rights, land control, tenancy, sharecropping, occupational and educational inequalities and insecurities, segregation of public facilities and residence, and the like. The recent rise of corporate organizations and public movements against this racial structure of inequality has evoked widespread hostile reactions in the South. Nonetheless, in the northern United States, where these movements won most initial support, parallel racial barriers persist with corresponding inequalities and tensions.

Negro acculturation in America has varied in degree and scope with differences of social circumstance. Negro and white professionals or bourgeoisie share many common institutional patterns; but these classes vary proportionately in both racial categories as a function of the prevailing inequalities of educational, economic, and political opportunity; further, the bourgeoisie and professionals in both races are structurally segregated and, with marginal exceptions, they are occupationally and socially restricted to their own racial categories. Thus, despite extensive institutional continuities across racial frontiers, Negro and white American professionals or bourgeoisie are not socially equivalent; rather, each group is isolated from the other within unequal, closed, and perpetual corporate categories which are racially defined and structurally contraposed. In consequence of this primary cleavage, Negro American professionals are defined first as Negroes, then as Americans, and only finally by occupation, in contrast with their white colleagues. How do the contexts and correlates of such phenomena illuminate the salient differences between pluralism and heterogeneity?

On their introduction to America, Negroes were racially, culturally, and socially distinct. Slavery categorized them as the property of their owners and systematically denied them civil, economic, political, and other social rights (Phillips, 1963; Stampp, 1964). Following the abolition of slavery after deep strife, effective substitute controls were developed by the dominant whites in the Deep South to perpetuate the categorical exclusions on which Negro subjugation and social inequality were based (Johnson, 1934; Davis, Gardner and Gardner, 1941). All persons of Negro descent were identified as members of the category excluded from participation in the public domains of Southern white society. In the North, to which many Southern Negroes emigrated, residential and social segregation produced broadly similar effects by simultaneously excluding them from white society and by constituting them in urban ghettos as a residual corporate category, irrespective of their internal institutional and social differentiations. Given these structural contexts, institutional continuities across racial boundaries, or institutional discontinuities within either racial category, have limited relevance, in the wider society, in either corporation, or to the individuals concerned (Myrdal, 1944).

Similar divergences between institutional and corporate boundaries are observed among the East Indians and Creole Negroes of Trinidad and British Guiana (Crowley, 1957, pp. 817–24; Smith, 1962, pp. 98–143; Despres, 1964, pp. 1051–77). In Trinidad, East Indians may identify many local Creole Negro dishes and other cultural items as elements of 'ancestral Indian culture'. Conversely, Negroid Creoles, having forgotten their cultural debts to East Indians for numerous items, including cuisine, ornaments, and so on, identify these as traditional Creole patterns. Such 'plural acculturation', cultural exchange, or assimilation merely highlights the distinction between strictly cultural and strictly social categorizations within this community. However incorrect these attributions may be in fact, the primary identification for any individual or cultural item as East Indian or as Creole Negro is prescribed by this corporate contraposition. Hybrids, distinguished as *doglas* (bastards), are excluded by East Indians from their collectivity. Though many middle-class East Indians and Negroes share common institutional forms and skills, they remain contraposed by their corporate identities.

Similarly, no American of either race fails to identify an American Catholic Negro bishop or bureaucrat as first and foremost a Negro—that is, by his primary corporate identity. In the United States, as in Guiana and Trinidad, the racial division is institutionalized as a specifically social boundary between two closed categories, irrespective of institutional continuities across boundaries or differences within either category. On either side of these corporate boundaries, each collectivity maintains its distinct 'public' organizations, for internal and external collective action in matters of common interest. In all three societies, the contraposed collectivities participate unequally and differently, but primarily as units in the public sector that includes them. As in Guiana or Trinidad, so in the United States, following an initial situation of marked differences between two structurally segregated collectivities, institutional modifications and assimilations have left intact their social boundaries, and social pluralism prevails, regardless of strictly cultural continuities between or differences within either category. In Trinidad and Guiana it is probable that a majority in either category remains unfamiliar with the other's institutional system, and perhaps also in the United States. However, exclusive categorical incorporations are clearly independent of cultural assimilation or internal differences. Likewise, in Senegal, despite official French doctrines of assimilation and association, similar categorical exclusions contraposed European and *évolué,* despite their common institutional allegiances (Crowder, 1962).

The principal conditions that ensure such persistence of social pluralism despite the prevalence of institutional continuities across social boundaries are inherent in the corporate organization itself. If a social boundary rigidly separates two corporate categories, as in the northern United States, both collectivities will then lack inclusive corporate organizations in which they participate as equals and to whose coordinated actions alone they can look for peaceful changes in the corporate structure. On the other hand, if one of the collectivities has categorical form, while the other is organized as a corporate group, as in the South, the latter is generally dominant, and by virtue of its organizational and other resources, can effectively contain pressures for the dissolution of the corporate boundaries on which its power, status, and privilege are based. Individual actions and alignments cannot demolish or transform these social divisions and corporate units; nor can the representative national government initiate such radical action without assurances of overwhelming support from both collectivities, and especially from the majority of the dominant one.

When two corporations are defined by virtue of a common boundary, this can be abolished only by their separate but joint determination, or by the radical action of one of them. Tokenism is the logical corporate response to external pressures by a national government for the elimination of inequalities by which corporate sections are mutually defined and segregated, as in the Southern states. Cultural continuities or variations can neither erode nor transform these corporate structures directly for the simple reason that sectional divisions and relations are based on other principles, such as power, race, or other criteria of exclusive corporate solidarity and autonomy.

All collectivities that are segregated as or within societies require special procedures and organization to coordinate and regulate their internal action and to guide their relations with external corporations. In consequence, the public domains of segregated collectivities develop specific modes of organization and action to handle their collective interests and problems. The more rigorous and institutionally extensive the segregation of the collectivity, the deeper and wider is its associational boundary, and the more exhaustively are its members socially identified with and dependent upon it. In the structural context of a plural society, each corporate section develops sectionally specific institutions, organizations, and procedures that constitute its distinctive public domain; and if the plurality contains two or more collectivities of equivalent or differing status, their segregation is further reinforced by these mutually distinctive collective organizations. If these social sections are also segregated spatially, as is often the case, then the public domain of either unit enjoys corresponding freedom from external competition or immediate internal challenge. In effect, any institutional development or systematic organization in the collective domains of either section in a context of pluralism tends to reinforce the already existing divisions and separatism of the sections as mutually exclusive, internally autonomous, contraposed corporations. Such structural developments proceed independently of cultural continuities or assimilation across sectional boundaries.

Thus in the Republic of South Africa, as in the United States, the 'black bourgeoisie' remain subject to the categorical identities and disabilities of their social sections (Kuper, 1965; Mitchell, 1960). In Trinidad, Guiana, and Mauritius (Benedict, 1962, pp. 1235–46), Indians and Creole Negroes have each developed and retained specific sectional structures; and when these social sections were simultaneously enfranchised, their distinctive organizations were quickly converted into political parties, as also in Surinam (van Lier, 1950) and Nigeria (Coleman, 1958; Post, 1963; Hodgkin 1961).

In sum, it seems that the decisive conditions that constitute and perpetuate social pluralism consist primarily in differences of institutional organization in the public domains of segregated collectivities identified as the basic corporate units of social structure, and contraposed in consequence of sharp initial differences in their political status and in their several public domains.

Under such conditions, it is irrelevant whether the inclusive social order emphasizes the functional differentiation and autonomy of institutional spheres within either section. If collectivities are rigorously segregated spatially and associationally, although the institutional structure may be highly differentiated within either collectivity, their separate public domains will each represent a sectionally specific and structurally distinctive organization. Under such conditions, the societally integrative effects of institutional differentiations and interdependences are restricted by and within the primary demarcation of collectivities as separate associational fields. Similarly, the opportunities for and implications of institutional assimilations or isomorphism are subject to the structural conditions and requirements of the prevailing corporate organization. [...]

We must thus distinguish three levels of pluralism and three related modes of incorporation. Structural pluralism consists in the differential incorporation of collectivities segregated as social sections and characterized by institutional divergences. Cultural pluralism consists in variable institutional diversity without corresponding collective segregation. Social pluralism involves the organization of institutionally dissimilar collectivities as corporate sections or segments whose boundaries demarcate distinct communities and systems of social action. The differential incorporation that institutes structural pluralism is found only in societies where institutionally diverse collectivities are set apart as corporate social sections of unequal status and resources. In these conditions, if the ruling sections forms a numerical minority of the aggregate, we find the plural society in the classic form described by Furnivall.

It is advisable to clarify the logical status and relations of these typologies before discussing their substantive bases. Despite their differing referents, these two typologies are not entirely independent of each other; nor does either distinguish a set of independent variables. As analytical categories, cultural, social, and structural pluralism refer to three levels of pluralism which differ in their properties, forms, intensity, and range. Though cultural pluralism may prevail without social or structural pluralism, these latter forms of pluralism cannot obtain without commensurate degrees of cultural pluralism. Moreover, while structural pluralism entails social and cultural pluralism, the converse is not necessary. As regards the alternative modes of incorporation, although analytically distinct, they are not necessarily exclusive and may be combined in various ways to constitute differing types of complex regime. Thus, in South Africa, whites are incorporated differentially from nonwhites, universalistically as citizens of the Republic, and consociationally through the provincial organization. Consociational and universalistic modes of incorporation can be found in societies that lack cultural or social pluralism, but in the latter context they are differentially associated with these different levels of pluralism. While universalistic regimes can accommodate cultural pluralism without substantive change, social pluralism generates a substantively consociational order within them; but neither of these two regimes, if substantively valid, accommodates a state of structural pluralism, which always requires differential incorporation for its constitution and maintenance.

The disjunctions of mutually exclusive collectivities involve differences of social structure which reflect corresponding differences in their basic institutional systems. By contrast, where cultural differences prevail without correlative social divisions, they must be equally consistent with direct individual participation in a common collective life under uniform conditions of incorporation. Whether regionally concentrated or dispersed, such cultural differences will then be individually optional, functional alternatives, restricted to the private domain and to secondary institutional spheres. The resulting combination of cultural diversity and social assimilation is normal in heterogeneous societies.

Societies that contain two or more institutionally dissimilar and mutually exclusive collectivities manifest substantively consociational or differential regimes, even under universalistic constitutions. This arises wherever individual identification with one or other of the associated collectivities is institutionally prescribed and prior, since this ordains individual dependence on representation in and through the collective organizations. Thus, whatever the constitutional form or the spatial distribution of social segments— given a society composed of institutionally distinct and exclusive collectivities —consociational or differential arrangements prevail, formally or informally, separately or together.

Though by no means restricted to contexts of social pluralism, consociation is formally appropriate for the union of institutionally diverse collectivities. However, multiethnic consociational regimes have certain structural weaknesses and face serious problems. In the absence of common external threats and widespread internal assimilations through intermarriage, they rarely endure. Persisting societies that contain institutionally distinct sections are commonly unified under conditions of differential incorporation as plural structures of radically unequal and disparate parts.

Structural pluralism intensifies and enhances the institutional disjunctions that social pluralism involves by prescribing collective differences of status and relation to the common public domain, and by transforming these differences into conditions of inequality and subordination. Whereas consociation assumes intersectional equivalence and encourages social assimilation, structural pluralism is constituted by the differential incorporation of such sections as superior and inferior, and to persist requires their continued disjunction. Where differences of collective organization and institutional practice antedate differential incorporation, pluralism increases and deepens these differences by establishing a new dimension of domination and subordination which imposes radically divergent societal contexts on the collectivities concerned. Moreover, in the absence of such antecedent differences of collective organization and institutional practice, differential incorporation generates them by prescribing distinct societal contexts to which collectivities must accommodate by appropriate socialization and institutional adaptation.

It is necessary, then, to distinguish social pluralism from cultural pluralism, though both assume systemic institutional differences among collectivities within a single society. Under formal or informal consociations, the institutionally distinct segments share identical status and relations with the common public domain, and thus share a common system of government and public law. This political and jural community modifies the institutional segregation of the sections accordingly, and defines their differences as equivalent alternatives. Under differential incorporation, one institutionally distinct collectivity regulates the others, having appropriated societal institutions of government, law, and force. Whereas the manifest equivalence of components—a condition that fosters intersectional association, mobility, and assimilation—is necessary for a stable consociation, the habituation of subordinate social sections to inferior status is equally essential for a stable system of differential incorporation. In short, structural pluralism, the corollary of differential incorporation, involves a special set of arrangements which either generates or extends the collective disjunctions of social pluralism by proscribing intersectional equivalence, mobility, and individuation.

Homogeneous and heterogeneous societies may equally well be based on uniform or universalistic conditions of incorporation. Differential incorporation obtains always and only with structural pluralism. Consociations may provide the bases for homogeneous societies, as for example Ashanti, Iroquois, or Nootka. Consociation may also constitute a heterogeneous society as among the Aztec, in Switzerland, or in Lebanon. It may unite two or more structurally distinct homogeneous societies, as in the Terik-Tiriki and Ga-Kpesi cases; or, as in Nigeria, it may unite institutionally heterogeneous collectivities distinguished by culture and social systems as mutually exclusive corporate sections. In the latter case, the consociation exhibits social and cultural pluralism in its sectional basis, while formally excluding structural pluralism by prescribing segmental equivalence. The result, illustrated by Nigeria, Uganda, or Cameroon, is a plural society of differing structure and type from that based on differential incorporation. Whether we apply the same term to both these models, or describe the Nigerian or Ghanaian types as 'composite' or as 'segmental' societies, following earlier writers, is not of major importance. The internal inconsistencies that threaten consociations of this sort with radical transformations or dissolution have been mentioned above.

Since these alternative modes of incorporation are always institutionalized as formal or substantive conditions of societal structure, their relations with other institutional sectors of the collective life are clearly important, however variable or indirect these may seem. Moreover, given their status as structural alternatives to which different levels and ranges of pluralism correspond, diverse combinations of these types of incorporation are not difficult to find. Perhaps the most complex and obvious example of this is the United States, incorporated constitutionally in explicitly universal terms as a consociation of territorially discrete collectivities, but substantively characterized by the differential incorporation of its Negro citizens. Such a society exhibits heterogeneity and pluralism together, but in differing proportions. In its white sector, cultural pluralism prevails without corresponding social and structural pluralism; across the race line social and cultural pluralism are institutionalized in direct contravention of the constitution. By its consociational form, despite its unreserved universalism, this constitution provides the essential resources for the defense of this system of differential incorporation by guarantees of states rights.

However different our formulations may seem, we have not abandoned Furnivall's problem; instead, we have merely attempted to clarify and generalize it. Though he confined his discussion to colonial pluralities, Furnivall identified and formulated the basic issues of social cohesion and development which characterize pluralism in all its many forms and dimensions. Since Furnivall wrote, most of these tropical colonies have attained independence, with greater or less turmoil. As independent states, their vicissitudes and upheavals declare their generic fragility, the product of their plural character and base. To anticipate the smooth development of such societies into nations, or even any rapid, continuous process of modernization within them, is antihistorical and antiempirical in the extreme. We need merely remember Latin America, Belgium, Spain, Portugal, and Germany, all of which have known independence far longer and under far more favorable conditions. For these new 'nonnational' states, with their 'multiple' societies, internal order and survival are surely the first formidable task; the promotion of internal loyalties and cohesion by the dissolution of sectional divisions, identities, and fears is the second. Though very closely connected, this latter presupposes the first condition.

Furnivall (1945) was seriously in error when he wrote 'there can be nationalism without a nation'. Does communalism exist without a 'community', or tribalism without a 'tribe'? Surely here Furnivall fell victim to the presuppositions, categories, and symbols of Western culture, which has long invested 'nationalism' with a moral supremacy and prevalence it does not always possess. True, leaders of colonial independence movements appealed to sentiments, ideals, and principles of nationalism and self-determination; the public acclaim and support they received was proportionate to popular dissatisfactions and desires to be rid of European rule; but desires for self-determination or independence may prevail without nationalism, and do not presuppose it. It is easier and more common for people to mobilize and unite in opposition to alien rulers than to construct and consolidate new societies under the influence of strictly national sentiments and ideals. It is surely uncommon for people divided by history, language, institutions, habitat, and in many other ways to unite voluntarily and in peace, in the absence of any serious external threat to their common security. The unity of negation is no more satisfactory a basis for assuming the moral solidarity and present or future cohesion of an aggregate in motion than the unity created by their differential incorporation. Even in the simplest situation, such as a lineage feud, this condition is evident. Thus in these new 'nonnational' states, it remains necessary to pursue policies that eliminate sectional barriers, identities, and fears among the collectivities that compose them. Ultimately this can be done only through the complementary or equivalent incorporation of these collectivities within the wider unit or by their effective extrusion from the common public domain through the universalistic incorporation of all individuals as citizens.

References

Benedict, B. (1962), 'Stratification in plural societies', *American Anthropologist*, vol. 64, no. 6.

Coleman, J. S. (1958), *Nigeria: Background to Nationalism*, Los Angeles.

Crowder, M. (1962), *Senegal: A Study in French Assimilation Policy*, Oxford.

Crowley, D. J. (1957), 'Plural and differential acculturation in Trinidad', *American Anthropologist*, vol. 59.

Davis, A., Gardner, B. B. and Gardner, M. R. (1941), *Deep South: A Social Anthropological Study of Caste and Class*, Chicago.

Despres, L. A. (1964), 'The implications of nationalist policies in British Guiana for the development of cultural theory', *American Anthropologist*, vol. 66.

Dollard, J. (1957), *Caste and Class in a Southern Town*, New York.

Frazier, E. F. (1940), *The Negro Family in the United States*, Chicago.

Frazier, E. F. (1949), *The Negro in the United States*, New York.

Frazier, E. F. (1962), *Black Bourgeoisie: The Rise of a New Middle Class in the United States*, New York.

Furnivall, J. S. (1945), 'Some problems of tropical economy', in R. Hinden (ed.), *Fabian Colonial Essays*, London.

Hodgkin, T. L. (1961), *African Political Parties*, Harmondsworth.

Johnson, C. S. (1934), *Shadow of the Plantation*, Chicago.

Kuper, L. (1965), *An African Bourgeoisie: Race, Class and Politics in South Africa*, New Haven.

Mitchell, J. C. (1960), *Tribalism and the Plural Society*, Oxford.

Myrdal, G. (1944), *An American Dilemma: The Negro Problem and Modern Democracy*, New York.

Phillips, U. B. (1963), *Life and Labor in the Old South*, Boston.

Post, K. W. J. (1963), *The Nigerian Federal Election of 1959: Politics and Administration in a Developing Political System*, Oxford.

Powdermaker, H. (1939), *After Freedom: A Cultural Study of the Deep South*, New York.

Smith, R. T. (1962), *British Guiana*, Oxford.

Stampp, K. M. (1964), *The Peculiar Institution: Slavery in the Ante-Bellum South*, New York.

Van Lier, R. A. J. (1950), *The Development and Nature of Society in the West Indies*, Royal Institute for the Indies, Amsterdam.

20 *M. Lofchie,* The Plural Society in Zanzibar

Political domination by an ethnically and culturally differentiated minority, and an unmistakable tendency for the broad social division of labor to exhibit a racial configuration, are the central ingredients in one concept of a 'plural society'. This usage of the concept is closely associated with the writings of the colonial historian, J. S. Furnivall, and the anthropologist, M. G. Smith. In extreme instances, a single racial group is predominant at each level of the plural society's class structure, especially at the elite level. As ethnic, economic, and political group boundaries tend to be identical, group memberships are culturally exclusive. The whole society, therefore, suffers from a high degree of nonintegration.

The concept of pluralism has also been employed by some sociologists to describe a different pattern of social organization. As Leo Kuper has pointed out in 'Plural Societies: Perspectives and Problems', a distinctively North American tradition of social science treats pluralism as an integrative mechanism and regards the plural society as characterized by restrained conflict, basic consensus, solidarity, and equilibrium. In the formulations of Lipset and Kornhauser, for example, the most important aspects of pluralism are that group boundaries continually cross and intersect one another and that, as a result, individuals experience multiple countervailing group loyalties. These multiple loyalties tend to prevent individuals from developing a total commitment to any single class or ethnic group. Because of their ties to a large number of social organizations, the members of society have an interest in the peaceful resolution of disputes. Thus, the segmentation of group affiliations tends to produce a political culture marked by attitudes of restraint, and conflict occurs through a political process of bargaining and compromise.

The term 'plural' society is employed in this essay in the same basic sense formulated by Furnivall and Smith and refers to those social systems characterized by a high degree of ethnic differentiation in the economic realm and by domination of a cultural minority in the political sphere. While

M. Lofchie, 'The plural society in Zanzibar', in L. Kuper and M. G. Smith (eds.), *Pluralism in Africa,* University of California Press, 1969, extracts from pp. 283–5, 293–309.

the Lipset-Kornhauser model of pluralism is highly useful in dealing with industrially advanced societies, it has limited utility in approaching traditional plural societies or plural societies in the developing nations. These plural societies exhibit a distinctive form of political conflict. Pervasively ideas of human equality and representative democratic government have made the conspicuous political and social inequalities of plural societies appear increasingly illegitimate both to the world community of nations and, more important for our purposes, to their internal majority populations. In domestic politics, this fundamental dissonance between a political culture of equality and prevailing sociopolitical arrangements has generated extreme conflict. This conflict is characterized by the quest of subordinated majorities for a political status reversal.

Until the African revolution of early January 1964,[1] Zanzibar's political and social arrangements corresponded closely to the theoretical model of a plural society. Culturally distinguishable racial and communal groups were differentially incorporated into the society's political system and differentially positioned in its economy. Political power was concentrated in the hands of a small Arab oligarchy which had formed Zanzibar's ruling class since the mid-nineteenth century. This group's position of political domination was based on its historical status as a landed aristocracy, its ownership of the best land, its near monopoly of the highest administrative levels of the Zanzibar government, and its privileged treatment by British colonial authorities. The Arab oligarchy comprised only a small proportion of the entire Arab community, which amounted to about 17 per cent of Zanzibar's total population; most Arabs did not have a position of influence or wealth in the society. Despite wide social differentiation among Arabs, the entire community possessed a high degree of political solidarity; the overwhelming majority of Arabs at all levels of the social structure not only identified themselves primarily as Arabs but considered themselves, as Arabs, to be members of a political and economic elite.

Asians (persons of Indo-Pakistani descent), comprising about 6 per cent of the population, were primarily a middle-class group and virtually monopolized trade, commerce, and the clerical levels of the civil service. Some Asians were extremely wealthy and those who owned the large import and export firms were by far the richest Zanzibaris. As a community, however, Asians were politically ineffectual, owing to a range of factors including communal fragmentation and a cultural disinclination toward political par-

[1] In April 1964, Zanzibar merged with Tanganyika to form the United Republic of Tanzania and thereby, in formal terms, ceased to exist as a sovereign independent nation. As a British protectorate and as an autonomous national unit, Zanzibar comprised the two East African offshore islands of Zanzibar and Pemba and a few adjacent islands. The total area is approximately 1,020 square miles: Zanzibar is roughly 640 square miles, and Pemba, about 380. For a full-length study of historical and political developments in Zanzibar, see Lofchie (1965).

ticipation, and were consistently unable to exert political influence commensurate with their economic status. The Asians' unwillingness to undertake concerted political action helped facilitate continuing political domination by a small minority of Arabs.

An African majority, including slightly more than three-fourths of the total population, formed the broad underprivileged mass of Zanzibar society. Of all the racial groups in Zanzibar, Africans were the least incorporated into the political structure and the most economically disadvantaged. By and large the occupational range of the African community was confined to rural fishing, petty agriculture, and unskilled manual labor. As the poorest Zanzibaris, most Africans were unable to afford higher education. This lack, together with a tendency by both the British colonial authorities and the Arab oligarchy to ignore the political interests of Africans, prevented them from gaining access to positions of political or administrative influence. [...]

Dimensions of Zanzibar pluralism

Ethnic consciousness was the most powerful determinant of group solidarity in Zanzibar, and prerevolutionary politics were conducted almost entirely in the idiom of communal conflict. The formation of racial groups did not, however, conform to strict genealogical lines. After the nineteenth century there was a certain amount of racial intermarriage, especially between Arabs and Africans, and many Zanzibaris were, in the purely genealogical sense, of mixed descent. But self-identification, common acceptance, and the general pattern of conduct almost invariably operated to locate such persons unambiguously in one racial group or another. The most accurate method of defining any ethnic or racial community in Zanzibar is to determine whether its members shared a sense of common racial identity. As these corporate units largely correspond to historical and genealogical reality, there are conspicuous cultural and physical differences among them. Thus, the most salient and important features of prerevolutionary Zanzibar were its social organization as a racially plural society and the high visibility of this pluralism to all Zanzibaris.

Arabs

The Arab minority of Zanzibar was, in proportion to the total population, the second-largest dominant alien minority in Africa. Constituting approximately one-sixth (16·9 per cent) of the total population, Zanzibar's Arab oligarchy was surpassed in percentage size only by the European community of South Africa. The data in table 1, drawn from the government census of 1948, indicate the numerical and proportional sizes of Zanzibar's principal racial communities.

Table 1: *Distribution of population by ethnic community, 1948*

Race	Zanzibar Island		Pemba Island		Total	
	Number	Per cent	Number	Per cent	Number	Per cent
African	118 652	79·3	81 208	70·9	199 860	75·7
Arab	13 977	9·3	30 583	26·7	44 560	16·9
Asian	13 107	8·8	2 104	1·8	15 211	5·8
Other[a]	3 839	2·6	692	0·6	4 531	1·6
Total	149 575	100·0	114 587	100·0	264 162	100·0

a Includes Europeans and Comorians, the latter a small group of approximately 3,000 persons who had migrated to Zanzibar from the Comores Islands.

* Source: *Notes on the Census of the Zanzibar Protectorate,* 1948 (Zanzibar: Government Printer, 1953).

The Arab oligarchy, a very small segment of the entire Arab community, was composed almost entirely of the descendants of a few hundred well-to-do Omani families. This group had constituted a self-perpetuating elite since the earliest days of Arab colonialism because its decisive advantages in income, style of life, and social contacts enabled successive generations to gain a superior education and thereby to qualify more easily for the highest commercial and administrative positions. With British indulgence, and through a variety of political practices including nepotism, favoritism, and outright corruption, Arabs established virtually monopolistic control over economically strategic sectors of the government. Indeed, Arab control in vital areas of public administration was so complete that the Arabs exercised a decisive influence over the whole social structure of the protectorate. By allowing Asians to monopolize middle levels of the civil service and the economy, and preventing Africans from advancing, the Arab oligarchy was able to safeguard its own dominant position.

The Arab oligarchy enjoyed enormous social prestige. Indeed, the Swahili term *u-arabu,* which literally means 'being like an Arab', was a common euphemism in Zanzibar for 'cultured'. As the true founders of the Faith, a historic landowning aristocracy, and a ruling elite deferred to even by the British, the Arab elite embodied the highest virtues of Zanzibar society. Deference to the Arab community became a major factor in prerevolutionary Zanzibar politics. It helps to explain why large numbers of Africans supported political organizations initiated and led by Arabs, despite the radical economic differences between the two communities.

The landed Arab aristocracy was nevertheless a rapidly declining group in Zanzibar, both in terms of landholdings and overall economic position. The decline was brought about by several factors. Many of the early Arab families had fallen heavily into the debt of Asian bankers and moneylenders during the nineteenth and early twentieth centuries. High rates of interest and falling clove prices made it impossible to repay these debts, and considerable Arab land was passing into Asian hands. The Islamic practice of partitive inheritance also led to a rapid decline in the economic position of many Arabs. After two or three generations, many of the largest Arab plantations had been fragmented into plots no larger than peasant holdings. These factors, combined with the Arab tradition of lavish entertainment, generous hospitality, and a tendency toward conspicuous consumption, siphoned off Arab wealth and significantly reduced the size and income of the landed Arab oligarchy. By the end of World War II, the Arab community was far more dependent upon its position in government administration and the professions than upon land for its position of social and political preeminence.

The overwhelming majority of the Arab community was in the middle and lower classes—petty shopkeepers, peasant farmers, and semiskilled craftsmen. There were several distinct groups among the poorer Arabs. One group consisted of the descendants of the original Omani families that had suffered declining economic fortunes as a result of indebtedness, partitive inheritance, and high expenditure. This group constituted a sort of ruined aristocracy. Many of these impoverished Arabs intermarried with indigenous Africans, since income and style-of-life differences were removed and African landholdings were an attractive economic incentive. An important result of such intermarriage was that in recent times the 'poor Arab' class was of mixed descent, with skin color noticeably different from that of the remaining Arab elite, which intermarried far less frequently.

Recent arrivals from Oman formed a second group of poorer Arabs. Known as 'Manga' Arabs (*Manga* is the Swahili term for the Omani region of Arabia), this group was distinguished from the older Omani settlers not only by its recent arrival but also by the fact that its members had no intention of establishing permanent residence in Zanzibar. By and large, the Manga Arabs stemmed from the lower classes of Arabian society and came to Zanzibar with the intention of earning enough money to improve their position at home. For this reason, they usually entered shopkeeping and urban trades rather than agriculture and lived modestly and frugally during their stay in Zanzibar. The Manga were of the purest Arab descent of all Zanzibar Arabs, because their average length of residence was less than a generation and because they usually did not intermarry with the local Arab or African communities. Before the era of open racial politics in Zanzibar, considerable tension and hostility marked the relations between the Manga Arabs and the older Omani elite, largely because of economic differentials and because the older settlers tended to remain indifferent to the economic hardships suffered by the newcomers.

The most numerous section of the Arab lower class consisted of persons who were not identified as Arabs by government census takers until fairly recent times. As late as the census of 1931, long after the establishment of the sultanate and the period of heavy Arab immigration, Arabs were officially recorded as less than 9 per cent of all Zanzibaris. Since the major upsurge in the Arab population occurred within a very brief period of time, from 1924 to 1931, when the Arab population rose from 8·7 per cent to 14·2 per cent of the total population, it is likely that the figures were affected by different census procedures and criteria. Moreover, many non-Arabs may have decided to identify themselves as Arabs in an effort to qualify for the social and economic privileges that the British government accorded members of the Arab community.

Most of the 'new' Arabs came from a single ethnic group, the Swahili. While the Arab community was gaining nearly 15 000 members between 1924 and 1931, the Swahili community declined by more than twice that figure, and nearly disappeared as a separate ethnic identity. Originally the term 'Swahili' had simply referred to persons of mixed Arab-African descent and Islamic faith, whose ancestors came from the East African coast. The Swahilis were thus not a tribe in the strict sense of the term, being joined only by common religion, common language (Swahili), and a vague sense of common geographical and historical origins. Ethnic solidarity among Swahilis was not strong enough to pose an obstacle to a change in ethnic self-description. More important, the ethnic term 'Swahili' had recently acquired a highly pejorative meaning which signified boorish manner, low pedigree, menial occupational position, and general social inferiority (Prins, 1961, p. 11). Being a Swahili thus meant substantial loss in status, and the negative stereotype of the term provided a strong incentive for Swahilis to seek a new and more respected ethnic identity. The dominant motivation behind the Swahilis' exodus from their own community was a search for a more prestigious self-identification; the fact that nearly half of this group chose 'Arab' as a category of self-description illustrates the high social esteem in which Zanzibar Arabs were held.

The Swahilis' ability to 'become' Arabs illustrates a basic difference between the Arab oligarchy of Zanzibar and other dominant racial minorities in Africa. Unlike the white oligarchies of South Africa and Rhodesia which have erected legal and social barriers to prevent trespass across racial boundaries, in Zanzibar the Arabs were not a completely closed community. One of the most noticeable physical features of Zanzibar society was the substantial number of persons who identified themselves as Arab and who were of darker complexion than many Africans. With few exceptions, however, these darker-skinned Arabs were of much lower economic status than the original Arab elite group. Regardless of differences in skin color or in economic position, persons identifying themselves as Arabs formed a highly solidaristic political unit whose cohesion was based on a sense of shared racial identity.

The openness of the Arab elite to penetration from below was the natural consequence of a situation in which all racial groups contained a certain number of persons of mixed descent. It was not a matter of deliberate Arab policy, but it had enormous political importance: the possibility of racial assimilation operated to preserve the racially plural character of social stratification. Those few Africans or persons of mixed Afro-Arab descent who managed to achieve a degree of upward economic mobility tended to change their self-identification accordingly and to become Arabs. The high status and prestige of the Arab community was a strong incentive for anyone possessing the economic wherewithal to pass as an Arab in his social and communal relations. Because these groups shared a common religion (Islam) and a common language (Swahili), because skin color was not an absolute criterion of racial community, and, most important, because the rising group never amounted to more than a very small number of persons, upwardly mobile individuals were usually able to gain entry into the elite structure of Zanzibar society, culturally and politically. As a result, Zanzibar's political elite tended to remain Arab in terms of self-description and general pattern of behavior. In this way, the movement across racial boundaries which resulted from individual economic mobility, however minimal in absolute numbers, reinforced rather than undermined the racial aspect of political domination and the social division of labor.

This form of racial passing also added to the overall stability of the society by providing a kind of safety valve. In the twentieth century, Zanzibar did not experience the emergence of a social class comparable to the bourgeoisie of prerevolutionary France or the African middle classes of southern Africa—a class that while rising economically, remained unassimilated culturally and socially into the political ruling group. Such alienation did not become politically significant until after World War II.

Few people were actually able to change their socioeconomic position. Economics, skin color, and social acceptance were, on the whole, immovable obstacles to upward mobility by Africans. While persons of mixed descent and, on a few occasions, Africans as well were able to alter their self-description to suit changing personal circumstances, not enough people were involved to alter the racial character of social stratification. Since very few non-Arabs ever achieved the highest level of Zanzibar society, the Arab oligarchy remained a highly differentiated entity, distinct from the mass of the population, not only economically, but also in being of visible Arab descent.

Asians

The Asian community furnished Zanzibar's middle class: Asians filled the clerical and technical levels of the civil service; owned and operated most of the protectorate's wholesale, retail, and import commerce; dominated the export of cloves; and managed and staffed the large international banking and insurance firms. By the mid-twentieth century, Asians had also become a significant landowning group. Asians had initially been unwilling to acquire rural property, largely because ownership of land would imply a more permanent relationship to Zanzibar than most were willing to acknowledge. Eventually, however, through foreclosures on indebted Arabs, they came into possession of many of Zanzibar's productive clove and coconut estates. Thus, though constituting only a very small minority of the total population, Asians owned a vastly disproportionate share of the nation's wealth; several Asian families had long since surpassed all Arabs as the wealthiest Zanzibaris. Like the Arabs, the Asians enjoyed advantages in income and style of life which gave their class position a self-perpetuating quality. Unlike the Arab community, however, Asians never became a major political force. Though able on rare occasions to act successfully as a pressure group, the Asian community was unable to translate its economic strength into corresponding political power.

The political weakness of the Asian community is traceable principally to three factors: divisive communalism and religious fragmentation, the vulnerability of middle-class status, and a pronounced tendency to remain culturally and emotionally oriented toward India.

The Asian community was composed of a myriad of religious and ethnic subgroups. The basic division was between Hindu and Muslim Asians, who formed approximately one-fourth and three-fourths of the Asian community, respectively. They were further divided along religious or caste lines. The Muslim Asian community, for example, included such diverse denominations as Ismailis, Bohoras, Ithna-Asharis, and Sunnis. Several small Asian groups (Parsees, Sikhs, and Goans) followed entirely separate and distinct religious practices. Most Asians felt far deeper loyalty to their particular subgroup than to the Asian community as a whole. This tendency was especially noticeable in recent years when the partition of Indian and Pakistan generated considerable antagonism between Hindu and Muslim Asians. The result of extreme fragmentation was that Asians were unable to cooperate with one another and thus could not function politically as a unified group.

The Asians' middle-class status also made their political position difficult. As a community of businessmen, traders, and shopkeepers, Asians were dependent on customer and client relations with the Arab and African communities; as a class of lower civil servants, Asians were usually under the jurisdiction of Arab superiors. Moreover, Asian civil servants lacked the economic autonomy that the Arab administrators derived from occupying a level of unchallengeable bureaucratic power or from large agricultural landholdings. The pressure of being located in sectors of the society where intercommunal relations were critical served to foster a nonpolitical ethos of deference, service, and profit within the Asian community. Most Asians tended to view political conflicts, not simply as largely irrelevant to their lives, but as potentially damaging to their social and economic status in Zanzibar society.

A marked tendency to remain culturally and emotionally attached to India and, more recently, to Pakistan also helps to account for Asians' noninvolvement in Zanzibar politics. Asian cultural separatism was reflected in a variety of ways: in a very low rate of intermarriage with local communities; in the maintenance of strong family and economic ties with the Asian subcontinent; in the tendency to speak Indian languages rather than Swahili in the home; and in the preference for segregated living areas which would permit a partial re-creation of Asian life.

Most Asians also looked to India and Pakistan, rather than to Zanzibar, for their ultimate political protection and security. Their homes were far more frequently adorned with photographs of Ghandi, Nehru, or Ayub Khan than with pictures of local leaders. In the past, this attitude had led to a peculiar indirect mode of political participation. Asians sought to exercise influence on the Zanzibar government through diplomatic pressures brought to bear by the government of India. When India announced that it could no longer protect its overseas minorities and told Asians abroad to accept the consequences of life in the diaspora, Zanzibar Asians were deprived of their sole mode of participation in local politics. Because they were unconcerned with local issues, Asians never sought to replace the diplomatic pressure of the Indian government with effective local organization.

Africans

Africans were a politically and socially disprivileged majority: they furnished the protectorate with its peasant farmers, fishermen, and manual workers. The Africans faced several major barriers to upward mobility. The presence of an Asian community culturally acclimated to middle-class status made it extremely difficult for Africans to compete successfully for more lucrative employment, even at the clerical level of the civil service or in commerce. Moreover, Zanzibar's educational system strongly favored the well-to-do at the expense of the poverty-ridden, especially at the secondary school level where school fees were usually beyond the means of the average African family. Overt discrimination also handicapped African mobility. Even qualified Africans had great difficulty in securing positions in government or business, since Arabs or Asians in authority strongly preferred to hire members of their own communities. Thus, the African community's overall position, like that of the Arab and Asian communities, had a self-perpetuating quality. Successive generations were unable to overcome the syndrome of impoverishment and discrimination.

Communal divisions among Zanzibar Africans assumed enormous political importance in the period preceding the African revolution. The African community's overwhelming numerical strength made it potentially the most powerful political group in Zanzibar under an elected form of government, but the chronic and long-standing ethnic tension between Shirazis and main-landers prevented Africans from becoming a unified electoral force. As a result, they consistently lost elections and thus failed to wrest power from the Arab oligarchy through the electoral process. Failure in the political arena was the immediate cause of the African revolution. A revolutionary army, composed principally of mainland Africans, overthrew Arab rule by force because the lack of overall communal solidarity among Africans had convinced many that Arab paramountcy never could be ended by orderly constitutional procedures.

Table 2: *African population in Zanzibar, 1948*

Community	Number	Percentage of all Africans
Hadimu	41 500	20·7
Tumbatu	44 000	22·0
Pemba	57 500	28·8
Total indigenous Africans (Shirazi)	143 000	71·5
Mainland Africans	57 000	28·5
Total of all Africans	200 000	100·0

Table 2 gives approximate population figures for the various African ethnic groups in 1948. Socioeconomic differentiation between mainlanders and Shirazis intensified and perpetuated the sense of estrangement between the two communities. The mainland African minority was predominantly an urbanized group, with the vast majority of its members manual workers. Zanzibar's dock workers, household servants, hotel and restaurant help, commercial laborers, and daily paid municipal workers were overwhelmingly of mainland African origin. The few mainlanders who lived in the rural areas were usually squatter-farmers on estates and plantations belonging to Arabs or Asians. In contrast, Shirazis were a predominantly rural group and their basic economic pursuits were agriculture and fishing. As agriculturists, Shirazis cultivated land which they themselves owned, privately or communally.

This pattern of social differentiation gave rise to markedly different attitudes toward Zanzibar on the part of mainlanders and Shirazis. The mainland Africans experienced life in Zanzibar as a combination of economic deprivation and political alienation. As landless manual workers, they were not only in Zanzibar's lowest economic stratum, but their urban residence placed them in proximity to the Arab and Asian elites whose affluence made their own poverty appear more extreme in comparison. Moreover, mainlanders were deeply aware of their historical origins in the slave trade or as migratory labor; their lowly background, together with their menial economic status, made it difficult for them to regard themselves as full-fledged members of Zanzibar society. Several generations removed from their countries of origin, the mainlanders were unable to return home and unable fully to accept life in Zanzibar. Despite being legal citizens of the protectorate, the mainlanders were stateless persons, psychologically and emotionally.

Shirazis, on the other hand, possessed a sense of national pride at being the first Zanzibaris, and their concept of mixed Persian descent created a profound awareness of an ancient cultural and historical heritage. Living in remote villages, they were less exposed to daily contact with Arabs and Asians than the mainlanders and were thus less aware of the economic and political domination of Zanzibar by alien elites. Moreover, as rural landowners and fishermen, Shirazis lived with a dignity denied to the mainlanders, and they viewed themselves as full citizens of Zanzibar society.

A social portrait of Zanzibar's class structure just before the era of competitive racial politics is presented in tables 3, 4, and 5. Three quantitative indexes of social structure—landownership, occupational status, and access to higher education—are used to illustrate the close coincidence between racial community and economic class in Zanzibar. The three tables are based on a social survey of Zanzibar conducted in 1948 by Professor Edward Batson of the University of Capetown, South Africa. Quantitative surveys of any developing country must be treated with considerable scepticism, and Zanzibar is no exception. Batson's survey figures, however, can, with the usual cautions, be regarded as fairly reliable[2]

The historic preeminence of cloves and coconuts as Zanzibar's basic cash crops has affected the manner in which Zanzibaris calculate the value of land. The only consideration taken into account is the number of trees on a particular plot. Other factors such as farm buildings, proximity to transportation, and even the quality of the soil have practically no influence on land values. As a result, Zanzibaris often measure a person's wealth according to the number of trees he owns. Following this tradition, both government and

[2] Professor Batson was commissioned to conduct the survey by the Zanzibar government, and had the cooperation of the colonial administration. He and his staff employed several means of checking the figures that fieldworkers collected. An official census had been taken earlier in the same year, and census figures were available, as were the files of various government departments. An important factor of reliability was that, in 1948, overt communal politics had not yet begun and matters of racial identification were far less sensitive than they later became. The Batsun survey has never been published but exists in Verifax form in Zanzibar and in South Africa.

private surveys of landownership have employed a 'number of trees' index to gauge the value of landed property in the hands of the different racial communities (Batson, 1948a, vol. 14).

Table 3, providing an estimate of landownership based on number of trees, shows that in 1948 Arabs owned more than two-thirds of Zanzibar's largest plantations, and that nearly one-third of the largest estates had passed into Asian hands. One of the most striking features of Zanzibar society revealed by the table is the limited size of the Arab landed aristocracy. Even if the top two categories of ownership are taken to constitute landed wealth, Zanzibar society in 1948 contained less than 500 Arab heads of families who enjoyed a position of social preeminence based on land. Given the low rate of profit of clove and coconut cultivation in the twentieth century, it is probably more realistic to employ only the top category of the table to indicate a position of real landed wealth. The total number of wealthy Arab agriculturists in Zanzibar after World War II, therefore, probably amounted to no more than 200. Table 3 thus helps to confirm the devastating toll being taken of the Arab elite group by its indebtedness and partitive inheritance practices.

Table 3: *Landownership in Zanzibar by racial community, 1948*

Number of trees	Percentage of parcels				Total number of owners
	Arab	Asian	Shirazi	Mainland African	
3000 or more	68·8	31·2	—	—	240
1000–2999	56·1	6·1	20·2	17·6[a]	570
250–999	51·9	5·2	33·8	9·1	3 635
50–249	14·5	0·3	74·2	11·0	13 680
Less than 50	16·0	0·1	66·6	17·3	10 250

[a] This figure, which represents 100 mainland African landowners, was recorded entirely in Pemba.

Table 3 also indicates fairly substantial African landholding in the second and third categories of ownership. Though some Shirazis, Pemba Shirazis in particular, had always retained possession of a certain amount of land, the Africans' overall position was significantly improved over the early part of the century. A government survey of landownership taken in 1922 indicated that 96 per cent of the owners of all plantations with 1000 or more trees, and 85 per cent of the owners of plantations with between 500 and 1000 trees, were Arabs (Batson, 1948b, p. 36). The resurgence of African landownership was directly related to the steady deterioration of the Arabs' position and occurred in two ways. First, land was being leased and sold to Africans by Asian financiers who had foreclosed on Arabs and who preferred African to Arab debtors because the Arabs' reputation had been damaged by the inability of earlier generations to repay loans. Second, in an effort to prevent further erosion of their position, the Arabs of Pemba had established a special procedure whereby Africans could acquire land. Under this procedure an African who agreed to plant and cultivate a virgin piece of Arab land for five years could, at the end of this period, assume legal possession of half of the area. In this connection it should be noted that the 100 mainland Africans who appear in category 2 of the table lived on Pemba Island. The deterioration of the Arabs virtual monopoly of Zanzibar's arable land was accompanied by an increase not only in Asian but also in African landownership.

The heavy preponderance of Arabs and Asians in elite Zanzibar society was also reflected in the pattern of occupational differentiation among the races. Table 4 ranks approximately 58 000 Zanzibaris following nonagricul-

Table 4: *Occupational distribution in Zanzibar by racial community, 1948*

Occupational level	Percentage of workers				Total number of workers
	Arab	Asian	Indigenous African	Mainland African	
Upper	4·2	95·8	—	—	120
Upper middle	26·0	59·2	6·3	8·5	710
Middle (nonmanual)	26·1	33·3	27·3	13·3	5 400
Middle (manual)	6·0	34·9	12·1	47·0	1 735
Lower middle	17·1	4·7	54·1	24·1	35 160
Lower	13·5	0·9	36·9	48·7	14 635

tural pursuits according to six occupational levels—(1) *upper,* including owners of large commercial firms, top professionals, and ranking administrators (e.g., heads of government departments, high school principals, doctors, lawyers, architects; (2) *upper middle,* comprising auxiliary professional workers (e.g., teachers, newspaper editors, retail shopkeepers); (3) and (4) *middle,* including nonmanual uncertified clerical and administrative personnel and skilled manual workers (e.g., koranic school teachers, clove inspectors, timekeepers, taxi drivers, carpenters, barbers); (5) *lower middle,* including semiskilled workers and itinerant workers (e.g., street vendors, coffee sellers, house servants, boat boys, builders of native huts); and (6) *lower,* composed of laborers (e.g., coconut, clove, and other agricultural workers, street sweepers, coconut huskers, porters) (Batson, 1948a, vol. 5). Table 4 reveals that Arabs and Asians monopolized Zanzibar's highest occupational category and constituted more than 85 per cent of the second highest. The most striking feature, however, is the extent to which Asians outstripped Arabs at the top professional levels of Zanzibar society. There can be little doubt that, by 1948, the Asian community was the most economically advantaged of all Zanzibar's racial groups.

This conclusion does not, however, qualify the proposition that Arabs formed Zanzibar's preeminent political stratum. Not only were Asians relatively quiescent politically, but the elite of the Asian community (categories 1 and 2) was concentrated overwhelmingly in the private sector of Zanzibar society, in commerce, industry, and finance. The Arab elite was composed primarily of top-ranking government administrators who functioned at the level of permanent secretary and district commissioner. Moreover, the wealthiest Arab landowners were also a part of the Arab 'political class'.

Table 5: *Access to higher education in Zanzibar by racial community, 1948*

Educational level	Percentage of students				Total number of students
	Arab	Asian	Indigenous Africans	Mainland Africans	
Standards I–VI	39·4	7·8	40·2	21·6	12 205
Standards VII–IX	29·9	41·3	12·8	16·0	1 440
Standards X–XII	31·4	46·8	3·2	18·6	620

The heavy Arab representation on the Legislative Council, on local government bodies, and on various governmental advisory committees was drawn from the landowner group. In contrast with the Asians' fragmented and basically apathetic attitudes toward politics, the Arab elite was a cohesive and assertive political force.

Access to higher education is a major determinant of a society's long-range pattern of social stratification. In this respect, as in landownership and occupational distribution, the differential incorporation of racial and communal groups into the institutional structures of Zanzibar society was highly conspicuous. The extent of this differential incorporation is indicated in table 5 (Batson, 1948a, vol. 10). Though the Asian community formed less than 6 per cent of the total population, almost half of the students at the highest levels of the secondary school system were Asian children. This radical disproportion was a consequence of urban residence, overwhelming preponderance in the clerical, managerial, and commercial sectors of the society, and a pervasive cultural emphasis on education rather than on politics as a vehicle for achieving and maintaining social status. Arab children accounted for nearly a third of the student body in the top three grades of secondary school, a figure almost double the Arab proportion of the total population. The Arabs' relative disadvantage vis-à-vis Asians in no way weakened the political status of the Arab elites. Because of the costs of secondary education, family wealth was a prime determinant of access to the upper grade levels, and nearly all the Arab students in secondary school were children of the oligarchic stratum of the community. Upon matriculation, they formed the intellectual core of the Arab political class, its administrators, journalists, and leaders. Though the number of Arab secondary school graduates was far smaller than the number of Asians, it was always sufficient to make the Arab political class a viable political force.

Though less than one-fourth of the total population, Arab and Asian children constituted well over two-thirds of the student population in the top three grades of Zanzibar's secondary school system. Their proportion was even higher in government secondary schools, since the large number of mainland Africans in Standards X–XII includes children of approximately 2000 Christians who received a high school education in missionary schools. The real character of the Zanzibar school system is to be seen in the position of the Shirazi community. Though constituting approximately three-fifths of the total population, Shirazis accounted for only about 3 per cent of the student body in the highest grades. In sum, Zanzibar's educational system did not function as a vehicle for social mobility through which subordinated racial groups could matriculate to the higher economic levels of the society, but was simply a mechanism by which already overprivileged racial communities were able to reinforce their control of elite socioeconomic status.

Tables 3, 4, and 5 show that Zanzibar's major communal groups were differentiated by economic and social status. Zanzibaris of different races did not share sufficient common occupational or economic interests to create politically meaningful bonds of solidarity across racial lines. The economic estrangement of racial communities extended into most other spheres of life as well. Zanzibar did not possess a network of noncommunal social clubs and voluntary associations. The only voluntary groups in the society which had significant numbers of members were organized along communal, not functional, lines: the Arab Association, the Indian Association, the Shirazi Association, and the African Association. Recreation, sports, and informal social relations were conducted almost wholly within the boundaries of these racial associations and, for this reason, Zanzibaris had little opportunity to establish interpersonal contacts and relationships across communal lines. When modern politics began, race was almost the only meaningful basis on which political organizations could be formed.

Factors of integration: language and religion

Two important aspects of Zanzibar culture, the Swahili language and the Islamic faith, cut across racial boundaries and, to a certain extent, constituted factors of integration among economically differentiated racial communities. Linguistic uniformity was especially characteristic of the Arab and African communities. All Zanzibaris spoke Swahili, and for Arabs and Africans a common version of this language was the first tongue. Although some Arabs spoke Arabic and there were regional dialects of Swahili within the African community, both groups were highly conscious of sharing a single mode of speech. The Asian community, however, was culturally differentiated along linguistic lines. With very few exceptions, members of the Asian community retained Indian languages as their first tongue and used Swahili only as a vehicle of communication with Arabs and Africans. As a result, the Swahili spoken by Asians was inferior and ungrammatical, and Asians could always be distinguished by their mode of speech as well as by their economic and physical characteristics.

The Islamic religion was the most important factor tending toward integration among Zanzibaris, furnishing as it did a powerful impetus toward the formation of political solidarities across racial boundaries. More than 95 per cent of Zanzibar's total population was Muslim, and there was a high degree of religious unity even along denominational lines. Sunni Muslims constituted nearly four-fifths of the total population and almost nine-tenths of all Muslims. Religious commonality, like linguistic commonality, was especially characteristic of the African and Arab communities. Nearly all Africans and the vast majority of Arabs were of the Sunni denomination.

Politically significant patterns of religious differentiation did exist in Zanzibar. Although approximately three-fourths of the Asian community were Muslims, the majority of these were Shia rather than Sunni, and the community was further fragmented by the presence of additional Muslim subgroups and a sharp cleavage between Muslim and non-Muslim. The Arab oligarchy was predominantly Ibadhi rather than Sunni, a division somewhat similar to the difference between Episcopalian and Baptist Protestant denominations, namely, 'high-culture' and 'low-culture' versions of the same faith. Perhaps most important, the mainland African community contained about 2000 Christians who actually represented only a small percentage of all mainlanders, but whose presence led to a widespread, though inaccurate, stereotype of the community as a Christian group. Arab political leaders were able to exploit this stereotype, stigmatizing the mainlanders as the real aliens to Zanzibar since they did not share the Islamic faith of other Zanzibaris.

The basic feature of Zanzibar's religious system, however, was that practically all Zanzibaris were Muslim and viewed a common religion as an important bond. The ubiquity of Islam meant that Zanzibaris shared not only a common theology but the pervasive religious environment that accompanied it. Shared institutions such as mosques, koranic schools, and Muslim charities, and common practices such as holidays, rituals, and ceremonies, were conspicuous symbols of a mutual religious identity.

The social and political values of Islam also contributed to a religious environment conducive to multiracial solidarity. The Koran treats racial diversity as a divine creation and endows it with sacred status as a means through which peoples of different races may come to share close social bonds. Two scriptural passages, frequently called to the attention of Zanzibaris, stress the Prophet's insistence on the divine imperative of harmonious race relations: 'Among his signs is the creation of the heavens and the earth and the diversity of your tongues and complections' (Koran: 30, 31); and, 'Men, we have... divided you into nations and tribes so that you might come to know one another' (Koran: 49, 13). Before the African revolution, Arab political leaders employed these passages in an effort to gain acceptance by Africans and to discredit African political organizations that sought to recruit support on the basis of economic antagonisms toward the Arab community.

The political theory of Islam also enabled Arab leadership to canvass for African acceptance and support. One important koranic passage reads: 'Obey God and His Apostle and those who have authority over you' (Koran: 4, 62). In terms of this passage, deference to established authority was, like racial harmony, a divinely imposed personal obligation. As a historic ruling elite, Arabs were able to derive therefrom a religious basis of legitimacy and to argue that any effort to reverse communal power relations was a violation of divine imperatives. They also argued that loyalty to the sultan was a religiously ordained obligation stemming from the principle of deference. Many Africans who supported Arab-led political groups did so in the firm conviction that this was a religious duty, believing that to support a politically radical African movement was against the sociopolitical teachings of their faith.

Common religion was therefore both consistent with and supportive of the plural pattern of Zanzibar society. By enjoining against racial conflict, and counseling acceptance and deference, it gave added strength to the Arabs' position as a political and economic elite. As Zanzibaris understood their religion, any effort to alter the pattern of stratification or to challenge Arab authority was a violation of religious obligation.

There were thus two basic and contradictory political tendencies in Zanzibar society: a tendency toward political equilibrium and multiracial harmony based upon common adherence to the Islamic faith; and a tendency toward extreme racial conflict stemming from the severe economic differentiation among the races. Islam operated to mute the racial antagonisms inherent in an economically plural society, and its articulated values caused many Africans to support the Arab elite or to refuse association with radical African movements. The racially plural aspect of the economy generated extreme antagonism, however, and accounts for the African community's bitter determination to overthrow the Arab oligarchy and establish an African government.

References

Batson, E. (1948a), *Social Survey of Zanzibar*, vol. 5, 'Occupations'; vol. 10, 'Educational achievements'; vol. 14, 'Land ownership' (Verifax).

Batson, E. (1948b), *Report on Proposals for a Social Survey of Zanzibar*, Government Printer, Zanzibar.

Lofchie, M. F. (1965), *Zanzibar: Background to Revolution*, Princeton.

Prins, A. J. H. (1961), *The Swahili-Speaking Peoples of Zanzibar*, International African Institute, London.

21 *N. Glazer and D. Moynihan,* Beyond the Melting Pot

When we wrote *Beyond the Melting Pot,* the alternatives seemed to lie between assimilation and ethnic group status; they now seem to lie somewhere between ethnic group status and separatism. Earlier assimilation seemed to us the unreal alternative, today it is separatism that holds that status. But unreal unfortunately does not mean impossible. Will makes almost all alternatives possible, even those that are disastrous and that seem sure to guarantee a substantial measure of misery and unhappiness.

We now have as alternatives two models of group relations, which we will name the Northern and the Southern. Both reject a total assimilation in which group reality disappears. In the Southern model, society is divided into two segments, white and black. The line between them is rigidly drawn. Other groups must choose to which segment they belong, even if, as many Southern Jews felt, they do not really want to quite belong to either. Violence is the keynote of relations between the groups. And 'separate but equal' is an ideology if not a reality.

The Northern model is quite different. There are many groups. They differ in wealth, power, occupation, values, but in effect an open society prevails for individuals and for groups. Over time a substantial and rough equalization of wealth and power can be hoped for even if not attained, and each group participates sufficiently in the goods and values and social life of a common society so that all can accept the common society as good and fair. There is competition between groups, as between individuals, but it is muted, and groups compete not through violence but through effectiveness in organization and achievement. Groups and individuals participate in a common society. Individual choice, not law or rigid custom, determines the degree to which any person participates, if at all, in the life of an ethnic group, and assimilation and acculturation proceed at a rate determined in large measure by individuals. This is at any rate the ideal—prejudice and discrimination often force people into closer association with groups than they wish. The Northern model in group relations is perhaps best realized in New York City.

N. Glazer and D. Moynihan, *Beyond the Melting Pot*, M.I.T. Press, 1970, pp. xxiii–xxiv.

We have begun to see the Northern model creep into the South. The politics of the city of Atlanta is now one in which various groups compete, bargain, and come to agreements in a style familiar to us from Northern urban politics. But the Southern style is now being brought into the North. Physically, by immigrants, black and white. Ideologically, by sections of the intelligentsia, black and white. Violence is beginning to play a frightening role in politics.[1] The demand for a rigid line between the races is now raised again, most strongly from the black side, this time. We believe the ethnic pattern offers the best chance for a humane and positive adaptation to group diversity, offering the individual the choice to live as he wishes, rather than forcing him into the pattern of a single 'Americanized' society or into the compartments of a rigidly separated society. The question is, can we still convince the varied groups of the society that this is still the best solution?

All the work of incorporating Negroes, as a group and as individuals, into a common society—economically, culturally, socially, politically—must be pushed as hard as possible. Negroes who want to be part of a common society —and these are still, from all evidence, the large majority, if a quiet one—must be given every aid and encouragement, and must be associated in every common enterprise. It is hard to believe that the genius for compromise and accommodation which has kept this a single city, despite the fact that it was made of minorities, will now fail. But the possibility, in 1970, is a haunting one.

[1] For a description of the Southern model, nothing will serve better than this letter, published in the *New York Times* on December 29, 1969. The writer, Mr Vincent S. Baker, is second vice-president, New York City Branch, NAACP. 'The Convention held in Harlem on the proposed state office building has implications far more important than the building, and the truth about what happened there should be known and remembered. Though the convention chairman, Judge James Watson, tried to be fair, free discussion could not take place in that atmosphere of violence and intimidation. The fact that an effort was made to drag me from the hall, and that my life was twice threatened by speakers on the convention floor without a word of reprimand from convention officials leaves no doubt that anyone wishing to disagree with the hooligan element could do so only at the risk of personal injury or even death [. . .]. The truth is that the Dec. 13–14 Convention, whatever the intention of its planners, was the opening phase of a drive by latter-day Fascists to impose on Harlem a despotic rule for their own power and profit. . . .' New York, Dec. 17, 1969.

Part 3 Institutions

The structure of community relations is often most clearly revealed through institutionalized discrimination, that is, discrimination as part of the economic, political, legal and educational arrangements within a society. Furthermore, such arrangements are frequently justified by reference to racist doctrines about the supposed genetic or cultural inferiority of subordinate minorities regarded as constituting a racially separate group. For sociologists adopting an 'order' perspective on such situations, these revealed inequalities are problematic insofar as they represent obstacles to the eventual integration (whether through absorption or some kind of pluralistic arrangement[1]) of particular minority groups. From a 'conflict' perspective, on the other hand, the inequitable distribution of wealth, power and justice between racial and ethnic groups reflects the substructural realities of domination and exploitation (see Katznelson, Extract 27). The institutional setting is the likely focus of those adopting an 'interactionist' approach. Here the circumstances of discriminatory activity may be seen as the context in which the mutual definitions of dominant and subordinate groups are constructed and reiterated.[2]

Liebow's *Tally's Corner* (Extract 22) is concerned, in his own words, with 'the inside world of the streetcorner Negro man'. By comparing these men's words with their actions an attempt is made to reveal his self-image and explain his responses to lower-class Negro life. With this intention in mind, Liebow goes on to argue that employment represents a key point of fusion between what he calls 'the inside world and the larger society surrounding it'. In the passage included here he attempts to provide insights, based on an interpretation of his own data, into the black man's response to economic discrimination in the United States.

The extract from Daniel's *Racial Discrimination in England* (Extract 23) is part of an account of the extent of racial discrimination based on an extensive study conducted by Political and Economic Planning (1967), a

---

[1] Rose (1969) and Coleman (1966) are illustrative of this approach.
[2] Coard (1971) perhaps comes closest to looking at how an institutional process is used to define a group as inferior. Liebow (Extract 22) may also be considered in the same terms.

report which led to the implementation of the Race Relations Act in 1968. Here the focus is on the question of accommodation in the private sector. The data are immigrants' claimed experiences of discrimination in applying for tenancy, the kind of data which elsewhere Rex and Moore (1969) analyse in terms of competition for scarce resources in an urban setting.

Like the P.E.P. Report, summarized by Daniel, Rose's *Colour and Citizenship* (Extract 24) was aimed at informing and influencing policy-makers, without necessarily challenging the existing social order in Britain. In revealing the special relationship between employment opportunities and social class position of 'coloured' immigrants in Great Britain, the report may be seen as extending a long-established sociological tradition associating social class with economic opportunities (for example, Glass, 1954).

Silberman's *Crisis in Black and White* (Extract 25) deals, in part, with the shifting power relations in American society, showing how the changing racial composition of the major American cities is putting more power into the hands of the urban black man as it hitherto favoured earlier immigrant ethnic groups. Silberman sees this as pushing to a crisis point the resolution of Myrdal's *An American Dilemma* when the American Dream is likely to be put to its ultimate test.

The American racial experience may be seen as historically and structurally distinct from the British situation, resulting in somewhat different black–white responses. Katznelson (1973) has recently pointed out that the white British response is an extension of a colonial tradition. Whatever colonial parallels may be drawn with South Africa, the distinctive policy of the Afrikaans-dominated government there, underpin a recognizably different domination pattern in that society. It is the peculiar South African mix of racial domination taken in conjunction with the process of racial integration which is the theme of Leo Kuper's *An African Bourgeoisie* (Extract 26). Kuper sees *apartheid* in practical terms as 'a policy of integration by means of racial stratification'. He takes 'integration' here to mean 'systematic coordination into a functional whole' of unequal racial units. In other words, the policy of *apartheid* aims at linking race with social role. The opportunity for blacks to affect this particular social policy is examined and is well worth contrasting with the U.S. situation discussed by Silberman.

The ability of blacks in Britain to influence their destinies through officially designated political channels is the central issue addressed by Katznelson. The context of his analysis is recent legislation in the field of race relations. He argues (Extract 27) that the establishment of the Community Relations Commission represents an extension of a classical colonial pattern of social control, 'indirect rule through a broker'. This has had the effect of depoliticizing the race issue, thus enabling Government to avoid making political policy decisions in this area, and hindering the Third World population from integrating within the existing party political structure. This, according to

Katznelson, buys short-term political quiescence at the expense of possible future racial polarization.

Those disenchanted with formal political institutions have sometimes put their faith in 'grass roots' organizations for the ironing out of racial discrimination. Harry Brill's *Why Organizers Fail* (Extract 28) focuses on the difficulties which such movements sometimes encounter. In particular he draws attention to the potential lack of unity among radical movements in what have elsewhere been designated 'open' or 'pluralistic' societies, where the ideological goals of the organizers were neither unified nor necessarily shared by those they set out to assist.

Shibutani and Kwan (Extract 29), in considering the patterns of migration and settlement, pinpoint some of the crucial factors and features of the geographic distribution of various groups as an aspect of ethnic stratification. They argue that 'The spatial distribution of people is seldom the product of deliberate design; after each migration new patterns of settlement develop through competition and natural selection. Once formed, each natural area develops its own universe of discourse, traditions of decency and propriety. The lines may then be enforced by custom and by law'. The manner in which natural resources are allocated, the degree and intensity of rivalry and conflict, the nature of the dominant system of production, the nature and rate of growth of urban industrial areas, the age-structure and the culture of different groups are all considered to be significant factors in the emergence of different settlement patterns among competing ethnic groups. Although they point out that 'ecological processes appear to be modified by law, [and] it should be remembered that such laws are enforced by authorities of the dominant group', it might be thought that Shibutani and Kwan tend to underplay the power which some groups are capable of wielding to impose patterns of residential segregation and restrict the free movement of minorities, as they appear to do so in South Africa and the Soviet Union.

The effects of institutionalized poverty on the differential distribution of residential groups is also underemphasized by Shibutani and Kwan, but highlighted by Lee Rainwater's sensitive account of the Pruitt-Igoe black community in *Behind Ghetto Walls* (Extract 30). The effects of limited resources and large families in holding American blacks imprisoned inside the ghetto and their 'pathological' consequences are systematically spelled out.

Much work has been done in recent years to show how, in a multi-racial society, even one formally committed to equality of educational opportunity as is the United States, black pupils all too often find themselves at the bottom of the educational heap, and confined within schools which are either formally or informally segregated. In this way the educational system has acted to reinforce inequalities between the races. But that 'desegregation' has not led inevitably to 'integration' is the burden of Thomas Pettigrew's paper (Extract 31). The desegregated school may take a variety of forms, and some may go little or no way towards altering patterns of domination and subordination maintained by more obviously discriminatory educational systems. Pettigrew's contribution to the debate raises the fundamental question of how far the school can affect wider patterns of inequality established over time within a particular community. In Pettigrew's own words, 'the racial implications of the Coleman Report [on educational opportunity in the United States, 1966] for both Negro and white children requires socially and radically integrated, not merely desegregated schools'. The implication is that this is a necessary rather than a sufficient condition for educational equality.

One response to revealed educational inequality between the races in America was to define cultural minorities, along with working-class whites, as 'culturally deprived'. The Poverty Program of the late 1960s in the U.S. was aimed in part at compensating children educationally through such schemes as Head Start. Murray and Rosalie Wax (Extract 32) examined such a scheme among American Indians and concluded that the ideology of cultural deprivation leads to deplorably fallacious characterizations of Indian life and is frequently used as a legitimation for attempting to replace Indian with white culture—with less than remarkable results.

The constraints and ill-effects of a white-dominated education system upon the West Indian child in Britain is the subject of a recent book by Bernard Coard (1971). Little, Mabey and Whitaker (Extract 33), however, strike a comparatively optimistic note from a less radical point of view. Their analysis of the achievement profile of children from the West Indies, India, Pakistan and Cyprus in London schools suggests that scholastic performance improves with length of time spent in the British school system. Christopher Bagley (Extract 34) shows how a subsequent press report of this piece of research distorted the findings, and offers his own interpretation of the situation by reference to the race relations literature.

Pettigrew and Wax and Wax have one thing in common—they argue, either explicitly or by implication, that 'liberal' educational policies are not enough; what is further required is a mode of implementing such policies so as to ensure that the ideologies of teachers and the forms of school organization do not reflect and reinforce wider patterns of dominance and subordination. Such an argument has implications which not only strike at the central principles on which education is organized (distribution of resources, modes of selection of pupils and methods of training teachers as well as curriculum content) in a multi-racial society, but also at the central principles on which society itself is organized.

Attitudes towards intermarriage between human groups often reflect patterns of dominance within a system of ethnic stratification. Simpson and Yingers' (Extract 35) overview of a wide range of sociological literature in their *Racial and Cultural Minorities*, considers its nature and incidence both in the United States and other countries. They consider its legal aspects and how sexual segregation between groups is rationalized as well as its consequences, and conclude that intermarriage on a large scale would produce a relatively homogeneous population, physically and culturally. The elimination of intergroup conflicts based on race and culture would have societal advantages, although some would lament the passing of cultural pluralism. One might add that some would also lament the passing of racial and ethnic stratification working to their own advantage.

References

Coard, B. (1971), *How the West Indian Child is made Educationally Subnormal in the British School System*, London.
Coleman, J. S. (1966), *Equality of Educational Opportunity*, Washington.
Glass, D. (1954), *Social Mobility in Britain*, London.
Katznelson, I. (1973), *Black Men, White Cities*, Oxford.
Political and Economic Planning (1967), *Report on Racial Discrimination*, London.
Rex, J. and Moore, R. (1969), *Race and Community Conflict*, Oxford.
Rose, E. B. (1969), *Colour and Citizenship*, Oxford.

22 *Elliot Liebow,* Tally's Corner

This study has been primarily concerned with the inside world of the street-corner Negro man, the world of daily, face-to-face relationships with wives, children, friends, lovers, kinsmen and neighbors. An attempt was made to see the man as he sees himself, to compare what he says with what he does, and to explain his behavior as a direct response to the conditions of lower-class Negro life rather than as mute compliance with historical or cultural imperatives.[1]

This inside world does not appear as a self-contained, self-generating, self-sustaining system or even subsystem with clear boundaries marking it off from the larger world around it. It is in continuous, intimate contact with the larger society—indeed, is an integral part of it—and is no more impervious to the values, sentiments and beliefs of the larger society than it is to the blue welfare checks or to the agents of the larger society, such as the policeman, the police informer, the case worker, the landlord, the dope pusher, the Tupperware demonstrator, the numbers backer or the anthropologist.

One of the major points of articulation between the inside world and the larger society surrounding it is in the area of employment. The way in which, the man makes a living and the kind of living he makes have important consequences for how the man sees himself and is seen by others; and these, in turn, importantly shape his relationships with family members, lovers, friends and neighbors.

Making a living takes on an overriding importance at marriage. The young lower-class Negro gets married in his early twenties, at approximately the same time and in part for the same reason as his white or Negro working- or middle-class counterpart. He has no special motive for getting married; sex

[1] There is, fortunately, a growing suspicion that 'culture' and 'historical continuity' may not be the most useful constructs for dealing with lower-class behavior. Hylan Lewis (1963, p. 43), for example, suggests that 'It is probably more fruitful to think of lower class families reacting in various ways to the facts of their position and to relative isolation rather than to the imperatives of a lower class culture.'

Elliot Liebow, *Tally's Corner*, Little, Brown and Co., 1967, extracts from pp. 208–14, 219–22, 230–1.

is there for the taking, with or without marriage, and he can also live with a woman or have children—if he has not done this already—without getting married. He wants to be publicly, legally married, to support a family and be the head of it, because this is what it is to be a man in our society, whether one lives in a room near the Carry-out or in an elegant house in the suburbs.

Although he wants to get married, he hedges on his commitment from the very beginning because he is afraid, not of marriage itself, but of his own ability to carry out his responsibilities as husband and father. His own father failed and had to 'cut out', and the men he knows who have been or are married have also failed or are in the process of doing so. He has no evidence that he will fare better than they and much evidence that he will not. However far he has gone in school he is illiterate or almost so; however many jobs he has had or hard he has worked, he is essentially unskilled.[2] Armed with models who have failed, convinced of his own worthlessness, illiterate and unskilled, he enters marriage and the job market with the smell of failure all around him. Jobs are only intermittently available. They are almost always menial, sometimes hard, and never pay enough to support a family.

In general, the menial job lies outside the job hierarchy and promises to offer no more tomorrow than it does today. The Negro menial worker remains a menial worker so that, after one or two or three years of marriage and as many children, the man who could not support his family from the very beginning is even less able to support it as time goes on. The longer he works, the longer he is unable to live on what he makes. He has little vested interest in such a job and learns to treat it with the same contempt held for it by the employer and society at large. From his point of view, the job is expendable; from the employer's point of view, he is. For reasons real or imagined, perhaps so slight as to go unnoticed by others, he frequently quits or is fired. Other times, he is jobless simply because he cannot find a job.

He carries this failure home where his family life is undergoing a parallel deterioration. His wife's adult male models also failed as husbands and fathers and she expects no less from him. She hopes but does not expect him to be a good provider, to make of them a family and be head of it, to be 'the man of the house'. But his failure to do these things does not make him easier to live with because it was expected. She keys her demands to her wants, to her hopes, not to her expectations. Her demands mirror the man both as society says he should be and as he really is, enlarging his failure in both their eyes.

Sometimes he sits down and cries at the humiliation of it all. Sometimes he strikes out at her or the children with his fists, perhaps to lay hollow claim to being man of the house in the one way left open to him, or perhaps simply

[2] And he is black. Together, these make a deadly combination and relegate him to the very bottom of our society.

to inflict pain on this woman who bears witness to his failure as a husband and father and therefore as a man. Increasingly he turns to the streetcorner where a shadow system of values constructed out of public fictions serves to accommodate just such men as he, permitting them to be men once again provided they do not look too closely at one another's credentials.[3]

At the moment his streetcorner relationships take precedence over his wife and children he comes into his full inheritance bequeathed him by his parents, teachers, employers and society at large. This is the step into failure from which few if any return, and it is at this point that the rest of society can wring its hands or rejoice in the certain knowledge that he has ended up precisely as they had predicted he would.

The streetcorner is, among other things, a sanctuary for those who can no longer endure the experience or prospect of failure. There, on the streetcorner, public fictions support a system of values which, together with the value system of society at large, make for a world of ambivalence, contradiction and paradox, where failures are rationalized into phantom successes and weaknesses magically transformed into strengths. On the streetcorner, the man chooses to forget [. . .].

Whether the world of the lower-class Negro should be seen as a distinctive subculture or as an integral part of the larger society (at the bottom of it, perhaps, but as much a part of it as those in the middle or on top) is much more than an academic question and has important consequences for 'intervention'. Marriage among lower-class Negroes, for example, has been described as 'serial monogamy', a pattern in which the woman of childbearing age has a succession of mates during her procreative years. The label 'serial monogamy' clearly has a cultural referent, deriving as it does from the traditional nomenclature used to designate culturally distinctive patterns of marriage, such as polygyny, polyandry, monogamy, and so on. 'Serial monogamy', then, as against the unqualified monogamous ideal of American

---

[3] This 'shadow system' of values is very close to Rodman's (1963, p. 209) 'value stretch'. Members of the lower class, he says, 'share the general values of the society with members of other classes, but in addition they have stretched these values, or developed alternative values, which help them adjust to their deprived circumstances'.

I would add at least two qualifications to Rodman's and other formulations that posit an alternate system of lower-class values. The first is that the stretched or alternative value systems are not the same order of values, either phenomenologically or operationally, as the parent or general system of values: they are derivative, subsidiary in nature, thinner and less weighty, less completely internalized, and seem to be value images reflected by forced or adaptive behavior rather than real values with a positive determining influence on behavior of choice. The second qualification is that the alternative value system is not a distinct value system which can be separately invoked by its users. It appears only in association with the parent system and is separable from it only analytically. Derivative, insubstantial, and co-occurring with the parent system, it is as if the alternative value system is a shadow cast by the common value system in the distorting lower-class setting. Together, the two systems lie behind much that seems paradoxical and inconsistent, familiar and alien, to the middle-class observer from his one-system perspective.

society at large, refers to and *is used as evidence for* the cultural separateness and distinctiveness of the urban, lower-class Negro.

When these same phenomena are examined directly in the larger context of American life, both 'serial monogamy' and cultural distinctiveness tend to disappear. In their place is the same pattern of monogamous marriage found elsewhere in our society but one that is characterized by failure. The woman does not have a simple 'succession of mates during her procreative years'. She has a husband and he a wife, and their hopes and their intentions—if not their expectations—are that this will be a durable, permanent union. More often, however, it is their fears rather than their hopes which materialize. The marriage fails and they part, he to become one of a 'succession of mates' taken by another woman whose husband has left her, and she to accept one or more men. While these secondary and subsequent liaisons are, for the most part, somewhat pale reflections of the formal marriage relationship, each is modeled after it and fails for much the same reasons as does marriage itself. From this perspective, then, the succession of mates which characterizes marriage among lower-class Negroes does not constitute a distinctive cultural pattern 'with an integrity of its own'. It is rather the cultural model of the larger society as seen through the prism of repeated failure. Indeed, it might be more profitable—again, especially for those concerned with changing it— to look on marriage here as a succession of failures rather than as a succession of mates.[4]

In summary, what is challenged here is not that the marriage pattern among urban low-income Negroes does not involve a 'succession of mates' but the implication that this succession of mates constitutes prima facie evidence for the cultural distinctiveness of those to whom it is attributed. [. . .] From this perspective, the streetcorner man does not appear as a carrier of an independent cultural tradition. His behavior appears not so much as a way of realizing the distinctive goals and values of his own sub-culture, or of conforming to its models, but rather as his way of trying to achieve many of the goals and values of the larger society, of failing to do this, and of concealing his failure from others and from himself as best he can.[5]

If, in the course of concealing his failure, or of concealing his fear of even trying, he pretends—through the device of public fictions—that he did not want these things in the first place and claims that he has all along been responding to a different set of rules and prizes, we do not do him or ourselves any good by accepting this claim at face value.

Such a frame of reference, I believe, can bring into clearer focus the

[4] 'It is important that we not confuse basic life chances and actual behavior with basic cultural values and preferences. . . . The focus of efforts to change should be on background conditions and on precipitants of the deviant behaviors rather than on presumably different class or cultural values' (Lewis, 1963, p. 43).

[5] '. . . concealment and ego-protection are of the essence of social intercourse' (Hughes, 1958, p. 43).

practical points of leverage for social change in this area. We do not have to see the problem in terms of breaking into a puncture proof circle, of trying to change values, of disrupting the lines of communication between parent and child so that parents cannot make children in their own image, thereby transmitting their culture inexorably, ad infinitum. No doubt, each generation does provide role models for each succeeding one. Of much greater importance for the possibilities of change, however, is the fact that many similarities between the lower-class Negro father and son (or mother and daughter) do not result from 'cultural transmission' but from the fact that the son goes out and independently experiences the same failures, in the same areas, and for much the same reasons as his father. What appears as a dynamic, self-sustaining cultural process is, in part at least, a relatively simple piece of social machinery which turns out, in rather mechanical fashion, independently produced look-alikes. The problem is how to change the conditions which, by guaranteeing a failure, cause the son to be made in the image of the father.

Taking this viewpoint does not reduce the magnitude of the problem but does serve to place it in the more tractable context of economics, politics and social welfare. It suggests that poverty is, indeed, a proper target in the attempt to bring lower-class Negroes 'into the mainstream of American life', and it supports the long line of social scientists, from E. Franklin Frazier and Gunnar Myrdal down through Kenneth Clark and Richard Cloward, in seeing the inability of the Negro man to earn a living and support his family as the central fact of lower-class Negro life. If there is to be a change in this way of life, this central fact must be changed; the Negro man, along with everyone else, must be given the skills to earn a living and an opportunity to put these skills to work.

No one pretends that this is an easy matter, to be accomplished at one fell stroke. For many Negro men, jobs alone are no longer enough. Before he can earn a living, he must believe that he can do so, and his women and children must learn to believe this along with him. But he finds it difficult to begin without their support, and they find it difficult to give their support until he begins. The beginning, then, will doubtless be a slow one, but, once started, success will feed on itself just as failure has done.[6] A beginning must be made, however, and it must be made simultaneously at all points in the life cycle. Children and young people must have good schools and good teachers who can give them the skills and the training to compete for jobs and careers, and they must have teachers who believe in them and help them believe in themselves. Jobs that pay enough to support a family must be opened up to

[6] 'Feed upon one another' suggests the model of 'the vicious circle'—the model which served as Gunnar Myrdal's main explanatory scheme for analyzing the Negro problem in the U.S. In Myrdal (1944, pp. 1065ff), the model of the vicious circle—refined as the Principal of Accumulation—is treated in detail. 'The theory of the vicious circle is a cause rather for optimism than pessimism. The cumulative principle *works both ways*.' (Emphasis added.)

the adult generation so that they can support their families, so that the young people can see the changed reality, so that young and old can experience it and gain a vested interest in the world they live in.[7] [. . .]

In a sense, we have already forfeited the power to initiate action in this area. The moral initiative has long passed over to Negroes and political initiative seems to be moving in that direction, too. This may be a disquieting, even fearful development to some segments of our society. In the long run, however, the sooner and the more effectively Negroes organize to promote their own self-interests, just as other ethnic and religious groups and the working class have done before them, the sooner and more effectively we can get on to other problems standing in the way of building a democratic society.

Since the great power lies with the white middle class, great decisions have to be made as to how this power is to be used in responding to action and demands initiated by the Negro masses and articulated by their leaders. Most of the time, the great federal power will best be used in direct support of the actionists. On some occasions, such as the outbreak at Watts, restraint will be the most judicious if difficult use of that great power.

In searching for guidelines to help us shape our responses, we would do well to keep in mind W. H. Auden's admonition to twentieth century man: 'We must love one another or die'.

Perhaps this is too much to ask of ourselves and others. Perhaps it will be enough if we just act as if we do.

References

Hughes, E. C. (1958), *Men and Their Work*, Glencoe, Ill.

Lewis, H. (1963), 'Culture, class and behavior of low income families', paper prepared for Conference on Views of Lower-class Culture, June 27–29, New York.

Rodman, H. (1963), 'The lower-class value stretch', *S.F.*, vol. XLII, no. 2, pp. 205–15.

Myrdal, G. (1944), *An American Dilemma*, New York.

---

[7] For some adults, perhaps many, it will be too late, but we will not know for which ones until it is tried for all. Those for whom it is too late should be bought off, with cash or sinecures, in much the same way and for much the same reasons as the Germans pay reparations to survivors of the Nazi persecutions or as we pay reparations to Japanese Americans disenfranchised, unpropertied, and interned during the war, or as our society sometimes indemnifies men wrongly imprisoned. It is a very small price to pay for their cooperation or neutrality, and there is comfort to be gained from the fact that, in this way, we may not have to buy off generation after generation as we do under our present welfare programs.

23 *W. W. Daniel,* Racial Discrimination in England

Private Letting

'No coloureds'; 'Sorry, no coloureds', 'Europeans only'. Such stipulations vie in frequency with 'no animals' or 'no pets' on cards advertising rented accommodation in newsagents' windows.

The fact that much private rented accommodation is not open to immigrants is obvious to anyone who reads the small advertisements in newspapers or on notice boards. The Milner-Holland Report on housing in London estimated that only 11 per cent of private lettings are both publicly advertised and do not specifically exclude coloured people.

We describe here what happened when we sent white and coloured applicants to seek this small minority of flats which did not exclude coloured people in advance. We recount the reasons landlords gave for refusing coloured people. We describe what happened when we sent out applicants to accommodation bureaux and estate agents and recount the explanations that they in turn offered for both their own behaviour and landlords' behaviour. Finally we show how coloured people were affected by the massive discrimination in this sector of housing, the types of people most severely affected by it and the ways the others avoided it.

First, then, we describe the findings of tests and follow-up interviews carried out with landlords, estate agents and accommodation bureaux. In general the procedure for the tests was as follows.

A West Indian, a white immigrant from Hungary and a white English tester applied for accommodation from landlords in each of the six Areas. In half their applications they adopted professional roles with appropriate levels of income and seeking appropriate accommodation (the West Indian was a hospital registrar, the Hungarian an accountant and the Englishman a school-teacher). In the other half they adopted working-class roles (the West Indian a bus conductor, the Hungarian a van driver, and the Englishman a builder's labourer). Similar teams also went to inquire about accommodation from estate agents and accommodation bureaux. Subsequently we talked to the landlords and staffs of both the accommodation bureaux and the estate agencies tested.

W. W. Daniel, *Racial Discrimination in England*, Penguin, 1969, pp. 154–69.

The applications to landlords showed that the West Indian was discriminated against two thirds of the time when flats which did not exclude him in advance were tested in practice. The Hungarian, on the other hand, experienced comparatively little discrimination.

Sixty landlords were approached in person and 120 by telephone.

In approaching landlords the testers obtained contacts through advertisements in the local newspaper or from notice boards, ignoring those advertisements that stipulated 'no coloureds' or 'Europeans only'. As the summary of their experiences in Table 1 shows, out of a total of sixty applications made in person the West Indian was offered accommodation on the same terms as the Hungarian and Englishman only fifteen times. On the other forty-five occasions some form of discrimination occurred.

Table 1: *Results of personal applications to landlords (60 applications)*

Occasions when discrimination occurred	45
Occasions when all three applicants were given similar information	15
	—
	60
Types of discrimination (45 occasions)	
West Indian told accommodation taken; both other applicants told it was vacant	38
West Indian asked for higher rent than both other applicants	4
West Indian and Hungarian told accommodation taken; Englishman told it was vacant	2
West Indian and Hungarian asked for higher rent than Englishman	1
	—
	45

Such discrimination was in most cases covert in the sense that the West Indian was just told that the accommodation had gone when it had not. On occasion, however, he had the door slammed in his face and once he was told 'get your black arse off my doorstep'.

The table does not include the occasions among the fifteen, otherwise non-discriminatory, when the Englishman was given such encouragement as 'Come round quickly, I've got a West Indian coming at 7 p.m., so get here by 6.30'.

The summary of experiences outlined in Table 2 shows that landlords' reactions when they were approached by telephone were very similar to those when they were approached in person. With the telephone applications it would of course have been possible for discrimination to have occurred at a later stage in the application even in those cases where it did not appear to occur at the initial telephone contact. This doubtless accounts for the fact that the West Indian experienced discrimination on three quarters of the occasions where he was making personal contacts but on only 74 of the 120 occasions when he was making telephone contacts. The figures combined show that the West Indian experienced discrimination in two thirds of his total of 180 applications to landlords whose advertisements did not specifically exclude him in advance.

Table 2: *Results of telephone applications to landlords (120 applications)*

Occasions when discrimination occurred	74
Occasions when all three applicants were given similar information	46
	120
Types of discrimination (74 occasions)	
West Indian told accommodation taken; both other applicants told it was vacant	50
West Indian asked for higher rent than both other applicants	5
West Indian and Hungarian told accommodation taken; Englishman told it was vacant	13
West Indian told rent 'monthly in advance'; both other applicants told 'weekly'	6
	74

From these findings emerges a picture of the types of experience that a West Indian moving into one of the Areas of our study can expect if he wants to rent a flat. Ignoring both those flats that are not advertised and those advertisements that exclude him by stating 'no coloureds', he can expect discrimination in about two thirds of his applications. Normally this will mean that the accommodation will be refused him altogether. But even on some of the occasions when he is not refused he can expect to be charged a higher rent: 'The advertised figure was a misprint. You know what newspapers are.' He can expect discrimination whether he is a bus conductor or a hospital registrar because there were no significant differences according to the type of role the tester occupied. Moreover, there was a remarkable similarity between the pattern of the results in the six Areas. Occasionally he will be met by brutal insults and, not infrequently, he will meet hostility and unpleasantness. Some explanation of why he would meet such receptions emerged from the interviews with landlords who had discriminated which we made following the tests. These interviews were designed to elicit the reasons for the discriminatory behaviour. A few landlords provided such reasons, of which the following were typical:

I've nothing against them but you've got to think of the neighbourhood. Nobody wants this to become little Jamaica, do they?

Well they aren't very clean and also they're noisy. All their friends come round. I don't think it's good for the children either to have them around.

I discussed this with my wife. She said she doesn't go for them much and anyway it would look bad with the neighbours. And, come to think of it, give me a good reason why we should?

This isn't that sort of neighbourhood.

This is a quiet house and they're too noisy.

It's in our lease that we can't sub-let to them.

They cause trouble, don't they?

Although only a minority gave their reasons, the responses of all the landlords interviewed confirmed that they had discriminated.

Further confirmation of the nature and extent of discrimination in private letting was provided by similar tests and follow-up interviews with staff of accommodation bureaux and estate agents. Each of the three applicants approached eighteen accommodation bureaux and thirty estate agents in all. The receptions they were given are summarized in Tables 3 and 4. The West Indian experienced discrimination at almost three quarters of the accommodation bureaux. Discrimination occurred at two thirds of the estate agents,

Table 3: *Results of personal inquiries at accommodation bureaux (18 inquiries)*

Occasions when discrimination occurred	14
Occasions when all three inquirers given similar information	4
	—
	18
Types of discrimination (14 occasions)	
West Indian offered nothing; Englishman and Hungarian given addresses	6
West Indian offered fewer addresses than both Englishman and Hungarian	3
West Indian refused; Englishman and Hungarian put on mailing list	4
'We do not let to non-English'	1
	—
	14

Table 4: *Results of personal inquiries at estate agents for accommodation to let (30 enquiries)*

Occasions when discrimination occurred	20
Occasions when all three inquirers given similar information	10
	—
	30
Types of discrimination (20 occasions)	
West Indian offered nothing; Englishman and Hungarian given addresses	5
West Indian offered fewer addresses than Englishman and Hungarian	3
West Indian refused; Englishman and Hungarian put on mailing list or encouraged to call back	11
'We do not let to coloureds'	1
	—
	20

although the position here was complicated by the fact that the agents had so little accommodation of the type testers were seeking, which, in the case of the agents, was unfurnished. A more complete picture of the extent of discrimination, the types of accommodation it affected most severely, and the reasons for discrimination emerged from the interviews with bureaux and agency staff, following the tests.

Nine times out of ten you can't do a thing for them. You can't help them and never will be able to. It's a waste of time to take down details of what they want when you know perfectly well their card will sit on your desk for months. I think it's better to be frank with them, otherwise you build up their hopes. Of course it's difficult for them to realize that you yourself aren't prejudiced. Let's face it, I'd like to fix everyone up. I make more money that way and it's no skin off my nose what colour they are.

The manager of a bureau in the North who had previously worked in London made this comment:

I used to work in a bureau in London and about three quarters of the property we handled was marked in our files as 'Whites Only'. That was four years ago and I think perhaps it's got worse. Up here there are fewer coloured people and most landlords haven't had experience of them. For this reason not so many properties are specifically marked as not being for coloureds. Still, if you send a coloured person around, the landlords go berserk. The phone never stops. They may not actually tell you not to send coloured people—they just assume you won't. They certainly never expect them.

Everyone we talked to agreed that difficulties were most severe with unfurnished accommodation or statutory tenancies. Some went so far as to say that the accommodation of this type which passed through their hands was almost altogether closed to coloured people:

Once they're in, they're there for ever. Landlords are worried about overcrowding. Also they are under pressure from their neighbours—people don't want coloured people living in their street, let alone their own building. As soon as one house or flat is let to coloured people, it's looked on as the first hole in the dyke. People think it's only a matter of time before the area becomes a slum. For this reason I'd say it's virtually impossible to get an unfurnished flat for, say, a Jamaican or a Pakistani.

There was, moreover, general agreement that the situation was becoming worse.

The consensus of opinion from agents' and bureaux' staff, then, was that they only very infrequently had an unfurnished flat on their books which they could offer to a coloured person. The proportion of furnished accommodation that did not specifically exclude coloured people was higher, but still less than 30 per cent.

In the light of these interviews, the fact that the estate agents and accommodation bureaux did not discriminate against the West Indians in over a quarter of the tests needs some explanation. Part of the cause lies in the type of accommodation testers were seeking. It had been apparent from the pilot survey that if the testers were to get any results at all they would have to apply for single accommodation, or at most, accommodation for a married couple. Consequently on those occasions when informants had been given similar details it was normally one or two bed-sitters which bureaux or agents had 'on their hands' at the time of application. This was confirmed by follow-up interviews with those agents and bureaux who had not discriminated. In each case their assessment was similar to that of those that had:

It's only rarely that we can offer something. There are certain streets where coloured people have a foothold and it's sometimes possible to get them something there. But if we do ever have something to offer, say, a Jamaican he should count himself particularly lucky. He's one in a hundred.

The bureaux staffs found their own position in all this very invidious. They were faced with substantial numbers of coloured applicants. Their estimates suggested that, in the South, between 10 and 15 per cent of all people seeking accommodation through bureaux are coloured. In the Areas in the North and the Midlands, bureaux said that 'just less than 10 per cent' of applicants were coloured: this was thought to be a 'slight increase' on five years ago. But the agents and bureaux were rarely able to offer the coloured applicants anything. They stressed, however, that they played a passive role in the process, being the landlords' agents and not free agents:

We ourselves have no reason to discriminate. Our business is to sell or to let property. That's how we make our money and naturally enough we'd like to be able to satisfy everyone who comes in. But we are governed by the specific wishes of the people whose property we handle. If a landlord doesn't want coloured tenants and we send one along, it isn't going to make him change his mind. All it's going to do is lose us business.

Nevertheless, because of their assessment of the low possibility of obtaining any accommodation for coloured people, they agreed that they were inclined to 'pay less attention' to them or 'be short' with them:

If you chat with them, you get all their friends in—even if you can't place them. They come in droves, you've no idea. It sounds a bit brutal, I know, but you've got to be short with them otherwise you never get a moment's peace.

I remember when I first started here. It used to really upset me that I couldn't help them. Many of them really were sweet and I used to worry about it. Then I realized that I couldn't change the world. Now I'm fairly brisk with them. This doesn't mean I don't care. It means I know I can't help them so there's no point in wasting time.

Moreover, there were cases in which the agents themselves had to make decisions about the suitability of a coloured applicant:

You have to ask yourself various questions. Can they pay? Will they wreck the place? Will they run up bills and then do a moonlight? Will they cause trouble with the neighbours? You have to ask these questions no matter who the potential tenant is. Any estate agent will tell you of his experiences in this field. On these standards, very few coloured immigrants are suitable. I know it's unfair to say they all create problems but a very high proportion of them do and you learn to be cautious.

Again, agents were under pressure from sources other than landlords. They mentioned that it was not unusual for members of the public to come into their office and ask them not to let property they were handling to coloured people:

On more than one occasion I've had someone come in to me and tell me that she lives down the street from a property I'm handling and would I please on no account let it to a coloured person as she and her neighbours want the area kept nice. I wouldn't say this sort of thing happens a lot but it happens.

These factors, combined with their assessments of the extent of discrimination, led the agents to make assumptions about whether or not their clients would accept coloured people:

It's a mistake you soon stop making. After a few people have bawled you out for sending a coloured chap along to look at the flat, you learn to check up first and ask whether they will take coloureds. You don't have to guess the answer. They just assume that you won't send them coloureds. You soon get to know the score.

Agents' assessments of the reasons why both landlords and neighbours or other tenants resisted the idea of coloured tenants were typically as follows:

The most important one is that people fear that surrounding property will lose its value, that the area will degenerate and become a slum. Also there's the worry of overcrowding and the question of noise. Also so many people are convinced that coloured people are dirty and don't wash. They don't like the idea of their kids mixing. On top of this there is the point that many coloured people won't or can't adapt to our way of life and I think we expect that they should. If they were more like us, less strange, then people wouldn't be so worried about them. There are two sides to it.

The accounts of both landlords and their agents show that two main justifications are put forward for discriminating against coloured people in private letting. They are directly parallel to those which were put forward in the employment sector. The first is that coloured people are unacceptable as neighbours to many white people and consequently letting property to them is resisted by other tenants in a block of flats or people in neighbouring property. The second is that, landlords allege, coloured people in general are inferior as tenants to white people. They cannot be relied upon to pay their rent, look after their flat properly or fulfil the requirements of their tenancy.

The information we collected permits us to make the following comments on these points. As far as resistance from neighbours is concerned there is no reason to doubt that some white people would be initially reluctant to accept coloured people as neighbours. As far as the inferiority of coloured people as tenants is concerned we have no way of measuring whether the charges made against coloured people are true of a majority or even of a minority. Two points can, however, be made with certainty.

The first is that from our interviews with immigrants it is clear that the groups of people for whom many of the charges are most likely to be true are least likely, in fact, to apply for a flat from a white landlord. That is to say, the findings of the survey, [. . .], showed that many coloured people (in the case of Asians nearly three quarters) had never applied for a flat from a white landlord who was a stranger. Most common among such people were Asians, the most recent arrivals, people at low occupational levels before coming to Britain and people with no educational qualifications.

Consequently those people most likely to have at least some of the characteristics that landlords attributed to all coloured people, particularly for instance an alien culture involving different methods and standards of hygiene which might appear 'dirty' by normal English standards, are just the people who are unlikely to be seeking houses from them. It is those less likely to have such characteristics who apply and suffer because landlords assume they do have them.

The second point which we can make with certainty is that the characteristics landlords attach to coloured people are developed and extended to all coloured people, whatever their history, occupation, income and personality, so that the coloured person no different from a white person in any way other than his colour suffers severely. Colour prejudice and the discrimination that follows from it operate in a blanket, indiscriminating way and there is no attempt to distinguish between coloured people. Consequently the educated, professional coloured person who is fully familiar with every aspect of British life is often treated in exactly the same way as the most recently arrived peasant immigrant. This point is particularly illustrated by two of the findings from the tests.

There was no less discrimination against the West Indian when he was applying for accommodation in a professional, educated role, as a hospital registrar, than when he was applying as a bus conductor. Indeed the only difference appeared to be that in his professional role he tended to be treated with more hostility than in his working-class role. Colour was being used by the discriminators as the sole criterion for evaluating the West Indian. That it was colour rather than 'foreignness' is demonstrated by the experience of the Hungarian. In both professional and manual working roles he experienced minimal discrimination, compared to the West Indian.

Here, however, there is a nice distinction which again emphasizes the importance of colour. In personal applications to landlords the West Indian's experience of discrimination compared to that of the Hungarian was in the ratio 15:1. In telephone applications it was in the ratio 6:1. This provides some indication of the reassurance the sight of a white face accompanying a slightly foreign accent brings to landlords. The West Indian was discriminated against more when he was seen (in personal applications) than when he was only heard (in telephone applications). On the other hand the Hungarian was discriminated against more when he was only heard than when he was seen. This finding emphasizes the point made when introducing the findings of telephone inquiries that the West Indian might have found further discrimination, following his initial inquiry, had he appeared in person.

The extent of the differences between the West Indian and the Hungarian in all housing tests (including the ones on purchase described in the next chapter) are in marked contrast to those in employment tests. Here the West Indian's experience of discrimination compared to that of the Hungarian was in the ratio 2:1.

This does suggest that colour, as a factor on its own, is more important in letting someone accommodation than in taking him on as an employee at a low level.

The tests and follow-up interviews, then, show massive discrimination in private letting, based solely upon colour. In view of this the main sources of interest in the interviews with immigrants lie in the impact which such discrimination has upon them, the types of people most severely affected and the way they cope with the discrimination.

The findings on the proportion of people in each group who claimed personal experience of discrimination are extracted from a sequence of questioning similar to that on experiences in employment. Informants were questioned on their beliefs about discrimination, whether those beliefs were based on personal experience or knowledge of other people's experience and, if only on other people's experience, why they thought they themselves had avoided it. Moreover, if they had said they were unsure about discrimination or did not think it occurred, then they were asked if they had ever applied for accommodation to a white landlord who was a stranger. The summary, composite findings of this sequence of questions, is presented in Table 5.

The chief feature of these findings is the way in which many of the informants, and in the cases of Pakistanis and Indians the large majority (72 and 71 per cent respectively), had never been in a position to be discriminated against. They had always applied where they knew they would be accepted, or they had always lived with friends or relations, and they had certainly never applied to a white landlord who was a complete stranger. Consequently they had never been exposed to the possibility of discrimination.

The percentage of those who had had 'no exposure to the possibility of discrimination' is calculated from

1. Those who had said that they knew of discrimination from the experiences of others but had avoided it themselves by applying only where they knew they were acceptable.

2. Those who did not know of discrimination but said they had never applied to a white landlord who was a stranger.

By excluding those who are known never to have been in a position to experience discrimination it is possible to calculate more realistic figures on the extent to which discrimination is perceived by the individuals who are discriminated against. This involves expressing the number who had perceived personal experiences of discrimination as a percentage of those who

Table 5: *Immigrants claimed experience of discrimination in private letting (composite table—all informants)*

	Total	West Indians	Paki- stanis	Indians	Cyp- riots
No. of informants	974	540	217	118	99
Weighted base for percentages	1,720	851	492	219	158
	%	%	%	%	%
Personal experience of discrimination claimed and evidence produced	26	39	15	19	8
No exposure to the possibility of discrimination through having only applied to places where known to be acceptable	53	40	72	71	25
Belief in existence of discrimination through knowledge of the experience of others—avoided discrimination personally through personal or racial characteristics or 'luck'	5	5	1	3	16
Belief in existence among others—no real reason given for having avoided it personally	9	12	4	3	25
Others: i.e. not sure about source of belief in discrimination, or not sure about type of accommodation applied for or no belief in discrimination while having applied to white landlord	7	4	8	4	26
	100	100	100	100	100

could ever possibly have been in a position to experience discrimination. The result of this calculation is as follows:

People having perceived personal experiences of discrimination as a percentage of those who could have been exposed to the possibility of discrimination	
West Indians	65 per cent
Pakistanis	54 per cent
Indians	66 per cent
Cypriots	11 per cent

These figures are more in line with what might have been expected in view of the findings of the tests. Two thirds of the Indians and West Indians who had sought privately rented accommodation on the open market claimed personal experience of discrimination, and over half the Pakistanis. In assessing these figures, it is necessary to remember that, as the tests abundantly demonstrated, much of the discrimination is not of the overt variety where the coloured immigrant can tell he is being discriminated against, so that his claims almost certainly represent only a part of the discrimination that is in fact practised against him.

Moreover the majority of people who claimed experience of discrimination claimed that it had occurred on more than one occasion. This emphasizes the significance of exposure and shows that, once people start to look for accommodation of this type on the open market, then they begin to experience the massive discrimination that awaits them. Informants who claimed personal experience of discrimination in this sector were asked on how many occasions they had been refused accommodation because of race or colour. The proportions giving each type of answer were as follows:

Number of times discrimination experienced	
On five or more occasions	35 per cent
On two–four occasions	44 per cent
Once	17 per cent
Uncertain	4 per cent

Although when only people who had sought accommodation on the open market are considered the proportions of West Indians and Asians having perceived instances of discrimination are similar, there are important differences between the West Indian and the Asian groups.

West Indians have both the highest level of exposure (60 per cent having sought privately rented accommodation compared to 28 per cent for Pakistanis and 29 per cent for Indians) and the highest proportion claiming personal experience of discrimination (39 per cent compared to 15 per cent and 19 per cent).

The West Indians were, moreover, keenly aware of discrimination although many had avoided it by not exposing themselves to the open market. Only about one half of the Indians and Pakistanis were aware of the existence of discrimination, because the pattern of their life did not expose them to it. To put it another way, awareness of discrimination by West Indians made many of them order their way of life to avoid it. For Pakistanis and Indians their ways of life, in many instances, protected them from even awareness of discrimination.

As in the employment situation this pattern is illustrated by local differences among the Pakistanis in particular. In Area III[1] 65 per cent were aware of the existence of discrimination. In Area IV the corresponding figure was 19 per cent.

In view of the massive discrimination which takes place in private lettings, and the overt form of much of it (for example in public advertisements), the fact that in Area IV only 19 per cent of Pakistanis were aware that a landlord would refuse someone accommodation purely because of race or colour can represent only an almost complete isolation of the majority of Pakistanis in that Area from the host community and an insulation from the effects of discrimination through the organization of their accommodation through their own community. Ninety-seven per cent of those in Area IV who were unsure about discrimination or did not believe it existed had never applied for accommodation to a white landlord who was a stranger. This practice is similar to that followed by the Pakistanis in relation to employment in that Area, but even more marked. Of course it is very much easier to pursue a way of life or to order one's way of life to avoid discrimination in private letting than in employment, because there are but few coloured employers in Britain. Nevertheless, despite the patterns of avoidance of discrimination, and despite the fact that much of the discrimination is not overt, significant proportions were aware of having experienced it. Their significance is highlighted by variations within the different groups.

The local differences in levels of awareness of discrimination mentioned above were reflected in actual experience of discrimination. Only 3 per cent of Pakistanis in Area IV claimed personal experience of discrimination compared to 20 per cent of Pakistanis in Area III. Regional differences among West Indians showed that, while in each of the three southern Areas 50 per cent claimed personal experience, this dropped to 12 per cent in the Midlands and 21 per cent in the northern Areas.

Claims of personal experience rose consistently with occupational level within each group, for example:

[1] Areas III and IV here are the same Southern and Northern towns having, respectively, the highest and lowest proportions of Pakistanis experiencing discrimination in employment.

West Indians: proportions having personal experience of discrimination by occupational level	
Non-manual	64 per cent
Partly skilled	45 per cent
Unskilled	37 per cent

Similarly claims rose with educational qualifications and length of time in Britain and this was particularly true with regard to Pakistanis, a trend which was partly responsible for the marked local differences among Pakistanis.

These differences demonstrate the point, made in evaluating landlords' reasons for discriminating, that it is the more able coloured people who experience the greater degree of discrimination.

This discussion of people's experience of discrimination has been carried on in terms of their claims. In view of the extent of discrimination revealed by the tests and interviews there is, in fact, no reason to doubt that people who had looked for rented accommodation on the open market had experienced discrimination whether they were aware of it or not. Nevertheless it is interesting and useful to look at the evidence, put forward to justify claims by those who made them, not so much to prove their validity but to illustrate further the types of experience people faced and the ways they justified claims.

As with regard to claims of refusal of employment because of race or colour, the most common reason given was that they had been told 'no coloureds'. The different types of justification and the proportion making each type of claim were as follows:

Grounds for claiming discrimination	%
Was *told* 'no coloureds'/'other tenants would object' etc.	43
Had door slammed in face as soon as seen	9
*(Sign up—'No coloureds', 'Europeans only' etc.) (6)	
Was told property was gone when knew it was vacant because:	
It continued to be advertised	15
Was told on the telephone	3
Knew person who eventually got it	4
'You just know'	8
Landlords asked exorbitant rent/made stupid excuses, etc.	9
No details given	9
	100

* These are informants who spontaneously said that there was no need to give details of personal experience because they had seen signs which provided conclusive evidence of discrimination.

24 *E. J. B. Rose,* Colour and Citizenship

Occupation

The occupational distribution of male immigrant groups in London shows a fairly wide spread over a number of occupations with considerable diversity between different groups. There are no overwhelming concentrations (except possibly for Cypriots) of any immigrant group in any occupation. Table 1, which shows those occupation orders[1] in which 7·5 per cent or more of any immigrant group were enumerated by the Census, illustrates this point. Contrary to popular belief, the majority of West Indians are not transport workers. Although the category of Transport and Communication workers is one of the most important, it only contains just over 15 per cent of economically active males.

Table 1: *Distribution in major occupations* for selected birthplace groups by percentage, by sex, 1966*

(a) *Males—Greater London conurbation*

	India	Pakistan	Jamaica	Rest of Caribbean	All Caribbean	British West Africa	Cyprus	Total population
Number economically active†	36 530	9 440	33 710	30 240	63 950	8 480	18 700	2 468 300
Selected occupations								
VII. Engineering and allied trade workers n.e.c.‡	13·7	11·0	17·4	15·4	16·4	12·1	9·1	12·6
VIII. Woodworkers	—	—	9·1	7·7	8·4	—	—	2·7
XI. Clothing Workers	—	8·1	—	—	—	—	9·3	1·1
XVIII. Labourers n.e.c.	—	—	20·7	15·1	18·1	—	—	6·0
XIX. Transport and communications workers	7·6	—	12·4	18·3	15·2	10·7	—	10·1
XXI. Clerical workers	17·9	12·9	—	—	—	21·8	—	11·3
XXIII. Service, sport, and recreation workers	—	13·2	—	—	—	—	33·9	7·6
XXV. Professional, technical workers, artists	18·1	12·3	—	—	—	17·5	—	11·0

[1] The Census divides the population into twenty-seven major divisions (occupation orders) and over 200 minor sub-divisions (unit groups).

E. J. B. Rose, *Colour and Citizenship*, Oxford University Press for the Institute of Race Relations, 1969, pp. 155–66.

(b) *Males—West Midlands conurbation*

	India	Pakistan	Jamaica	All Caribbean	Total population
Number economically active†	*12 630*	*11 470*	*13 530*	*16 910*	*777 490*
Selected occupations					
V. Furnace, forge, foundry, rolling mill workers	15·9	—	8·6	7·8	4·3
VII. Engineering and allied trades workers, n.e.c.	19 2	22·3	25·3	25·7	28·3
XVIII. Labourers n.e.c.	26·6	53·1	22·9	22·5	7·8
110. Labourers n.e.c. in engineering and allied trades§	*9·9*	*37·4*	*11·8*	*11·9*	*3·6*
XIX. Transport and communications	—	—	9·8	10·3	6·3

c) *Females—Greater London conurbation*

	India	Jamaica	Rest of Caribbean	All Caribbean	British West Africa	Cyprus	Total population
Number economically active†	*16 220*	*23 510*	*20 340*	*43 850*	*5 150*	*8 170*	*1 611 140*
Selected Occupations							
XI. Clothing workers	—	15·6	10·8	13·4	7·6	64·5	4·7
XX. Warehousemen, storekeepers, packers, bottlers	—	—	—	—	11·1	—	3·5
XXI. Clerical workers	45·5	7·5	13·4	10·2	21·4	8·1	35·7
139. Typists, shorthand writers, secretaries	*26·9*	*—*	*—*	*—*	*7·8*	*—*	*13·9*
140. Clerks, cashiers	*16·5*	*—*	*—*	*—*	*10·3*	*—*	*18·9*
XXIII. Service, sport, and recreation workers	9·9	27·9	22·2	25·3	17·5	13·6	21·4
XXV. Professional, technical workers, artists	18·6	13·5	22·0	17·4	19·0	—	10·4
183. Nurses	*—*	*12·8*	*14·3*	*13·5*	*13·4*	*—*	*3·9*

(d) *Females—West Midlands conurbation*

	Jamaica	All Caribbean	Total population
Number economically active†	*7 720*	*9 670*	*447 110*
Selected occupations			
VII. Engineering and allied trades workers, n.e.c.	39·5	37·8	15·0
XXIII. Service, sport, and recreation workers	14·2	14·5	20·4
XXV. Professional, technical workers, artists	15·9	16·4	7·4
183. Nurses	*15·8*	*16·3*	*2·7*

* Percentages have been shown for immigrant groups only in those occupations where 7·5% or more of the economically active are enumerated. A dash (—) does not mean that no members of that group were in that particular occupation but only that less than 7·5% were enumerated.

† Figures for the number economically active have been multiplied by ten as the size of the sample was 10% of the total population.

‡ 'n.e.c.' after an occupational description means 'Not Elsewhere Classified'.

§ Unit groups (identified by 3-digit code numbers) are sub-divisions of the occupation order (identified by Roman numerals) directly above them.

Sources: 1966 10% Sample Census, Special Tabulations; figures for total population from Table 13, *Economic Activity Tables*, Part I, H.M.S.O.

In the West Midlands the pattern for male immigrants shows greater concentration and less difference between each immigrant group. Over one-fifth of the males of each immigrant group are labourers and this rises to over one-half for Pakistanis. A large percentage of these labourers work in engineering and allied trades. Contrasts which appear between London and the West Midlands are most apparent for the Indian and Pakistani-born populations. Whilst both groups in London are fairly well represented in clerical and professional jobs and have low percentages in labouring jobs, the reverse occurs in the West Midlands.

There is a certain similarity between male and female patterns. Indian-born women are very well represented in clerical and professional jobs in London; the most important occupations for West Indian women are service jobs (over one-quarter). Cypriot women are the great exception, where nearly two-thirds are clothing workers. In the West Midlands, engineering occupations are the most important for West Indian women (over one-third). Nursing, whilst it is an important occupation for West Indian women, is not the largest in either conurbation.

Table 2: *Over- or under-representation* of different immigrant groups in different occupations, 1966*

(a) *Males—Greater London conurbation*

Occupation	India	Pakistan	Jamaica	Rest of Caribbean	All Caribbean	British West Africa	Cyprus
VIII. Woodworkers			+	+	+		
XI. Clothing workers		+					+
XVIII. Labourers n.e.c.			++	+	++		
XIX. Transport and communications workers				+	+		
XXI. Clerical workers	+		−	−	−	++	−
XXII. Sales workers			−	−	−	−	
XXIII. Service, sport, and recreation workers		+					+++
XXIV. Administrators and managers			−	−	−		
XXV. Professional, technical workers, artists	+		−	−	−	+	−

b) *Males—West Midlands conurbation*

Occupation	India	Pakistan	Jamaica	All Caribbean
V. Furnace, forge, foundry, rolling mill workers	++			
VII. Engineering and allied trades workers n.e.c.	−	−		
XVIII. Labourers n.e.c.	++	++++	++	++
110. Labourers n.e.c. in engineering and allied trades	+	+++	+	+
XIX. Transport and communications workers	−			
XXI. Clerical workers			−	
XXII. Sales workers			−	−
XXV. Professional, technical workers, artists	−		−	−

* Over- or under-representation has been calculated from the difference between the percentage of those in employment for the immigrant group in question in a particular occupation and the percentage of the total population in the same occupation. Only differences of 5% or more are shown and plus (+) denotes over-representation, minus (−) under-representation of the immigrant group in comparison to the total population.

+ or −	Difference between 5% and 9·9% inclusive
++ or − −	Difference between 10% and 19·9% inclusive
+++ or − − −	Difference between 20% and 34·9% inclusive
++++ or − − − −	Difference between 35% and 49·9% inclusive

Sources: 1966 10% Sample Census, Special Tabulations; Table 13, *Economic Activity Tables*, Part I, H.M.S.O.

How does the occupational distribution of the immigrants compare with that of the population as a whole? In Table 2 some of the major differences are shown for men, and some indication is given of those occupations in which immigrants are either heavily under- or over-represented. In London, the greatest over-representation is for Cypriots in service occupations and, to a lesser extent, for West Indians as labourers. Africans and Indians are over-represented and West Indians under-represented in clerical and professional occupations. Other occupations in which immigrant groups were over-represented include West Indians as woodworkers and transport and communications workers, and Pakistanis and Cypriots as clothing workers. In the West Midlands, there was a very large over-representation of all male groups, especially of Pakistanis, as labourers. The other major over-representation was of Indians as furnace, forge, foundry and rolling mill workers.

For women (not shown in Table 2), in London the greatest over-concentration was as clothing workers for Cypriots and, to a much less degree, for West Indians. In the West Midlands, West Indian women were very heavily over-represented in engineering jobs. They were also over-represented in both conurbations as nurses.

One way of contrasting the occupational distribution of immigrant groups with that of the total population is to compare their numbers in the main 'white-collar' jobs—that is, clerical, sales, administrative, and professional jobs. The 'white-collar' analysis is shown in Table 3, and it will be seen that for males in London there were very considerable differences between the different groups. Both Indians and Africans were better represented than the total population, and Pakistanis were only slightly under-represented compared with the total population. The representation of the West Indian groups (especially Jamaicans) and Cypriots was markedly inferior to that of the total population in 'white-collar' occupations.

In the West Midlands, all the male immigrant groups were badly under-represented in 'white-collar' jobs and all were less successful in this respect in the West Midlands than in London, even allowing for the differences in occupational structure between the two areas. Indians were the best represented of all immigrant groups in these jobs, their percentage being about half the percentage of the total population, but Pakistanis and West Indians were hardly represented at all in these occupational categories.

For women, the 'white-collar' or 'white-blouse' analysis in Table 3 includes and excludes nurses; throughout the text nurses will be excluded when referring to 'white-blouse' occupations.[2] In London, Indian women were better represented in these jobs than the total population, whilst all the other immigrant groups were heavily under-represented. Women born in Africa

[2] Nurses are excluded from the analysis of 'white-blouse' occupations in order to highlight a position which might otherwise be masked by their inclusion. This is especially so in view of the high concentrations of certain immigrant groups in this occupation.

Table 3: *Distribution in main 'white-collar' occupations of selected birthplace groups by percentage, by sex, 1966*

(a) *Males—Greater London conurbation*

	India	Pakistan	Jamaica	Rest of Caribbean	All Caribbean	British West Africa	Cyprus	Total population
Number economically active*	36 530	9 440	33 710	30 240	63 950	8 480	18 700	2 468 300
Occupation								
XXI. Clerical workers	17·9	12·9	1·9	5·6	3·6	21·8	3·3	11·3
XXII. Sales workers	5·9	4·8	0·8	1·0	0·9	1·3	5·7	8·9
XXIV. Administrators and managers	3·4	2·0	0·2	0·5	0·3	1·3	1·4	5·7
XXV. Professional, technical workers, artists	18·1	12·3	1·6	4·7	3·0	17·5	3·6	11·0
Total % of E.A. in above occupations	45·3	32·0	4·5	11·8	7·8	41·9	14·0	36·9

(b) *Males—West Midlands conurbation*

	India	Pakistan	Jamaica	All Caribbean	Total population
Number economically active*	12 630	11 470	13 530	16 910	777 490
Occupation					
XXI. Clerical workers	1·7	0·9	0·5	0·7	5·5
XXII. Sales workers	3·6	1·2	0·4	0·4	6·7
XXIV. Administrators and managers	0·9	0·1	—	0·1	4·6
XXV. Professional, technical workers, artists	5·9	1·0	0·8	1·4	8·0
Total % of E.A. in above occupations	12·1	3·2	1·7	2·6	24·8

(c) *Females—Greater London conurbation*

	India	Jamaica	Rest of Caribbean	All Caribbean	British West Africa	Cyprus	Total population
Number economically active*	16 220	23 510	20 340	43 850	5 150	8 170	1 611 140
Occupation							
XXI. Clerical workers	45·5	7·5	13·4	10·2	21·4	8·1	35·7
XXII. Sales workers	5·7	1·3	1·5	1·4	1·4	3·3	10·0
XXIV. Administrators and managers	1·2	0·2	0·1	0·1	0·8	0·4	1·1
XXV. Professional, etc.,	18·6	13·5	22·0	17·4	19·0	1·8	10·4
of whom 183 Nurses†	*1·0*	*12·8*	*14·3*	*13·5*	*13·4*	*0·5*	*3·9*
Total % of E.A. in above occupations	71·0	22·5	37·0	29·1	42·6	13·6	57·2
Total % of E.A. in above occupations (excluding nurses)	70·0	9·7	22·7	15·6	29·2	13·1	53·41

(d) *Females—West Midlands conurbation*

	Jamaica	All Caribbean	Total population
Number economically active*	7 720	9 670	447 110
Occupation			
XXI. Clerical workers	2·3	2·5	26·3
XXII. Sales workers	0·9	1·2	11·1
XXIV. Administrators and managers	—	—	0·5
XXV. Professionals, etc.,	15·9	16·4	7·4
of whom 183 Nurses†	*15·8*	*16·3*	*2·7*
Total % of E.A. in above occupations	19·1	20·1	45·3
Total % of E.A. in above occupations (excluding nurses)	3·3	3·8	42·6

* Figures for the number economically active have been multiplied by ten as the size of the sample was 10% of the total population.
† Unit Group 183 nurses is a sub-division of occupation order XXV Professional, Technical Workers, Artists.

Sources: 1966 10% Sample Census, Special Tabulations; Table 13, *Economic Activity Tables*, Part I, H.M.S.O.

and the Rest of the Caribbean fared about half as well as the total population, but Cypriots and Jamaicans only one-quarter as well. In the West Midlands, West Indian women did very much worse than the total population in 'white-blouse' jobs and were much worse represented than their sisters in London in these jobs.

Up to now we have only discussed occupational distribution at one moment in time (1966). To assess the nature of change over time we need to examine 1961 data as well, but unfortunately these are available for London only, therefore limiting this aspect of our study. Whilst the percentage of men in the total population in 'white-collar' jobs increased between 1961 and 1966, all the immigrant groups showed a drop in the proportion of males in these jobs (Table 4). This decrease was greatest for the Indians and least for the West Indians. For women, all groups, including the total population, showed increases in the percentage in 'white-blouse' occupations between 1961 and 1966. However, Jamaicans, who in 1961 were the least well-represented group, showed the smallest increase in the five-year period (Table 4).

Table 4: *Comparison of percentage in 'white-collar' occupations in the Greater London conurbation, 1961 and 1966, for selected birthplace groups and the total population*

	Males		*Females**	
	1961	*1966*	*1961*	*1966*
India	50·2	45·3	66·8	70·0
Pakistan	34·5	32·0	—	—
Jamaica	4·8	4·5	7·5	9·7
Rest of Caribbean	11·9	11·8	15·1	22·7
All Caribbean	8·0	7·8	10·6	15·6
Total population	35·8	36·9	51·1	53·4

* Female data exclude persons enumerated in sub-unit 183 nurses at both dates.

Sources: 1966 figures from Table 13.5; 1961 figures calculated from Table A.4 Census 1961, England and Wales, Commonwealth Immigrants in the Conurbations, H.M.S.O.

As far as other occupations are concerned West Indian men became slightly more concentrated and over-represented as woodworkers, transport workers, and engineering workers in London. These occupations were three of the four most important for West Indians, but in the fourth, labouring, there was a decline both in concentration and in over-representation. The concentration of West Indian women in nursing also declined between 1961 and 1966.

Before attempting to draw any conclusions from the analysis of occupation,

R.A.E.R.—I

certain points need to be made concerning the nature of the enumerated groups. The problem of interpreting census data concerning persons born in India has already been referred to. The evidence on occupational distribution, especially the comparison for men between London and the West Midlands, seems amply to confirm the suspicions that persons born in India enumerated in London are atypical. This is not only because of the large numbers of white Indians but also because there is a heavy concentration of middle-class and professional Indians in London. Thus, the data for the West Midlands give a much truer representation of the profile of the typical Indian immigrant. This conclusion applies—although to a more limited degree—to the Pakistani immigrant as well. Certain inferences can also be drawn regarding the African population which seem to differentiate that group from the typical immigrant situation. Approximately one-third of the male African population (15 and over) are students, and it would seem fair to hypothesize that a very large proportion of the African working population are ex-students whose educational attainments are very much higher on average than those of any other immigrant group or of the total population. The occupational distribution of Africans would tend to confirm this assessment of the nature of the African population. We propose, therefore, in what follows, to refer rather less to Indians, Pakistanis, and Africans in London and more to what are regarded as typical immigrant groups.

Certain general assessments of the position of coloured immigrants are possible. The occupational distribution of immigrant groups differs not only from the general population but also from each other. In general terms, immigrants are less well represented than the total population in those occupations usually considered most desirable, and over-represented in those occupations considered most undesirable. In many respects the over-concentration of immigrants in labouring jobs is even more disturbing than their virtual absence in 'white-collar' jobs, especially in the West Midlands. Again, occupationally, coloured immigrants are not a homogeneous group; one must discuss the separate situations of Indians, Pakistanis, and West Indians. Even this is often a gross over-generalization, as can be seen for West Indians, where persons born in the Rest of the Caribbean consistently show higher percentages in 'white-collar' jobs and lower percentages in labouring jobs than Jamaicans, and this is so in both conurbations.

Within immigrant groups there are also differences in occupational structure between London and the West Midlands that are not wholly explicable by the overall differences of the occupational structure of the two areas. All immigrant groups show a less favourable occupational structure in the West Midlands, and whilst this may be due in part to a difference in the kind of persons enumerated and in the overall occupational structure in the two areas, it may also indicate the differing attitudes of the population in the two areas to the employment of coloured immigrants.

Implicit in this discussion is the assumption that before any immigrant group can be regarded as having achieved some sort of reasonable *modus vivendi* within the field of employment, its members must have a comparable opportunity to that of the general population. It must be equally possible for them to achieve a wide variety of occupations, especially those that are generally regarded as the elite occupations. We know that this stage has certainly not yet been reached, but there is no direct information from the Census as to the causes. In general, the unfavourable occupation distribution of the immigrant can be ascribed to two reasons. Firstly, inadequate skills, education, or, in general, factors personal to the immigrant, and secondly, the attitudes of the general population to the employment of the immigrant.

One can approach this question obliquely by examining the fact that West Indian women are heavily over-represented in nursing. It seems fair to state that the skill and educational levels of nurses are certainly not less than the majority of 'white-blouse' occupations examined in Table 3. It is therefore pertinent to note that in the West Midlands nurses were four times as numerous as 'white-blouse' workers for West Indians, but for the total population the situation was completely reversed and there were sixteen times as many 'white-blouse' workers as nurses. The reasons for these immense differences are complex, but it seems fair to suppose that the reasons why West Indian women are markedly under-represented in 'white-blouse' occupations cannot be solely their lack of suitable qualifications, but must also include in some measure the disinclination of the general population to see them in these occupations. It is also unlikely that the skill levels of West Indian men and women are so disparate that the under-representation of West Indian men in 'white-collar' jobs is not also due in part to the same reasons.

Finally, and most crucially, an examination of the data for London in 1961 and 1966 showed no sign of the occupational structure of immigrants coming any closer to the occupational structure of the total population. What changes there were, as far as West Indian men were concerned, showed very slight moves to greater concentration in certain occupations; there was no evidence that between 1961 and 1966 they were moving into those occupations in which they were markedly under-represented.

25 *Charles E. Silberman,* Crisis in Black and White

The Negro migration to the city actually began about seventy-five years ago, when the Jim Crow system first began to take shape in the South and white men moved actively and brutally to force the Negro back into his pre-Reconstruction place. Contrary to the popular view that Southern folkways are immutable, the quarter-century following the Civil War had seen a considerable relaxation of the barriers between the races as the South accommodated itself to a new order. Negroes were accepted at the polls, in the courts and legislatures, in the police and militia, and on the trains and trolleys. Col. Thomas Wentworth Higginson of Boston, a noted abolitionist who had been one of John Brown's 'Secret Six' before Harper's Ferry, went south in 1878, and reported in *The Atlantic Monthly* his pleasant surprise at how well Negroes were being treated, as compared with his native New England. 'How can we ask more of the states formerly in rebellion', he wrote, 'than that they should be abreast of New England in granting rights and privileges to the colored race?' In 1885, T. McCants Stewart, a Negro newspaperman from Boston, returned to the South for a visit and found traveling 'more pleasant than in some parts of New England . . . I think the whites of the South', he reported, 'are really less afraid to [have] contact with colored people than the whites of the North'. Negroes were treated particularly well in Virginia. Thus in 1886 the Richmond *Dispatch* took what today would be considered a pro-Negro position:

Our State Constitution requires all State officers in their oath of office to declare that they 'recognize and accept the civil and political equality of all men'. We repeat that nobody here objects to sitting in political conventions with negroes. Nobody here objects to serving on juries with negroes. No lawyer objects to practicing law in courts where negro lawyers practice . . . Colored men are allowed to introduce bills into the Virginia Legislature; and in both branches of this body negroes are allowed to sit, as they have a right to sit.

Racism was still widespread, of course, in all its ugliness. But it was held in check by a number of forces: Northern liberal opinion; the prestige and

Charles E. Silberman, *Crisis in Black and White*, Random House, 1964, and Jonathan Cape, 1965, pp. 20–35.

influence of Southern conservatives, with their tradition of *noblesse oblige* and their distaste for the venomous race hatred of the poor whites;[1] and the idealism of Southern radicals, who for a time dreamt of an alliance of all the propertyless against the propertied class. As a result of these competing pressures, Negroes were able to retain the suffrage they had won during Reconstruction. While Negroes were increasingly defrauded and coerced, they did continue to vote in large numbers, and Southern conservatives and radicals competed for their support. 'The Southern whites accept them precisely as Northern men in cities accept the ignorant Irish vote', Colonel Higginson wrote, 'not cheerfully, but with acquiescence to the inevitable; and when the strict color line is once broken, they are just as ready to conciliate the Negro as the Northern politician to flatter the Irishman. Any powerful body of voters may be cajoled today and intimidated tomorrow and hated always', the abolitionist added, 'but it can never be left out of sight'.

Beginning around 1890, however, the forces that had kept Southern racism and fanaticism in check rapidly weakened and became discredited. In the North, the desire for sectional reconciliation persuaded liberals to drop their interest in the Negro, who was the symbol of sectional strife; increasingly, liberals and former abolitionists began espousing the shibboleths of the Negro's innate inferiority in the pages of *The Atlantic Monthly, Harper's, The Nation,* and *The North American Review*; and this, in turn, encouraged the more virulent Southern racists. 'Just as the Negro gained his emancipation and new rights through a falling out between white men', wrote historian C. Vann Woodward (1957), 'he now stood to lose his rights through the reconciliation of white men'. Not only did the Negro serve as a scapegoat to aid the reconciliation of Northern and Southern white men; he served the same purpose in aiding the reconciliation of estranged white classes in the South itself. The battles between the Southern conservatives and radicals had opened wounds that could be healed only by the nostrum of white supremacy.

The first and most fundamental step was the total disfranchisement of the Negro; disfranchisement served both as a symbol of 'reform' and as a guarantee that no white faction would ever again seek power by rallying Negro votes against another group of whites. Because of the Federal Constitution, the Southern states had to rob Negroes of their vote through indirection: through the use of the poll tax, the white primary, the 'grandfather clause', the 'good character clause', the 'understanding clause', and other techniques, some of which are still in use in states like Mississippi and Alabama. But while the methods were roundabout, the purpose was not.

---

[1] 'It is a great deal pleasanter to travel with respectable and well-behaved colored people than with unmannerly and ruffianly white men', a Charleston, South Carolina, paper observed, suggesting that 'the common sense and proper arrangement ... is to provide first-class cars for first-class passengers, white and colored'.

When the Mississippi Constitution was revised in 1890, for example, the purpose of revision was stated quite baldly: 'The policy of crushing out the manhood of the Negro citizens is to be carried on to success'. Addressing the Virginia Constitutional Convention eleven years later, the young Carter Glass, then a member of the Virginia State Senate, was no less blunt: 'Discrimination? Why that is precisely what we propose; that, exactly, is what this convention was elected for—to discriminate to the very extremity of permissible action under the limitations of the Federal Constitution, with a view to the elimination of every Negro voter who can be gotten rid of, legally, without materially impairing the numerical strength of the white electorate'. By the winter of 1902, the Convention had achieved its purpose. By 1910, the Negro was disfranchised in virtually every Southern state. In Louisiana, for example, the number of registered Negro voters dropped abruptly from 130 334 in 1896 to only 1342 in 1904.

Disfranchisement was preceded and accompanied by an intensive campaign of race hatred, designed in good measure to allay the suspicions of the poor whites that they, too, were in danger of losing the vote. Although the regime of the carpetbaggers had been over for twenty years or more, all the old horror stories were revived and embroidered; the new generation of Southerners (and each succeeding one) was made to feel that it, too, had lived through the trauma of Reconstruction. Newspapers played up stories of Negro crime and 'impertinence'. The result was a savage outbreak of anti-Negro violence. In Atlanta, white mobs took over the city for four days, looting and lynching at will; in New Orleans, mobs rampaged for three days. And rigid segregation rapidly became the rule. Until 1900, Jim Crow laws had applied only to railroad travel in most Southern states; indeed, South Carolina did not require Jim Crow railroad cars before 1898, North Carolina before 1899, and Virginia before 1900. Until 1899, only three states required separate waiting rooms at railroad terminals. In the next six or eight years, however, Jim Crow laws mushroomed throughout the South, affecting trolleys, theaters, boarding houses, public toilets and water fountains, housing; in Atlanta Jim Crow extended even to the ultimate absurdity of providing separate Jim Crow Bibles for Negro witnesses to swear on in court, and, for a time, to requiring Jim Crow elevators in buildings.

In short, the South, whose leaders today deny the possibility as well as the desirability of rapid change, transformed the pattern of race relations almost overnight. Men's hearts changed as swiftly as their actions. As late as 1898, for example, the Charleston, South Carolina, *News and Courier*, the oldest newspaper in the South, ridiculed the whole idea of segregation of the races. 'As we have got on fairly well for a third of a century, including a long period of reconstruction', the editor wrote, 'we can probably get on as well hereafter without it, and certainly so extreme a measure [as Jim Crow railroad cars] should not be adopted and enforced without added and urgent cause'. The editor went on to discuss the absurd consequences that would follow, once the principle of Jim Crow were accepted. 'If there must be Jim Crow cars on the railroads, there should be Jim Crow cars on the street railways. Also on all passenger boats'. Warming to his task, he continued: 'If there are to be Jim Crow cars, moreover, there should be Jim Crow waiting saloons at all stations, and Jim Crow eating houses . . . There should be Jim Crow sections of the jury box, and a separate Jim Crow dock and witness stand in every court—and a Jim Crow Bible for colored witnesses to kiss', and separate Jim Crow sections in government offices so that Negroes and whites would not have to mingle while paying their taxes. In resorting to the tactics of *reductio ad absurdum*, Professor Woodward has commented, 'the editor doubtless believed that he had dealt the Jim Crow principle a telling blow with his heavy irony'. But the real irony was unintended: what the *News and Courier* editor regarded as an absurdity in 1898 very rapidly became a reality, down to and including the Jim Crow Bible. So rapidly did the change occur, in fact, that in 1906—only eight years later—the paper had swung completely around. Segregation was no longer ridiculous; it was merely inadequate. Only mass deportation could solve as grave a problem as the presence of Negroes in South Carolina. 'There is no room for them here', the paper declared.

There *was* room in the North—and thus began the great migration. There had been a steady trickle of Negroes from the eleven states of the Old Confederacy since the end of the Civil War; emancipation had cut many Negroes loose from the land and started them wandering from place to place. In the last decade of the century, however, the number of Negroes leaving the Old Confederacy jumped to more than two hundred thousand from fewer than sixty thousand in the 1880–1890 period, and the number of migrants increased somewhat in the first decade of the twentieth century. The migrants included a great many of the preachers and politicians who had sat in Southern legislatures during Reconstruction and its aftermath, as well as less distinguished Negroes who had occupied minor political posts. But the majority were half-educated or illiterate country folk too restless or too proud to accept life on Southern terms.

It was World War One that broke the social and economic fetters that had bound Negroes to the rural South almost as effectively as slavery itself, for the war created an enormous demand for previously untapped sources of labor. Business was booming as the United States supplied the Allies with weapons and matériel; but combat had cut off the flow of immigrants from Europe. With labor the scarce factor of production even before American entry into the war, Northern industries began sending labor agents into the rural South, recruiting Negroes just as they had recruited white workers in Ireland and Italy during the nineteenth century. The labor agents promised jobs and frequently offered free railroad tickets. Negroes began to move

North in such numbers—emigration from the eleven states of the Old Confederacy jumped from 207 000 in 1900–1910 to 478 600 in 1910–1920— that white Southerners began to fear a shortage of labor in their own region and took measures to stop the Northern labor recruiters. In Macon, Georgia, an ordinance was passed requiring labor recruiters to pay a license fee of $25 000 and barring their admission unless recommended by ten local minsters, ten manufacturers, and twenty-five businessmen. In Montgomery, Alabama, fines and jail sentences were imposed on anyone found guilty of 'enticing, persuading, or influencing labor' to leave the city, and throughout Mississippi, agents were arrested, ticket agents were intimidated to keep them from selling tickets to Negroes, and trains were actually stopped.

The Negroes kept leaving nevertheless. Besides the agents for Northern firms, Northern Negro newspapers also encouraged the migration editorially, as well as through advertisements offering employment. *The Chicago Defender*, in particular, exhorted Negroes to leave the oppression of the South for the freedom of the North. Copies of the *Defender* were passed from hand to hand, and from all over the South, Negroes wrote to its editor, Robert S. Abbott, asking for help and advice. 'I would like Chicago or Philadelphia. But I don't Care where so long as I Go where a man is a man', wrote a would-be migrant from Houston, Texas. From the Black Belt of Mississippi came this letter, showing the hopes that moved the migrants:

Granville, Miss., May 16, 1917

Dear Sir:

This letter is a letter of information of which you will find stamp envelop for reply. I want to come north some time soon but I do not want to leve here looking for a job where I would be in dorse all winter. Now the work I am doing here is running a guage edger in a saw mill. I know all about the grading of lumber. I have been working in lumber about 25 or 27 years. My wedges here is $3.00 a day, 11 hours a day. I want to come north where I can educate my 3 little children, also my wife. Now if you cannot fit me up at what I am doing down here I can learn anything any one els can. also there is a great deal of good women cooks here would leave any time all they want is to know where to go and some way to go. please write me at once just how I can get my people where they can get something for their work. There are women here cookeing for $1.50 and $2.00 a week. I would like to live in Chicago or Ohio or Philadelphia. Tell Mr Abbott that our pepel are tole that they can not get anything to do up there and they are being snatched off the trains here in Greenville and a rested but in spite of all this, they are leaving every day and every night 100 or more is expecting to leave this week. Let me here from you at once.

America's entry into World War One stimulated migration still more. As men were drafted, the labor shortage was intensified. And the draft brought thousands of Negro soldiers to Army bases in the North, opening a vision of a world beyond that of the small town in which, until then, their lives had been bound. The heavy traffic of Negroes moving North in turn persuaded others living along the main routes to join the trek. A migrant from Decatur, Alabama, reported that perhaps a third of the city's Negro population decided to leave after seeing all the migrants riding through. 'And when the moving fever hit them', he said, 'there was no changing their minds'.

While Negroes were being pulled to the North by job opportunities, they were also being pushed off the land in the South. The full impact of the agrarian revolution was reaching the Southern cotton farmer, and the Negro was hit hardest of all. Farmers in the hot, dry climate of New Mexico and Arizona were producing a longer staple, better quality cotton than the farmers in the old Black Belt could produce, and so cotton production of Negro-operated farms east of the Mississippi began to decline. Mechanization of agriculture also hurt the Negro farmers, most of whom were sharecroppers and tenants. Finally, the ravages of the boll weevil, which plagued the Black Belt after 1910, intensified the Negro cotton farmer's already desperate plight. 'The merchant got half the cotton, the boll weevil got the rest', went a Negro ballad. And as if the boll weevil weren't enough, a series of floods during the summer of 1915 added to the Negroes' woes.

The Negro was pushed off the land—but he could find no place in the cities of the South, for poor whites who were also being forced off the land preempted the jobs opening up in Southern industry. Indeed, not only were Negroes barred from jobs in the new textile mills and other industries springing up in the South, but they found their traditional occupations as well—as barbers and waiters, as carpenters, masons, and painters, as saw-mill operators—taken over by the desperate whites. And so the North, for all its faults, looked more and more like the promised land.

Once the forces of ignorance and inertia were overcome and a new pattern of behavior opened up, the movement northward rapidly gained momentum. The pull of demand continued after the end of the First World War, when the Immigration Exclusion Acts of the early twenties ended once and for all the immigration from Southern and Eastern Europe. And the agrarian revolution continued to push Negroes off the land, while discrimination barred them from jobs in Southern industry. Nearly 800 000 Negroes left the eleven states of the Old Confederacy during the 1920s, and almost 400 000 moved away during the Depression of the 1930s. Thus, the 1940 Census revealed that the Negro population outside the Old Confederacy had more than doubled in the preceding thirty years, increasing from 1·9 to 4 million. Within the Old Confederacy, by contrast, the Negro population had increased only 12 per cent. Yet these eleven states still contained over two-thirds of all Negro Americans.

World War Two really opened the floodgates. With ten million men in uniform and industry operating in full blast, labor again was a scarce and precious commodity. Negroes flocked to the assembly lines in Detroit, now turning out tanks and jeeps instead of autos; to the shipyards in Oakland, New York, and Camden; to the steel mills in Pittsburgh, Gary, and Chicago; to the aircraft plants in Los Angeles. After the war had ended, industry continued to boom; in the late forties and early fifties the auto companies sent labor agents fanning through the South to recruit Negroes for the busy assembly lines. In New York, Philadelphia, Chicago, and most other big cities, employment agencies still do a brisk business directing a steady flow of Negro women and girls to work as domestic servants in a newly affluent society.

Within the South itself, moreover, mechanization of agriculture has been forcing millions of people, black and white, off the land, even when there are no jobs in the cities. Thus, the number of farms in the United States declined by one-third during the fifties. As always, the Negro farmers were hardest-hit: the number of Negro farm operators dropped 41 per cent in the five years from 1954 to 1959, the latest year for which figures are available. Share-cropping—once the predominant method of Negro farming—has almost disappeared: the number of sharecroppers, black and white, dropped from 541 000 in 1940 (and 776 000 in 1930) to a mere 122 000 in 1959.

The result has been an enormous shift of population from rural to urban areas: no fewer than 78 per cent of the counties of the United States suffered a net out-migration of population during the decade of the fifties. In the South itself, nearly four and a half million whites and two million Negroes moved from rural to urban places in the 1950s. The rural whites, for the most part, moved to Southern cities and towns, (though some 1·4 million left the South). Negroes on the other hand, left the South altogether: only 150 000 Negroes moved to Southern cities during the 1950s, since competition from white migrants, when added to traditional Southern discrimination, made it impossible for Negroes to find jobs in the Southern cities. In all, some 2·75 million Negroes left the South between 1940 and 1960.[2] Thus, the Negro population outside the Deep South has increased five-fold since 1910; it has nearly tripled just since 1940. Part of this expansion, of course, has come from natural increase rather than migration; but it is the migration of Negroes of child-bearing age that enabled the natural increase to occur outside the South. Within the South itself, migration has caused a substantial decline in the Negro population in rural areas; as a result, the population living in cities has jumped from 21 per cent in 1940 (and only 7 per cent in 1910) to 41 per cent in 1960.

Most of the Negroes moving to the North have crowded into the slums of the twelve largest cities, which in 1960 held 60 per cent of the Negroes living

[2] The statistics, of course, refer to *net* changes in population. A good many rural Southern Negroes moved to Southern cities, taking the place of Negroes who had moved to the North.

outside the Deep South. Between 1940 and 1960 the Negro population of New York increased nearly two and a half times to 1·1 million, or 14 per cent of the city's population. The Negro population of Chicago increased more than two and a half times to 890 000, or 24 per cent. In Philadelphia, between 1940 and 1960, the number of Negroes doubled to 529 000, or 26 per cent. The Negro population of Detroit has more than tripled to nearly a half-million, or 29 per cent of the city's population; and the Negro population of Los Angeles County has increased a phenomenal 600 per cent between 1940 and 1960, from 75 000 to 464 000. In recent years, moreover, Negro migration has fanned out to a host of smaller cities—Buffalo and Rochester, Toledo and Akron, Newark, New Haven, Fort Wayne, Milwaukee, Kansas City, Wichita.

The migration continues; Newark, which was 34·4 per cent Negro at the time of the 1960 Census, is now over 50 per cent Negro. But even if Negro migration were to stop completely (and it's bound to slow down), the Negro population of the large cities would continue to grow at a rapid rate, and Negroes would account for a steadily increasing proportion of the cities' population. For the Negro population is considerably younger than the white population of these cities; in addition, the Negro birth rate is considerably higher than the white. (In New Haven and Buffalo, for example, Negroes represent one person in eight out of the total population, but account for one birth in four.) Thus, Professor C. Horace Hamilton of the University of North Carolina, has predicted that Negro population outside the South will have doubled again by 1980, and that by the year 2000, nearly three Negroes in four will be living in the North and West.

Were it not for the increase in their Negro population, the large cities would be losing residents at a rapid clip. For the stream of Negroes moving into the big cities has been paralleled by a stream of whites moving out to the suburbs. In the twenty-four metropolitan areas with a half-million or more residents, for example, the 'central cities' lost 2 399 000 white residents between 1950 and 1960, a drop of 7·3 per cent.[3] They gained 2 641 000 new Negro residents in the same period, a rise of over 50 per cent; Negroes now account for over 20 per cent of the population of these cities. In the suburbs, by contrast, the white population grew by nearly 16 million, or 65 per cent; Negro population increased by 800 000, or better than 60 per cent, but remained a small proportion—under 5 per cent—of the total suburban population.

The dimensions of the suburban population explosion, incidentally, make it clear that the white exodus from the city has *not* been due primarily to the

[3] The twenty-four are New York, Los Angeles, Chicago, Philadelphia, Detroit, San Francisco–Oakland, Boston, Pittsburgh, St Louis, Washington, D.C., Cleveland, Baltimore, Newark, Minneapolis–St Paul, Buffalo, Houston, Milwaukee, Paterson–Clifton–Passaic, Seattle, Dallas, Cincinnati, Kansas City, San Diego, and Atlanta.

Negro influx, as sensitive Negroes (and a good many white liberals) frequently assert. On the contrary, the flight to the suburbs has been one of the dominant facts of city life for a century or more. Almost as soon as city dwellers become members of the middle class, they seem to long for a house and a patch of land, no matter how small. Hence the middle class has always been on the move, abandoning its homes near the center of town for sites farther out. The opening of an Illinois Central railway station at Fifty-fourth Street and Lake Park Avenue in 1856, and another at Forty-seventh Street, in 1859, led to the creation of the first suburbs south of Chicago's Loop; Hyde Park Village was incorporated in 1861, and by 1890, shortly before its annexation by the city of Chicago, boasted that its population of 85 000 made it the largest village in the world. In New York, as early as the 1870s, citizens were lamenting the exodus of men of 'moderate income to the suburban towns', and complaining that the city was becoming the habitat only of the very rich and the very poor. (Manhattan reached its peak population in 1910 and has been losing residents ever since.) To be sure, until the 1930s or 1940s, cities were able to recapture a large portion of their self-exiled residents by annexing the new suburbs to which the former urbanites had moved. But they depended for their growth on the steady stream of immigrants.

Like all previous immigrants groups, the Negroes have settled in the traditional 'port of entry'—the oldest, least desirable section of the city, generally in or around the central business district. That is where the cheapest housing usually is to be found; more important, that is the only place the newcomers can find a place to live, since prejudice as well as income keeps them out of the 'better' neighborhoods. (Immigrants, Negroes included, have always paid more for their housing, comparatively, than the established city dwellers. No urban industry is quite as profitable as slum manufacturing.) In Detroit, for example, the number of Negroes within an eight-mile radius of the central business district has increased eightfold since 1930, while the number of white residents has been halved.

As did each European immigrant group, moreover, the new Negro residents also figure disproportionately on the police blotters, the relief rolls, the truant officer's case load, the registers of rundown housing, the commitments for drug addiction, etc. In St Louis, for example, Negroes represented 29 per cent of the population in 1959, but accounted for over 50 per cent of the crime. In Detroit, where Negroes make up about 30 per cent of the population, they comprise some 80 per cent of the people on relief. (One Negro in four in Chicago is receiving public assistance of some sort.)

To be sure, it is not Negroes alone who find the move painful. In New York, the Puerto Rican population has swelled from perhaps 100 000 in 1940 to over 700 000 in 1960; with this increase has come a host of social problems. And Cincinnati, Baltimore, St Louis, Columbus, Detroit, and Chicago, among other cities, receive a steady stream of impoverished white hillbillies from the Southern Appalachian Mountains. These Appalachian whites—the oldest and purest Anglo-Saxon stock in the United States—have at least as much initial difficulty adjusting to the city as do the Negroes and Puerto Ricans. Consider this report, from *Harper's* (Votaw, 1958, pp. 65–6), on the hillbillies in Chicago:

Settling in deteriorated neighborhoods where they can stick with their own kind, they live as much as they can the way they lived back home. Often removing window screens, they sit half-dressed where it is cooler, and dispose of garbage the quickest way. Their own dress is casual and their children's worse. Their housekeeping is easy to the point of disorder, and they congregate in the evening on front porches and steps . . .

Their children play freely anywhere, without supervision. Fences and hedges break down; lawns go back to dirt. On the crowded city streets, children are unsafe, and their parents seem oblivious. Even more, when it comes to sex training, their habits—with respect to such matters as incest and statutory rape—are clearly at variance with urban legal requirements, and parents fail to appreciate the interest authorities take in their sex life . . .

'Skid row dives, opium parlors, and assorted other dens of iniquity collectively are as safe as Sunday school picnics compared with the joints taken over by clans of fightin', feudin' Southern hillbillies and their shootin' cousins', said one ferocious exposé in the Chicago *Sunday Tribune*. 'The Southern hillbilly migrants', the story continued, '. . . have the lowest standard of living and moral code (if any), the biggest capacity for liquor, and the most savage tactics when drunk, which is most of the time'.

It is the explosive growth of their Negro populations, however, that constitute the large cities' principal problem and concern. The Puerto Rican and Appalachian whites affect only a limited number of cities, usually only in a limited way; but every city has a large and growing Negro population. In every city, white residents and civic leaders are concerned about the physical deterioration of neighborhoods inhabited by Negroes; about the rising adult crime and juvenile delinquency rates in Negro neighborhoods that spill over into the rest of the city, making the parks and sometimes even the streets unsafe; about the tensions unleashed by suits to force school desegregation, and the fiscal strain of building classrooms fast enough to hold the mushrooming enrollments in Negro areas, and the difficulty of hiring teachers to teach in these schools; about the burden of welfare payments and the horror they feel as they watch second- and third-generation relief recipients grow up without ever knowing, or even seeing, what it means to be self-supporting. And in every city, Negro residents are bitter about the high rents they have to pay for rundown and shamefully neglected tenements in segregated sections of the city; about the discrimination by businesses and trade unions alike that bars them from skilled crafts and white-collar jobs; about the overcrowding and lack of standards in the schools their children attend; about the snubs and hurts and humiliations—big and small, real and imagined—that are their daily lot; about the general indifference to their plight. There is no large city, in short, which does not have a large and potentially explosive Negro problem.

References

Votaw, A. N. (1958), 'The Hillbillies invade Chicago', *Harper's*, February.
Woodward, C. V. (1957), *The Strange Career of Jim Crow*, New York.

26 *Leo Kuper,* An African Bourgeoisie

Racialization is a dominant process in South African society, but there is also a process of racial integration. Indeed, the South African choice, in terms of political goals actually pursued, is not between racial separation and racial integration, as the alternatives are normally phrased. It is between different modes of integration.

Integration may be conceived on the model of 'nonracialism', in which each individual has the right to participate fully and as an equal in all spheres of social activity: in other words, race is irrelevant, and the unit of integration is the individual. Or the unit of integration may be the racial group, not the individual, in which case there is a variety of models. Thus different spheres of activity may be distinguished, and a policy advocated of, say, economic integration but social separation. Or the model may be that of a racial partnership or a balance of power between the racial groups. Or racial integration may rest on stratification, with the subordinate racial groups either leveled or themselves differentially ranked.

The various modes of integration may be ordered in a continuum, ranging from the present policy of maximum emphasis on racial groups as the units to be integrated to the disappearance of race as a criterion and maximum emphasis on the individual as the basic unit, the variable being the degree of emphasis on the group. Alternatively, the continuum may be conceived as extending from maximum racial discrimination (or stratification) to racial equality, the variable being discrimination. The Government's policy of apartheid (racial separation), *considered in its practical implications rather than in its ideological formulations,* is in fact a policy of integration by means of racial stratification. The unequal racial units are to be systematically coordinated into a functioning whole. So-called separation between White and non-White is largely an intellectual device to define the units, their role in the total social system, and their manner of relationship in different spheres, although as between the non-Whites themselves there is an attempt to raise real vertical barriers against unification.

Leo Kuper, *An African Bourgeoisie*, Yale University Press, 1965, extracts from pp. 42–51.

From the point of view of the Government, the most important areas for control are the political and economic. In these fields, the Government pursues a policy of integration by stratification. Indeed, the same policy is applied to the general pattern of social relations. Apartheid is in fact a very tightly knit system of integration, extending to numerous aspects of the lives of the groups involved.

Politically, non-Whites are removed from the major sources of national power—the vote and direct representation in Parliament. Only Colored voters in the Cape Province still have the right to elect four White representatives to the House of Assembly. A high level of integration is sought administratively by the delegation of non-White affairs to special departments of state. In the case of the White population, control is distributed among many departments, with a division of function according to type of activity. For the Coloreds and Indians, on the other hand, separate Departments of Coloured Affairs and of Asiatic Affairs have been established, and the trend of policy is to centralize control over Coloreds and Indians in these departments. Their scope is defined in racial terms, not functionally. African affairs are already largely centralized in two departments, the Department of Bantu Administration and Development, and the Department of Bantu Education. Hence the administrators are in a position to implement policy toward non-Whites in a systematic and unified way.

The system of Bantu Authorities, with its promise of self-governing African linguistic communities, developing along their own lines, would appear to be a departure from the general principle of centralized bureaucratic control; and so it may prove in the future.[1] But at present, it is essentially an administrative device for harnessing the traditional tribal authorities to the state machine, and for absorbing the chiefs into the state bureaucracy. The potentially disruptive forces of tribal authority, and of tribal traditions in conflict with the requirements of a modern industrial state, are thus controlled. Tribalism is integrated into the total social system, and the African majority, which might otherwise threaten and indeed overthrow the established order, is fragmented—at least in theory.

The political system provides a basis for almost total racial integration. Education for Africans can be harmonized with their prescribed political and economic status, with the system of tribal and White authority, with the idealization of tribal life, and with the philosophy and practice of apartheid. The same general principle of harmonious development within a predetermined framework can be applied to the other non-White groups. Moreover, the heads of the racial bureaucracies are in a position to coordinate the affairs of the different racial groups with each other and with the total racial

---

[1] It is still early to assess the new constitutional developments in the Transkei: the indications are that the Transkei and its leaders will not be easily contained within the framework of apartheid.

strategy of the Government. Greater consistency of control may be expected from a bureaucracy than at the parliamentary level of compromise between contending interests.

Integration of economic activity is also based on the stratification of racial groups, on the differentiation of role by the criterion of race. This is most marked in the public sector. In Natal, for example, in the Provincial Architects Department, Africans were employed as general laborers, cleaners, and messengers; Indians as gardeners for semiskilled work, sirdars, and tractor and lorry drivers; while Europeans held the administrative positions. On the railways, there was a clear racial demarcation of posts. In the Local Health Commission, the general principle was that Indians should be employed to serve in Indian communities, Africans to serve in African communities, save that rough labor in all communities was reserved for Africans, and the higher administrative and executive positions for Europeans. To an appreciable extent, roughly similar patterns of racial differentiation prevail in the private economy. Europeans hold the managerial, executive, and skilled occupations; Africans the unskilled and to some extent the semiskilled; while Indians and Coloreds fall somewhere between the Africans and Europeans. This racial organization of the economy was beginning to change as a result of rapid industrialization. The powers assumed by the Government to reserve occupations for particular racial groups have provided the legal means for restoring the pattern, at any rate in those circumstances where the privileged position of the White worker might be threatened.

By contrast, integration in a free economy (considered as an ideal type), is based on the mobility of labor, capital, and resources, and on freedom to contract. The society is a unit from the point of view of employment, in the sense that competitive wage rates prevail throughout by virtue of the mobility of workers who would otherwise move to areas of higher remuneration (other factors being equal). It is a unit in terms of investment, in the sense that, capital and resources are not restricted to particular areas or particular uses but move freely into enterprise in any area or any sector. It is a unit in the sense that all members of the society, regardless of race, may be brought into all manner of contractual relations with each other, and that each sector of the economy is responsive to changes in every other sector.

In the racially ordered economy of South Africa, on the other hand, there are extensive restrictions on the geographical mobility of African and Indian labor, and on the occupational mobility of all non-Whites. There are limitations on the use of capital in terms of area, race, and type of investment. Freedom to contract is limited by reference to the race of the contracting parties and the nature of the contract. And as for the sensitive interrelations between sectors of the economy, a poor harvest in the African reserves has limited repercussions on the general economy, save to ensure a supply of migrant labor—which is guaranteed in any event by the poverty of the reserves.

A further distinction between a free economy and a racially organized economy may be phrased as follows. In both types, there is economic stratification of positions and of occupations, in the sense that these positions and occupations carry different rewards and prestige. In a racially organized economy, the stratification of positions is likely to be more extreme, with greater differences in the rewards for skilled and unskilled work, where the former is reserved for the racially dominant, and the latter for the racially subordinate group. And the same positions may be rewarded differently because of the race of the incumbent, as for example, in the case of European, Indian, and African teachers with the same qualifications. Both economic systems then are stratified. In a free economy, however, there is open recruitment. Theoretically, no rigidities restrict the mobility of workers: recruitment is based on the universally applicable criteria of aptitudes and training. In the racially controlled economy, there is a stratification of the groups which provide the potential recruits to the economy. The particular criterion of race becomes central, so that members of the different racial groups are recruited at different levels of the economic hierarchy, and the different levels themselves are highly stratified.

This added element of stratification does not imply a lack of integration, provided of course that sentiments of injustice do not threaten the entire system or the privileges of the White group. Even then, conflicts may give rise to mechanisms which more firmly integrate the system, as, for example, the machinery of industrial conciliation. The conflicts are contained within the system and the threat of disruption removed. Thus, the Labor Boards established by the South African Government are designed as a means of resolving labor disputes between employers and their African workers, while at the same time impeding African use of the challenging power of trade union organization.

Indeed, racial stratification in South Africa may assist the process of integration, if integration is conceived as involving the precise interweaving of the parts into a functioning whole. Control over the movement of Africans and the systems of influx and efflux control and of labor bureaus permit, in theory, the exact integration of African labor into the economy. African labor can be treated as a commodity and fed into the economy in the precise quantities and qualities desired, without any redundancies in the urban areas. Surplus workers will move out of sight into the reserves to provide a labor pool for new or changing demands, and their poverty will not be a charge on the industrial areas. This is a most exact form of economic integration.

Apart from the political and economic integration of the racial groups, there is the broader problem of integrating the wide range of social relationships, both formal and informal, into the system of apartheid, and of securing a measure of agreement on supporting values. It would seem fantastic to attempt to integrate such varied bonds between individuals and groups.

And yet this is precisely what the apartheid laws seek to accomplish: the harmonizing of social relations with the over-all ideology. The laws move in a planned way through the range of human contacts, controlling and regulating both the racial identity of the parties and the content of the relationship between them.

The model for social relationships in societies with a minimum of hereditary stratification of races is presumably the same as for a free economy or a democratic political system—the mobility of the individual and his freedom to participate in all manner of relationships. There are no special norms governing interracial relationships, and members of different races are distributed randomly in social groups. Companionship with schoolmates, spiritual affinity with fellow worshippers, and shared occupational interests stimulate loyalties cutting across those of race, and supporting a common value system.

In a racially stratified society, a consistent pattern of inequality in social relationships between members of different races may be expected to promote appropriate common values, since contact on the basis of inequality reinforces the sentiments supporting inequality. Where contacts begin to develop on a basis of equality, there is a challenge to the whole system of stratification, since the experience of equality in a particular situation negates the assumption of a general inequality. Hence the maintenance of racial stratification requires the integration of social relationships within one consistent pattern. If this were acceptable to all the groups, then presumably there would be a self-perpetuating system. Failing acceptance, the policy must be imposed by force, or a new supporting value system must be created. Both methods have been adopted by the South African Government. The volume of repressive laws and the application of force have rapidly increased, while educational policy is directed toward the forging of a common value system. The increased interest of the Dutch Reformed Church in the evangelization of Africans also has the potential function of inculcating the appropriate apartheid values.

The policy of total integration by separation has been applied since 1948, but the pattern is not yet established. There are inherent contradictions. Africans are promised the establishment of independent African states within the boundaries of South Africa, yet power is increasingly centralized, and the rights of the individual are increasingly curtailed. In these circumstances, it is inconceivable that the Government would simultaneously follow a policy of decentralizing power and extending individual rights. There is little reason to believe that authoritarian states wither away by a process of self-immolation. And yet the myth of independence engenders a measure of reality. The Government, by virtue of the sheer force of its own propaganda and the hostility of the outside world is obliged to lay the foundations for a façade of independence, while some chiefs, by accepting the myth as reality, are unleashing a truly separatist movement. An ideology to sustain apartheid unleashes forces which may destroy it, though no doubt the National Party calculates that it is not threatened by tribal Africanism, but only by national Africanism.

A large urban housing program for Africans accompanies the preservation of the urban and developed areas of South Africa for the Whites. Separation of the races in theory means, in practice, the increasing urbanization and industrial employment of Africans. Racial conflict sharpens and threatens to disrupt the entire system. Indeed, the contradictions of apartheid are widely pervasive. And there is much evidence to suggest that they arise because present policy is incompatible with the structure of South African society in many essential respects.

This incompatibility may be assessed by the number and the nature of the laws passed to lay the basis for racial separation. If miscegenation were foreign to the structure of South African society, there would not have been any need to define miscegenation between White and non-White as a criminal offence. So too, if the White group had enjoyed a monopoly of amenity and profit in the urban areas, there would have been less demand for the spatial separation of the races. Hence the Immorality Amendment Act, prohibiting miscegenation, and the Group Areas Act, providing for the compulsory segregation of the races, are evidence of the incompatibility of apartheid with the structure of South African society.

The laws passed since the accession of the National Party Government provide controls for almost every conceivable social situation, involving members of different races—marriage; 'illicit carnal intercourse'; proximity between traders and neighbors; inclusion on a common electoral roll; school education for Africans (and now for Coloreds); industrial conciliation machinery for Africans; trade unions; reservation of occupations; control of contact in trade; control of contact with Africans in schools, hospitals, clubs, places of entertainment, public assemblies, and churches (under certain conditions); occupation of premises for a substantial period of time; university education; partaking of refreshments; and (pending) all aspects of African life and work. The wide range of these laws, and the penal sanctions they incorporate, demonstrate the extensive incompatibility of racial separation with the nature of South African society.

Campaigns and their objectives, disturbances and their causes, yield further measures of incompatibility. Since the 1952 campaign against the systematic application of racial separation, that is, the Defiance Campaign against Unjust Laws in which over 8000 non-Whites voluntarily served prison sentences, there has been a continuous succession of protest campaigns, following set patterns, and persisting despite mounting repressive action. At the same time, disturbances have become endemic, from the East London riots in 1952, through the series of conflagrations in Durban at Cato Manor, to the destruction of African life by the police in Sharpeville, and assault and murder in the tribal area of Pondoland. The systematic attempt by the Government to impose a totally integrated pattern of race relations throughout the country has had the effect of drawing in wider and wider circles of protest and despair. Even the most improbable segments of the population have become involved—African women in rebellion against low wages, liquor raids, and the beer hall system, and rural Africans in revolt against influx control and the role of the chiefs as Government servants.

Increasing rule by force is further evidence of the incompatibility of Government policies. If these policies were compatible, the ultimate power of the State would not be evident: the populace would hardly be aware of the State's armory of violence. As it is, force is so manifest that even small African children in Cato Manor readily distinguished between the Saracen armored car and the troop carrier. Police with sub-machine guns appear at public gatherings, and even on the university campus. During the stay-at-home demonstration by non-Whites, at the time of the inauguration of the Republic, troop carriers and soldiers with bayonets drawn were to be seen traveling along the peaceful holiday Esplanade of Durban.

There has been a whittling away of civil liberties, proscription of organizations, long treason trials of innocent people, midnight raids and arrests, and the terror of secrecy and mystification. Men and women are deported, banished, banned, and imprisoned without trial, and now they are condemned to the 'civil death' of house arrest, 'interrogated', or tortured. The declaration of a state of emergency has set the pattern for the arbitrary suspension of the rule of law. The police are armed with Saracens and improved weapons for killing people. Military forces are mobilized for police duties. Refugees flee the country along established escape routes and seek asylum in other countries. There are the beginnings of a government or governments in exile. All this indicates that systematic racial stratification so conflicts with current trends in South Africa that it can only be maintained by the extraordinary use of force. And as a result, opposing forces are released.

The process of imposing racial separation has unleashed racialisms which seem to threaten the disintegration of South African society. These racialist reactions are inevitable because the official policies are grounded in racialism, are incompatible with certain trends in South African society, and do not rest on consent. At the same time, new adjustive mechanisms are arising to contain the threatening conflicts. These structures cross racial lines and bring together individuals on the basis of a community of interest, not as representatives of racial groups. In other words, racial policies have stimulated not only a massive reaction of racialism, but also some movement toward integration on a nonracial basis.

The opposition of the official policy of racial separation is not confined to a single group. On many issues, Whites and non-Whites have come together, finding shared values and an identity of interest. New patterns of organization are emerging to resolve racial conflicts, to promote better understanding, and to plan for a shared future, such as the multiracial conferences of churches and the multiracial political organizations. There has been a slight breach of the taboo against joint political action with non-Whites. The founding of two political parties with membership open to all racial groups, the Liberal Party and the Progressive Party, coincided with the systematic application of racial separation. The multiracial church conferences and the multiracial political parties are a response to the threatened conflict of racialisms. The threat of disruptive racialism promotes new forms of nonracial integration.

A further stimulus in the same direction is the common subjection of racial groups to the total plan. Resentment against the attendant discrimination forges new links. This is most marked among non-Whites, though White persons are not exempt from its influence.

Political developments among the Colored people demonstrate the complexity of the new alignments. Traditionally, the Coloreds have identified with the White group, since the Whites are at the apex of the system of stratification, and the Coloreds enjoyed the highest racial rating and privileges among the non-White groups. Coloreds tended to accept their position as appendages of the Whites, and to guard their privileges by maintaining an extreme social distance in relation to Africans. This is beginning to change as a result of new discriminations against the Colored people, which were motivated partly by the total nature of the plan for racial differentiation, and partly, perhaps mainly, by the fear that the Afrikaners might merge into the Coloreds, with whom they had already intermingled their blood. For some of the same reasons that Coloreds maintained their exclusiveness in relation to Africans, the National Party Government is increasing the social distance between Whites and Coloreds, so that Coloreds now find difficulty in maintaining their traditional attitudes. The result has been a movement among Coloreds toward cooperation with Africans. This change so conflicts with their traditional attitudes that it is difficult to assess its significance. It may be a passing phase with only a small section of the Coloreds drawn into enduring relationships with Africans, or it may be extensive in its effects and inaugurate a basic reorientation in racial attitudes. In any event, some new links will be forged between Coloreds and Africans.

Indians are particularly threatened by the competing racialisms of Afrikaners and Africans, since they are a small minority, with a few conspicuously wealthy men, and with some commercial interests to which the new trading classes in both the African and Afrikaner communities aspire. The promise by the Government that Africans would enjoy a monopoly of trade in their own areas has helped to focus African commercial antagonism against Indians, who had largely pioneered this trade. There is much hostility, latent, but sufficiently near the surface to be readily inflamed by African or White politicians. The 1949 African riots in Durban emphasized the vulnerable position of Indians, and their need to forge closer links. At the political level, the South African Indian Congress worked as a member of the Congress Alliance, which included the proscribed African National Congress, the South African Coloured People's Congress, the South African Congress of Trade Unions and the Congress of Democrats (also proscribed).

Cooperative approaches by Coloreds and Indians involve the Africans themselves in new interracial contacts. There is some reciprocity—Africans derive help from the greater political experience and resources of the Indian political leaders, and strength from non-White unity. These new political relationships act as a measure of restraint on African racialism. At the non-political level, there is increasing contact, with visiting of homes and the forming of friendships. And some significance should be attached to the assistance Indian lawyers have rendered African political leaders by making available to them facilities for legal training.

The sociological principle involved in these tendencies toward non-White integration is the unifying effect of a common subordination. The Government has chosen to reduce the hierarchical distance between the non-White groups. Suffering a common subordination, sections of the non-White groups are showing signs of drawing together. Such are the antagonisms and prejudices between them that the strongest pressure was needed to forge political cooperation. Apparently the Government provided this. The aversion felt for the Government by some members of the non-White groups is seemingly greater than the aversion they feel for each other. In direct contravention of its goals, apartheid is effecting a measure of non-White unification which might otherwise have been delayed for decades.

27 *Ira Katznelson,* Black Men, White Cities

Racial Buffering: Colonial Relationships in the Mother Country

'How is it possible', Cobbett inquired in 1808, 'for us to justify our conduct upon any principle of morality? Conquests in India are not at all necessary to our safety or comfort' (see Bennett, 1953, p. 65). The imperialist response to this gnawing moral question was an affirmation of moral idealism—the backward races needed civilizing.[1] Exploitative racist and humanitarian impulses fused to produce an ennobling paternalist doctrine. The colonized were pictured as children, the offspring of the family of Empire, later the Commonwealth, headed by the benevolent matriarch Britain.[2]

Contemporary racial attitudes have been shaped by the colonial experience, forged in the crucible of imperialism. A nation's culture, both social and political, is the outcome of a unique historical process. Though not all learning is culture, all culture is learned, and Britain, in particular, is characterized

---

[1] The Empire, Lecky (1893, pp. 22–3) argued in his inaugural lecture at Cambridge, had expanded because Englishmen 'have largely employed their redundant energies in exploring, conquering, civilising, and governing distant and half-savage lands', and spoke of 'an Empire planted amid the shifting sands of half-civilised and anarchial races'. Racism, Epstein (1964, p. 13) observed, 'seems an almost inevitable component of imperialism. In its crude form, as that the only good Indian is a dead Indian, it accompanied cruel and bloody conquests, and in its less ferocious form it went along with benevolent paternalism'.

[2] The ennobling theme of benevolent paternalism was adopted by socialist and Tory, imperialist and anti-imperialist alike. Thus while the Governor-General of Nigeria, in 1922, asserted that 'the standard which the white man must set before him when dealing with the uncivilised races must be a high one', the Labour party in 1926 declared as its official policy 'with regard to the native races' that 'the Empire should be, in the words of the Covenant, a Trustee for the well-being of the natives'. The death of Empire and the birth of the Commonwealth did not dim these sentiments. In 1953, for example, when the migration of West Indians to Britain was beginning to increase in numbers, Salisbury spoke of 'that portion of the Empire which is not yet grown up, which is not yet in a position to manage its own affairs, internal or external, without guidance from us. . . . We are dealing with people's of an infinite variety of races and colour and gradations of civilisation.' Similarly, the Conservative Commonwealth Council argued in 1955, 'A worthy colonial power has to perform the supreme and often thankless task of the old nobility and middle classes of the better kind: to keep civilisation alive and hand it over sound and safe to rising new bodies of men and women who previously were incapable of fending for themselves in the modern world'.

Ira Katznelson, *Black Men, White Cities*, Oxford University Press for the Institute of Race Relations, 1973, pp. 178–88.

by a hereditary culture.[3] As a consequence of the heritage of imperialism, British feelings of racial superiority became part of the country's cultural baggage, not always consciously felt, but always potentially operative. Most Englishmen alive today have grown up nurtured by a press, literature and education that promoted the related notions of the civilizing mission and racial paternalism.[4]

Distinguishing between folk prejudice, politically relevant prejudice, and its structural-systemic expression, the history of the politics of race in Britain since 1948 is the paradoxical history of the politicization of prejudice and its national and local systemic expression in political consensus arrangements calculated to take race off the two-party political agenda. The operative phrase, nationally and locally, has been 'for immigrants', as the colonial ethos of racial paternalism found domestic rhetorical and institutional expression.

A key feature of classic colonial patterns of social control—indirect rule through a broker, native leadership—has been replicated in the mother country. Indirect rule, as Apter (1955, pp. 120–1) notes, is not a precise term; it refers, in an omnibus way, to a variety of colonial practices of governing in different areas. The essential feature of indirect rule is that native chiefs were an integral part of the colonial administration. As Lugard put it, 'There are not two sets of rulers—British and native—working either separately or in cooperation, but a single government in which the native chiefs have well defined duties. . . . They must be complementary to each other and the chief himself must understand that he has no right to place and power unless he renders his proper services to the state'. Where traditional chiefs did not exist (for the Kikuyu or the Plateau Tonga of Northern Rhodesia, for example), they were invented (Worsley, 1967, p. 38). 'The colonial administrator turned to them basically because he was faced with the problem of creating an administrative system where none existed'; to communicate and to control the colonized, the colonizers needed authority-figures who could provide 'a

---

[3] For discussions, see Barbu (1960, pp. 6, 13, 42, 203, 212), Kluckhohn (1966, pp. 40–53), and the comparative report on anti-semitism by Tumin entitled, 'Intergroup Attitudes of Youth and Adults in England, France, and Germany' (1963), based on a report prepared for a conference on the subject at Munich in October 1962.

[4] The ingrained stereotypes of backward races and white superiority have been perpetuated by British schools. Attlee recalled the great map at school 'with large portions coloured red. It was an intoxicating vision for a small boy, for, as we understood it, all these people were ruled for their own good by strong silent men, civil servants and soldiers as portrayed by Kipling. We believed in our great imperial mission'. The assumptions and language of racialism were incorporated into school histories. The widely used sixth edition of Raynor's textbook (1946, pp. 386, 395), for instance, discusses 'the peculiar qualities in the Englishman that make him so successful as a colonist and a ruler of backward races', and later states, 'The traditional policy of non-interference which had such happy results in the great self-governing dominions had not been so suitable for those colonies which, situated in the tropics and inhabited chiefly by backward races, were unfitted for democracy'. Attlee (1960, p. 6).

bridge of legitimation', and enable 'an administration to divide and rule: popular resentments and hatreds could be deflected on to the local officials while the ultimate authority could remain remote, unseen and "above the battle" ' (Worsley, 1967).

The arrangements of the 1965 White Paper institutionalized indirect rule with respect to the Third World immigrant population. 'In one sense', Eric Irons (1962, p. 2) wrote in his 1961–2 report to the Nottingham Council, 'the organiser looks upon his functions as being that of an "interpreter" between the new and the established communities and his advice and help are often sought by statutory and voluntary bodies in their approach to these sections of the population'. The national and local liaison committees were not meant to be spokesmen for the newcomers or organized pressure groups. Rather, their orientation was consensual. N.C.C.I.'s (1967) guidelines on the formation of local committees stressed that 'it should be emphasized at every stage that this is *not a committee to serve the interests of one section of the community but a committee to promote racial harmony. It is therefore beneficial to all*' [italic in original]. Local representation, the guidelines urged, should include party representation, service organizations and clubs (Rotary, Chamber of Commerce, working men's clubs, etc.), voluntary and statutory service organizations (Council of Social Service, Family Welfare Association, probation office, the police, the welfare officer, etc.), and *visible* immigrant leadership: 'There may already be immigrant associations in the area which can be approached for representation, but if not, the officers of appropriate High Commissions may be able to supply some names, as also may the National Committee for Commonwealth Immigrants' (N.C.C.I., 1967).

Seen in these terms, most of the literature on British race politics misses the significance of the critical structural decision to link the Third World population to the polity through buffer institutions, replicating key features of traditional colonial relationships. Thus, to cite only a few examples, Abbott (1971) has written, in the context of his critique of John Rex's work, 'It is probably not very important to decide whether or not the N.C.C.I. had a general "political" role' [the important political issues are raised later in the essay, p. 318]; and Kramer (1969), Deakin, and Bourne (1970) distinguish between deleterious (political) immigration control features of the White Paper, and its (non-political) 'constructive' institutional arrangements. Yet, as we have seen, the 1965 document was the outcome of the building of a *political* consensus, aimed at depoliticizing race.

In their attempt to create a stable, coherent, predictable politics (or non-politics) of race, British politicians had to deal with the immigrant–colonial amalgam. Hence it was necessary both severely to curtail immigration from the Third World Commonwealth and to create quasi-colonial institutional structures to deal with the issues of race outside of the traditional political arenas. As a result, the Third World population has been institutionally separated from the society-wide, largely class-based network of political institutions and associations, and has been unable to compete effectively for the scarce resource of political power.

From its founding, the instruments of indirect rule—N.C.C.I. and its local affiliate committees—were put in an impossibly ambiguous position: sponsored and financed by the Government, established by a document that gave systematic expression to cultural-folk prejudices, yet expected to somehow speak and act 'for immigrants'. Thus one N.C.C.I. development officer has complained, 'We have no policy', adding, 'We are caught in a bind. What can you expect from a government agency? We must be careful' [from an interview with Anne Evans, N.C.C.I. and C.R.C. Development Officer for Northern England, 21 Jan. 1969]. The organizations' general secretary accepted the politicians' non-political definition of N.C.C.I.'s role ('Politics is not my line') (cited in Heineman, 1972). As a consequence of its anomalous position, the organization, Dipak Nandy (1967, p. 6) has observed, has generated 'an atmosphere of superficial liberalism and of generalized goodwill. . . . Its characteristic style is paralysis and non-statement'.

A recent study of the work of ten local liaison officers revealed clearly the way in which the structural arrangements of the White Paper limited behavioural choices to a relatively meaningless set of alternatives. The liaison officers found that goodwill on their part could not be translated effectively into action; they felt constrained by the structural limitations they did not create. The officers uniformly found their financial dependence on the local authority led to embarrassment and ambiguity; most criticized the tri-partite obligation of liaison officers: they are paid by central government funds, and responsible both to the local authority and the executive committee of their organization (Levy, unpub., pp. 5, 8).

'Looking back upon the whole period from 1955 to the present day', the authors of *Colour and Citizenship* (Rose, *et. al.*, 1969, p. 391) maintained, 'it is clear that it was too much to expect that "integration" could be decisively promoted or affected by the local voluntary committees unless they had more political backing'. But the very origins and structure of the buffer institutions militated against this level of political support; the White Paper institutional network was created only incidentally to promote integration. Rather, it was meant to structure and deflect immigrant political participation into nonthreatening activity.

At their best, buffer institutions can, despite their shortcomings, under certain circumstances, become significant arenas of inter-group accommodation in themselves which may be more accessible to new potential partisans than traditional established institutions. To assume this role, the buffers must have the capacity to affect the distribution and allocation of scarce resources. They must be descriptively representative in membership, responsive in policy, and efficient in policy-execution. To prevent the process of bargaining from becoming one of dictation, they must link groups that, in terms of power capacity, are relatively equal.

As we have seen, however, the race relations buffers established in Britain do not meet these standards. Though they have attempted at times to be responsive (substantively representative), their descriptively unrepresentative membership and their lack of efficacy have combined to resemble closely the ideal-type of ineffectual paternalism (see Katznelson, 1973, chap. 3, s. III). At their best, buffering institutions are an inadequate substitute for direct, bi-directional political participation. In Britain these structures, by rewarding complaisant 'leaders', by inhibiting the development of Third World political consciousness, and by permitting politicians to claim that integration is successfully being promoted (see, for instance, Ennals, 1968, pp. 435–6), have actually obstructed the development of more viable immigrant polity relationships. The N.C.C.I. (and its successor the Community Relations Commission) and the committees it supervises have produced neither productive nor distributive justice.

The 1965 political consensus has taken race out of politics, then, in two respects. Immigrants' felt needs and demands are dealt with by quasi-political bodies like the Community Relations Commission and the Race Relations Board, which administer the country's anti-discrimination legislation, rather than by Parliament and the Government directly. In neither institution are Third World representatives selected primarily by the immigrant communities themselves.[5] Secondly, since 1965 the Front Benches of both parties have accepted the dual framework of very strict immigration controls coupled with anti-discrimination legislation and quasi-political buffering institutions. These institutions (there are now over eighty local committees) have pursued an elite, consensual strategy, leaving the mass of the Third World immigrants politically unanchored.[6]

Both aspects of the depoliticization of race have permitted the Government to avoid making political policy decisions in this field, some of which must be made if anti-discrimination legislation, which at present lacks adequate enforcement provisions, is to have any meaning at all. In the area of housing

[5] At a special general meeting of the Camden Committee for Community Relations on 4 April 1968, the Rev. Wilfred Wood, a West Indian, proposed that N.C.C.I. be replaced by a National Commission for Racial Equality with 25 per cent of its members to be nominated by the Government, 25 per cent elected by existing voluntary liaison committees, and 50 per cent elected by the Third World ethnic communities on the basis of registered membership. After some discussion in the national press, these proposals have been ignored by the media and by policy-makers.

[6] In preparing his Ph.D. thesis, Daniel Lawrence found, in a random sample of 122 male coloured immigrants drawn from Nottingham's central parliamentary constituency that 75 per cent had not heard of the Consultative Committee; 19 per cent claimed to have knowledge of the organization, but in fact knew almost nothing about it; of the 6 per cent who knew something of the committee, two were members of immigrant organizations that had served on the committee. I am indebted to Mr Lawrence for this information.

for example, the Race Relations Act of 1968, according to Moore (1968, p. 390) 'will be rendered nugatory unless the Government takes a number of political decisions in an unambiguous manner (a major change in policy itself). . . . Local authorities must be prevented from discriminating in their housing allocation and planning policies, or by selective application of over-crowding regulations'. Like the pre-political consensus of the 1950s, the political consensus of the late 1960s (and early 1970s) encourages elite defer-ment of policy questions of this kind.

Ironically, despite the broad area of bi-partisan agreement codified by the White Paper, race has only partially been depoliticized, for the effort to maintain the political consensus has entailed repeated concessions to those who have continued to appeal to the public's folk prejudices in demagogic fashion. The reaction to Enoch Powell's first major speeches on immigration in the spring and autumn of 1968 instructively illustrates the point.

In Birmingham on 20 April, Powell, then Shadow Minister of Defence, spoke in emotive terms about Third World immigration: 'It is like a nation busily engaged in heaping up its own funeral pyre'. He suggested not only that 'the total inflow for settlement should be reduced at once to negligible proportions', but also urged 'the encouragement of re-emigration. . . . In short, suspension of immigration and encouragement of re-emigration hang together, logically and humanely, as two aspects of the same approach'. (Text of the speech in *Race*, 1968, pp. 94–9.) Edward Heath issued a statement the following day announcing that Powell had been dropped from the Shadow Cabinet:

I have told Mr. Powell that I consider the speech he made in Birmingham yesterday to have been racialist *in tone* and liable to exacerbate racial tensions. This is un-acceptable from one of the leaders of the Conservative Party and incompatable with the responsibility of a member of the Shadow Cabinet. (Italic added, p. 99.)

Heath, however, made it clear that he did not differ with the substance of Powell's remarks: 'I have repeatedly emphasized that the policy of the Con-servative Party is that immigration must be more stringently limited and that immigrants wishing to return to their own countries should be helped financially to do so'. The Labour Home Secretary indicated that the Govern-ment accepted this position too. On B.B.C. television on 29 April, James Callaghan stated that 'the Ministry of Social Security is willing to repatriate any immigrant family unable to pay for itself and wanting to return home'. He added that he was aware of unrest in the country regarding coloured immigration, declaring 'that is why I introduced the Commonwealth Immi-grants Act in February[7] in order to limit the number of people coming into this country' (*The Times*, 1968, 30 April, p. 1).

[7] Mr Callaghan, of course, was referring to the bill rushed through Parliament in February 1968 which introduced a voucher system for Kenyan Asians (1500 per year) even

Powell repeated his proposals at Eastbourne in November, this time calling for a special Ministry of Repatriation and announcing a new doctrine of citizenship based on colour: 'The West Indian or Asian does not by being born in England become an Englishman. In law he becomes a United King- dom citizen by birth; in fact he is a West Indian or Asian still (*Sunday Times*, 1968, 17 Nov., p. 8). This time Heath condemned 'the character assassination of any racial group in this country' but called too for stricter controls based on the amalgamation of aliens and Commonwealth immigration legislation (*The Times*, 1968, 18 Nov., p. 1). He repeated these proposals at Walsall in January 1969 (and moved to enact them in 1971). The Government responded by revoking the right of Commonwealth citizens to enter the United Kingdom to marry their fiancees regardless of whether the woman was born in the United Kingdom or not; this concessionary right was not revoked in the case of aliens (*The Times*, 1969, 31 Jan., p. 1). Powell's substantive proposals, if not Powell himself, were on the legitimate agenda of political discourse and accommodation. The maintenance of the political consensus required con- tinued systemic concessions, for the substance of the consensus was less important than the fact of consensus. (See Lipjhart, 1969, pp. 207ff., for a discussion of analogous 'cartel of elites' arrangements.)

Britain's Third World population could have been linked to the polity either by a legitimately colour-blind policy that would have permitted them to divide, like other Englishmen, as individuals based largely on class affiliation (individual integration) or by a recognition that the immigrants constituted, at least in the early decades of contact, a discrete political conflict collectivity, thus making possible bi-directional group linkages of boundary management and direct bargaining (collective integration).[8] The first alternative clearly would have been preferred by a majority of the West Indian immigrants who were moving away from colour-ascriptive societies; they wanted and expected to be accepted as Englishmen. Black (as opposed to coloured) West Indians have suffered most in their home islands from the white-bias legacy of colonial rule; in Thornton's (1968, p. 320) telling phrase, they have only one world to belong to and are not at home in it. Some reacted to this intolerable situation by affirming their blackness. Members of the Ras Tafari cult, for example, believe that Haile Sellassie (Ras Tafari) of Ethiopia is the living God, that the black man must seek salvation by returning to Africa (see Smith, Augier and Nettleford, 1960; Simpson, 1955). The West Indian blacks

---

though they held British passports. The bill was introduced after a brief but frenzied campaign, led by Powell and Duncan Sandys, that talked in the familiar terms of an uncontrollable flood of immigrants. It is noteworthy that Lord Butler has indicated that he would have voted against the bill had he been present at the vote in the House of Lords. Interview with Lord Butler, Cambridge (2 March 1968).

[8] I am referring here, of course, to structural, not cultural, integration.

who came to Britain were afflicted by the same frustrations and feelings of inadequacy. Like the Ras Tafarians, they too seek to resolve those feelings through migration. But significantly, they have looked to and moved to England. Like the Ras Tafari movement, the migration to Britain was 'a lower-class thing; it was a black thing' (Naipaul, 1962, p. 230). But unlike their Ras Tafarian countrymen, the migrants to England moved toward 'whiteness', to the mother country.

To be sure, the West Indian migrants chose to come to Britain for economic reasons, for their frustrations at home have most often been defined in economic terms. The average migrant will state when asked that he has come to work, to better his economic position (for extended discussions, see Peach, 1968; Davison, 1962). Yet, the migrants have come not simply for economic reasons, but for social and cultural ones as well. In moving to Britain, the West Indian migrant rejects implicitly the whole inhibiting colour-ascriptive network of his island's social structure. That system of relationships condemned him to inferior status, prevented him from achieving what the culture defined as good, and offered few compensations. He had little chance to achieve the positive cultural norms of 'whiteness' and 'respectability'. He could not assimilate; the middle-class solution was beyond his reach. As Philip Mason has put it:

There is a sense in which the Caribbean displays the essence of colonialism. It is true that in one respect this region is different from most of the colonial world; there are only fragmentary remains of a native population subjugated by invaders. But it is the essence of colonialism . . . that the few impose on the many a spiritual yoke which comes to govern their day to day actions, more constantly and pervasively, if less obtrusively, than the physical force which lies in the background. Nowhere did this happen more completely than in the Caribbean. Whole societies were persuaded to imitate a way of life that was quite unfamiliar to them, one they had little hope in attaining and not in itself particularly estimable; what was more serious, they came to despise themselves and their own way of life.[9]

The migration from the West Indies to Britain can be seen in part as an attempt to achieve social, cultural, as well as economic and political assimilation into the 'superior' society. The black migrant hoped to do one better

[9] Mason (1970, p. 274). The dual theme of the rejection of European culture and colour values and the search for an African identity is the central issue in West Indian literature. According to Coulthard (1962, p. 52) there have been four principal variations on this theme: 'First, the feeling that the Caribbean Negro is somehow constricted in the moulds of European thought and behaviour patterns which are not fitted to his nature. Linked with this is the interest in African cultures, past and present, both in Africa and their remains in the West Indies. Second, the feeling that European civilisation has failed, by becoming excessively concerned with the production of happiness for the human individual. African, or Negro culture, is presented as being nearer to nature and nearer to man. Third, the rejection of Christianity as an agent or ally of colonialism; and finally, the attack on European civilisation for the brutality and cynicism with which it enslaved and exploited the Negro while still maintaining high-sounding principles of freedom and humanitarianism'.

than his coloured countryman—he would become English. To the West Indies, the Englishman had brought the prestige of his association with England. It was this esteem by association that the West Indian migrants wanted to share, and it was this ambition that caused most to reject agricultural and domestic work in England, though they had been farmers and domestics in the Caribbean (Oakley, 1968, p. 6). It was this too that occasioned their surprise when they found that many white Englishmen did unskilled, even menial work. And it was this, ultimately, that contributed to the bitterness and frustrations of life in England, for there too they were and are defined by their colour. Seeking to escape the oppressions of colour, they found they were still black.[10]

Thus, the increasing political relevance and systemic expression of the folk prejudices of British society made impossible individual integration for most of the migrants. The realities of discrimination, the political conciliation of those who advocated colour-based immigration policies, and the development of a political consensus by white elites at the Third World immigrants' expense clashed too sharply with the hopes of individual acceptance. Yet the second possibility, that of collective integration, has been achieved only in the highly inadequate form of uni-directional buffering institutions.

The fluid period of the politics of race in Britain is over. The trend towards stricter immigration controls (and perhaps ultimately a programme of forced repatriation) aimed at reducing the number of black Englishmen appears irreversible. Two anti-discrimination laws have been passed, both with loopholes and weak enforcement provisions (see Dickey, 1968, pp. 338–41; Rex, 1968, pp. 78–80). The buffer institutions created and sustained by the White Paper consensus have been put on a more permanent basis; section 25 of the 1968 Race Relations Act established the Community Relations Commission as the successor to N.C.C.I. Unlike N.C.C.I., the C.R.C. is a statutory body responsible to the Home Office.[11]

In conclusion, I have argued that British race relations can only be understood as an amalgam of the colonial and voluntary migrant cases. The most

[10] The most comprehensive survey of racial discrimination in Britain concluded, 'Of the three coloured groups, the experiences of the West Indians have been the worst. To a considerable extent this is due to their higher expectations on arrival and their greater desire to participate in a British pattern of life. This has caused them greater exposure to rejection and rebuff, and therefore to have a greater feeling that discrimination occurs'. Political and Economic Planning (1967, p. 8).

[11] For an extended discussion, see Community Relations Commission (1970). In a letter to the Bexley Community Relations Council on 28 May 1970 (at the onset of the election campaign), Edward Heath indicated strong support for the C.R.C., noting that it was not 'likely that we would favour a merger between the Community Relations Commission and the Race Relations Board'. Ioan Davies (1971, p. 439) has recently commented, 'The retention of the Community Relations Commission is also an indication that—in one area at least—the Conservatives intend to try to keep the lid on'.

significant feature of the politics of race in Britain has been its non-integration into an institutionalized class conflict framework. Thus, the Labour Government's White Paper of August 1965, 'Immigration from the Commonwealth', gave political expression to the immigrant-colonial amalgam in an effort by national and local party leaders to channel the issues of race to institutions outside of the usual political arenas. The issues of race, for British politicians, were incoherent and anomic. This central feature of domestic racial politics produced a political consensus that strictly controlled Third World immigration, and that—in the key structural decision of the period—linked the immigrants to the polity indirectly through quasi-colonial buffer institutions. These arrangements made impossible meaningful immigrant political participation, produced a group of broker leaders, formalized the institutional separation of the black population, and made it highly unlikely that Britain's Third World population would secure an equitable share of the scarce resource of political power.

This discussion is a corrective to the dominant research foci in the literature on immigrant assimilation, prejudice, and discrimination, and points the way to neglected research concerns. As such, it represents the beginning, not the end, of analysis. In part, then, this section should be read as an implicit research agenda. Much needed are additional studies (hopefully with some actional consequences) of the buffering institutions and their consequences for social and economic mobility, political participation rates, perceived satisfaction or deprivation, patterns of conflict and accommodation; in short, on the ways in which the political consensus buffer institutions define the limits of choice and racial justice.

A few speculative comments may be hazarded. The perceptual field of the Third World population, it is reasonable to assume, changes in reaction to changes in the response of the white population, at the mass and elite levels, to them. It is to the institutionalized politics of race of the political consensus that the black population does and will respond. For many of the immigrants, the events of the last two and a half decades have been profoundly alienating. A recent study of the reaction of West Indian leaders to the national and local politics of race concluded that there was no doubt that most were convinced that there had been a rapid deterioration in race relations (Manderson-Jones in Abbott, 1971, based on unstructured interviews with twenty-one West Indians, most living in London). A Nottingham Jamaican put his reactions this way:

In 1944 I was a serviceman in the British air force fighting for freedom and democracy. In 1947 I became a settler in Nottingham. In the 1958 race riots I became a coloured man. In the 1962 Commonwealth Immigrants Act I became a coloured immigrant. And in 1968 I am an unwanted coloured immigrant. You tell me what's going to happen to me in 1970. (Quoted in Heilpern and Hiro, 1968, p.11.)

The buffering institutions may have bought social peace in the short term. But, typically, when buffers lose their legitimacy, when one of the groups linked by the buffer breaks its connection with it, there is, to use Halpern's (1968, p. 52) opaque terminology, a lapse into political incoherence. Present evidence indicates the likelihood of this rejection of officially sanctioned buffers by most blacks; 'more and more, to put it succinctly, the immigrant sees himself less a West Indian or a Sikh in English society, and more as a black man in a white society' (Lewis, 1970, p. 89). Writing in 1970, Gordon Lewis observed,

Not to collaborate is to lose financial aid, even more, is to abjure the English conviction that the way to get things done is to know the 'important people' at both the national and local government levels. To collaborate, on the other hand, is to run the risk of absorption, of being killed by official patronage, of seeming to betray the immigrant interests to a career of comfortable opportunism. It is not too much to say that most of the organizations in the field have decided by now in favour of complete independence, after a long experience of disillusionment (p. 91).

The short term peace bought by the buffers may soon yield to a continuing, and increasingly bitter, corrosive politics of racial confrontation and despair. This development, it might be argued, is not inevitable, but it surely is more likely than when the Third World immigrants first came in large numbers. In the 1950s, the problem was one of folk prejudices expressed in private acts of discrimination; by the late 1960s, the problem had become one of the political institutionalization of racism, a problem more resistant to change. In the United States, the change from black quiescent acceptance of the migration period linkages to non-violent protest to the Black Power Movement of the 1960s to violent ghetto rebellions to urban guerilla activity has taken place over a period of seven decades. In Britain, as a result of the unitary state (which provides fewer access points than the American Federal system), increased communications, awareness of the American experience, and the internationalization of Third World anti-colonial conflicts, the consequences of the unsatisfactory political linkages are liable to be felt much more rapidly as the process of disenchantment will be accelerated.

Institutions and linkages created by men can be reconstructed by men. This much is clear: existing political-structural race relations arrangements must not merely be tinkered with but transformed. The institutions created 'for immigrants' must be both representative of and made responsible to the constituency they claim to represent—black Englishmen themselves. At present, members of the C.R.C. are appointed by the Home Secretary, the majority of local committee representatives are white delegates of community organizations, and though the salaried local officers are hired by the local committees, the C.R.C. openly uses its control of funds to quash potentially embarrassing activism (Dummett, 1970). If the existing elaborate race relations structures are to be transformed, they must shed their ethos of benevolent paternalism; the dominant, controlling voice must be black.

Secondly, given the fact of pervasive racial discrimination in Britain, the C.R.C. and its committees (if they are to have any meaningful role at all) must, at the expense of their presently cherished pose of respectability (Reddaway, 1970; Taylor, 1970), become far more outspoken and active in seeking an equitable allocation of jobs, houses, and schooling for their Third World constituency. In short, if they are to be more than sham instruments of social control, these institutions need to become representative in all dimensions. At present, the C.R.C. and its affiliate local committees insulate politicians from the black community and permit them to handle the issues of race on politically manageable terms for them. Instead, I am suggesting that these organizations be transformed into vigorous advocates for the Third World population in a continuing process of boundary management and direct bargaining.

Given present political realities, of course, including the financial and statutory position of these organizations, these proposals are hopelessly utopian. But this reality only indicates the scope of present and future tragedies, for only if just collective integration is made possible through transformed political relationships will future generations of black Englishmen not be strangers and afraid in a world they never made.

References

Abbott, S. (ed.) (1971), *The Prevention of Racial Discrimination in Britain*, London.
Apter, D. (1955), *The Gold Coast in Transition*, Princeton.
Attlee, C. (1960), *Empire into Commonwealth*, London.
Barbu, Z. (1960), *Problems of Historical Psychology*, London.
Bennett, G. (ed.) (1953), *The Concept of Empire: Burke to Attlee*, London.
Community Relations Commission (1970), Report for 1969/70, London.
Coulthard, G. R. (1962), *Race and Culture in Caribbean Literature*, London.
Davies, I. (1971), 'Pretty political devices', *New Society*, 18 March.
Davison, R. B. (1962), *West Indian Immigrants*, London.
Deakin, N. and Bourne, J. (1970), 'Powell, minorities, and the 1970 election', *Political Quarterly*, vol. 41, July.
Dickey, A. (1968), 'The Race Relations Act, 1968', the Institute of Race Relations *Newsletter*, November/December.
Dummett, M. (1970), 'Race and colour in Great Britain', talk given to the Society for Philosophy and Public Affairs, Columbia University, 21 November.
Ennals, D. (1968), 'Labour's race relations policy', the Institute of Race Relations *Newsletter*, November/December.
Epstein, L. D. (1964), *British Politics in the Suez Crisis*, London.
Halpern, M. (1968), 'Conflicts, violence, and the dialectics of modernization', unpublished paper.

Heilpern, J. and Hiro, D. (1968), 'The town we were told was tolerant', the *Observer*, 1 December.

Heineman, B. W. (1972), *The Politics of the Powerless: A Study of the Campaign against Racial Discrimination*, London.

Irons, E. (1962), 'Report of the organiser for work amongst the coloured communities', February 1961–March 1962, City of Nottingham, Council Education Committee.

Katznelson, I. (1973), *Black Men, White Cities*, Oxford.

Kluckhohn, C. (1960), 'The Study of culture', in L. Coser and B. Rosenberg (eds.), *Sociological Theory*, New York.

Kramer, D. C. (1969), 'White versus colored in Britain: an explosive confrontation?' *Social Research*, vol. 36, Winter.

Lecky, W. E. H. (1893), *The Empire: Its Value and Growth*, London.

Levy, M. (unpub.), 'The work of liaison officers'.

Lewis, G. (1970), 'Protest among the immigrants: the dilemma of a minority culture', in B. Crick and W. Robson (eds.), *Protest and Discontent*, London.

Lipjhart, A. (1969), 'Consociational democracy', *World Politics*, vol. 21, January.

Mason, P. (1970), *Patterns of Dominance*, London.

Moore, R. (1968), 'Labour and Colour—1965-68', the Institute of Race Relations *Newsletter*, October.

Naipaul, V. S. (1962), *The Middle Passage*, London.

Nandy, D. (1967), 'The National Committee for Commonwealth Immigrants: an assessment', C.A.R.D. Position Paper, London.

N.C.C.I. (1967), 'Notes for guidance on the formation of a voluntary liaison committee', unpublished, April.

Oakley, R. (ed.) (1968), *New Backgrounds*, London.

Peach, C. (1968), *West Indian Migration to Britain: A Social Geography*, London.

Political and Economic Planning (1967), *Racial Discrimination*, London.

Race (1968), vol. X, July.

Raynor, R. (1946), *England in Modern Times*, London.

Reddaway, J. (1970), 'What happened to the CRC?', *Race Today*, vol. 2, 7 July.

Rex, J. (1968), 'The race relations catastrophe', in T. Burgess, *et al.*, *Matters of Principle: Labour's Last Chance*, London.

Rose, E. J. B., *et al.* (1969), *Colour and Citizenship: A Report on British Race Relations*, London.

Simpson, G. E. (1955), 'The Ras Tafari movement in Jamaica: a study in race and class conflict', *S.F.*, vol. 34, December.

Smith, M. G., Augier, R. and Nettleford, R. (1960), 'The Ras Tafari movement in Kingston, Jamaica', report for the Institute of Social and Economic Research, University College of the West Indies.

Taylor, W. (1970), 'Aerial's revolt: community relations in the 1970s', *Race Today*, vol. 2, 7 July.

Thornton, A. P. (1968), *For the File on Empire*, London.

Worsley, P. (1967), *The Third World*, London.

28 *Harry Brill,* Why Organizers Fail

We have just completed a painful examination of the failure of the Neighborhood Action Committee organizers to move effectively toward winning the
rent strike. Forcing the Housing Authority to accede to their demands had
a dual purpose for them. They believed that the conditions under which the
tenants lived were abhorrent, and they considered it a major task to force
the agency to change its practices and policies. NAC also wanted to build a
radical black nationalist movement, and believed that a victory over these
'white exploiters' would advance this long-range aim.

But NAC never developed the political muscle and influence to win. The
organizers failed to build an effective organization. Tenant membership did
not increase, and the striking tenants did not participate. In fact the tenants
who were relatively uninterested in the first place, became even less committed as the strike progressed. And because they did not participate and no
gains were made, the strikers formed no attachment to the organization.
In the city-wide community, the organizers were almost politically friendless
toward the end of the strike; by then, they had fairly thoroughly discredited
themselves. Finally, despite the organizers' own impressions, they never
really intimidated the Housing Authority.

While losing the strike, the organizers still might have educated the tenants
politically and brought them around to their point of view. Radicals often
use issues for this purpose, and NAC certainly gave lip service to that goal.
To have worked in this way would have brought the organizers a step closer
to their ideological aims. But NAC failed to make any progress in this regard
and in fact lost a good deal of ground. The tenants were more discouraged
after the strike than when they originally joined. If they learned any lessons
at all, it was that 'you can't fight City Hall', to say nothing about battling
the system at large.

NAC's main immediate goal, winning the strike, was certainly a difficult
one; even the effective mobilization of political resources carried with it no
guarantees of success. Though some tenant unions have been rewarded for

Harry Brill, *Why Organizers Fail: The Story of a Rent Strike*, University of
California Press, 1971, pp. 140–52.

their efforts, many have not. Even among well-organized groups, factors such as the lack of sufficient resources, the power and ruthlessness of government agencies, and internal dissension within the community have caused incalculable political damage. Nevertheless, there is a very serious difference between organizations that 'fight the good fight' and those that are too weak internally to ever stand a chance. Unfortunately, the difference often escapes the public. The media often conveys the impression that some of these groups are towers of strength, when in reality there is more noise than substance to their movement. The failure of the public, and particularly the poor, to realize this feeds the illusion that the establishment cannot be beaten. How can they, if even the strong are unable? This is tragic, but not only because it is terribly pessimistic; it is inaccurate as well.

For the sake of political clarity, then, let us admit that NAC was more noise than substance. Though it received a great deal of publicity, and many imagined it a poor man's Goliath, it suffocated internally, and despite sincerity and good intentions its armor was slight for the many battles it took on. NAC's failure to develop an effective political program was, to a great extent, a function of the behavior of the organizers. Their behavior, in turn, was shaped by two major factors: the character of their radical black nationalist ideology, and the pervasive influence of a style of relatedness based upon their social background. Both factors conspired to generate a self-defeating political pattern. In the remainder of this essay, we shall look at how these factors operated, independently and in relation to each other, in order to explain the political conduct that has been described earlier. (See Brill, 1971.)

NAC defined itself as a radical, black nationalist, militant organization. Its radicalism spoke to a conviction that the problems of black people could not be significantly changed without overhauling America's 'racist economic and social institutions'. Ghettos were more than enclaves of poor blacks; they were colonies serving white imperialism. Further, this system of exploitation could not be reformed nor compromised. The kind of new society NAC had in mind was never very clear. Though the organizers occasionally talked about socialism, this was never seriously or carefully incorporated into their ideology.

Their radicalism was linked instead to their black nationalism. They called for all-black control of the institutions that affected black people. NAC, in contrast to other black organizations which have also been demanding various forms of control, opposed seating black tenants on the Housing Authority's policy-making commission. According to NAC, it would not alter the fact of white domination, and blacks would therefore be lackeys. Their black nationalism, then, was linked to a radical perspective. But it also shared in common with other black nationalist groups a commitment to building all-black organizations. Though willing to accept white support under certain conditions, NAC was extremely distrustful of alliances with whites. With regard to militancy, the organization believed that disruptive activities, whether peaceful or not, were indispensable to achieving social change.

NAC's radicalism had a decidedly sectarian or in-group character, which greatly influenced how the organizers perceived and behaved toward others, and how others related to them. As might be expected, many organizations and individual citizens would refuse to cooperate with radicals under any conditions. But NAC appreciably exacerbated this difficulty by adopting a stance that was more often moralistic than political. Though desiring to build a movement, NAC generally did not think in terms of moving people politically. Instead, believing strongly in the moral correctness of their position, they hammered out their point of view without ever considering that the manner in which they communicated had unfavorable political consequences for them.

In presenting their ideas without being politically sensitive to their various audiences, the burden of responsibility fell upon others, for the organizers assumed that convincing others reflected not how they operated or presented themselves, but whether those whom they addressed were decent political types. Another important aspect of their moral radicalism was the tendency to believe that those more moderate than themselves were either 'sell-outs' or dupes, and were therefore potential enemies or at best untrustworthy allies. These perspectives, which were taken very seriously, generated indifference and antagonism between themselves and others.

Several key groups who were quite sympathetic to the aims of reforming the Housing Authority refused to associate themselves with NAC. An outstanding example was the refusal of the militant issue-oriented South Peak Tenants Union to respond favorably to NAC's overtures. There was some ambivalence and hedging at first, but NAC was finally rejected because it was considered by the tenant union as 'too far out in left field'. Its leaders were disturbed both by the radical politics of NAC and by the brazen style in which the organizers communicated their views. The South Peak Tenants Union, which eventually won its own strike, had feared that associating with NAC would injure its own reputation. So, interestingly enough, even a militant group willing to use direct action tactics still considered a connection with NAC politically damaging.

There were, nevertheless, some moderate black groups who were interested in cooperating with NAC, but they were treated with what appeared to be crass expediency because they were defined as liberal organizations. NAC's relationship with a moderate black rent-strike leader, whose concern with his own rent strike did not extend beyond winning reforms, was noted earlier. Not only were his goals too limited for NAC, but the organizers resented his willingness to meet privately, all alone, with the Housing Authority. On the other hand, he was quite willing to engage in a joint venture with NAC. Their outspoken radical politics and abrasive style did not trouble him. He apparently believed, perhaps naively, that a great deal was to be gained, or certainly nothing lost, by assuming that almost everyone was a potential ally.

The Rogers Point organizers were greatly troubled by his liberal politics. His views were treated with disdain, anger, and mockery. Privately, they referred to him as a 'fink'. What made their attitude toward him significant was that they never took his views and formal proposals seriously, and when it was to their advantage they ignored him. Without his knowledge, they excluded him from meetings that had a direct bearing on his own situation. They rarely attempted to try to convince him in a patient way that he was erring politically.

The reason they carried on any sort of relationship with the 'fink' was because they found him occasionally useful. When they needed pickets or a delegation to meet with public officials, they were able to count on their liberal ally, who was also affiliated with the city-wide Tenant Council, to bring people along. However, despite his patience, he eventually became disillusioned. It became apparent to him that the gains achieved by allying with NAC were one-sided, and probably more important, he resented NAC's discourteousness. He broke off his ties with NAC, which did not regret the move.

The nationalist character of NAC further narrowed its range of potential allies. The organizers were opposed to building political ties with white citizens and organizations in a city where blacks were in a minority. Their nationalist ideology, which interpreted basic cleavages in racial terms, not only tended to make them shun alliances with influential middle-class groups but even caused them to avoid ties with some poor people's organizations.

Generally speaking, black nationalist organizations have occasionally drawn upon the support of white radicals, who have been about the only group ready to offer blacks unqualified support. But aside from the students in Presentation City, with whom the organizers preferred not to associate politically, there was really no radical community they could have readily drawn upon. It was not their policy to automatically reject white support, but the terms they would impose for accepting any assistance were so stringent that very few white citizens or groups would be willing to accept them. They were willing, for example, to ally with white lawyers, but only on their own terms.

A more complicated consequence of this nationalist ethos was the impact it had upon the internal character of NAC. The commitment to black nationalism was a major factor in maintaining cohesion and even preventing the organization from falling apart. At the same time it made NAC more politically rigid. We have already seen how Curtis Jones gained the political loyalty of the other organizers in his battles against the poverty program administrators by interpreting major political differences, that existed between NAC and those with whom they disagreed as based on racial antagonism. As the oldest and most experienced of the organizers, Curtis was able to shrewdly link nationalist issues to his radical politics. This was no cynical maneuver; it reflected his political views. Nevertheless, if any of the organizers had challenged Curtis, who was putting himself out on a limb in his battles with non-black members of the community, it would have been interpreted by all as a betrayal. Curtis succeeded in creating a political atmosphere within his organization that made it virtually impossible to openly challenge any of his political positions.

However, there were differences in political opinion between the individual organizers, and a great deal of personal tension between them as well. These factors exerted a centrifugal pull on the organization. On the whole, maintaining the unity of the organization by stressing black nationalism was successful. But the nationalist ethos tended, though not always successfully, to relegate personal tensions and political differences to a covert level, which in turn prompted an overt behavioral pattern that may be characterized as rigid.

What seems to have occurred was this: the gap between the black unity norms of the nationalist ethos and the organizers' actual estrangement from each other prompted them to over-conform. Sensing their own differences and interpersonal tensions, they cautiously avoided letting on to others and themselves the fragile character of their social bond. Frequent and intense discussions among the organizers on the importance of black people getting along and working together left no doubt about the great meaning they attached to the nationalist value. In political terms, this meant having good working relations with each other and being united behind a single political perspective. For blacks to be incompatible, either personally or politically, was anathema to their commitment to black unity.

In their personal relations with each other, there were two major signs of trouble. First, they were extremely competitive. Though acting as a team in public, privately each of the organizers would enjoy boasting about his own individual contributions as compared to those of the others. George Franklyn, for example, continually exclaimed that he, more than the other organizers, was really responsible for the strike. He reasoned that the good reputation he had earned as a tenant in the project explained why some tenants were willing to join the strike. Believing that he excelled the others, though, was not only a boast. George also felt it as a burden. He thought that he carried too large a share of the load and that his efforts were unappreciated by the others. So when discussing his contributions as an organizer, the tone of his remarks reflected anger as well as vanity.

Second, the mutual distrust between the organizers seemed deep; I had the distinct sense that they really didn't like each other. Elliot Liebow (1967, p. 180) made a similar observation in his study of a black street-corner group. He noted that despite frequent claims of close personal ties, 'friendship does not often stand up well to the stress of crisis or conflict of interest when demands tend to be heaviest and most insistent'. He also observed that friendship, though often addressed as if it is a sacred covenant, is at another level recognized as the locus of cynical exploitation (p. 181). As with Liebow's street-corner men, there was often a substantial gap between the claims and the behavior of the organizers.

In private, they often spoke about each other in highly critical terms, and even believed themselves to be victims of the others' deviousness. For example, Jerry Cook once suspected that Eddie Daniels was plotting to get him fired. He imagined, among other things, that Eddie was jealous because he and George were then getting on well with each other. On another occasion, Jerry and Eddie were outraged by George's temper tantrums. Something was always going haywire between them, and these tensions posed a serious threat to NAC's unity.

Curtis finally instituted 'bitching sessions' to provide the organizers with an opportunity to unload their tensions. These meetings would continue until their differences were at least formally resolved. Curtis would always stress at these meetings, as well as on other occasions, how important it was for blacks to get along with each other. For whatever their apparent differences, those with their enemies were much greater. But the interpersonal tensions that surfaced at these meetings hardly exhausted the harsh feelings that they harbored toward each other. Occasionally shaking hands afterward to show that all was forgiven often seemed more a formality than a relaxed exchange. And no matter how much tension was released on these occasions, it would invariably develop again soon.

It is not surprising that they strained to show a unified political perspective, particularly when we consider that political differences, like their interpersonal tensions, existed between them despite their unwavering commitment to black unity. For the organizers, political differences posed a more sensitive issue than personality matters, and how this was handled reflected that sensitivity. Interestingly enough, though the organizers expressed opinions that were departures from the prevailing views, they were, somehow, able to shut out the realization that their opinions did in fact clash.

For example, George once mentioned to me the importance of stressing a cultural as opposed to a political orientation in improving the conditions of black people. When I told him that this view stood in opposition to NAC's official political position, he seemed startled and became visibly embarrassed. More dramatic was Eddie Daniel's reaction when I confronted him with the differences between his own expressed views and those of the other organizers on a particular issue. He actually panicked, became visibly shaken, and blurted out how dedicated he was to the organization. He apparently interpreted having any difference of opinion as a sign of disloyalty.

In public, they always seemed to be of one mind, with each always reinforcing the others. A perceptive observer would notice that even when one of the organizers would make a remark that was too inaudible or rambling to be heard, at least one of the other organizers would still shout approval. These confrontations often appeared to others as vigorous and overacted performances. It seems that a sensing of their differences generated internal psychological pressure for each to play the proper role demanded by the nationalist ethos, with its stress on black unity.

The role-playing that characterized their behavior when confronting outsiders also guided their behavior toward each other. There was an unstated agreement not to be critical of each other's behavior, and whenever possible to be highly supportive. So George Franklyn would praise Eddie Daniels for a leaflet he had written, though he privately expressed concern that the statement had overlooked a major issue. And when one organizer proposed a plan of action, unless tempers were high the others tended to avoid directly challenging its advisability. This situation severely limited their political flexibility by narrowing down the range of political alternatives that they could feel comfortable about considering.

On one major policy, however, they all genuinely agreed—that beating the establishment required moving beyond the framework of conventional politics. Black people had to engage in militant or direct action tactics. They were convinced that the chances of significantly improving conditions in public housing were directly related to the extent to which they could continually disrupt the normal operation of the Housing Authority and the City. So although it was not reflected in practice, they firmly believed that their main task was to build a large organization of tenants who were ready, willing, and able to cooperate and take risks.

The barriers to building an organization in this ghetto community were formidable. The neighborhood was fairly atomized, with little formal or informal group life. Tenant apathy was pervasive, and few were normally willing to take any action that might bring eviction. Under these circumstances, the day-to-day task of organizing tenants was bound to be extremely difficult and tedious. To stand even a chance of putting together the kind of organization that NAC had in mind would necessarily require a considerable amount of organizing skill, self-discipline, and personal endurance.

NAC's reputation as a revolutionary organization further minimized its chances of increasing tenant participation. Tenant dissatisfaction with conditions did not, of course, necessarily imply a readiness to favor radical solutions to social problems. Tenants were interested in immediate improvements in housing conditions. Though the energies of the organization were oriented mainly around this goal, it was difficult for tenants to ignore NAC's radical character. The kind of leaflets the organizers distributed and the political commitments they expressed to tenants undoubtedly frightened many away. On the other hand, NAC offered only slogans and made no systematic efforts to radicalize the tenants.

NAC's ideology, then, under the conditions in which it operated, worked against its own interests in winning the strike. With very little potential for building their own political base or winning allies in the City, and lacking the kind of organization that could encourage open discussion among its organizers, which then might have increased its tactical flexibility, NAC was rendered virtually powerless and without influence. Lacking political power, influence, and even a good reputation, NAC was placed in a political box in which almost anything it did would tend to be politically self-defeating; no activities the organizers engaged in would bring them closer to winning the strike. It is not surprising, then, that their powerlessness, to which they contributed considerably, would produce enormous feelings of frustration and anger, which in turn were reflected in their political behavior.

In other words, their powerlessness generated behavior that was often motivated by a sense of frustration rather than by norms of political expediency. They would engage in activities that served to gratify various immediate needs, such as release of tension. Ironically just as the ideological straight-jacket encouraged expressive behavior, their ideology also fostered non-utilitarian behavior by liberating them from restrictions. By not developing allies in the City or a substantial base in their own community, they were not subject to the expectations of others, who might have demanded that they pursue a different political course of action as a price for their support.

At the end of the strike, George Franklyn said that it could have continued if many of the tenants had not stopped turning over their rent payments to NAC. The tenants were rebelling against NAC, which caused the organizers to close shop perhaps earlier than they had wanted. No matter what the organizers thought of the tenants, they were in some ways subject to their pressure. Had the tenants been organized and meeting together all along, they would have been in a position to ask questions, make suggestions, and even challenge the conduct of the strike itself. NAC might have been forced to behave differently.

Indeed, having no significant ties encouraged them to become not active organizers but angry spokesmen. Their activities became largely confined to exercises in radical and militant rhetoric. Rather than engaging in the unquestionably arduous task of organizing tenants, they took on the highly visible spokesman role of making speeches—usually dramatic ones—issuing press releases, holding press conferences, and engaging in heated verbal exchanges with establishment officials. In truth, they were organizers in name only.

References

Brill, H. (1971), *Why Organizers Fail*, Berkeley.
Liebow, E. (1967), *Tally's Corner*, Boston.

29 *T. Shibutani and K. Kwan,*
Patterns of Migration and Settlement

Patterns of Land Use and Occupancy

The geographic distribution of various groups within a community is an important aspect of ethnic stratification. Members of a small minority group may be scattered throughout an area. Sizable ethnic groups, however, are frequently segregated, although there is considerable variation in the patterns that develop and in the harshness with which the boundaries are enforced. All ethnic groups tend to congregate into natural areas, natural in the sense that they are not planned. The spatial distribution of people is seldom the product of deliberate design; after each migration new patterns of settlement develop through competition and natural selection. Once formed, each natural area develops its own universe of discourse, traditions, and standards of decency and propriety. The lines may then be enforced by custom and by law.

The distribution of ethnic groups within a community is related to the prevailing system of land use, the manner in which natural resources are allocated. Each method of converting energy requires a somewhat different use of land and other resources; hence, most migrations disturb the previously existing allocation. In Brazil and the United States, for example, the arrival of peasants from Europe and Asia resulted in the transformation of waste lands and swamps into fertile fields. Immigrants from barren soil were overjoyed to find rich virgin land and built agricultural empires. If the interests of the groups in contact happen to be complementary, they become interlocked in a common, more diversified economy. Throughout the world ethnic groups with different cultures, using different tools and utensils, have settled in the immediate neighborhood of each other. In the Sahara the Tuareg are camel herders, while the Berbers and other Africans have entirely different economies. Their huts and settlement patterns differ, but they coexist without conflict. (Thurnwald, 1932, pp. 26–7, 79–84.) Once such patterns are established, the groups may retain their identity for centuries, each occupying territory that is defined in tradition and carrying out customary roles.

When the interests of the groups are incompatible, however, competition

---

T. Shibutani and K. Kwan, 'Patterns of migration and settlement', in *Ethnic Stratification*, Macmillan, 1965, pp. 159–67.

is intensified into rivalry or conflict. In New Zealand the Maori resisted the incursion of Europeans in a series of bloody wars; the Hawaiians defended their land by legislation and political bargaining. (Condliffe, 1959, pp. 28–31, 62–74.) In the end the victorious group imposes its system of land use upon the entire community, and the minority groups must adjust or leave. Even when the losers are not driven off the land, the introduction of new techniques of exploiting the resources often disrupts their culture. In many cases food, shelter, family ties, and social organization are inextricably bound up with particular ways of occupying and cultivating soil. Social bonds based on ancient systems of landholding collapse. Those who are unable to compete on equal terms are shunted into menial jobs and occupy the least desirable areas. They thereby become incorporated into the lower rungs of the new economy. In Kenya, for example, the European settlers seized the most fertile lands for their farming operations, and the natives were forced to farm elsewhere as best they could. Hunting and food-gathering activities were also curtailed in the choice areas, and many of the dispossessed were forced to work for the colonists to eke out a livelihood. (Leakey, 1955; cf. Franck, 1960, pp. 64–86.) Thus, the resolution of the conflict results in the formation of a common system of land use.

There are several kinds of communities, and somewhat different patterns of land use and spatial segregation develop in each of them. Many cases of inter-ethnic contact occur in areas in which population density is low, as in agricultural settlements, small villages, and nomadic communities, and the formation of systems of ethnic stratification is somewhat circumscribed by the type of social contacts that take place. A distinctive mode of life develops in sparsely-settled areas where many people know one another on a personal basis. In small communities social control is largely traditional; the societies are made up more of families than of individuals. (Cf. Redfield, 1947, pp. 293–308.) Contacts between ethnic groups tend to be friendly, and superficial associations such as those found in trade and bartering are relatively easy to establish. Since each group has a strong sense of mutual identification and solidarity, however, the barriers of social distance are not likely to be relaxed. In the contacts of nomadic groups with each other and with people in rural settlements, social distance is retained to the point where they can intermingle for centuries without altering their respective ways of life.

In this type of context conflicts frequently arise between agricultural people and those who depend primarily on pastoral or hunting pursuits. Farmers need to occupy land for fairly long periods, and they must have some assurance of keeping it under control until their crops have been harvested. Hunting, collecting, and pastoral economies require freedom of movement and extensive areas, for only superficial use is made of available plant life. Much of the struggle between the settlers and the Indians on the American frontier was a conflict between groups with different patterns of land use. In Canada this issue resulted in a series of disturbances culminating in the Riel rebellion of 1885. During the century after trappers and traders went in large numbers into the Canadian northwest, offspring of these frontiersmen and their Indian wives developed into an ethnic group—known as 'half-breeds', *bois brulé*, or Méti. Although these people dressed like white men and spoke either French or English in addition to an Indian language, they lived apart in their own communities. After 1860 the westward movement of Canadian settlers led to demands that the territory be annexed by Canada, and fur trading and hunting were increasingly brought under legal control. The Méti claimed territorial rights by virtue of their Indian ancestry; they felt that the country was theirs and resented the intrusion. When they realized that their buffalo hunting and carefree way of life were coming to an end, they rebelled. (Stanley, 1936, pp. 3–11, 48–66.)

Another type of community in which inter-ethnic contacts take place is the settlement that is the by-product of large-scale production: plantations and mines. These commercial enterprises require the concentration of a large and reliable labor force, whether the workers be slaves, immigrants, or migratory laborers. The pattern of land use is clearly defined; plantation boundaries are marked and guarded, and within the boundaries activities are coordinated to maximize the profits of the owners. Although plantations differ from medieval manors in that production is not diversified and self-sufficient, as social units they are much like the feudal communities. The labor force is cared for by a paternalistic regime. There are sharp and clearly defined differences of status, usually between a literate owner class and an illiterate working class, and the privileges and responsibilities of each rank are noticeably different. The workers are dependent upon the owners to the point where they cannot exercise initiative without great risk to themselves. The plantation is also a place in which minority groups become acculturated to the standards of their rulers. Sanitation standards are administered by the owners not only to maintain a reliable working force but also to protect their own health. Workers become acquainted with the language of the dominant group, and if their children are educated at all, it is often in the culture of their rulers. There is a tendency for plantation and mines to develop and perpetuate a rigid system of stratification. When more than one ethnic group is involved, the conflicting class interests tend to coincide with ethnic lines.

In most communities of this type each ethnic group is clearly segregated except during working hours. In spite of the separation, however, close contacts are inevitable among those who work together. The frequency with which a large population of mixed parentage develops in such communities suggests that illicit relations and the exploitation of minority-group women is commonplace. (Freyre, 1946; Frazier, 1957, pp. 235–52.)

Another type of community is the city, which has a high population density and distinctive land use. Large cities have existed from the dawn of recorded history, and inter-ethnic contacts have been going on in them for many centuries. Roman artisans, merchants, and mining engineers often migrated beyond the confines of the empire; cities such as Constantinople, Alexandria, and Palermo received large numbers of immigrants and were known for the heterogeneity of their population. (Cf. Clari, 1936, p. 105; Sjoberg, 1960, pp. 25–79.) Since the Industrial Revolution there has been a spectacular growth of urban centers, for large-scale production requires a large labor force within commuting distance from the factories. In recent times growing cities have encroached upon the surrounding regions, and in some areas there is little countryside left. Cities have always played an important part in the history of inter-ethnic contacts.

In industrial cities, especially in one that is growing rapidly, the segregation of ethnic groups develops through a selective process. People of low status settle in those areas where the rent is low and there is least opposition to their presence; those who can afford better housing usually live in mixed areas with the more successful members of their minority groups. In Great Britain approximately two-thirds of the colored population live in ethnic islands. The dockland areas have a heavier concentration of West Africans. The more ambitious, especially among the immigrants from the West Indies, strike out into districts with fewer minority peoples. In London the concentration is in Stepney. (Banton, 1955, pp. 68–9, 104; cf. Hatt, 1945, pp. 352–6.) In Kampala, Uganda, there is no zoning by ethnic groups, but most natives live in the 'African area'. African civil servants and professional men live in neighborhoods that are predominantly Asian or among Europeans (Elkan, 1970, p. 17). Where the conquerors are greatly outnumbered, they establish their own enclaves. In Batavia during the colonial days of the Dutch East Indies, the administrators and traders lived in spacious villas in the most desirable areas; the Indonesian middle class and some Chinese lived in brick houses in more crowded areas; and throughout the city, wherever they were tolerated, there were kampongs for the lower-class Indonesians (Keyfitz, 1961, pp. 348–54). In Durban to a noticeable degree, different ethnic groups live in separate quarters. The distinctive character of each region of the city reflects the cultural life of the inhabitants as well as their economic standing. The Europeans, having the highest average income, occupy the most desirable residential areas in terms of view of the sea, altitude, and accessibility to the center of the city. (Kuper, Watts and Davies, 1958, pp. 110–58; cf. Reader, 1961, pp. 10–35.) The spatial distribution of ethnic groups develops through competition; the patterns develop as the members of each group settle in the best housing they can find.

Industrial cities frequently have a characteristic biotic pattern and psychological orientation. The population is made up largely of young people who migrate there from the surrounding countryside, spend most of their productive years there, and then retire elsewhere. The population of Livingstone,

Northern Rhodesia, for example, shows an overloading in the age groups from 20 to 40, a preponderance of male over female, and the relative absence of older people of both sexes (McCulloch, 1956, p. 15). What is significant about very large cities is that the concentration of so many people into a limited area makes it impossible for anyone to know everyone else on a personal basis, and the anonymity results in the formation of a distinctive way of life. City-dwellers are in constant association with other people, but a large proportion of their contacts are with nodding acquaintances and strangers. Social relationships tend to be categorical, and people are identified in terms of the uniform they wear—ethnic or otherwise. Hence, the bonds of kinship, neighborliness, and friendship that arise from sharing numerous experiences do not enter into many transactions. City life is marked by a utilitarian accent. People tend to be highly rational and individualistic, and each goes about pursuing his own interests. Men often stand in a relationship of reciprocal utility toward one another; the pecuniary nexus often replaces personal preference as the basis for association. Where people use each other in the pursuit of their own ends, each person has to protect himself against exploitation; hence, urbanites tend to be more sophisticated and less idealistic. Timbuctoo, for example, is large enough so that the status of an individual is not known outside the immediate area in which he lives, and economic dealings with strangers are often ruthless. Outside the circle of his family and friends, each person expects this kind of treatment and remains on guard. (Miner, 1953, pp. 24–5, 245–6.) When young people away from home live together in this type of atmosphere, there is a relaxation of traditional standards. This relative freedom from the moral controls often facilitates the establishment of contacts across the color line (Simmel, 1950, pp. 409–24; Wirth, 1956, pp. 110–32).

There is some kind of ethnic segregation in virtually all cities, and the formation of natural areas is easiest to see in the growing industrial city, where the distribution of peoples and institutions develops through competition on the open market. There are other cities, however, which are old, well established, and not in an industrial economy. Many of these are collections of self-contained villages. Many of the old cities of Asia are as much political as economic centers; they constitute the point from which rulers control the numerous villages around it. Their location depends more upon the will of the prince than upon economic convenience. The location of institutions and peoples is traditional, although at times the internal arrangement is determined by decree. Religious and political institutions are usually found in the center of the city, along with the homes of the wealthy. The poorer people usually live on the periphery. There are special quarters for each ethnic group; in many cases they are virtually self-sufficient units with their own regulations. (Sjoberg, 1960, pp. 95–103, 133–7.) In Timbuctoo, for example, there are four traditional quarters, with additional areas with bad reputations on the outskirts of the city. Although there is no clearcut segregation, a preponderance of people of a given class or ethnic group are found in each quarter. Furthermore, there are widely-held beliefs about the kind of people who supposedly dwell in each of these areas. (Miner, 1953, pp. 32–47.) Social control is not as impersonal as it is in an industrial city, and the lines of demarcation between ethnic categories tend to be more stable.

In all types of communities the most desired areas belong to the ethnic group whose culture provides competitive advantages in that particular environment. In Swat, in northwestern Pakistan, the Pathan, sedentary farmers who speak an Iranian language, inhabit the valley. They are the most powerful group, but their territorial expansion is limited by their culture; they must remain at an altitude in which two crops can be raised each year. The Kohistani, who speak a Dardic language, have a two-fold economy, and they are not limited by this barrier. They plant on narrow terraces with irrigation and also keep herds; in season they leave their lands and go up as high as 14 000 feet. Since the size of their herd depends on the supply of winter fodder, they must have some fields. The Gujars, who are Gujiri-speaking nomadic herders, can survive on any part of the land, but they move about in small bands and do not have the military strength to challenge the others. Hence, they must carve out their niche from what is left by the others. (Barth, 1956, pp. 1079–89.) If the culture of a minority group is better suited to the environment, it may eventually displace the dominant group. In eastern Canada and in New England the French-Canadians have been spreading at the expense of the English-speaking Protestants. The French work on the soil and buy farms whenever they can, while the English farmers are too ambitious for their sons and find themselves without successors. Thus, their large-family farm system has enabled the French to compete successfully against the dominant group. Human beings compete with their sentiments and customs as well as with their technical skills and money. (Hughes, 1943, pp. 16–21.)

These ecological processes are sometimes complicated by political policies. In some European colonies, for example, there was a view that the colonial administration was responsible for opening up the resources not only for the homeland but also for the benefit of the indigenous people. In some British colonies there were laws prohibiting the sale or transfer of land from natives without the consent of the governor; these laws were designed to protect the native proprietor. When Great Britain assumed protection of Uganda in 1900, the crown took as its share about half of the territory, mostly uncultivated land. The cultivated area was considered the property of the native chiefs, and the colonial government maintained control over these aristocrats so that they could not sell freely. Various decrees favored small freehold tenure, and a system of peasant proprietorship developed. British policy in Nigeria also supported the indigenous form of land ownership. The effect was to keep out foreign capital and to prevent the growth of a European settler community. Thus, individual members of the dominant group are not always free to exploit their advantages. Although ecological processes appear to be modified by law, it should be remembered that such laws are enforced by authorities of the dominant group.

References

Banton, M. P. (1955), *The Coloured Quarter: Negro Immigrants in an English City*, London.

Barth, F. (1956), 'Ecologic relationship of ethnic groups in Swat, North Pakistan', *American Anthropologist*, vol. LVIII.

Clari, R. (1936), *The Preindustrial City: Past and Present*, Glencoe, Ill.

Condliffe, J. B. (1959), *New Zealand in the Making*, London.

Elkan, W. (1960), *Migrants and Proletarians*, London.

Franck, T. M. (1960), *Race and Nationalism: The Struggle for Power in Rhodesia—Nyasaland*, New York.

Frazier, E. F. (1957), *Race and Culture Contacts in the Modern World*, New York.

Freyre, G. (1946), *The Masters and the Slaves*, New York.

Hatt, P. K. (1945), 'Spatial patterns in a polyethnic area', *A.S.R.*, vol. X.

Hughes, E. C. (1943), *French Canada in Transition*, Chicago.

Keyfitz, N. (1961), 'The ecology of Indonesian cities', *A.J.S.*, vol. LXVI.

Kuper, L., Watts, H. and Davies, R. (1958), *Durban: A Study in Racial Ecology*, New York.

Leakey, L. S. B. (1955), *Mau Mau and the Kikuyu*, London.

McCulloch, M. (1956), *A Social Survey of the African Population of Livingstone*, Manchester.

Miner (1953), *The Primitive City of Timbuctoo*, Princeton.

Reader, D. H. (1961), *The Black Man's Portion*, Cape Town.

Redfield, R. (1947), 'The folk society', *A.J.S.*, vol. LII.

Simmel, G. (1950), *The Sociology of Georg Simmel*, trans. K. Wolf, Glencoe, Ill.

Sjoberg, G. (1960), *The Preindustrial City: Past and Present*, Glencoe, Ill.

Stanley, G. F. G. (1936), *The Birth of Western Canada: A History of the Riel Rebellions*, New York.

Thurnwald, R. (1932), *Economics in Primitive Communities*, London.

Wirth (1956), in E. W. Marvick and A. J. Reiss (eds.), *Community Life and Social Policy*, Chicago.

30 *Lee Rainwater,* The Pruitt-Igoe Community

The Dumping Ground

Pruitt-Igoe houses families for which our society seems to have no other place. The original tenants were drawn very heavily from several land clearance areas in the inner city. Although there were originally some white tenants, all of the whites have moved out and the population is now all Negro. Only those Negroes who are desperate for housing are willing to live in Pruitt-Igoe—over half the households are headed by women; over half derive their principal income from public assistance of one kind or another; and many families are so large they cannot find housing elsewhere. The project has proved particularly unappealing to 'average' families, that is, families in which there is both a mother and father and a small number of children. Thus, while the overall vacancy rate ran between 20 and 25 per cent for several years, the vacancy rate in two-bedroom apartments was in the 35 to 40 per cent range.

In the slum people are continually confronted with dangers from human and non-human sources. Public housing removes some of the latter (like rats and faulty electrical wiring) but may leave others (like high windows and exposed elevator shafts in Pruitt-Igoe's tall buildings, exposed steam pipes and broken glass outside). After two years of intensive field observation, a questionnaire was administered to a representative sample of Pruitt-Igoe tenants to discover how extensive were the problems of this nature that were revealed in the field work. Some of the troubles that were characterized as 'very big problems' by over half the respondents in this sample are listed below. A few of these had to do with the design and maintenance of the project:

There's too much broken glass and trash around outside.
The elevators are dangerous.
The elevators don't stop on every floor, so many people have to walk up or down to get to their apartments.
There are mice and cockroaches in the buildings.
People use the elevators and halls to go to the bathroom.

Lee Rainwater, 'The Pruitt–Igoe community', in *Behind Ghetto Walls*, Penguin and Aldine, 1970, pp. 9–14.

However, by far the greater number of complaints had as much to do with human as with non-human sources of danger and difficulty:

Bottles and other dangerous things are thrown out of windows and hurt people.
People who don't live in the project come in and make a lot of trouble by fights, stealing, drinking, and the like.
People don't keep the area around the incinerator clean.
Little children hear bad language all the time so they don't realize how bad it is.
The laundry rooms aren't safe: clothes get stolen and people get attacked.
The children run wild and cause all kinds of damage.
People use the stairwells and laundry rooms for drinking and things like that.
A woman isn't safe in the halls, stairways, or elevators.

Given these experiences, it is hardly surprising that only a minority of the tenants demonstrate any real attachment to the project community. The great majority feel that their present apartments are better than their previous dwellings, but most would very much like to move out, to a nicer and safer neighborhood.

Most Pruitt-Igoe residents liked their apartments very much. Seventy-eight per cent said that they were satisfied with their apartments; 62 per cent indicated that their present apartments met their needs 'much better' than their previous dwellings and an additional 18 per cent found their needs met 'a little better' in Pruitt-Igoe. But they did not like the project community to anything like the same extent: 51 per cent said they were dissatisfied with living in the project. In contrast, those living in private housing were more often dissatisfied with their apartments or houses (45 per cent), but more satisfied with the neighborhood in which they lived (only 26 per cent were dissatisfied).

Given their limited resources and the special burdens of their large families, it is not surprising that in Pruitt-Igoe 69 per cent of the household heads said either that they planned to stay in public housing indefinitely or that they had no idea when they would be able to leave, although 86 per cent indicated a preference to live elsewhere.

Only 38 per cent of the households had a male household head, most of the female heads had been married but were now separated, divorced, or widowed: 56 per cent of the female heads of households said that they were separated, 10 per cent said they were divorced, and 17 per cent said they were widowed. Twelve per cent indicated that they were still married but that their husbands were elsewhere, often in the armed services, and five per cent had never married.

It is also understandable that many tenants develop a rather jaundiced view of the public housing program. Thus, when we asked tenants what the government was trying to accomplish by building public housing and how well this had in fact been accomplished, we got answers like these:

They were trying to put a whole bunch of people in a little bitty space. They did a pretty good job—there's a lot of people here.

They were trying to better poor people (but) they tore down one slum and built another; put all kinds of people together; made a filthy place.

They were trying to get rid of the slum, but they didn't accomplish too much. Inside the apartment they did, but not outside.

Other troubles make life difficult for the project tenants. For example, we asked our respondents to indicate how serious and how frequent they felt various kinds of aggressive and deviant behaviors to be. The following items were judged by most of the tenants to be very serious and very frequent:

Holding somebody up and robbing them.
Being a wino or an alcoholic.
Stealing from somebody.
Teenagers yelling curse words at adults.
Breaking windows.
Drinking a lot and fooling around on the streets.
Teenagers getting in fights.
Boys or girls having sexual relations with a lot of different boys or girls.

In short, though some social scientists have quarreled with Kenneth Clark's emphasis on the 'tangle of pathology' in the ghetto, it would seem that at least this sample from one federally-supported ghetto shared his views.

Ordinary Lives

Despite the world of troubles that Pruitt-Igoe and the ghetto generally present to their inhabitants, systematic observation of family life in the community impresses the observer also with its ordinariness. The basic pattern of life is simply the ordinary American way of family living. The Pruitt-Igoeans get up in the morning like everyone else, the men put their pants on one leg at a time, the women cook meals, someone shops for groceries, brothers and sisters bicker with each other, children go off to school and straggle home at the end of the day, mothers worry about their children's behavior as they try to live up to their responsibilities for socializing them—all like everyone else. There are variations sometimes slight, sometimes major, on the basic themes of American life that are distinctive to this place and time and to these people, and these variations will be treated problematically in the analysis that follows because we must understand them if we are to understand the particular suffering that ghetto life represents and thereby help to eliminate this special suffering. But we cannot appreciate daily life, family life, child-growing-up life in Pruitt-Igoe without realizing that it mixes in complex and ineffable ways the ordinariness of all American life (indeed of all human life) with the special qualities of the ghetto, and the even more special qualities of the Pruitt-Igoe community.

Indeed, the very ordinariness of it all contributes to the suffering of the Pruitt-Igoeans because while they regard themselves as 'people like everyone else' they must also and continually confront the way they are disadvantaged by and deviant in the larger society. The following analysis highlights that which is special about life in Pruitt-Igoe, but from a perspective that seeks to take into account also its ordinary, taken-for-granted qualities. The case studies which are interspersed among the analytic chapters, will help to make the contrapuntal qualities of ordinariness and special suffering as clear to the reader as they are to the observers working with all of the data from Pruitt-Igoe tenants.

The Family Demography of Pruitt-Igoe

Pruitt-Igoe has a rather unusual demographic structure. In September 1965, toward the end of our field work, some 9952 people lived in the project; 3067 were adults and 6895 were minors. The adult sex ratio was heavily weighted in favor of women; there were two-and-a-half times as many women as men living in the project. The minors were heavily weighted toward the lower ages, 25 per cent were under six and 70 per cent under twelve.

At that time there were 2760 apartments available but only 74 per cent of them were occupied. During its 12-year history the project had proved particularly unattractive to small families, the vacancy rate in the one or two bedroom apartments was much higher than in the three bedroom apartments. Over the years the Housing Authority had converted a number of one bedroom apartments into four and five bedroom apartments, and these were always heavily in demand, seldom vacant for long. Thus the average number of minors in households with any minors at all was 4·28, and 40 per cent of the households included five or more minors.

Once in the project, families tended to stay for a fairly long time; in 1965 the average family had lived there for six years, compared to an average tenancy of only three years for families in the private housing neighborhood just to the west. Women headed 62 per cent of the families, compared to only 50 per cent in the private housing to the west. The households were heavily dependent on public assistance; 38 per cent included no employed person, and many of those who were employed produced income only intended to supplement assistance payments. In only 45 per cent of the households was employment the sole source of income.

In 1966 the median income for households in Pruitt-Igoe was $2454, the second highest among the seven St Louis public housing projects. However, because of the large numbers of minors, average per capita income in Pruitt-

Igoe was the lowest of all the projects, only $498 per year, $78 below the next lowest, and $234 below the per capita figure for the project with the highest income.

Only 30 per cent of the households with children included all the members of our society's typical grouping: husband, wife, and children. Fifty-seven per cent included only mother and children. Six per cent were three-generational female-headed households.

The median education of household heads was nine years. Of those who worked, over half held unskilled jobs, about one-third had semi-skilled jobs, and fewer than 10 per cent worked at skilled or white collar occupations.

Characteristically, the majority of household heads (62 per cent) were born in a southern or border state; only one-third were born in the St Louis metropolitan area.

The apartments in Pruitt-Igoe were larger (2·9 bedrooms) than the private housing to the west (1·9 bedrooms). The residents of the private housing area were slightly older, more of them were southern-born, and they were less educated. Their family incomes were slightly higher than those in Pruitt-Igoe, though they had the same occupational distribution. In part this resulted from the presence of more adults in the households, and money stretched further because there were fewer children.

31 *T. F. Pettigrew,* Race and Equal Educational Opportunity

In racial terms, the complex concept of 'equal educational opportunity' translates into *effective integrated schooling*. That anything less than this has not proven to be truly equal opportunity for Negro American children is a demonstrably harsh fact of the current scene—and there is reason to believe that the same holds true for white American children as well. There are many reasons for this translation, a number of which receive considerable support from the extensive Coleman data. This brief summary will utilize analyses of the data from the Coleman Report itself (1966) and the U.S. Commission on Civil Rights report (1967), *Racial Isolation in the Public Schools.*

The Social Class Climate of the School

The most significant school correlate of achievement test scores uncovered by the Coleman study is the social-class climate of the school's student body. This variable is measured by the social-class origins of all of a school's students; and it appears most critical in the later grades and somewhat more important for Negro than white children. Put bluntly, children of all backgrounds tend to do better in schools with a predominant middle-class milieu; and this trend is especially true in the later grades where the full force of peer-group influence is felt. This basic finding of the Coleman Report has been vigorously challenged by a number of methodological critics, none of whom seem aware that the identical finding had been attained by four other studies which employed sharply different measures and samples from those used by Coleman. Interestingly, three of these replications were in print several years before the appearance of *Equality of Educational Opportunity* in 1966.

The importance of this key Coleman conclusion warrants further mention of these supporting studies. In a research paper published in 1959, Alan Wilson (1959, pp. 836–45) demonstrated the special significance of school social class in determining college aspirations in eight high schools in the

T. F. Pettigrew, 'Race and equal educational opportunity', *Harvard Educational Review*, vol. 38, Winter, 1968, pp. 66–76.

San Francisco–Oakland Bay area of California. He found higher percentages of college aspirants in higher-status schools even after controlling for other determinants of college aspirations: father's occupation and education, mother's education, median academic grade, and intelligence-test score. For example, among those boys whose fathers and mothers were high-school graduates and whose fathers held manual occupations, 60 per cent in upper-status schools wanted to go to college compared to 54 per cent in the medium-status schools and only 32 per cent in the working-status schools. Likewise, among those boys with a modest 'C' academic grade record, 72 per cent from upper-status schools aspired to college in contrast to only 55 per cent from medium-status schools and 41 per cent in working-status schools. Finally, for those in the 100 to 119 I.Q. test range, 93 per cent in the upper-status schools, 72 per cent in the medium-status schools, and 51 per cent in the working-status schools aimed for college.

Differential college aspirations are not the only outcomes of school social class uncovered in this Wilson study. Controlling for father's occupation, he found that both occupational aspirations and political party preferences are also influenced. Hence, among boys whose fathers occupied manual positions, 44 per cent in the upper-status schools wanted to be professionals and 50 per cent preferred the Republican Party compared with 31 per cent and 32 per cent in the medium-status schools and 27 per cent and 24 per cent in the working-status schools, respectively.

A second early attack on the problem was mounted at Harvard University, though it substituted the social-class level of nine Boston suburbs for a direct measure of the schools' social-class levels (Cleveland, 1962, pp. 453–4). Controlling for father's occupation, the researchers found that boys from the higher-status communities were more likely to go to college. In addition, community status, which determined the status level of the schools, had its crucial impact only at the high-school level, the level at which Wilson was working. Consequently, community status predicted neither primary-school grades nor entrance into the college preparatory courses in high school from junior high school, a finding that resembles the Coleman result that the social status of schools gained in predictive value in the secondary-school grades.

The most definitive early study was conducted by John Michael (1961, pp. 585–95). He analyzed the aptitude test scores (on a test not unlike those used by Coleman) as well as the career and college plans of 35 436 seniors in a nationally representative sample of 518 American public high schools. Michael classified the students on an index of family social class using such information as the father's occupation and education and whether older siblings had attended college. Further, he classified the high schools into five status ranks according to the percentage of seniors in each school who fell into his two top family status classifications, a method similar to the school social class measures of Coleman.

The first finding showed that with family status controlled, the higher the status of the school, the higher the average score on the scholastic aptitude test. Further analysis revealed that the variation in the percentages of students scoring above the national average on the test was roughly equally attributable to the individual and school social class indices. But the variation in the percentages scoring in the top quarter was considerably more related to individual social class than school social class—a result directly in line with Coleman's finding that school social class is most important for the more deprived students and in line with the Commission's (1967, p. 85) re-analysis finding that among whites in the metropolitan Northeast, school social class was least important for the highest-status students. The little-known Michael research, then, provided early evidence for most of the major Coleman Report conclusions.

On the matter of plans to attend college, the Michael study, like the Wilson and Harvard investigations, demonstrated that school social class makes a difference. But Michael's larger sample allowed deeper analysis and, as did the Coleman analysis, revealed that these effects are strongest for students from lower individual class backgrounds. Consider first those seniors who score in the top quarter of the aptitude test distribution. Among these talented youngsters from the lowest individual social class group, only 44 per cent who attended the lowest-status high schools planned to go to college compared with 57 per cent who attended the highest-status high schools. By contrast, among the talented seniors from the highest individual social class group, 80 per cent who attended the lowest-status high schools planned to go to college compared with 86 per cent who attended the highest-status high schools. In other words, the high-status school exerts a far greater influence on college plans among talented lower-status than talented higher-status children.

Much the same phenomenon is true for Michael's entire sample. The percentage differences in college plans between individual social class groups is essentially the same at each type of school; but the percentage differences in college plans between scholastic aptitude test levels is far higher in the high-status than the low-status high schools. Put simply, attendance at a low-status school does not deter seniors from upper-status families in planning for college, but attendance at a high-status school is an important aid to able seniors from lower-status families.

These three early investigations, however, suffered from two interrelated methodological weaknesses that also limit the Coleman survey: the results are neither longitudinal nor corrected for initial achievement and aspirations upon entering school in the primary grades. These limitations open the studies to the possibility that their findings are merely the result of special selection biases. That is, lower-class children in predominantly middle-class schools may achieve more and aspire higher not because of the school climate but only because they are as a group brighter and more ambitious to begin with than lower-class children in general.

Robert Nichols (1966, pp. 1312–14) has been a particularly vehement critic of the social-class climate finding of the Coleman Report on precisely these grounds of possible selection biases. He and other critics apparently choose to ignore a fourth replication of the Coleman result reported at length in the U.S. Commission on Civil Rights report (1967, pp. 165–206). Wilson, in a follow-up to his earlier research, studied the social-class climate variable on a probability sample of junior- and senior-high-school children in California's Bay area. He had the advantage of longitudinal data and initial scores upon entering school, thus overcoming Nichols' objections. In this study, Wilson finds a strong effect of the social-class context at even the elementary-school level. After carefully 'allowing for individual differences in personal background, neighborhood context, and mental maturity at the time of the school entry', he notes that the social-class level of elementary schools has a significant effect upon subsequent academic success at higher grade levels.

The Racial Composition of the School

The racial significance of this social-class climate finding of the Coleman Report becomes obvious as soon as we recall that, at most, only about one-fourth of the Negro American population can be accurately described as 'middle-class'. Apart from strictly racial factors, then, extensive desegregation is necessary to provide Negro pupils with predominantly middle-class school settings. On these class grounds alone, Negro children in interracial classrooms would be expected to achieve more than similar Negro children in all-Negro classrooms, and these expectations are supported in the Coleman data (1966, p. 332). Negro children from 'more than half' white classrooms score higher on both reading and mathematical achievement tests than other Negro children; and this effect is strongest among those who began their interracial schooling in the early grades. In addition, Negro students in 'more than half' white classrooms yield as a group higher standard deviations in test scores than Negroes in classrooms with fewer whites—that is, desegregated Negroes reveal a wider spread in test performance (Coleman, 1966, p. 333).

But are these achievement benefits of the interracial classroom *completely* a function of the social-class climate factor? Or are racial composition factors independently related *in addition?* The text of the Coleman Report (1966, pp. 307, 330) is equivocal on this point; it speaks of the desegregation effect being 'largely, perhaps wholly, related to', or 'largely accounted for by', other student-body characteristics. The Civil Rights Commission's re-analysis of these data (1967, p. 90), however, focuses further attention upon this particular question and finds that there *is* indeed a critical racial composition correlate. The re-analysis uncovers relatively large and consistent differences in favor of those twelfth-grade Negroes who are in 'more than half' white classrooms even after the two major factors of the Coleman analysis have been controlled—family social class and school social class. The apparent benefits of interracial classrooms are not linear; in other words, Negroes in predominantly-white classrooms score higher on the average, but those in classrooms with 'less than half' whites do no better than those in all-Negro classrooms. Once again, this effect of improved performance appears greatest for those Negro children who begin their biracial training in the early grades. Moreover, this is not a zero-sum game; that is, white performance in predominantly-white classrooms does not decline as Negro performance rises. The achievement scores of white children in biracial classes with 'more than half' white students average just as high as those of comparable children in all-white classes.

The Commission Report also makes a crucial distinction between a merely desegregated school and an integrated one. Desegregation involves only a specification of the racial mix of students—preferably, more than half white. It does not include any description of the *quality* of the interracial contact. Merely desegregated schools can be either effective or ineffective, can boast genuine interracial acceptance or intense interracial hostility. In short, a desegregated school is not necessarily a 'good school'. Recall the greater spread of test scores of Negro children in desegregated classrooms. Many of these children are doing extremely well, but others are not doing nearly as well. What accounts for the difference? The Commission's reanalysis of the Coleman data suggests that the explanatory intervening variable is *interracial acceptance*. In the schools which can truly be described as 'integrated', where most teachers report no racial tension whatsoever, Negro students evince higher verbal achievement, more definite college plans, and more positive racial attitudes than comparable Negro students in tense, merely 'desegregated' schools (pp. 157–8). Desegregation, then, is a necessary but not sufficient condition for integration, for integration involves in addition to racial mix a climate of interracial acceptance.

While important, high achievement-test scores are surely not the sole goal of education. Indeed, many advocates argue for integrated education only in terms of the nonacademic benefits of diverse contacts. Preparation for the interracial world of the future, they insist, demands interracial schools today for both white and Negro youth. The Coleman data speak to this issue, too. The Coleman Report (1966, p. 333) itself shows that white students who attend public schools with Negroes are the least likely to prefer all-white classrooms and all-white 'close friends'; and this effect, too, is strongest among those who begin their interracial schooling in the early grades Consistent with these results are data from Louisville, Kentucky on Negro pupils. In an open-choice situation, Negro children are far more likely to select predominantly-white high schools if they are currently attending predominantly-white junior high schools (U.S. commission on Civil Rights, 1963).

A Civil Rights Commission survey (1967, pp. 111–13) of urban adults in the North and West suggests that these trends continue into adulthood. Negro adults who themselves attended desegregated schools as children tend to be more eager to have their children attend such schools and do in fact more often send their children to such schools than comparable Negro adults who attended only segregated schools as children. They are typically making more money and are more frequently in white-collar occupations than previously-segregated Negroes of comparable origins. Similarly, white adults who experienced as children integrated schooling differ from comparable whites in their greater willingness to reside in an interracial neighborhood, to have their children attend interracial schools, and to have Negro friends. For both Negro and white adults, then, it appears that desegregated schooling does in fact prepare its products for interracial living as adults.

Two Psychological Processes

Most discussion to date of these results has centered upon their immediate implications. But of greater psychological significance are the questions they raise concerning the actual dynamics of the interracial classroom and the precise individual processes which undergird these crude aggregate findings. A number of fascinating clues concerning these psychological processes are provided in the Coleman Report, two of which deserve special mention: 'fate control' and 'social evaluation'. The former is essentially Rotter's (1966) 'internal-external control of reinforcement' variable; while the latter refers to the cross-racial comparisons made possible by the interracial classroom (Pettigrew, 1968).

Student personality variables are surprisingly strong independent correlates of test performance in Coleman's data for all groups of children, though different measures predict white and Negro achievement. An 'academic self-concept' variable (measured by such items as 'How bright do you think you are in comparison with the other students in your grade?') proves more significant for white performance. But a brief scale of 'fate control' (indicated, for example, by disagreeing that 'Good luck is more important than hard work for success') is much more important for Negro performance. Not surprisingly, this sense of internal control among Negroes tends to be greater in desegregated schools—a vital finding that contradicts those who would distort the 'fate control' results as evidence for separate all-Negro schools under 'black control'.

Clearly, these personality-achievement findings result from tapping into a complex process involving a two-way causal pattern. Not only do those

Negro children with a sense of internal control subsequently do better in their school achievement, but those who do well in school achievement undoubtedly begin to gain a sense of internal control. Nevertheless, it is tempting to speculate with Coleman that each child faces a two-stage problem: first, he must learn that he can, within reasonably broad limits, act effectively upon his surroundings; and, second, he must then evaluate his own relative capabilities for mastering the environment. The critical stage for white children seems to be the second stage concerning the self-concept, while the critical stage for Negro children seems realistically enough to involve the question of manipulating an often harsh and overpowering environment. In any event, more detailed experimental work along the lines of Rotter's research and Coleman's speculation appears warranted.

A number of theoretical considerations from social psychology suggest a broad social evaluation hypothesis: *Many of the consequences of interracial classrooms for both Negro and white children are a direct function of the opportunities such classrooms provide for cross-racial self-evaluation.* It follows from such an hypothesis that the more opportunities for cross-racial self-evaluation a school provides, the greater the consequences. And it also follows that those children for whom peers of the other race become referent should evince the largest changes.

These predictions are consistent with the analyses of the Coleman and Commission reports and with the conceptual framework and experimental results on biracial performance of Irwin Katz (1964, pp. 381–99). Hence, the repeated indications of the special potency of desegregation in the early elementary graces fit well with the self-evaluation view. Young children have less rooted self-conceptions and have not yet adopted uniracial school cliques as their chief peer referents. So, too, do the Coleman conclusions that the most significant school correlate of test scores is the social-class climate of the school's student body; and that this factor is especially important for Negro children. Schools with a middle-class milieu furnish higher comparison levels for achievement and aspirations; and these higher levels will be especially influential for disadvantaged Negro youngsters whose referents otherwise might well have lower levels. And the special efficacy of 'more than half' white classrooms and schools, particularly those characterized by cross-racial acceptance, is also consistent with these predictions. The integrated class and school are unique in the range of opportunities they provide Negro children for maximal self-evaluation against higher comparison levels.

The inclusion in Coleman's student schedules of a question about cross-racial friendships makes possible direct tests of the social evaluation hypothesis. All students tested in the sixth, ninth, and twelfth grades were asked: 'Think now of your close friends. How many of them are white? None less than half, about half, more than half, all'. Assuming 'close friends' to be referent, the social evaluation hypothesis predicts that the major consequences of interracial schools for both Negroes and white will be found among those who report 'close friends' of the other race.

The published analyses employing the 'close friend' variable confirm this hypothesis. Thus, with the family and school social-class variables controlled, Negro children with close white friends far less often prefer all Negro friends and an all-Negro school than other Negro children regardless of the racial composition of their classrooms (U.S. Commission on Civil Rights, 1967, pp. 97–9). Classrooms with half or more white students relate strongly to these interracial preferences solely because Negroes in them more often have close white friends. In addition, Negroes who participate in extra-curricular activities more frequently report close white friends.

Negro achievement scores and college aspirations present a slightly different picture from the attitude data. Having close white friends is related neither to higher scores nor aspirations in all-Negro classrooms. But in 'more than half' white classrooms, Negro students with close white friends tend to have both higher achievement scores and college aspirations.

Friendship operates in a similar fashion for white students. Hence, with father's education controlled, having close Negro friends is strongly and positively related to white preference for an interracial school (U.S. Commission on Civil Rights, 1967, pp. 100–3, 141). And, as noted, white pupils who begin their interracial schooling in the early grades are more likely to have close Negro friends when they reach the ninth and twelfth grades (Coleman, 1966, p. 333).

In short, integrated education in the early grades seems to have important benefits for both Negro and white children in terms of improved interracial attitudes and preferences—not an unimportant consequence in a nation torn by racial strife and bigotry. And if social evaluation processes during inter-racial contact are as critical contributors to these benefits as they appear in these data, even the most academically-successful 'compensatory program' in ghetto schools cannot rival genuine integration.

A Final Word

Let it be clearly stated that Coleman and his associates achieved a landmark contribution in an amazingly short span of time. Though not without its problems of sampling, non-response, and analysis, this massive and ambitious study should influence educational research and practice for years to come. It is of necessity a broad-gauged, aggregate survey of what exists now in American public schools. It could neither detail precise learning processes nor test what American public schools could potentially become in the future. Similar to the naked eye compared with an electronic microscope, the Coleman Report outlined the gross facts of American public education today, while the precision of the limited experiment is now needed to detail the undergoing processes that go unseen by the survey. From fate control to social evaluation, the results of the Coleman Report are rich and suggestive for fruitful experimentation. In the meantime, the racial implications of the Coleman Report for practical school policy are reasonably clear: equal educational opportunity for both Negro and white children requires socially and racially integrated, not merely desegregated, schools.

References

Cleveland, S. (1962), 'A tardy look at Stouffer's findings in the Harvard Mobility Project', *Public Opinion Quarterly*, vol. XXVI.

Coleman, J. S. *et al.* (1966), *Equality of Educational Opportunity*, U.S. Government Printing Office, Washington.

Katz, I. (1964), 'Review of evidence relating to effects of desegregation on the performance of Negroes', *American Psychologist*, vol. XIX.

Michael, J. A. (1961), 'High school climates and plans for entering college', *Public Opinion Quarterly*, vol. XXV.

Nichols, R. C. (1966), 'Schools and the disadvantaged', *Science*, vol. CLVI, 9 December.

Pettigrew, T. F. (1968), 'Social evaluation theory: covergences and applications', in D. Levine (ed.), *1967 Nebraska Symposium on Motivation*, Lincoln, Neb.

Rotter, J. B. (1966), 'Internal versus external control of reinforcement', *Psychological Monographs*, vol. LXXX, no. 609.

U.S. Commission on Civil Rights (1963), *Civil Rights USA: Public Schools, Southern State, 1962*, U.S. Government Printing Office, Washington.

U.S. Commission on Civil Rights (1967), *Racial Isolation in the Public Schools*, U.S. Government Printing Office, Washington.

Wilson, A. B. (1959), 'Residential segregation of social classes and aspirations of high school boys', *A.S.R.*, vol. XXIV.

32 *Murray and Rosalie Wax,* Federal Programs and Indian Target Populations

Head Start and Hind End

Between American Indians and the people and organizations who wish to help them exists an almost inpenetrable wall. As social scientists and as teachers, we have until recently believed that proper means of communication could breach that wall: if the Indians who need help could learn how to plug into the right channels—if the White People who man these channels could come to understand Indians—then the stalemate of Indian helplessness, isolation, and bitter poverty might be broken. We realize, of course, that as compared to other people in the US, the Indians had very little power, and, ourselves being professors, we had good reason to appreciate that knowledge is *not* power. Nevertheless, we reasoned, power is hard to acquire without knowledge and knowledge rests on communication.

It was in the spirit of this belief that we participated in many workshops and conferences—both for Indians and for the teachers of Indian children. It was also in the spirit of this belief that we designed and carried out an intensive study of a reservation school situation where academic achievement was notoriously low (Wax, Wax, and Dumont, 1964; Wax and Wax, 1965; Wax, 1967). There we observed that in some classrooms the children were learning virtually nothing of a scholastic nature. By the fifth or sixth grade they had become adept at disrupting and inhibiting the process of instruction. They feigned stupidity, refused to listen, sharpened pencils loudly when asked to recite, and wrote on the board in letters so small no one could read them. When asked to read aloud they held their books before their faces and mumbled a few incomprehensible words. (The teacher was not aware that other pupils were teasing the reader, by signs and whispers in their native language.)

The efficiency of social organization of these children excited our admiration. Nonetheless, when we talked to their parents we found that most wanted their children to acquire education and, moreover, believed that they were getting it. Investigating further, we found that the parents rarely entered

Murray and Rosalie Wax, 'Federal programs and Indian target populations', in N. R. Yetman and C. H. Steele, *Majority and Minority: The Dynamics of Racial and Ethnic Relations*, Allyn and Bacon, 1971, pp. 491–502.

the school and never saw what went on in the classrooms; whereas the teachers, on their part, never visited the parents or attended any of the local Indian social events, such as fairs, dances, give-aways, or bingo-parties. Indian elders were not permitted to use the schools for gatherings or entertainments, lest they dirty the floors and destroy government property. Around each consolidated school was a compound in which the teachers lived and kept to themselves.

It seemed to us that if the teachers genuinely wished to educate the Indian children and if the parents genuinely wished their children to be educated, they might do well to break down this elaborate system of *dharma*, get together, and devise means by which the spirited youngsters could be controlled. Among the more radical of our recommendations (though we now consider it the most sensible) was the suggestion that the Indian communities run their own schools with monies from the federal government (Wax, Wax and Dumont, 1964, chap. 7). Eccentric and off-beat such schools might be, but they could not teach the children less than now. Among our other or less radical suggestions were that mothers be hired as classroom aides, that parents be invited to social gatherings held at the school, that teachers be given time off to visit parents in their homes, and that Indians sit on the school board.

Having spoken so strongly in favor of involving the Indian parents and communities in the education of their children, we subsequently welcomed the opportunity to observe and report on Head Start Projects among the Indians living in the Dakotas and Minnesota. In these projects, or so it seemed to us, the OEO was sponsoring exactly the kind of grassroots activity that would help to dissolve the wall between the Indian parents and the schools. For example, communities needing aid were to request it. If funds were granted, the projects were to be directed and carried on by the people who had asked for assistance—and not, primarily, by outsiders. Should outside professional assistance be required, the professionals were directed to involve the parents. We were particularly eager to see what was happening in the several Indian communities which, a year before, had been visited by a representative of the Community Action Programs, who had urged the people in the various districts to form committees, make plans for community improvement, and submit them to Washington. We had heard that several communities had prepared such plans and had ourselves seen the one submitted by the Standing Man Community. So far as we know, it is the only Poverty Program introduced by a poem:

> Go in search of the people
> Live with the people
> Learn from them
> Love them
> Serve them

> Make plans together with the people
> Begin with what they know
> Build on what they have.

It further explains that:

Many members (of the community) expressed that they had not realized that poverty existed, as so many of them grew up in conditions which are now described as poverty but was not identified as such prior to this time.

and that:

The older people have given their consent to let the young people plan the future of the community. They have said that the younger generation is the one who will have to live with the proposed programs.

The plan included such items as a summer youth program, adult education, and self-help housing. Its budget was extremely modest, and it emphasized that:

the community feels that the programes for the POVERTY PROGRAM COM- MITTEE can be effective in establishing a foundation for stabilizing the impact of the dominant culture if administered by the people themselves, and thus, maintain the dignity and respect for themselves as Indian people.

It requested, in addition, a professional personnel

who will help and work with the people in the community (and help) develop able trainees from the local people in the community.

So far as we knew, this program had not yet been funded. On the other hand, we were informed that the OEO expected to establish Head Start projects on this reservation and, this being so, we were to investigate and report on how this might best be done. Accordingly, on our arrival we began to visit Indian friends and acquaintances in the districts and ask them what they thought about a play-school for four and five year olds. Most parents and elders opined that if the hours were not too long and if the teachers were young and happy instead of old and crabby, a school in which the little children could learn and play might be a good thing. Some felt that the children should be taught something about 'Indian things', and others, that it would be a good idea if some of the teachers or teachers-helpers spoke the native language. Asking about recent developments, we were told that the newly established program of work for youth (Neighborhood Youth Corp) was a good thing—but that, of course, what the people really needed was work for the adult men who had to support families. When we asked about the new and handsome looking Old Peoples Home erected since our last visit, we were told that the old people didn't like it and so nobody was living in it now but Vista Workers and some nurses aides.

After three days, this phase of our investigation was brought to an abrupt close when we discovered, quite by accident, that an elaborate program of

Head Start and Child Development Centers was already funded and under way. Curious as to how such a program could exist without any of the people knowing anything about it, we inquired further and were referred to 'The Vista Workers'. These young people, looking wan and harassed, told us that they had been so busy doing paper work and arranging for the delivery of Head Start supplies, that they had not had the time to leave the Agency Town and get out on the reservation. From them we learned that the existing program had been spearheaded by the (White) Tribal Attorney, with the consent of the Tribal Council. It was now being directed by another White man who was supervising their work. A highly qualified young White woman with a Master's Degree in child development had been hired to take charge of instruction. Several of the Head Start schools would be ready to open within a few weeks.

We expressed sincere astonishment at the amount of progress which had been made through the efforts of so few people. Nonetheless, we suggested that the program as it was now being conducted seemed somewhat lacking in community involvement and parental participation. Would it not still be possible to arrange a few meetings at which hours, curriculum, transportation, and other matters might be discussed with the parents? The young people explained that they had suggested this, especially since one of the schools was about to open, and, ' "the people out there" must be beginning to wonder what it's all about'. But the temporary director had vetoed the idea, because, he said, 'As soon as "the people out there" discover that a program has been funded, they will come to my office in droves trying to get jobs for their relatives'.

We pointed out that the contract with OEO specifically called for the involvement of parents in the planning of the program, and went on to ask to what extent community leaders had been involved. 'We haven't been able to find any', said the young folk rather aggrievedly. When, later in the conversation, we named several of the men who had helped to prepare the original 'Poverty Programs', the young peoples' faces hardened with distaste. These men, they confided, were selfish politicians who wanted only to help their family and kin but cared little for the reservation as a whole. 'They're not going to get a thing from us.' Warming to the subject the young folk informed us that 'we have decided' that the Standing Man Community, which had been making the most fuss of all (apparently, we gathered, by asking what had happened to their Poverty Program of the year before), was to be taught a lesson. It was to be the last district on the reservation to be granted a Child Development Center.

In subsequent discussions we tried to point out to the young Vista Workers that the grand, over-all reservation community with which they were trying to interact, did not exist. Instead, the reservation always has been and still is divided into people who call each other Fullbloods and Mixedbloods. Most of the Fullbloods live out on the reservation in small, local, communities, which they themselves call *tiyospaye* and which are predominantly composed of kin. Each of these small communities maintains an internal organization and economy of extraordinary efficiency. They are extremely poor, but they are also extremely tough and tenacious. On the other side are the Mixed-bloods who, for three generations have served as mediators between the local bands, or *tiyospaye*, and the larger society. First existing as scouts and traders, they later became entrepreneurs; and in recent years, many have become liaison men and federal administrators. Their social organization is much more diffuse than that of the Fullbloods, and while they are seldom wealthy, they are usually better off than the latter. Since the White and Mixedblood members of the bureaucracy insist (and sometimes believe) that there is only one reservation-wide community, they can and do monopolize all the influential and well-paid jobs. This is not to say that they do not need jobs. But the Fullbloods, who rarely get within reach of a good job, are, for the most part, bitterly poor. As in many symbiotic relationships, neither side trusts the other. The Mixedbloods consider the Fullbloods unreliable and backward, because 'they are always favoring their relatives'. The Fullbloods mistrust the Mixedbloods because they have no (local) community allegiance and so are 'not really Indian'.

We did not tell the Vista Workers that the Fullbloods do not always regard the members of the Tribal Council as their 'representatives', and that though able and honorable men sometimes sat on the Council, it had been created by the Indian Bureau to operate according to the White Man's rules. Nor did we tell them that we had small confidence that the Tribal Attorney or the incumbent Director of the Community Action Program had any real under-standing of the social dynamics of reservation life. The Attorney—who is dedicated to helping Indians but has never striven to understand them or to grasp their values—had recently involved the Tribal Council in several elaborate and expensive ventures—like the then uninhabited Old Peoples Homes.[1] The Director has devoted a lifetime to trying to change the Full-

---

[1] Such ventures are the topic of considerable self-congratulation at ceremonial, political occasions, and it is true that they have the important effect that, during their construction, employment and monies are brought into the reservation area. On the other hand, honesty requires that we note their defects. Since these projects are heavily underwritten by the federal government and do promise employment and temporary prosperity, as well as providing a symbolic opportunity to do good, it is difficult for the tribal government to assess them rationally and critically. Thus, this government is propelled into ventures which require a significant share of its income both for maintenance and for servicing the debt. Meantime, the more traditional Indians, who exist on a narrow margin of subsistence, are not inclined to devote tribal monies or energies to projects in which they have no real emotional investment.

To be more specific, almost all persons on the reservation, and of whatever background, would be inclined to favor projects to assist the aged Indians who are impoverished. But it is doubtful if these aged would have defined their needs in terms of institutional housing ('A Home') and it is equally doubtful whether they or their kin were polled on the matter.

bloods into his conception of good citizens, but he pointedly refrains from attending their social or ceremonial affairs (which would put him on a level of parity with them), and participates instead in the Rotary Club, the Kiwanis, the American Legion and other organizations whose cultural basis is non-Indian; nor has he learned the native language in which Fullbloods carry on most of their social, economic, and political affairs. We did recommend most strongly to the young people that they get out of the Agency Town and make the acquaintance of the so-called Fullbloods, feeling that if they obtained a more complete picture of the situation, they would be able to make their own judgments. One of the Vista Workers accepted Rosalie's invitation to make some home visits together. But talking to the Fullblood mothers about their children seemed to make little impression on this young lady. On the ride back to the Agency Town she expressed concern because she had been doing something contrary to the local program, namely, consulting the parents beforehand.

Some five months later, we were again given the opportunity to visit Thrashing Buffalo Reservation and report on the now functioning Head Start Program. By this time the Vista Workers had been replaced by a considerable staff of White People and Mixedbloods. These persons talked about 'selling the program to the Indian people and pointed out that a great deal of work would have to be directed toward the Indian people 'in order for them to comply with our attempts and efforts, as workers, to help them'. They also stressed the 'lack of communication' and complained about the difficulty of making 'an effective penetration into the Indian areas'. Meanwhile the Fullbloods were voting with their feet. Some pointed out to us that the Community Action Program directorate in the Agency Town had, as usual, hogged all the funds that might otherwise have flowed directly from the federal government to the people of the *tiyospaye*. When asked what their neighbors thought of the Head Start Programs, they remarked delicately: 'Since these programs are not their own programs, they are not too much interested'.

At one indoctrination meeting, the few local people who attended were less diffident. They told the CAP representatives that they did not want a nursery school, because four year old children would not grow as they should if taken from their mothers. Besides, without her little children to care for, a mother would feel lost and useless. They regarded with strong disfavor the suggestion that they donate their community building to serve as Head Start classrooms, because (we suspect) they feared that if the school authorities took it over they would never give it back.

A year after its inception, the Thrashing Buffalo Head Start Program was limping along with neither 'side' giving an inch. Indeed, the director, an energetic specialist in child development, openly announced that the purpose of the program was to change Indian culture. When members of a *tiyospaye* approached her with the suggestion that some older Indian people be hired to teach some elements of Indian culture, she explained that this is not possible because 'nursery age-levels do not permit factual and conceptual learning'.

We visited many other Head Start Projects for Indian children, and in most of them we found that the programs had been funded, planned, staffed, and put into operation with virtually no involvement of the children's parents. At several schools the parents had subsequently approached the directors and teachers with complaints and suggestions concerning the operation of the schools. But in every case, the professional staff regarded this parental interest with distress—as if it reflected a failure either in planning or procedure. Parental involvement was defined as the parents complying with the suggestions of the teachers. Thus, the directors were pleased when the parents made blocks for the children according to the specifications laid down by the teachers, or when the parents, as requested, would 'volunteer' to accompany the classes on bus trips.

To the directors and teachers we remarked that the complaints and suggestions of the parents could profitably be viewed—not as judgments on their professional competence—but as opportunities to involve the parents in participation. Meetings might be held in which the various problems and proposals could be discussed and the advice and assistance of the parents might be solicited. If, for example, the parents felt that their children were being 'picked-on' during free play periods, they might be willing to send more volunteers to watch the children. At this time we did not realize that we were preaching heresy. But two weeks later, when we made the same suggestion at a workshop for teachers of Indian children, we were summarily rebuked by a high school principal, who pointed out that 'consulting with parents would detract from the authority of the schools'.

Cultural Deprivation as an Ideology

Rationalizing the kinds of behaviors we have just described and pervasive throughout the history of White relationships with Indians is the ideology of cultural inferiority. From the earliest Spanish missionaries in Middle America until the most recent federal program runs the theme that the European and the White is the civilized and the norm to which the Indian must be brought—peaceably and through conversion, when possible; forcibly, otherwise. White society is the point toward which the Indians must be moved, despite the resistance that such stubborn and traditional peoples offer to the process of change.

When the ideology is elaborated specifically for children, it becomes visible as 'cultural deprivation': the Indian home and the mind of the Indian child are described as if they were empty or lacking in pattern. A high official of Bureau of Indian Affairs expressed the view—and the problem as he saw it—in the following words:

The school get this child from a conservative home, brought up speaking the Indian language, and all he knows is Grandma. His home has no books, no magazines, radio, television, newspapers—it's empty! He comes into school and we have to teach him everything! All right. We bring him to the point where he's beginning to know something in high school, and he drops out. . . . Because at this time he has to choose between Grandma and being an educated member of the community.

Another official put the matter to us this way:

The Indian child has such a *meager* experience. When he encounters words like 'elevator' or 'escalator' in his reading, he has no idea what they mean.
  But it's not just strange concepts like those. Take even the idea of *water*. When you or I think of it, well, I think of a shining, stainless steel faucet in a sink, running clean and pure, and of the plumbing that brings it, and chlorination and water purification, or of the half-million dollar project for the reservation water supply. But the Indian child doesn't think of water as something flowing into a bathtub.

Carried far enough, this Ideology of Cultural Deprivation leads to characterizations of Indian life which are deplorably fallacious. One person who had worked on the Thrashing Buffalo Reservation for many years asserted in a public meeting that 'Indian children have no home experiences in art or music' and that Indian children are not told stories by their parents. (Even a music teacher in secondary school stated that Indians had no musical experience.) Another person, also of many years' experience, remarked, 'We must go back to the (Indian) home to find the lack of patterns that should have been learned'.

In the face of this repetitive and rigid usage of such terms as empty, meager, and lacking in pattern, we at length began to feel that these administrators were perceiving the Indian mind as the land-hungry settlers had perceived (La Flesche, 1900, p. xx) the continent:

The White people speak of the country at this period as 'a wilderness', as though it was an empty tract without human interest or history. To us Indians it was as clearly defined then as it is today; we knew the boundaries of tribal lands, those of our friends and those of our foes; we were familiar with every stream, the contour of every hill, and each peculiar feature of the landscape had its tradition. It was our home, the scene of our history, and we loved it as our country.

So far as we could see, this reservation Ideology of Cultural Deprivation serves the following functions: First, it places the responsibility for scholastic defeat on the Indian home and the Indian child; since the child is seen as entering school with an empty head, then surely it is a great achievement if he is taught anything whatsoever. Second, the Ideology is a *carte blanche* that justifies almost any activity within the school as being somehow 'educational'; for, if the child is presumed deficient in every realm of experience, then the task of the school can properly be defined as furnishing him with vicarious experiences to compensate in every aspect of his life. Finally, the Ideology justifies the educators in their isolation from the ignorance of the Indian community; for, if the child actually had a culture including knowledge and values, then they ought properly to learn about these so as to build on his present status, but if he is conceived of as a vacuum on entering school, then the educators may properly ignore his home and community.

Before continuing with a description of the Indian scene, we should like to add that we believe that a similar constellation of attitudes and relationships currently plagues schools in urban settings (cf. Leacock, 1970). Children who come from lowerclass and impoverished ethnic groups are regarded as empty and culture-less rather than as having a culture and social life of their own which educators must learn about in order to be competent in their jobs. Children from lowerclass Negro homes have especially been subjected to this mishandling, since many 'liberals' have refused on political grounds to recognize that their families have a distinct subculture.

Commentary and Critique

Like many other ideologies, that of Cultural Deprivation does not stand close scrutiny. The image it purveys of a static and unchanging traditional Indian culture does not accord with the ethnohistorical reality. Indian societies underwent great innovative transformations in response to the inventions and opportunities accompanying the White invasion of the Americas. The Iroquoian peoples responded to the fur trade by banding together as a great confederacy, the Six Nations. The Cherokee organized themselves as a republic with a bicameral legislature, and one of their number—a man who spoke no English—was stimulated by the sight of the missionaries, their Scriptures, and their schools, to the invention of a syllabary that proved so congruent with native ways of procedure that in a short time his entire people were literate. The Navajo oriented themselves about the horse and the sheep (both introduced by the Spanish) and today they and the Whites think of their woollen rugs and their mutton as wholly 'traditional'. Other groups of Indians responded to the horse by rapidly elaborating a brilliant culture as horse-nomads, and today the popular stereotype of the Indian is precisely the mounted warrior chasing the buffalo and harassing the Anglo settlers.

Certainly it is true that the subsequent confinement to reservations and existence in a condition of severe poverty and subordination has not been conducive to further brilliant innovation by Indian peoples. Yet it is equally true that reservation life has its drama and its vitality, its arts and its culture, so that in comparison the life of the middleclass child may well seem 'culturally deprived'. We well remember the day when we stepped from a Quonset hut where Indian children were being drilled offtune in those eviscerated folk songs that are considered appropriate to the nursery and moved but a short distance to a local fair where powwow singing and dancing of the highest esthetic intensity were being exhibited, and we thought how deprived were the musical and esthetic senses of those presumably well trained Head Start teachers. And this experience was not confined to the musical realm. Before we began work on Indian reservations, we had read accounts in which Indians were characterized as passive, apathetic, and hostilely dependent. In opposition to these terms, we must state that our own observations are that BIA and federal personnel are as hostile toward the Indians as the latter are toward them (and on both sides there are individuals who are not hostile); also, that federal personnel are utterly dependent upon the continued existence of the 'backward' Indians, because if Indians managed their own affairs then the local Indian agencies or programs would provide no employment (this dependency is therefore especially marked among the lower and less skilled echelons). Our own observations again are that 'apathy' is a convenient label to apply to people who don't happen to agree with the program that a government official or other reformer happens to be pushing. Frankly, when we went to the reservation, we did expect to see apathetic people. Instead we saw people whose lust for life reminded us of the descriptions of Restoration England or Dostoevskian Russian, and today we are inclined to feel that it is the urban lowermiddleclass who are culturally deprived and whose children have such meager experiences.

Possibly we may need to reemphasize that neither we as observers nor most Indians as actors are satisfied with the conditions of their lives and neither we nor they are seeking to preserve a mythically static, traditional, Indian society. What we are arguing is that Indian communities have been continuing the function in very positive ways, although their existences are often hidden by the vagaries of federally drawn boundaries to Indian reservations. As organized and functioning communities, they have as much right to exist within the U.S. as do communities of Irish Catholics, Hutterites, Old Order Amish, Chasidic Jews, or Japanese-Americans; and, as in the case of these communities, if they should be dissolved by the acids of supposedly benevolent (but quite authoritarian) programs, the consequences are more likely to be the creation of a deracinated *lumpen proletariat* than the emergence of conventional lowermiddleclass urban Anglos (cf. Wahrhaftig, 1966; Gans, 1962, chap. 7). (The conspicuous presence in urban localities of alcoholic and disorganized Indians should caution us as to the consequences of eroding the bonds of Indian community organization.) Insofar as Indian communities are impoverished, they can utilize assistance—mostly they want jobs. But, instead of jobs they are given programs, and despite the fact that their membership includes persons of wisdom, talent, and experience, the programs are headed by those who use the mantle of professional training to derogate what they do not perceive or comprehend.

References

Gans, H. J. (1962), *The Urban Villagers*, Glencoe, Ill.

La Flesche, F. F. (1900), *The Middle Five: Indian Schoolboys of the Omaha Tribe*, Madison.

Leacock, E. B. (ed.) (1970), *The Culture of Poverty: A Critique*, New York.

Wahrhaftig, A. L. (1966), 'Community and the caretakers', *New University Thought*, vol. 4, no. 4, pp. 54–76.

Wax, R. H. (1967), 'The warrior dropouts', *Trans-Action*, vol. IV, pp. 40–6.

Wax, M. L. and Wax, R. H. (1964), 'Cultural deprivation as an educational ideology', *Journal of American Indian Education*, vol. III, no. 2, pp. 15–18.

Wax, M. L. and Wax, R. H. (1965), 'Indian education for what?', *Midcontinent American Studies Journal*, vol. IV, no. 2, pp. 164–70.

Wax, M. L., Wax, R. H. and Dumont, R. V. J. (1964), 'Formal education in an American Indian community', *Social Problems*, vol. XI, no. 4, Society for the Study of Social Problems.

33 *A Little, C. Mabey and G. Whitaker,* The Education of Immigrant Pupils in Inner London Primary Schools

Educational authorities in many urban areas have, over the past ten years, provided school places for a growing number of 'immigrant' pupils. It would be unrealistic to deny that this creates or intensifies for the school system a range of educational problems. Some are akin to the general difficulties of educating young people from culturally disadvantaged backgrounds, others are more specific problems of the linguistic handicaps of youngsters coming from non-English-speaking countries. Because of these types of problem a working party of the Inspectorate was set up by the ILEA to inquire into the needs, attainment and contribution of immigrant pupils in ILEA's schools. The following paper is an analysis of a special investigation into the attainment of immigrant pupils; the working party's general report has been published by the Authority.

Definition of Immigrant

The official Department of Education and Science definition of 'immigrant' was used in the survey and in this report includes:

1. Children born outside the British Isles who have come to this country with or to join parents, other relatives or guardians whose country of origin was also abroad.

2. Children born in the United Kingdom to parents whose country of origin was abroad and whose parents, to the best of the head teacher's knowledge, have not been in this country more than ten years.

Children from Northern Ireland or Eire were excluded. Where the term 'non-immigrant' (or sometimes 'indigenous') is used in this paper it is intended to cover all children in the schools surveyed who are not 'immigrants' in the terms of the above definition.

Sample

As the main object of the investigation was to examine the problems of, and effect on, schools with a high proportion of immigrant pupils, the question-

A. Little, C. Mabey and G. Whitaker, 'The education of immigrant pupils in Inner London primary schools', *Race*, vol. 9, no. 4, 1968, pp. 439–52

naire was sent only to those schools with a high proportion. A 'high proportion' was defined as those schools in which more than one-third of the children were immigrant. The chief reason for the choice of this percentage was the view put forward by the Department of Education and Science in its circular 7/65 that 'experience suggests . . . that if the proportion (of immigrant children) goes over about one-third either in the school as a whole or in any one class, serious strains arise'. The investigation was further limited to schools with junior departments since one of the chief objectives was to examine the effect on attainment standards at 11 years of age.

Fifty-two schools fell into the category mentioned above, that is, schools with junior departments whose total roll was composed of more than one-third immigrant pupils, and these schools had 1068 such pupils transferring to secondary education in 1966. This represents more than one-quarter of the immigrants of the relevant age in the Authority's primary schools (in September 1966 there were 3952 immigrants of 10+ and 11+ in primary schools). Obviously this cannot be claimed as a random or representative sample of pupils of this age, because it was specifically taken from schools with a high concentration of immigrants. Some indication of representativeness can be obtained by comparing the country of origin of the sample of immigrants due for transfer with the origin of immigrant pupils of this age in all the Authority's schools.

	% All authority	% Sample
West Indian	44	56
Indians and Pakistanis	10	7
Cypriots	21	23
Others	25	14

The sample of immigrant school-leavers was not completely representative of the immigrant population of the same age in the Authority. The sample had a significantly higher proportion of West Indians and fewer 'Other' immigrants. Because of the importance of the 'Other' group the schools were asked in January 1966 to complete returns listing the exact nationality of their immigrant pupils. The composition of the 'Other' immigrant group for 10+, 11+, 12+ pupils (that is, excluding West Indians, Indians, Pakistanis, and Cypriots) for the fifty-two sample schools was about one-third Europeans, one-third Africans, one-fifth Guyanese, and the remainder for all other places with no substantial proportion from any one country.

Performance Ratings

Information was collected on the groupings of children in the sample schools in the three 'subjects' (English, Verbal Reasoning and Mathematics) given in the 'profile' used in the ILEA transfer procedure from primary to secondary schools. All pupils due for transfer to secondary education are placed in one of seven 'profile groups' (from 1 down to 7) for English, Mathematics and Verbal Reasoning. A pupil's groups for English and Mathematics are based on the school's assessment of his attainment from its whole knowledge of his work in these fields as well as scores on specific tests. Within the school the head teacher may adjust the number placed in the various groups in the light of information about the school's distribution of attainment obtained from county comparability tests but these tests do not directly determine the groupings of individual pupils since the tests are taken anonymously. A pupil's grouping for Verbal Reasoning is also based on the school's cumulative knowledge of the child, but in this case the school also takes into account the results of Verbal Reasoning tests taken by each pupil. One of these, taken during a specified period in January, is a closed test devised each year for London schools. It will be seen from this account that the groupings are based very considerably on the school's general knowledge of the child, though the standards in English and Mathematics applied to the school can be related to general standards in the ILEA by reference to comparability tests, and those for Verbal Reasoning to the scores obtained by individual children in Verbal Reasoning tests throughout the Authority.

Statistical Tests Utilized in the Report

Statistical Tests of significance were applied to the results reported in this paper. The test chosen was the Kolmogovov-Smirnov One Sample Test. This test is designed to compare the whole distribution of scores of different groups rather than comparing individual parts of a distribution. The underlying principle of it is to take the largest difference between the cumulated proportions of two distributions and assign a probability of this difference occurring by chance alone for a given sample size. The smaller the sample size, the larger the difference that is required before it can be considered statistically significant. Throughout comparison has been made at the 0·05 and the 0·01 levels: if differences are *not* significant at the 0·05 level the table has been marked **. If the difference *is* significant at the 0·05 level it has been marked *. Tables without an asterisk show differences which are significant at the 0·01 level (that is, are highly significant). What these tests show is the probability of difference arising by chance: at the 0·01 level (which for our purposes has been taken as the level of significance necessary) the difference observed between a population and a sub-sample would occur by chance in one sample out of a hundred drawn from that population. To say a difference is significant at the 0·05 level means that this difference would be expected in 5 samples out of every hundred drawn. The test does not tell us whether the differences are real or not, it merely indicates the probability of them arising by chance. In a sense there are no tests of significance, but only levels of confidence with which observations can be accepted.

For one set of comparisons (for immigrant entrants in 1959 and 1960 and non-immigrants in the same schools) an additional test of significance was used, the Chi square. This is a test that attempts to assess the extent to which observed differences in the distribution of sets of observations could have arisen by chance. Again the 0·05 and 0·01 levels have been used. Again it must be emphasized that these tests tell us the probability of a difference arising by chance, they do not tell us if the difference is real or meaningful. For the purposes at hand it is assumed that if a difference could occur in one sample out of a hundred, then the difference is real. But this is merely an assumption for the analysis.

Immigrants' Performance

The proportions of all the Authority's and of immigrant pupils falling into the seven groups are shown in Table 1. Complete information about all immigrant pupils was not provided; this was largely due to the fact that some children had arrived too recently to be placed into profile groups. A comparison of immigrant and all the Authority's scores shows clearly that the distribution of the immigrant pupils is very different from that of all the pupils in the Authority's area. In no sense is the immigrant pupils' distribution a normal one: in fact, in each descending group more pupils are found. Only 2 per cent of the immigrant pupils were placed in the top group,

Table 1: *Percentage of Pupils Falling in the 7 Profile Groups*

Group in profile	English		Verbal Reasoning		Mathematics	
	Immigrants	All Authority	Immigrants	All Authority	Immigrants	All Authority
1	2	11	2	11	2	12
2	4	15	4	14	4	15
3	7	15	7	15	8	15
4	14	19	11	17	15	18
5	16	15	15	15	16	15
6	23	15	25	15	23	15
7	33	11	36	12	32	11
No. for whom information received	1 051	31 723	1 038	31 706	1 051	31 722

Note: In the tables in which the figures are expressed as percentages, the percentages have been rounded up so that in some cases they do not total exactly 100.

1, in any of the three 'subjects', and approximately one-third fell into the bottom group, 7. Whereas, the average child in the Authority was placed in the middle of group 4, the average immigrant pupil was placed in the lower third of group 6. The figures can also be expressed in terms of the proportions of pupils of below average performance ('average' in this context is related to the average of all the Authority's pupils). Whereas, half of all the Authority's pupils can be termed as below average performance (those placed into the bottom half of group 4 and into groups 5, 6 and 7), approximately four-fifths of the immigrant pupils fell into this category (79 per cent in English, 82 per cent in Verbal Reasoning, and 79 per cent in Mathematics). The differences in the distributions on all three ratings are significantly different at the 0·01 level.

Perhaps the most striking illustration of the comparative performance of immigrants is that whereas roughly one pupil in four in the Authority (including it must be remembered immigrants), falls in the top two ability groups in each 'subject', the percentage for immigrants is 6 per cent or roughly one pupil in seventeen. It must be remembered that all the Authority's ratings include (and may therefore be depressed by) the immigrant pupils both in the sample schools and in other Authority schools.

Performance Related to Nationality

Although the overall performance of immigrants was found to be significantly lower than that of all Authority pupils, differences might have existed in the performance of the different national groups. As Table 2 shows there are significant differences between the distributions of the different nationalities, but no one nationality group has a normal distribution. The chief point which should be noted is the relatively low performance of the West Indians compared with the other groups and, in particular, as compared with the 'Other' immigrants. This difference is particularly marked in Mathematics for which 85 per cent of the West Indians were placed into the lower half of group 4 and lower groups; 68 per cent of the Indians and Pakistanis, 75 per cent of the Cypriots and 65 per cent of the 'Other' immigrants fell into this category. The overall results are, on the surface, somewhat surprising in view of the fact that a greater proportion of West Indians were English-speaking, and might have been thought to have an advantage on that account.

The differences between each national group and 'all Authority' are significant at the 0·01 level.

Perhaps important in determining the level of a pupil's performance is his knowledge of English: the immigrant population includes youngsters from diverse countries of origin and therefore their knowledge of English is likely to vary widely. Because of this an analysis was completed on the performance of all the immigrant pupils divided into three groups: the English-speaking pupils,

Table 2: *Pupils falling in each Profile Group by Nationality*

(a) *English*

Nationality	No. of pupils for whom information received	% of group in profile						
		1	2	3	4	5	6	7
West Indian	590	1	3	6	15	14	24	37
Indian and Pakistani	74	3	5	14	8	15	24	31
Cypriot	237	3	3	7	12	18	23	34
Other	150	3	7	12	17	20	22	20
All Authority	31 723	11	15	15	19	15	15	11

(b) *Verbal Reasoning*

Nationality	No. of pupils for whom information received	% of group in profile						
		1	2	3	4	5	6	7
West Indian	583	1	3	6	10	14	26	41
Indian and Pakistani	73	3	10	11	14	15	15	33
Cypriot	232	1	5	7	13	17	25	32
Other	150	5	7	9	13	15	27	24
All Authority	31 706	11	14	15	17	15	15	12

(c) *Mathematics*

Nationality	No. of pupils for whom information received	% of group in profile						
		1	2	3	4	5	6	7
West Indian	590	1	3	5	12	14	25	40
Indian and Pakistani	74	5	7	11	19	16	11	31
Cypriot	237	3	4	8	19	17	25	23
Other	150	5	6	14	20	19	19	17
All Authority	31 722	12	15	15	18	15	15	11

those with some English and those with little or no English. The results of this analysis are shown in Table 3 and show very clearly the much lower attainment of those children with inadequate English. Whereas only about one-quarter of the English-speaking pupils fell into Group 7 in the three subjects, about one-half of those children with some English and between 64 per cent to 92 per cent of the non-English-speaking category were placed in this group. It is interesting to note that, perhaps not surprisingly, English is a smaller handicap in Mathematics than in other subjects. However, it should be pointed out that even the English-speaking pupils do not achieve a distribution comparable with that of all Authority pupils. For English, only 8 per cent of them are in the top two groups (which should account for 25 per cent of the pupils) and the median pupil falls into the lowest quarter of group 5 rather than into the middle of group 4. Again the differences between the

Table 3: *Immigrant Pupils falling in each Profile Group related to their Knowledge of English*

(a) *English*

Knowledge of English	Number for whom information received	% of group in profile						
		1	2	3	4	5	6	7
English-speaking	752	3	5	10	18	18	24	22
English-speaking but needing further teaching	244	—	1	2	6	11	25	55
Little or no English	55	—	—	—	—	4	4	92
All Authority	31 723	11	15	15	19	15	15	11

(b) *Verbal Reasoning*

Knowledge of English	Number for whom information received	% of group in profile						
		1	2	3	4	5	6	7
English-speaking	750	2	6	8	14	16	26	27
English-speaking but needing further teaching	238	—	—	4	7	10	26	53
Little or no English	50	—	—	2	—	8	6	84
All Authority	31 706	11	14	15	17	15	15	12

(c) *Mathematics*

Knowledge of English	Number for whom information received	% of group in profile						
		1	2	3	4	5	6	7
English-speaking	752	3	6	9	19	16	23	25
English-speaking but needing further teaching	244	1	—	4	7	16	22	50
Little or no English	55	—	2	4	—	4	27	64
All Authority	31 722	12	15	15	18	15	15	11

distribution of all Authority pupils and the 3 'immigrant' groups are statistically significant at the 0·01 per cent level.

A further analysis was undertaken on the three groups subdivided by
country of origin. Because the number of non-English-speaking pupils was
so small there were too few in each of the four nationality groups and so this
analysis was concentrated on pupils speaking English and those speaking
some English but needing further intensive language training. The results of
this in the case of those regarded by the teachers as English-speaking are
shown in Table 4. This table shows even more clearly than Table 2 the low

Table 4: *English-speaking Immigrant Pupils of each Nationality
falling into each Profile Group*

(a) *English*

Nationality	Number for whom information received	% of group in profile						
		1	2	3	4	5	6	7
West Indian	478	2	4	7	18	16	25	28
Indian and Pakistani	43	5	7	21	12	14	26	16
Cypriot	124	5	6	10	18	26	21	14
Other	107	4	8	17	19	21	24	7
All Authority	31 723	11	15	15	19	15	15	11

(b) *Verbal Reasoning*

Nationality	Number for whom information received	% of group in profile						
		1	2	3	4	5	6	7
West Indian	476	1	4	7	13	15	26	35
Indian and Pakistani	43	5	16	9	16	16	21	16
Cypriot	124	2	10	9	17	22	27	14
Other	107	7	9	12	16	16	25	14
All Authority	31 706	11	14	15	17	15	15	12

(c) *Mathematics*

Nationality	Number for whom information received	% of group in profile						
		1	2	3	4	5	6	7
West Indian	478	1	4	6	14	16	27	32
Indian and Pakistani	43	9	12	9	28	12	9	21
Cypriot	124	6	8	12	27	15	19	12
Other	107	7	7	18	22	22	15	8
All Authority	31 722	12	15	15	18	15	15	11

attainment of the West Indians compared with the other groups. The differences can be seen at both ends of the scale. While only about 5 per cent of the English-speaking West Indians fell into the top 2 groups in each of the three subjects, between 12 per cent and 21 per cent of the rest of the English-speaking immigrants were placed in these groups. Conversely, groups 6 and 7 accounted for between 53 per cent to 61 per cent of the West Indians but only for between 23 per cent to 42 per cent of all the other immigrants. The English-speaking immigrants, with the exception of the West Indians, have a distribution in Mathematics which does not differ significantly from that of all the Authority pupils. In particular, the 'Other' immigrants have a distribution over the seven groups which is very similar to that of all the Authority pupils. Examination of the results of the pupils with only some English underlines the differences between the West Indians and the rest. Groups 6 and 7 accounted for about 92 per cent of the West Indians but only for between 45 per cent (Indians and Pakistanis in Mathematics) to 78 per cent ('Other' immigrants in Verbal Reasoning) for all other nationalities. It is difficult to detect significant differences between the three nationality groups (excluding the West Indians, that is) although there seems to be a slight tendency for the 'Other' immigrants when they are English-speaking to rank slightly higher than the other groups.

Performance Related to Date of First Entry to an English School

There were two main reasons for attempting this analysis. The first was to try to discover if there was a relationship between length of English education and performance at age eleven. The second was to determine, if a positive relationship were found, whether there was a critical period of English education necessary for immigrant children to achieve, in academic terms, an equivalent performance level to all the Authority pupils.

The results of this analysis are set out in Table 5. All children who started school in, or before, 1960 have been both grouped together, and divided into a 1960 and a '1959 or earlier' cohort. The first point to be made is that quite clearly those pupils who had started school in, or before, 1960 (and, thus, had had a complete or almost complete primary education in the U.K.) had a much higher performance than, for example, those entering in 1966. Whereas 57 per cent of the 1966 cohort entry fell into group 7 for Verbal Reasoning, only 16 per cent of the 1959 and 1960 cohort were in group 7. Even a superficial examination of the tables shows that, in fact, as the length of English education decreases so the standard of performance declines. However, when the performances of the 1959 and 1960 cohorts, either together or separately, are compared with all the Authority pupils it can be seen that the immigrant pupils, even with a full or nearly full English education, do not have a distribution of performance which one would expect from a sample of London schoolchildren. Further it is very difficult, from the analysis done so far, to detect any particular length of English education as being critical to a child's performance. There appears to be an almost regular decline in performance as length of English education decreases. However, a more marked decline seems to be shown for those pupils first starting in 1964: that is, those pupils who had between one year two terms and two years two terms of English education.

In previous comparisons when various 'immigrants' subgroups' ratings were compared with the distribution of ratings for all Authority pupils, differences were found to be consistently statistically significant at the 0·01 level. However, a more complex set of results is found in Table 5:

1. When the '1959 or earlier' group are compared with all Authority pupils the difference in the distribution of Verbal Reasoning scores was not statistically significant. Further the differences in the distribution of both English and Mathematics although statistically significant at the 0·05 level were not so at the 0·01 level (which was the level of significance selected at the outset).

2. Similar comparisons for the 1960 cohort and the combined 1959 and 1960 cohort in each case with all Authority pupils yield differences in the distribution that are significant at the 0·01 level.

Therefore the results of the statistical comparison are by no means clear cut when all Authority pupils and the 1959 cohort are compared. Visual comparison suggests differences: rigorous statistical testing suggests that the differences are too small to be considered significant. But it must be remembered that there are only fifty-two members of the '1959 or earlier' cohort, and because of this relatively small sample size differences have to be large to be statistically significant. This point can be demonstrated by a hypothetical example: given the difference in the distribution shown in the tables, had the sample been eighty people the differences would have been statistically significant at the 0·01 level for the English test. Sample sizes of 200 for Mathematics and 300 for the Verbal Reasoning would have yielded 'statistically significant' differences for the distributions as shown in Table 5.

The same problem of small differences and small sample size bedevils another comparison which further complicates this situation. If the 1959 and earlier cohort and the 1960 cohort are compared the distributions are not significantly different at the 0·05 level. Therefore we are confronted by a situation in which statistically the 1959 and 1960 cohorts can be considered the same, the 1959 cohort and all Authority pupils can be considered the same, but the 1960 cohort and all Authority pupils can be considered different. This point will be returned to later. Earlier it was shown the country of origin affected performance: in particular the attainment of West Indian pupils appeared to be lower than other groups. Of the 219 pupils who completed all or most of their primary education in the U.K., 101 were from the West

Indies, and Table 6 compares their attainment in the three areas with those of other immigrant groups. On the whole, the gap between them and other immigrant groups has been maintained in Verbal Reasoning and Mathematics but not in English. In both Mathematics and Verbal Reasoning there are rather fewer in the top two groups, and more in the bottom two than for other immigrant groups. For example, 8 per cent of West Indian and 16 per

Table 5: *Performance of Immigrant Pupils related to their Year of Entry to U.K. Education*

(a) *English*

Year of entry to U.K. education	Number for whom information received	% of group in profile						
		1	2	3	4	5	6	7
1959 and 1960	219	5	8	12	17	21	25	13
1959 or earlier*	52	6	15	8	15	21	21	15
1960	167	5	5	12	17	20	26	14
1961	112	2	4	10	21	14	28	21
1962	152	3	5	10	18	21	20	22
1963	102	1	4	9	14	17	26	29
1964	175	—	2	5	11	10	26	46
1965	192	1	2	3	7	10	22	56
1966	72	—	—	—	8	15	14	62
No information	29	—	10	7	24	31	14	14
All Authority	31 723	11	15	15	19	15	15	11

(b) *Verbal Reasoning*

Year of entry to U.K. education	Number for whom information received	% of group in profile						
		1	2	3	4	5	6	7
1959 and 1960	218	4	8	12	15	18	26	16
1959 or earlier**	52	5	11	13	17	17	22	14
1960	166	4	7	11	16	18	26	18
1961	112	1	4	9	15	15	33	22
1962	151	3	5	9	13	21	26	23
1963	101	—	5	6	15	17	19	39
1964	170	—	2	2	8	10	26	51
1965	190	1	2	4	5	9	21	58
1966	69	—	—	4	7	10	22	57
No information	29	3	10	—	21	24	24	17
All Authority	31 706	11	14	15	17	15	15	12

(c) *Mathematics*

Year of entry to U.K. education	Number for whom information received	% of group in profile						
		1	2	3	4	5	6	7
1959 and 1960	218	6	8	8	20	19	24	16
1959 or earlier*	52	7	11	7	20	19	20	15
1960	166	4	7	9	20	19	24	18
1961	112	2	4	12	22	17	19	25
1962	152	3	7	11	18	20	22	20
1963	102	2	3	9	17	19	22	29
1964	175	1	2	5	11	11	25	46
1965	192	1	2	5	8	9	26	50
1966	72	—	1	3	4	12	24	56
No information	29	3	3	10	21	34	21	7
All Authority	31 722	12	15	15	18	15	15	11

Table 6: *Performances of Immigrants from West Indies and other countries who entered schools 1959–60*

	% in each profile group													
	1		2		3		4		5		6		7	
	WI	other	WI	other	WI	other	WI	other	WI	other	WI	other	WI	other
English	3	7	9	7	9	13	22	12	20	21	25	24	12	17
V.R.	2	6	6	10	15	10	12	18	20	15	30	22	15	18
Maths	2	8	9	7	6	10	17	23	20	17	29	19	17	16

cent of other immigrants were in groups 1 and 2 on the Verbal Reasoning, and 11 per cent compared with 15 per cent in similar mathematics group. At the other end, groups 6 and 7 on the mathematics profile contained 46 per cent West Indian compared with 35 per cent of other immigrants.

The Standards of the Non-immigrant Pupils

One final, general question remains, namely the performance of the non-immigrant pupils in the fifty-two schools in 1966 as compared with the general pattern of performance of all Authority pupils. Two qualifications should be made, however, when considering this evidence. The first is that, of course, it gives no information about whether the performance of the native children in these schools has changed over the last five years. Secondly, the distribution of performance of all Authority pupils includes that of the immigrant pupils, and they make up roughly 12 per cent of the age group covered in this paper. It is known from the survey that the performance of immigrant pupils in the fifty-two schools concerned was much lower than that of all London pupils. Therefore it might be that the performance of all English pupils in the Authority is significantly higher than that of all the Authority pupils, the overall figures given in this paper being depressed by the performance of immigrants.

Visual inspection of the table shows the striking similiarty in the two distributions: and statistical testing did not indicate that any of the differences shown were statistically significant. Therefore it can be concluded that the distribution of ratings of non-immigrant pupils in schools with high immigrant concentration are the same as for all Authority pupils. However, as has been pointed out the latter distribution may be depressed by the inclusion of immigrant ratings within it. Nevertheless given the frequently expressed anxiety about the performance of non-immigrants in schools where there is a concentration of immigrants, the similarities reported in Table 7 are of great importance. It must also be remembered that the figures for all Authority pupils will include those for areas which are more fortunate than those in which most of the sample schools occurred.

Immigrants'—Non-immigrants' Performance in the Fifty-two Sample Schools

Because of the apparently illogical findings when making comparisons between all Authority, the '1959 or earlier', and 1960 cohorts, a further analysis of these findings was undertaken. Instead of the original test of significance the Chi square was used. Further, scores for all Authority pupils

Table 7: *Performance of the Non-immigrant Pupils in the 52 Schools in the Survey*

Group in profile	English**		Verbal Reasoning**		Mathematics**	
	Non-immigrants	All ILEA	Non-immigrants	All ILEA	Non-immigrants	All ILEA
1	9	11	10	11	10	12
2	14	15	15	14	14	15
3	17	15	16	15	15	15
4	19	19	17	17	20	18
5	16	15	15	15	15	15
6	14	15	16	15	16	15
7	10	11	11	12	11	11
No. of pupils put into a profile group	1 564	31 723	1 569	31 706	1 553	31 722

were replaced by the distribution of scores of non-immigrant pupils in the fifty-two sample schools. The results were still not clear cut:

1. The 1960 cohort distribution for all three 'subjects' was significantly different from that of non-immigrants in the sample schools at the 0·01 level.

2. The 1959 and 1960 immigrant cohorts were not significantly different, although there was some evidence of a difference that was nearly significant at the 0·05 level for English ratings.

3. The '1959 and earlier' cohort and non-immigrant distribution were not significantly different for Mathematics and Verbal Reasoning but were (at the 0·05 level, not the 0·01 level) for English.

Conclusions

1. Clear, consistent and significant differences were found between the performance of immigrants taken as a whole and all Authority pupils.

2. Immigrant performance was related to knowledge of English, country of origin and length of education in the U.K.

3. There is a consistent and marked improvement in immigrant performance with increasing length of English education.

4. No difference was found between the distributions of groupings for non-immigrants in the sample schools and all Authority pupils.

5. The evidence on completed primary schooling and immigrant performance is not clear cut, and it would be unwise to conclude that even with full English primary education the performances of immigrant pupils is the same as non-immigrants in these schools. Statistical tests suggest that the differences are not wide enough to be statistically significant, but it would be safer to conclude only that the distribution of scores fits closer to that of non-immigrants the longer the length of education in the U.K.

6. The empirical findings and problems confronting schools with high concentrations of immigrants can be illustrated by Table 8, in which are

Table 8

	% in groups 1 and 2				% in groups 3, 4, 5				% in groups 6 and 7			
	Recent Arrivals	*Long stay*	*Non-immigrants in sample*	*All Authority*	*Recent arrivals*	*Long stay*	*Non-immigrants in sample*	*All authority*	*Recent arrivals*	*Long stay*	*Non-immigrants in sample*	*All Authority*
English	1·6	13	23	25	23·3	50	52	50	75·1	38	24	25
Verbal												
Reasoning	1·9	12	25	25	19·7	45	48	50	78·4	42	27	25
Mathematics	2·3	14	24	25	23·3	47	50	50	74·4	40	27	25

summarized the distributions for: recent arrivals (immigrants who entered English education in 1964 or after); long stay immigrants, beginning their English education in or before 1960; non-immigrants in the sample schools; all Authority pupils.

The magnitude of the problems facing schools with large numbers of recent arrivals is shown by the performance of these pupils at 11 years of age: the impact of full or nearly complete schooling on performances is indicated by the improvement shown in those entering in 1960 or earlier: the continuing educational problem is indicated by the gap between the 1960 group and non-immigrants in the same schools.

34 *C. Bagley,* The Educational Performance of Immigrant Children

The present political climate in Britain is one in which information and opinions concerning coloured people tend to be seized upon by newspapers and some politicians, and often treated in a semi-sensational and alarmist fashion. An example is to hand. In the April 1968 issue of *Race* (vol. IX, no. 4) an article was published, under the authorship of A. Little, C. Mabey and G. Whitaker, entitled 'The Education of Immigrant Pupils in Inner London Primary Schools'. The tone of this article was moderate and scholarly, and the conclusions tempered by a number of qualifications.

The article in question studied the performance of 1068 immigrant pupils in inner London schools where more than one-third of the pupils were immigrant. The 11 + profiles of the immigrant children were compared with those of non-immigrant children, and the profiles of various kinds of immigrant children (West Indian, etc.) were compared. A finding which has been made by a previous study emerged—that the performance of immigrant children was inversely related to the number of years they had spent in the British school system. Poor profiles were also related to poor command of English.[1] One encouraging finding was that the performance of non-immigrant pupils in these schools with a high proportion of immigrant children was in no way different from the performance of non-immigrant children in the ILEA as a whole.

On 10 May 1968 under a three-column headline, 'How Immigrant Children Fall Behind', a 600-word summary of this article appeared in the *Financial Times*, accompanied by a single selected table giving gross results only. The first paragraph of this report stated: 'A most disturbing research report on the performance of immigrant children in London schools, judged on Eleven

---

[1] Approximately 5 per cent of the immigrant children in the Little *et al.* study were said to have 'little or no English'. Cf. the report by Wolfinden (1968), that in 57 immigrant children specially studied attending primary schools where there were 35 per cent or more immigrant children, 5·26 per cent had 'language difficulties severe enough to interfere with their education'.

C. Bagley, 'The educational performance of immigrant children', *Race*, vol. 10 no. 1, 1968, pp. 91–4.

Plus criteria, seems to suggest that they are doing consistently worse in school than their English schoolfriends. . . .'

In the present writer's opinion the judgment that the article by Little *et al.* is a 'most disturbing research report' cannot be sustained; nor can the generally pessimistic tone of the newspaper article be justified.

There are a number of reasons why this finding should be perfectly explicable. Firstly, in the case of Indian, Pakistani and Cypriot children their first language is not English; and in the case of West Indian children, the customary linguistic constructions of their language are different from those of English. Given these facts it is not surprising that these children do not fare well on tests of English and Verbal Reasoning, which of necessity require a good command of English. Mathematics too requires a reasonable knowledge of English before number concepts can be handled.

Secondly, while these children can acquire a knowledge of English by means of the school system, their parents cannot. There is a wealth of research in the field of educational sociology which shows the paramount importance of the child's home background (see, for example, Douglas, 1964) and the linguistic constructs used by his parents (Bernstein, 1961, p. 288) for his intellectual achievement. What is surprising is that immigrant children who have spent all their primary education years in Britain should make sustained progress towards some level of parity with English children. Indeed, the research by Wiles (1968, pp. 81–7) showed that in secondary education (in a large London comprehensive school) there is actually a preponderance of immigrant children who have spent all their secondary school years in Britain, in the top streams, in comparison with English children. This finding (which did not receive any press publicity) is in keeping with other research which has shown the greater motivation to achieve educational and vocational success in the immigrant, as compared with the English teenager (Milson, 1966; Beetham, 1961).

The discussion has so far assumed that the 11 + profiles for English, Verbal Reasoning and Mathematics are objective measures of the ability of the children to manipulate the English language. This *may* be so, but the information given by Little *et al.* suggests that some doubt may be cast upon this.

The educational profiles were the standard 11 + assessments used in the ILEA. Little *et al.* write

'A pupil's groups for English and Mathematics are based on the school's assessment of his attainment from his whole knowledge of work in these fields as well as scores on specific tests . . . a pupil's grouping for Verbal Reasoning is also based on the school's cumulative knowledge of the child, but in this case the school also takes into account the results of verbal reasoning tests taken by each pupil . . . it will be seen from this account that the groupings are based very considerably on the school's general knowledge of the child, though the standards in English and Mathematics applied to the school can be related to general standards in the ILEA by reference to comparability tests, and those for Verbal Reasoning to the scores obtained by individual children in Verbal Reasoning tests throughout the Authority (p. 441).

Now, there is a good deal of careful work (for example by J. W. B. Douglas and his colleagues at the M.R.C. Unit, London School of Economics) to show that low social class depresses a childs performance in school *independently* of his actual intelligence. The child's basic intelligence—as measured by the Wechsler or Stanford-Binet tests, or the relatively culture-free Draw-a-Person test (Datta, 1967, pp. 626–30)—is hardly ever known to the schools. The teacher's own estimate of a child's intelligence is not a reliable indicator of the child's actual intelligence.

I can best illustrate this by reference to a recently completed study of epileptic children in London (Bagley, 1968). Epileptics have some similarity to individuals whose skin is not white—they are a group subject to prejudice and discrimination. In America for instance, a national opinion survey found that responses to an attitude question about epileptics were somewhat similar to responses about coloured people (Caveness, *et al.*, 1965, pp. 75–86). In 1964, 23 per cent of respondents objected to their child playing with an epileptic child, and 18 per cent advocated employment segregation. The most liberal responders were younger, more educated, living in towns rather than in the country, and living in the north rather than the south. These are exactly the characteristics of those who show liberal attitudes with regard to race.

In the London study, 118 epileptic children were given the Wechsler Intelligence Scale for Children. The teachers were then asked to estimate the child's actual intelligence (in broad groupings—average, above average, well-above average, etc.) from their own knowledge of the child. In 28 cases the teachers in these London schools, seriously underestimated the child's true ability. For example, a 13-year-old girl with an I.Q. of 120 had failed her 11+ examination, and was in the 'D' stream of a secondary modern school. Her teacher considered that she was of 'below average' intelligence.

Another case is particularly relevant for the article under discussion. A 10-year-old girl who came from a disordered background was found to have an I.Q. of 132—she was in fact a very bright child indeed. Her father was in prison. She had six brothers and sisters and the family lived in circumstances of extreme poverty; on several occasions the family had split up. The mother was prone to fits of depression, and on the occasion of her husband's last imprisonment had attempted suicide. The child did not present, to her primary school teachers, a likely candidate for high-stream secondary education, and they were unanimous in putting her in low 11+ profiles. However, on the intervention of the hospital psychologist the child was in fact transferred to a grammar school.

It is possible that many immigrant children are in just such a situation. Their teachers do not perceive them as good academic material and in consequence they are given neither stimulating teaching nor optimistic academic profiles. The possible processes at work can be illustrated by a recent American study (Rosenthal and Jacobsen, 1968, pp. 19–23), in which intelligence tests were given to all children attending a primary school (grades one to six) for 'culturally disadvantaged' children. Twenty per cent of all children were designated as 'high flyers' (children with particularly high intelligence) on the basis of random numbers, and *not* on the basis of their actual I.Q. tests: that is, the teachers were told that some children were particularly bright who were *not* in fact bright. They were not told about those children who actually were bright.

At the end of the school year the teachers completed a number of schedules for the children, whose real I.Q. was retested. The authors state, 'The children from whom intellectual growth was expected were described as having a better chance of being successful in later life and as being happier, more curious and more interesting than the other children.' These children were in fact *not* objectively bright, but had only been designated so by the researchers. Moreover, the 20 per cent of the children to whom the label 'high flyer' had been attached made larger objective I.Q. gains than the children who were not so designated.

Those children who were not described as high flyers but who made some objective I.Q. gains were in fact described in generally negative terms by their teachers: 'Evidently it is likely to be difficult for a slow-track child, even if his I.Q. is rising to be seen by his teacher as well-adjusted and as a potentially successful student'.

The results of this study, which suggest that the teacher's perception of the child in his care is of fundamental importance for this child's intellectual status, confirm much English work in this field.

Returning to the study by Little *et al.*, the final 11+ profiles were made up of both teachers' reports (with all their danger of bias) and an 'exam' type test. It should be noted that there is some reliable work showing that the race of the examiner can have a significant effect on the child's performance.[2] Thus coloured children (in America) have a better performance on some types of I.Q. tests when the examiner is coloured, rather than white.

The field of the intellectual achievement of immigrant children in British schools is a microcosm of the problems with which educational sociology is concerned. Very little research in this area has so far been carried out. Future studies will need to control the effects of social class, and investigate the linguistic concepts of immigrant parents as in the studies of Bernstein (1961)

[2] For example, the study by Baratz (1967, p. 194) showing higher levels of anxiety in Negro students when tested by a white examiner, in comparison with those groups tested by a Negro examiner.

and his colleagues with working-class English families; and investigate also the value structure of different immigrant groups with respect to education and achievement, using models and procedures such as those advocated by Swift (1965, pp. 224–350).

Finally, to return to the original newspaper article. A report such as this, one suspects, may bolster the ideology that coloured children are intellectually inferior. The issues are precisely the same as those in the debate about whether working class children are intellectually inferior. They are not. But some evidence in unsophisticated or semi-sensationalist hands can be made to appear to prove that such inferiority is a reality, perhaps even a biological reality.

References

Bagley, C. (1968), Ph.D. Thesis, University of London.

Baratz, S. (1967), *Journal of Personality and Applied Psychology*, vol. 7.

Beetham, D. (1967), *Immigrant School Leavers and the Youth Employment Service in Birmingham*, Institute of Race Relations, London.

Bernstein, B. (1961), 'Social class and linguistic development', in A. Halsey, J. Floud and C. Anderson (eds.), *Education, Economy and Society*, Glencoe, Ill.

Caveness, W. *et al.* (1965), 'A survey of public attitudes to epilepsy in 1964', *Epilepsia*, vol. 6.

Datta, L. (1967), 'Draw-a-person test as a measure of intelligence in pre-school children from very low income families', *Journal of Consulting Psychology*, vol. 31.

Douglas, J. W. B. (1964), *The Home and the School: A Study of Ability and Attainment in the Primary School*, London.

Milson, F. (1966), *Operation Integration Two: The Coloured Teenager in Birmingham*, Westhill College Occasional Paper no. 13, Birmingham.

Rosenthal, R. and Jacobsen, L. (1968), 'Teacher expectations of the disadvantaged', Scientific American, no. 218, April.

Swift, D. (1965), 'Educational psychology, sociology and the environment: a controversy at cross purposes', *British Journal of Sociology*, vol. 16.

Wiles, S. (1968), 'Children from overseas', *Institute of Race Relations Newsletter*, February.

Wolfinden, R. P. (1968), 'Immigrant children in Bristol', *Nursing Times*, 23 February.

35 *G. Simpson and M. Yinger,* Intermarriage: Interracial, Interfaith and Interethnic

Intermarriage here will include interracial, interfaith, and interethnic unions. The extensive sexual association of majority and minority men and women outside of marriage will also be considered.

Race Mixture during the Slavery Period[1]

Sexual association between Whites and Negroes began with the introduction of Negroes into the colonies. Intercourse between the two races was not limited to white males and Negro females, and a considerable number of bastard children by Negro men were born to indentured white women. Marriages of Negroes and Whites occurred frequently enough to cause laws against such unions to be enacted. Later in the colonial period, censure and penalties were imposed almost exclusively on the association of Negro men and white women.

The evolution of slavery as a social institution did not decrease the sexual association of Negroes and Whites. The sale of mulatto women for prostitution became part of the slave trade in southern cities, and there were many casual relationships between white men and free Negro women. Where the associations became more or less permanent, as they did in Charleston, Mobile, and New Orleans, a system of concubinage developed. Intermixture of the races also occurred under various types of associations between the men of the master class and slave women on the plantations. At one end of the scale was physical compulsion and rape, with the Negro woman becoming separated from her mulatto child at an early date. At the other extreme was the slaveholding aristocrat who took a mulatto woman as concubine and lived with her and their children affectionately and permanently. Between these two extremes were all degrees of attachment and involvement. Some men of the master class sold their own mulatto children. Others quickly abandoned their mistresses. The prestige of the white race was a factor in

[1] This section is based largely on Frazier (1948, chaps. 3–4).

G. Simpson and M. Yinger, 'Intermarriage: interracial, interfaith and interethnic', in *Racial and Cultural Minorities*, Harper and Row, 1953, pp. 488–516.

bringing about compliance of black and mulatto women. In many cases certain advantages came to the Negro woman, including freedom from field labor, better food and clothing, special privileges for her half-white child, and perhaps his eventual freedom.

Negro–White Extramarital Sexual Relations in Recent Years

Emancipation brought profound social and personal disorganization to the former slaves. Promiscuity was common, and interacial sexual relations in the decades immendiately following the Civil War were at least as frequent as they were during slavery. It is more difficult to ascertain early twentieth-century and present trends. (Myrdal, 1944, pp. 127–8; Klineberg, 1944, pp. 276–300.) Most of the sociological investigations have brought the conclusion that interracial sexual relations have decreased. In 1943 Charles Johnson found that the practice of sex relations, including the 'keeping' of Negro 'second wives', had been continued, particularly in the rural areas of the South (Johnson, 1943, pp. 147–8, 292).

The taboo on interracial sex relations seemed to be as strong in the border areas as in the South, although the penalties were not always so severe (p. 291). The taboo continues in the North, although it is often violated. Some interracial marriages occur and common-law alliances are more frequent. According to Johnson, '... The associations, while much limited and frowned upon in practice, are not as dangerously unnatural as in the South or in border areas; and this applies especially to the Negro residence districts in northern cities' (p. 150).

Incidence of Intermarriage in the United States

Racial intermarriage does not occur frequently in the United States. Religious intermarriage is somewhat more common, and ethnic intermarriage occurs most often. [. . .]

Interethnic Marriages

Nationality groups do not long remain endogamous in the United States. For example, in examining the rates—for sample years 1930–1960—at which residents of Buffalo, New York, with Polish or Italian names married persons of similar backgrounds, Bugelski (1961, pp. 148–53) found that ingroup marriages among Italians fell from 71 per cent in 1930 to 27 per cent in 1960, and among Poles from 79 per cent to 33 per cent. The parallelism of the trends for the two groups is striking, but the following differences are noted: (1) Polish males have always been slower to outmarry, but by 1960 they reached a 50 per cent point and were not far behind other categories;

(2) Italian women started out more slowly, but by 1950 they passed Polish women, and in 1960 they had a slight lead; and (3) Italian men were the most rapid assimilators from the beginning of the period under study. On the basis of present data on Buffalo, Bugelski, does not draw the conclusion that assimilation along ethnic lines is proceeding so rapidly that national origins will soon become matters of indifference and that the groups studied were selecting marriage partners along lines of religious affiliation (Catholics, Protestants, and Jews). He does conclude (1) that the likelihood of Pole marrying Pole or Italian marrying Italian is diminishing at a faster and faster rate; (2) that intermarriage will result in even greater intermarriage on the part of children of such marriages; and (3) that before 1975, the 'Polish Wedding' and the 'Italian Wedding' will be a thing of the past.

An analysis of 7492 marriage licenses issued in Los Angeles County during 1963 includes all marriages in which one or both spouses carried a Spanish surname. By the definition adopted, a total of 9368 Mexican-American individuals were identified. Of these, 2246 (24 per cent) were first-generation (born in Mexico); 3537 (38·2 per cent) were second-generation, with one or both parents born in Mexico; and 3585 (38·2 per cent) were third-generation, defined as Spanish-surname individuals whose parents were born in one of the five southwestern states where Mexican-Americans are concentrated. The overall rate of exogamy in these marriages was considerably higher than expected. Forty per cent of the 7492 marriages involving Mexican-Americans were exogamous, and 25 per cent of the Mexican-American individuals outmarried. Exogamy is much higher for Mexican-Americans in Los Angeles than it was in the past or in other urban areas. According to Mittlebach and Moore, the Mexican-American exogamy rate in Los Angeles approximates that of the Italian and Polish ethnic populations in Buffalo, New York a generation ago. Their data indicate that both men and women of the second and third generations are more likely to marry Anglos than to marry immigrants from Mexico. Among third-generation persons, the chances are higher that they will marry Anglos than either first- or second-generation Mexicans. Mexican-American men and women with both parents born in Mexico are more likely than those with mixed perantage to marry first- and second-generation spouses and less likely to marry third-generation spouses. Thus, the social distance between some categories of Mexicans is greater than between some categories of Mexicans and Anglos. In general, this study found that the higher the socio-economic status of the groom, the greater the rate of exogamy. For Mexican-American women, slightly more than half of those marrying high-status grooms married exogamously. (Mittlebach and Moore, 1968, pp. 50–62.)

In a study of every marriage in the city of New York of a first- or second-generation Puerto Rican in the years 1949 and 1959 (22 118 Puerto Ricans),

Fitzpatrick (1966, pp. 395–406) found a significant percentage increase in outmarriage among second-generation Puerto Ricans. Nearly one-third of the second-generation brides and grooms married outside the Puerto Rican group. The increase was as great for grooms and greater for brides than the increase in outmarriage among second-generation immigrants in New York City in the period 1908–1912. In these marriages, the correlation between higher occupational status and outgroup marriage is not consistent. Generation rather than occupational level is the significant variable among grooms, but among brides outmarriage increases as the occupational level of their husbands rises. Data on color were obtained from the marriage records, but Fitzpatrick says that it is difficult to make any reliable judgment about color in the case of Puerto Ricans. The designation of color on the marriage record is as it was given by the person who declared it, and the overwhelming majority of Puerto Ricans declared themselves white. It may or may not be significant that 90 per cent of the marriages in the 1949 series were listed as 'white-white', compared with 85 per cent in 1959.

The other percentages are (Fitzpatrick, 1966, p. 396):

	1949	1959
White/brown	0·35	1·99
White/colored (Negro)	1·66	3·17
Brown/brown	2·37	4·14
Brown/colored	0·11	2·64
Colored/colored	3·06	2·21
Other	2·20	1·12

A. I. Gordon (1964, pp. 296–301) found that ethnic considerations play a minor or passive role, if any at all, in the lives of people in the major religious groups as well as those who are unaffiliated. He says that among American Jews today, little thought is given to national origins. The division between Jews of Eastern and Western European descent are no longer significant. Marriages between the two groups occur regularly. Reference is made above to studies by Hollingshead and Bugelski indicating that in Catholic marriages ethnicity is receding as a factor to be given serious consideration. Interethnic marriages among the American people are becoming more common, but such marriages do not take place indiscriminately.

Interracial Marriages

From 1900 until the end of World War II, the Negro-white intermarriage rates in New York City, New York State, Boston, and Los Angeles were from 1 to 5 per cent of all marriages in which Negroes participated.

Perhaps the fullest data on Negro-white intermarriages in the United States are for Boston. Stone found that there were 143 such intermarriages for the period 1900–1904, or an average of 28·6 per year. The rate per 100 Negro marriages was 13·6.

The considerable decrease in Negro-white intermarriage in Boston cannot be explained by the hypothesis that the smaller the proportion of a minority race in the total population the higher will be the rate of intermarriage. The percentage of the Negro population in Boston was practically constant from 1900 to 1920 (1900, 2·1; 1910, 2·0; 1915, 2·1; 1920, 2·2). It was not markedly higher in 1930 (2·6). The Boston rate of Negro-white marriages in all Negro marriages in the period 1914–1938 was 3·9 as compared with 3·4 for New York urban areas exclusive of New York City in 1919–1937. The Boston rate changed little after 1919, whereas the New York rate, except during the period 1922–1924, dropped steadily. Whereas the former high rate of intermarriage in Boston was unique, the later Boston rate does not seem to be atypical. (Wirth and Goldhamer in Klineberg, 1944, p. 280.)

In his study of the four states with recent data, Heer (1966, pp. 265–6, 273) shows that Hawaii has the highest reported incidence of Negro-white intermarriage. In this respect the other states, in descending order, are California, Michigan, and Nebraska. For Whites of both sexes the rates were: Hawaii, 0·38 per cent; California, 0·21 per cent; Michigan, 0·15 per cent; and

Table 1: *Intermarriage in Hawaii, 1957–1959*

	Grooms				Brides			
	Total	Out	% Out	Group Intermarried Most and Number	Total	Out	% Out	Group Intermarried Most and Number
Caucasian	5 204	2 058	39	P.H. 921	3 889	743	19	P.H. 366
Part-Hawaiian	2 312	894	39	Cauc. 366	3 244	1 781	55	Cauc. 921
Chinese	641	313	49	Ja. 150	659	331	50	Cauc. 126
Filipino	1 736	842	49	P.H. 382	1 539	645	42	Cauc. 317
Puerto Rican	328	188	57	P.H. 83	380	240	63	Cauc. 129
Korean	142	105	74	Ja. 56	159	122	77	Cauc. 49
Negro	145	90	62	P.H. 48	62	7	11	Cauc. 3
Hawaiian	227	62	27	Cauc. 38	269	149	55	Cauc. 60
Others	219				215			
Japanese	3 628	408	11	P.H. 185	4 166	826	20	Cauc. 398
Total	14 582	4 960	34		14 582	4 844	33	

Note: P.H. = part Hawaiian; Cauc. = Caucasian; Ja = Japanese. Out = Married out of group.

Nebraska, 0·02 per cent. For Negroes of both sexes the interracial marriage rates were: Hawaii, 16·16 per cent; California, 2·58 per cent; Michigan, 1·56 per cent; and Nebraska, 10·67 per cent. The Negro-white intermarriage rate for Negroes in Hawaii during 1964 was higher than in any part of the United States at any period. The proportion of Negro men marrying white women in Boston in the period 1900–1904 was 13·7 per cent as compared with 20·3 per cent in Hawaii in 1964, and the proportion of Negro brides marrying white grooms was 1·1 per cent in Boston during 1900–1904 as compared with 8·6 per cent in Hawaii in 1964. Heer concludes that racial intermarriage in the United States appears to be increasing, but that it is unlikely that Negro-white marriage rates will increase rapidly in the next 100 years. He argues that trends such as reductions in residential and school segregation may operate directly to decrease Negro-white status differences and indirectly to increase Negro-white intermarriage. On the other hand, the recent increase in black awareness, and the emphasis on 'black is beautiful' will tend to have the opposite effect.

According to Barron (1948, p. 189), the 'other colored' races in the United States, especially the Filipinos and American Indians, have had considerably higher intermarriage rates than the Negro. Also, there has been a greater variation in rate among the Chinese, Japanese, Indians, and Filipinos than among Negroes. In some places there these minority races have had very small numbers, intermarriage has exceeded inmarriage. (See also Roy, 1962, pp. 548–51; Berry, 1963.)

Between 1945 and 1954, 28·4 per cent of those entering marriage in Hawaii married outside their group (Caucasian, Part-Hawaiian, Chinese, Filipino, Puerto Rican, Korean, Negro, Hawaiian, Japanese). During the years 1957–1959, 34 per cent of the grooms and 33 per cent of the brides in Hawaii outmarried (see Table 1). (Cheng and Yamamura, 1957, pp. 77–84.)

Burma's (1963) study of interracial marriages in Los Angeles County, 1948–1959, covered 3150 mixed marriages in over 375 000 total marriages. Mixed marriages here refers to taking out a marriage license in a county where about 5 per cent of licenses applied for are not used within the time span of their validity. 'Interethnic intermarriages' were defined as cases in which an Anglo or Mexican married either a Negro, Filipino, Japanese, Chinese, Indian, or member of another non-European racial-ethnic group (pp. 156–65). The above table shows that the number of interracial marriages that took place immediately after the old law was declared unconstitutional in October, 1948 was small, and it indicates that there was no great increase of interracial marriages during the next several years. By the mid-1950s an increase became apparent and it had become impressive by 1958 and 1959. Burma remarks that 'even at its highest the rate is small but since some seven per cent of Los Angeles County population is non-white, the rate conceivably could be eight to ten times as great as it actually is. On the other hand,

Table 2: *Interracial Marriages in Los Angeles County, 1948–1959*

Year	Total Marriages	Interracial Mar- riages	Interracial Interracial Marriages per 1000 Marriages
1948 (2 mo.)	5 376	28	5·2
1949	31 779	187	5·8
1950	31 915	168	5·3
1951	29 459	187	6·4
1952	30 178	171	5·7
1953	31 980	197	6·2
1954	32 095	238	7·4
1955	33 996	264	7·8
1956	36 365	268	7·4
1957	38 333	346	9·1
1958	37 700	465	12·3
1959	39 300	631*	16·1*
		3 150	

* In the 8 and one-half months of 1959 in which race could be recorded, there were 447 intermarriages, which were prorated to 631 for 12 months and 16·1 per 1000 per year. The 12-year total also includes this proration.

Source: Burma (1963, p. 157).

this is a high rate compared to most of the remainder of the nation where the rate is practically zero' (p. 158). The total number of marriages increased by approximately 22 per cent from 1953 to 1959, but the number of inter-marriages during the period increased by approximately 220 per cent. Since the 1959 law forbids asking race on licenses, there is no way of determining whether this rapid rate of increase has continued. It appears that the inter-marriage rate per 1000 marriages in Los Angeles County is now about three times as high as it was in the late 1940s and early 1950s. Since this report does not include marriages between American Indians and any group except whites, marriages between two ethnic groups neither of which is white (for example, Chinese-Filipino), or the Mexican-Anglo or Anglo-Mexican marriages, this is a minimal rate. The following two tables from Burma's study provide additional data on interracial marriages in Los Angeles County, 1949–1959. Summarizing, Burma says:

This study indicates that in Los Angeles intermarriages are increasing significantly; the largest number of marriages include Whites and Negroes, but proportionately the smaller groups intermarry tremendously more than the larger groups; some evidence of intermarriage by cultural homogamy exists; intermarried couples are on the average somewhat older than are persons intramarrying, except if they themselves are the products of intermarriage; and, except for Whites, in most cases there was a greater likelihood that one party had been divorced than in comparable intramarriages (p. 165).

Table 3: *Percentage of Males and Females in the Total Population, 1960, and Percentage of Total Intermarriages, for Selected Groups, Los Angeles County, 1948–1959*

	Male			Female		
Group	Percent in Total Pop.	Percent in Inter-marriage	Index	Percent in Total Pop.	Percent in Inter-marriage	Index
White	90·2	42·0	0·47	90·4	58·0	0·64
Negro	7·6	21·5	2·83	7·7	6·5	0·84
Japanese	1·3	7·4	5·70	1·2	12·6	10·50
Chinese	0·4	4·2	10·50	0·3	4·4	14·66
Filipino	0·3	13·7	45·67	0·1	8·1	81·00
Indian	0·1	3·8	38·00	0·1	4·0	40·00
Other	0·1	7·4	74·00	0·1	6·4	64·00

Note: The percentage of intermarriages divided by the percentage of population gives the index of probability of intermarriage by a person within that group.

Source: Burma (1963, p. 160).

Table 4: *Intermarriage by Ethnic Classification and Sex; 1958–1959*

Classification	Total Number	Percent of Total
Negro-white	256	21·5
Filipino-white	163	13·7
White-Japanese	150	12·6
White-Filipino	96	8·1
Japanese-white	88	7·4
White-Negro	77	6·5
Hawaiian-white	63	5·3
White-Chinese	52	4·4
Chinese-white	50	4·2
White-Indian	48	4·0
White-Hawaiian	47	4·0
Indian-white	45	3·8
White-Korean	11	1·0
Korean-white	7	0·6
Other	36	3·0
Total	1 189	100·1
Anglo-Mexican	1 433	
Mexican-Anglo	1 226	

Note: Male listed first in all cases.

Source: Burma (1963, p. 162).

Except for the 25 000 Japanese war brides, Kitano (1969, pp. 137–43) reports that marital assimilation for the Japanese has been limited. One sample showed that Nisei parents overwhelmingly preferred that their children marry only other Japanese, but intermarriage brings little opprobrium. Among the Sansei (third generation), intermarriage is increasing. According to Kitano, undoubtedly the general direction of assimilation will include biological as well as social integration.

The 'black is beautiful' theme in the current black nationalist movement, as well as in the continuing Black Muslim group, discourages association with Whites and, in those circles, may serve to reduce both extramarital Negro-white sexual relations and intermarriage.[2]

Greater Tendency for Minority Men to Outmarry

There is a general tendency for the men of a racial, religious, or ethnic minority to outmarry to a greater extent than the women. Although the sexes in the Jewish group in Canada are almost equally divided, the number of Jewish men who marry non-Jews is regularly larger than the number of Jewish women who marry non-Jewish men (Rosenberg, in Cahnman, 1963, pp. 62–3). Likewise, Jewish women in Europe have been more conservative than Jewish men in intermarrying (Barron, 1946, p. 9). In Koenig's Stamford, Connecticut study, the overwhelming majority of the Jewish partners in Jewish-gentile marriages (40 out of 59) were male. In Minneapolis, Gordon (1950, pp. 206–7) found that in nearly all cases of intermarriage, 'it is the Jewish youth who marries the non-Jewish girl . . . in most instances the Jewish youth is financially better off than the girl he marries'. Sklare (1964, p. 422) says that at least seven out of every 10 Jews who intermarry are men. The majority of intermarriages in which the 'other colored' races in the United States participate are between nonwhite males and white females (Barron, 1948, p. 189).

Barron reports that the most common type of Negro-white intermarriage is that of Negro men and white women (p. 190), and Heer (1966, pp. 265–6) found this to be the case in Hawaii, California, Michigan, and Nebraska. For example, for California in 1959 the intermarriage rate of white grooms was 0·09 per cent and that of white brides 0·33 per cent. Similarly, the interracial rate for Negro grooms was 3·96 per cent and of Negro brides 1·16 per cent.

After California's antimiscegenation law was nullified by a state court, in 1948, the intermarriage rate was not high. During a 30-month period (November, 1948, to April 30, 1951), 78 266 licenses were issued in Los Angeles County, of which 445 were between persons of the white and some

[2] For an account of actual experiences with Negro-white intermarriage, including child-rearing, see Larsson (1965).

other race (Mexicans are considered white). This rate of 56 per 10 000 marriages is slightly more than one-half of 1 per cent of all marriages. Of the marriages between Whites and other races, 41 per cent involved Filipino men; 20·5 per cent, Negro men; 20·4 per cent, Anglo men (because Mexicans are legally 'white', the term 'Anglo' is used to denote whites of non-Mexican descent); 7·6 per cent, Chinese men; 5·3 per cent, Mexican men, and 4·5 per cent, Japanese men. For the women, 44·4 per cent involved Anglo women; 29·2 per cent, Mexican women; 7·4 per cent, Negro women; 7·4 per cent, Japanese women; 5·9 per cent, Filipino women; and 3·9 per cent, Chinese women. The rates of intermarriage according to race or nationality are shown in Table 5.

Table 5: *Rates per 1000 Marriage Licenses issued to Mixed Couples of White and Nonwhite Races in Los Angeles County, November 1, 1948, to April 30, 1951, by Race or Nationality*

Filipino-Anglo	217
Filipino-Mexican	193
Negro-Anglo	146
Anglo-Japanese	67
Anglo-Negro	58
Negro-Mexican	59
Chinese-Anglo	54
Anglo-Chinese	34
Anglo-Filipino	34
Japanese-Anglo	27
Mexican-Filipino	25
Chinese-Mexican	22
Japanese-Mexican	18
Mexican-Negro	16
Anglo-Korean	11
Mexican-Japanese	7
Mexican-Chinese	5
Other mixtures	7
Total	1000

Note: Male listed first in all cases.

The study did not record separately interracial marriages not including Whites, but the estimate of the total rate of intermarriage if these are included is 65 per 10 000 marriages. The sample seems to indicate that in the marriages of Whites to Whites about 3·5 per cent, are between Anglos and Mexican-Americans, with marriages of Anglo males to Mexican-American females constituting about four-fifths of this total. The sample of 1000 marriages indicates that of the marriage licenses issued in Los Angeles County, about 75 per cent are Anglo-Anglo, approximately 11 per cent are Mexican-

Mexican, almost 10 per cent are Negro-Negro, and the other 4 per cent are intraracial marriages involving other racial groups or interracial marriages. Since Los Angeles has a relatively large number of minority groups and of intermarriages, it should not be concluded that it is a typical city in the matter of intermarriage. (Burma, 1952, p. 587.)

Exceptions to the greater tendency for minority men to outmarry are found in several studies previously cited. The atypical instances include: Mexican and Japanese women in Burma's 1948–1951 study in Los Angeles County; Yamamura's 1957–1959 report on Part Hawaiian, Puerto Rican, Hawaiian, and Japanese women in Hawaii; and Japanese and Chinese women in Burma's Los Angeles County study, 1948–1959.

Lewis F. Carter (1968, pp. 347–50) questions whether the preponderance of racial caste hypogamy in the United States is a sociological myth. A 1939 national sample reported 559 cases of hypogamy and 583 of hypergamy. A 5 per cent sample, taken by the Census Bureau in 1960, showed 25 496 Negro males married to white females and 25 913 white males married to Negro females. Carter says that the major empirical studies of intermarriage in the United States have involved data from large urban areas and that these urban areas have been drawn exclusively from the northern and western sections of the country. It is his hypothesis that racial caste hypergamy, that is, white males marrying Negro females is more frequent in nonurban areas than is hypogamy, and, further, that these nonurban interracial marriages may be more numerous than urban ones.

The factors responsible for the tendency of the men in a minority racial, religious, or ethnic group to out-marry more than the women do may be summarized as follows:

1. The women in these groups have fewer opportunities for meeting the men in other groups than the minority men have for meeting outside women.

2. Religious and other institutional controls may exert a stronger influence on minority women than on minority men.

3. Men take the initiative in dating and courtship.

4. Marrying a woman in the majority group, or a woman in the minority group whose appearance and manners closely approximate those of majority-group women, is a symbol of success, of prestige, of being accepted in the larger community. In the case of the Negro in the United States, it may also mean the realization of a wish, perhaps an unconscious wish, to have children who will be nearer to the ideal physical type of this country. Majority women who intermarry typically are of lower socioeconomic status than the minority men they marry. They exchange majority prestige for higher socioeconomic standing. The woman in the minority group who is least visible from the standpoint of minority status has many competitors for marriage among majority women. Within the minority group she has marked advantages maritally.

In summary, we may say that people in the United States and elsewhere have been predominantly endogamous with respect to race, religion, and ethnic group. Of these three types of intermarriage, racial intermarriage has usually been the least common and ethnic intermarriage the most frequent. Time, place, and conditions have affected the incidence of each type of intermarriage. There is no single pattern in the trend of intermarriage incidence.

The Legal Aspects of Intermarriage

The legal history of intermarriage in the United States is fascinating (see Mangum, 1940, chap. 10; Klineberg, 1944, pp. 358–64; Johnson, 1943, pp. 162–9). For example, until recently Mississippi had a criminal statute providing for the punishment of anyone who published, printed, or circulated any literature in favor of or urging interracial marriage or social equality, and the Texas court upheld an ordinance enacted by Fort Worth that it was unlawful for Whites and Negroes to have sexual intercourse with one another within the city limits (Mangum, 1940, pp. 256–7).

There has been so much intermixture in Louisiana that it was said that a marriage license would be refused only in cases where mixture was obvious from the appearance of the person making the application. Ordinarily the marriages of white persons to individuals with a small amount of Negro ancestry were questioned only by those interested in property succession, and the courts have dealt leniently with children of mixed ancestry.

California's antimiscegenation law was declared unconstitutional by a state court in 1948. Two Catholics, one Negro and one White, declared that their religious freedom was hampered by the law; the sacrament of marriage was being unconstitutionally denied them by the law (Burma, 1952, p. 587).

In 1964, the U.S. Supreme Court unanimously struck down a Florida law that made it a crime for persons of different races to cohabit (Graham, 1966).

Laws barring intermarriage were on and off the statute books of at least six southern states during the nineteenth century. Louisiana seems to have been the first state to enact such a law (1810), North Carolina followed in 1830, Arkansas in 1838, and Mississippi and South Carolina in 1865. These laws were repealed for longer or shorter periods of time during Reconstruction, but all had reappeared by 1894.

At one time or another, 41 states had miscegenation laws. In the 1940s, 30 states prohibited, through constitutional provision or statutory law or both, the marriage of white persons and those who were defined in varying ways as 'Negro'. By 1963, through the repeal of statutes prohibiting interracial marriages or their nullification by state court decisions, the number was reduced to 21.[3] In the 1940s, 15 states possessed laws that expressly or im-

---

[3] The states prohibiting Negro-white marriages were: Alabama, Arkansas, Delaware, Florida, Georgia, Idaho, Indiana, Kentucky, Louisiana, Mississippi, Missouri, Nebraska, North Carolina, Oklahoma, South Carolina, Tennessee, Texas, Utah, Virginia, West Virginia, and Wyoming.

pliedly prohibited the marriage of Caucasians and Mongolians, 10 states did likewise for Whites and Malays, and five forbade the marriage of Whites and Indians. Lousiana and Oklahoma prohibited unions of Indians and Negroes, and North Carolina banned the marriage of Cherokee Indians of Robeson County with persons of Negro ancestry to the third generation inclusive. Maryland forbade the marriage of Malays and Negroes.

States differed with respect to the amount of Negro ancestry that would prevent a person from entering a valid marriage with a white person. Mulattoes were specifically mentioned in the statutes of Arkansas, Delaware, Idaho, Kentucky, Mississippi, South Carolina, Tennessee, and Wyoming, but in most cases there was no reference to the amount of Negro ancestry that was considered to come within the law. Two states (North Carolina and Tennessee) prohibited the marriage of Whites to persons of Negro 'blood' to the third generation inclusive. This was equivalent to making it illegal for a white person to marry an individual whose ancestry is one-eighth Negro. Five states (Indiana, Mississippi, Missouri, Nebraska, and South Carolina) had the same provision, but the language of the statutes was in terms of the marriage of Whites with persons of one-eighth or more Negro 'blood'. Florida had contradictory rules, the constitution prohibiting marriage to the fourth generation inclusive (one-sixteenth Negro ancestry), whereas the definition of Negro in the statutory law prohibiting intermarriage was a person of one-eighth or more 'Negro blood'. Five states, (Alabama, Georgia, Oklahoma, Texas, and Virginia) prohibited marriages of Whites with persons who had any Negro ancestry. In Utah and West Virginia the statutes did not indicate what amount of Negro ancestry would make a person ineligible to marry a white person.

When the U.S. Supreme Court ruled against state laws prohibiting interracial marriage, 17 states still had such laws. The final decision of the Court against the state laws came in the case of the Lovings versus the Commonwealth of Virginia. Richard Terry Loving and his part Negro, part Indian wife, Mildred Jeter Loving, were married in Washington, D.C., in 1958, because they could not get a license in Virginia. They returned to their home state, were indicted for violation of the antimiscegenation law, and pleaded guilty. They were sentenced to one year in jail, but the prison term was suspended for a period of 25 years upon the condition that they leave the state and not return together for 25 years. In announcing the suspension of the sentence, the trial judge stated: 'Almighty God created the races white, black, yellow, malay, and red, and he placed them on separate continents. And but for the interference with his arrangement there would be no cause for such marriages. The fact that he separated the races shows that he did not intend for the races to mix.' (*The United States Law Week*, 1967, 13 June, pp. 4679–82.) They left for a time, but in 1963 returned to challenge the conviction. In March, 1966, the Supreme Court of Appeals of Virginia held that nothing in the federal courts decisions of the previous 15 years had infringed upon the 'overriding state interest in the institution of marriage'. To upset the law in the courts would be 'judicial legislation in the rawest sense of that term', the court said. It suggested that any change would have to come from the legislature. The decision left the conviction of the Lovings in effect, but said that they could return to Virginia at the same time, as long as they did not cohabit (Graham, 1966).

In June, 1967, the U.S. Supreme Court held that the Virginia law to prevent marriages between persons solely on the basis of racial classification violated the Equal Protection and Due Process Clauses of the Fourteenth Amendment.

Barron (1951, p. 255)—among others—has pointed out the inconsistency in the conservative attitudes toward intermarriage held by many Americans and their activities in creating social and cultural conditions favoring inter-marriage. The reference here is to public-school attendance, children being sent to colleges away from home, the campaigns against discrimination in employment and housing, and participation in interfaith activities. Inevitably an increase in intergroup contacts will lead to some intermarriages.

Rationalizations of the Opposition to Intermarriage

The taboo against intermarriage varies from section to section in its com-plexity and in the sanctions that enforce it. To many persons in the South such unions are unthinkable, and southern sentiments, attitudes, myths, dogmas, and customs work to prevent them. As Charles Johnson (1943, p. 222) pointed out, 'In this culture area the proscription involves not merely a "climate of opinion" but a total ideology incorporating moral perspectives'.

The widespread opposition to Negro-white intermarriage finds expression, especially in the South, in the slogan of 'no social equality'. The term is vague; at times it covers and justifies all types of segregation and discrimina-tion, whereas at other times it seems to be limited to intimate personal and social relations and intermarriage. Any questioning about the doctrine will bring a stout insistence on preventing amalgamation and 'preserving the purity of the white race'. The ban on intermarriage is concentrated on white women, and it covers both formal marriage and illicit sexual relations. When the possibility of intermarriage is used to defend the whole caste system, 'it is assumed both that Negro men have a strong desire for "intermarriage", and that white women would be open to proposals from Negro men, *if* they are not guarded from even meeting them on an equal plane. . . . The conclusion follows that the whole system of segregation and discrimination is justified. Every single measure is defended as necessary to block "social equality" which in its turn is defended as necessary to prevent "intermarriage".' (Myrdal, 1944, p. 587.)

Myrdal concluded that the doctrine of 'no social equality' is a rationalization of social segregation and discrimination that enables white people to avoid making 'an open demand for difference in social status between the two groups for its own sake'. In other words, *'what white people really want is to keep Negroes in a lower status'* (p. 591).

Gross exaggeration of the likelihood of intermarriage has been utilized as a device for keeping the Negro 'in his place'. It has been utilized as the justification for not hiring Negro men in certain jobs, or as an excuse for separation in places of public accommodation, separate schools, or residential segregation. As Drake and Cayton (1945, p. 129) say, 'The ultimate appeal for the maintenance of the color-line is always the simple, though usually irrelevant question, "Would you want your daughter to marry a Negro?" To many white persons this is the core of the entire race problem'.

Sklare and Greenblum (1967, pp. 309–13) found that relatively few of their respondents justify their feelings of being unhappy or somewhat unhappy in the event of an intermarriage on the basis of a concern with Jewish identity, Jewish survival, or the Jewish religion. Only 14 per cent of those who opposed intermarriage explicitly based their reaction on such grounds. Most Jews in Lakeville, a midwestern suburb of 25 000 with a Jewish population of 8000, explain their opposition in terms of the discord they say is inevitable in an interfaith marriage. These persons maintain that a Jewish-Gentile marriage is inherently an unstable union, emphasizing disturbed relations between husband and wife, or difficulties created for the offspring of an interfaith marriage, or the problematic relationship of the married couple to relatives, friends, and society at large. Concerning these respondents, Sklare and Greenblum say that they are far from being unbiased students of marital problems and that their opposition 'seems to be a safe way of expressing the desire to continue the chain of tradition while at the same time avoiding the appearance of ethnocentrism'.

'Social Types' who Intermarry

For a sample of 1167 persons between the ages of 20 and 59, obtained in the Midtown Mental Health Project of Manhattan, five hypotheses were tested:

In general, the intermarried as compared with the intramarried are characterized by: (1) non-religious parents, (2) greater dissatisfaction with parents when young, (3) greater early family strife, (4) less early family integration, and (5) greater emancipation from parents at time of marriage. The Catholic data supported all of these hypotheses. In the Protestant group, only two received substantial support —relatively weak ties to religion and to family. Most of the general hypotheses do not seem to apply to Jews. Heiss says: 'The data suggest that intermarried Jews differ from intramarried Jews only in the strength of their family ties—while young and at the time of marriage'. (Heiss, 1960, pp. 48–54.)

In Honolulu, Schmitt and Souza (1963, p. 267) found that interracial households occupy a somewhat lower socioeconomic position. The members of such households hold, on the average, poorer jobs, have lower incomes, and live in less desirable housing than do those in unmixed households. They think it likely that the traditional Hawaiian tolerance toward intermarriage is more common among lower-income families, adding that 'many Island parents still discourage intermarriage, a practice that may be more frequent (or effective) in the wealthier groups'.

Problems of the Intermarried

The intermarried, especially the racially intermarried, in the United States face certain trials not faced by the homogamous. First, there is the matter of keeping a job. It may be necessary for both partners to keep their marriage a secret. Those who seem least vulnerable to economic reprisals are civil service employees, independent business people, Negro physicians, and labor leaders. Second, it is often difficult to find a place to live. The editors and correspondents of *Ebony* found that residential patterns for interracial families vary considerably from city to city. In Los Angeles mixed couples live in nearly every part of the city. In Chicago they spearheaded the drive that brought Negroes into Hyde Park for the first time. In Washington they settled in Negro areas. In Detroit they live in mixed communities. In New York they reside in Harlem and St Albans, L.I., but many live in 'white' sections of the metropoltian area. According to Larsson (1965, pp. 44–5), generally the sex of the white partner determines where an interracial couple lives. When the husband is white, the couple will ordinarily live in a white neighborhood; when he is Negro the reverse is usually true. Third, the intermarried couple will at times face ostracism from both the white and the black communities, including, in some cases, relatives and friends. Blood (1969, p. 96) says that the main question for the white partner is whether he or she is prepared to join the Negro race. It may be difficult for each partner to maintain friendships with persons of his race. For some of the inter-married, outside pressures have had at least occasional inside repercussions. One study found that 'after marriage the Negro partner tended to be touchy about seeming racial slurs and to insist on the white partner's need to learn to "understand" Negroes'. Fourth, children of an intermarriage may create problems.

One of these [problems] is the attitude of the parents and relatives of the white partner. To them, the Negro spouse is a difficult enough problem to adjust to, but still is not a blood relative. The child of the intermarriage, however, is a blood relative, and must be either accepted or rejected. This can be a real emotional crisis. Some couples reported that they had not informed white relatives of the existence of children for this reason. (Drake and Cayton, 1945, p. 155.)

Some interracial couples have refrained from having children because of possible difficulties or embarrassments, but they seem to have been the exceptions. Most of the Negro-white couples in Chicago have children, but they are Negro children. According to Drake and Cayton, good adjustment for the children of interracial marriages is difficult but not impossible. Such persons are usually not accepted by the white community unless they pass, but, in Chicago at least, the stigma of having a white parent is not very strong and the community may forget the interracial background completely. If the child of an interracial marriage wishes to pass but cannot do so, he may become seriously maladjusted. In Chicago such 'inbetweens' constitute a small percentage of the children of mixed parentage. Most make a successful adjustment to life in the Negro community; a few pass completely over into the white group. (Pp. 154, 158.)

Rosenthal (1963, p. 53) says that intermarriage usually means the end of belonging to the Jewish group, citing the fact that in at least 70 per cent of the mixed families in Greater Washington the children were not identified with the Jewish group. He writes: 'This finding, which repeats earlier European experiences, takes on special significance if viewed against the fact that the fertility of the Jewish population in the United States is barely sufficient to maintain its present size'. [. . .]

Passing

One of the results of marital and extramarital race mixture is the appearance of a number of persons who cannot be distinguished physically from members of the majority group. Such individuals may or may not 'pass' for Whites. [. . .]

There are no accurate figures on the extent of passing that occurs in the United States. Estimates of those who leave the Negro group permanently and are absorbed by white society vary from a few thousand to tens of thousands annually (Stuckert, 1958, pp. 155–60). It is impossible to estimate the number of Negroes who pass only temporarily or occasionally. Probably most of those who 'cross to the other side' remain in the white group, but thousands have returned after a trial period has shown that life for them in the Negro community is more enjoyable and more comfortable.

Factors that Facilitate Intermarriage

A number of factors seem to facilitate intermarriage. One is the attitudes of individuals toward intermarriage. The nature and the effectiveness of these attitudes are determined by the marriage mores and the other influencing factors to be mentioned shortly. In his study of intermarriage in Derby, Connecticut, Barron (1948, p. 326) found that attitudes alone are not responsible for intermarriage patterns. There were general similarities between intermarriage attitudes and practices, but the attitudes were more liberal than the practices.

The second group of factors are demographic, and include the sex ratio and the numerical size of minority groups. A marked disparity in the distribution of the sexes, as is the case with the Filipinos in the United States, favors intermarriage. Generally speaking, intermarriage varies indirectly and breadth of selection varies directly with the relative size of the minority group. This tendency is seen clearly among the Jews of Iowa. They live in relatively small Jewish communities and, during a seven-year period, the intermarriage rate fluctuated between 36·3 and 53·6 per cent. While the average rate was 42·2 per cent, in cities of 10 000 or more, the intermarriage rate was 34·2 per cent, it was almost twice as high in towns and rural areas. For the Jewish community of about 80 000 persons in Greater Washington the intermarriage rate was found to be 13·1 per cent. However, the intermarriage rate of in-migrants from larger communities, particularly from the New York metropolitan area, was significantly lower. (Rosenthal, 1963, pp. 51, 53.) Although the Jewish population of 20 000 in Providence, Rhode Island is relatively large, the intermarriage rate in that city is relatively low. According to Goldstein and Goldscheider (1968, p. 169):

The Providence Jewish community is an old one and has strong roots and strong organizational structure, and therefore it provides the framework for a close identification with the community, and . . . compared to such other communities as Washington and Los Angeles . . . Providence has a much more stable population and one that contains a higher proportion of first and second-generation Americans. But even among third-generation Jews in Providence the intermarriage rate was lower than that for the comparable group in Washington, D.C.

In the case of the Jews, not only does the small size of the group facilitate intermarriage, but the low birth rate of native-born Jews, at a time when the general population of the United States is growing, probably will mean further attrition by randomization (Sklare, 1964, pp. 422, 433).

In the Chinese population in metropolitan New York there is a general excess of males. For example, when men aged 25–29 are compared with women aged 20–24, there is an excess of 54 men in the sex ratio of the Chinatown population and of 20 in the non-Chinatown population. In general, the non-Chinatown population has a better income, education, and occupational status than the Chinatown population; hence the former group is more likely to be accepted by the majority population. Yuan (1966, pp. 321–32) says that some Puerto Rican girls in New York and some Mexican girls in Los Angeles marry Chinese men in order to support their families, adding that this practice is perhaps more acceptable to the lower-class Chinese and to the lower-class Puerto Ricans and Mexicans due to economic necessity.

A demographic factor of some importance in facilitating intermarriage is the high spatial mobility of the American people. More than one-fifth of the native-born population live in states other than those in which they were born. Thirty million persons changed their residence during World War II. In the age group 7 to 13 years, more than a third live in places other than where they were born. Changes in recreational habits, including increased travel, as well as the increased emphasis on higher education, new employment opportunities, and the requirements of military service, expose younger people to contacts with different backgrounds, and, also, weaken the hold of old group controls. (Bossard and Boll, 1957, pp. 6, 60.)

The third set of factors that affect intermarriage rates are the propinquous factors. They include place of residence, place of work, place of recreation, place of education, etc. Segregated minority groups tend to inmarry, whereas dispersed minorities tend to intermarry. (One should not infer a causal connection here. It may be that dispersed minorities intermarry more for the same reason that they are dispersed, namely, a lower prejudice against them.)

The fourth category of factors influencing the incidence of intermarriage consists of cultural similarities. Included here are similarity of cultural background, length of residence in the United States, occupational and economic class, amount and type of education, church affiliation or lack of it, and linguistic similarity. The Washington data show that the most important social factor influencing Jewish intermarriage is distance from immigration. Among the third and subsequent generations, the intermarriage rate was 18 per cent. (Rosenthal, 1963, p. 31.) In Providence, the reaction of the third-generation Jews of East European origin differed little from the second and the first: about one-fifth in each generation would be indifferent to an intermarriage in their own family and none would be happy with it. Among those of German or mixed descent, more than half of the fourth generation feel indifferent or even happy about their child's intermarriage, compared with much smaller proportions among the less advanced generations. (Sklare and Greenblum, 1967, p. 309.) To a greater extent than formerly, Jews are now working with Gentiles as colleagues occupationally instead of serving them as merchants or free professionals (Sklare, 1964, pp. 430–1).

To these rather specific factors might be added the general social conditions of 'political emancipation, intermingling of culture, and the spread of tolerance and growth of fellowship' in modern times (Goldstein, 1942, p. 161). Thomas' investigations lead him to believe that there will be a gradual but steady increase in the number of marriages between Catholics and non-Catholics. His reasons are as follows: First, the decline in immigration, the horizontal and vertical mobility of our population, and the increased cultural contacts due to modern means of communication will reduce the influence of ethnic groups over individuals choices of marriage partners; second, mixed marriages have a cumulative effect because the children of mixed marriages tend to marry outside their religious group more often than do the children of in-group marriages; third, the attitude of young people, both Catholic and Protestant, appears to be increasingly tolerant; and fourth, both the family and the church have less control over youth than they did in former years. Although Burma's (1963, p. 160) data on interethnic marriage in Los Angeles give no causal inferences, it is the author's opinion that assimilation, decreasing social distance, improved social status of minorities, and decreasing intolerance are likely to be found among the causal factors for all intermarrying groups.

Despite sharp segregation from both Anglo whites and Negroes in Los Angeles, including the existence of three high schools that are predominantly Mexican-American, Mittlebach and Moore (1968, p. 52) concluded that prejudice against the Mexican-American population is comparatively low and opportunities for status advancement quite high in comparison with other parts of the Southwest. They say: 'Los Angeles is an environment which facilitates interaction with the larger system'. [. . .]

Gordon's (1964, pp. 54, 60) assessment of intermarriage seems judicious. He sees it as the product of urbanization, mobility, propinquity, and related factors that play such an important role in present-day American society. As the generations succeed each other, he predicts that intermarriage will become more frequent because people 'by some fortuitous circumstance, happen to meet, fall in love, and—as the result of the general weakening of contemporary family and religious ties as well as the possession of similar educational, economic, and social backgrounds—decide to marry'.

Factors that Retard Intermarriage

Many of the parents of persons considering intermarriage use their influence to prevent it. There are no laws in the United States forbidding interfaith or interethnic marriages, and in June, 1967 the U.S. Supreme Court struck down the laws in 18 states that forbade Negro-white or other interracial marriages. With the exception of certain subcultures in the United States, the mores contain a strong taboo against interracial marriages and, to a lesser degree, against interfaith marriages. Some religious faiths, through teaching and the personal influence of clergymen, have always tried to discourage inter-marriage. (See Gordon, 1964, chaps. 5–7; Barron, 1948, pp. 22–47; Bossard and Boll, 1957, chap. 5.)

As far as Negro-white marriage is concerned, many white people will continue

. . . to exploit the fear of intermarriage as a means of retaining economic dominance, and as a devastating question to be raised in connection with any concessions, no matter how small, which the Negro community requests. A few intermarriages will no doubt continue to take place, as well as clandestine 'affairs', but 'crossing the line' is not uppermost in the minds of the Negroes. Relaxation of the taboos against intermarriage is something white people are most reluctant to grant. It is also the 'concession' which Negroes, as a group, are least likely to request. That it looms so large in the white mind is the irony of race relations in Midwest Metropolis [Chicago]. (Drake and Cayton, 1945, p. 173.)

Contrary to a widespread belief among white persons that Negroes are strongly interested in intermarriage, a Chicago study showed that very few parents would encourage their children to marry whites (1·1 per cent of a Negro slum sample and 2·5 per cent of a Negro middle- and upper-class sample). About half of the respondents said they would tolerate inter-marriage, stating that 'it made no difference', and the other half opposed it. 'Eighty per cent or more of Negro parents would permit their child to marry a white person if the romance had already developed without their knowledge but there is no evidence of a desire for miscegenation or even interest in prom-oting it, except among a very tiny minority'. (Bogue and Dizard, 1964, p. 7.)

Where integration increases, it is likely to be accompanied by an increase in Negro-white marriage. The recent growth of black consciousness and racial pride will tend to discourage intermarriage. In the near future, the rate of increase probably will be slow.

The Success or Failure of Intermarriage

Evidence concerning the success or failure of intermarriage is not extensive. Intermarriage—like inmarriage—does not always turn out well. In the event of marital difficulty, it may be difficult to discover whether the racial factor is directly or indirectly involved. Few studies control for class, education, residence, or other variables that influence the stability of marriages. Hence it is difficult to measure the possible impact of the factor of intermarriage. [. . .]

A study in Hawaii of 324 war brides and husbands of European and Japanese ancestry found that the Japanese wives of non-Japanese were the happiest group, followed by the European wives of Japanese husbands. As a group, European wives of non-Japanese husbands were third in marital adjustment, and Japanese wives of Japanese were fourth. (Kimura, 1957, pp. 70–1.) An exploratory study of 20 American-Japanese couples did not confirm the belief that such marriages would have a high rate of failure because they were hasty and involved sharp cultural conflict.

The serviceman's stay in Japan averaged over four years, and courtships averaged about two years. Severe cultural conflict was not found in in-group and out-group relationships; husbands identified themselves with their wives' circles; there were no regrets and no serious in-law problems. Cooperation and adaptation were common, wives were learning English, and there were no religious conflicts. A study of age at marriage, educational attainment, residence separate from in-laws, first marriage, and average number of children all indicated stability rather than conflict. (Schnepp and Yui, 1955, pp. 48–50.)

In a study in Chicago, Strauss (1954, pp. 99–106) found more harmony than strain in the American-Japanese war bride marriages he investigated. However, he says: 'This is not to . . . claim that homogamy between husband and wife is of no importance in marital selection. . . . However, the easy assumptions that interracial marriages are doomed to destruction or that the couples must have something extra-special to make a go of the marriage are much over-simplified notions'. He recommends a reappraisal of this type of intermarriage in the light of the special conditions of contact, selection, and living conditions that make mixed marriages more vulnerable to difficulty.

Banton (1955, p. 152) says a minority of the white wives who have married colored men in Britain could equally well have married white men but happened to have fallen in love with a colored man and married him despite opposition. He sees as the outstanding characteristics of most of the white women who associate with colored men: 'firstly, an inferior economic position and low earning power; secondly, emotional insecurity, and a background of personal rejection'. Egginton (1957, p. 114) says that 'many mixed marriages are successful in Britain'. Collins (1951, pp. 796–802) shows that white women in Britain who marry colored men from British West Africa and the West Indies play an important role as intermediary between the wife's family and the white community, seeking to gain concessions from the privileged group. Little (1954, p. 62) points out that disapproval and ostracism of white friends and acquaintances lead the white wife to identify with the colored group, but when the child leaves school he may find it difficult to develop friendships with white persons at work without giving up the colored friends of his earlier years. [. . .]

Blood (1969, p. 97) lists the same prerequisites for mixed marriages as for other marriages: compatibility, skill, effort, commitment, and support.

Conclusion

Our conclusion on intermarriage may be stated briefly as follows:

1. From a statistical standpoint, the chances for success in marriage seem to be somewhat less for intermarriage than for inmarriage in the United States at the present time. Without the control of other variables, however, it is not clear how much the intermarriage factor itself produces this result.

2. The legality of intermarriage is an important aspect of equal civil rights. During the past two decades state laws against miscegenation have been repealed and/or declared unconstitutional by state courts in nine states, and in 1967, the U.S. Supreme Court struck down the laws forbidding interracial marriages in the 17 states that still had such legislation.

3. Race mixture is not biologically inadvisable.

4. Opposition by fervent church members to religious intermarriage has not decreased, otherwise, resistance to all types of intermarriage, except Negro-white, has declined significantly during the past three decades.

5. Religious intermarriage and ethnic intermarriage are increasing rapidly and, with continued acculturation, will continue to increase in the United States. Racial intermarriage is also increasing, with Negro-white marriages increasing more slowly than other kinds of racial intermarriage.

6. Intermarriage on a large scale would produce a relatively homogeneous population, physically and culturally. The elimination of intergroup conflicts based on race and culture would have societal advantages, although some would lament the passing of cultural pluralism.

References

Banton, M. (1955), *The Coloured Quarter*, London.

Barron, M. L. (1946), 'The Incidence of Jewish intermarriage', *A.S.R.*, February.

Barron, M. L. (1948), *People Who Intermarry*, New York.

Barron, M. L. (1951), 'Research on intermarriage: a survey of accomplishments and prospects', *A.J.S.*, November.

Berry, B. (1963), *Almost White*, London.

Blood, R. O. (1969), *Marriage*, London.

Bogue, D. J. and Dizard, J. E. (1964), *Race, Ethnic Prejudice and Discrimination as Viewed by Subordinate and Superordinate Groups*, Community and Family Study Center, University of Chicago.

Bossard, J. H. S. and Boll, E. S. (1957), *One Marriage, Two Faiths*, New York.

Bugelski, B. R. (1961), 'Assimiliation through intermarriage', *S.F.*, December.

Burma, J. H. (1952), 'Research note on the measurement of interracial marriage', *A.J.S.*, May.

Burma, J. H. (1963), 'Interethnic marriage in Los Angeles, 1948–1959', *S.F.*, December.

Cahnman, W. J. (ed.) (1963), *Intermarriage and Jewish Life*, New York.

Carter, L. F. (1968), 'Racial-Caste hypogamy: a sociological myth?', *Phylon*, Winter.

Cheng, C. K. and Yamamura, D. S. (1957), 'Interacial marriage and divorce in Hawaii', *S.F.*, October.

Collins, S. F. (1951), 'The social position of white and "half-caste" women in colored groupings in Britain', *A.S.R.*, December.

Drake, S. and Cayton, H. (1945), *Black Metropolis*, New York.

Egginton, J. (1957), *They Seek a Living*, London.

Fitzpatrick, J. P. (1966), 'The intermarriage of Puerto Ricans in New York City', *A.J.S.*, January.

Frazier, E. F. (1948), *The Negro Family in the United States*, New York.

Goldstein, S. E. (1942), *The Meaning of Marriage and the Foundations of the Family*, New York.

Goldstein, S. and Goldscheider, C. (1968), *Jewish Americans: Three Generations in a Jewish Community*, Englewood Cliffs, N.J.

Gordon, A. I. (1950), *Jews in Transition*, Minneapolis.

Gordon, A. I. (1964), *Intermarriage*, Boston.

Graham, F. P. (1966), 'Miscegenation nears test in High Court', *The New York Times*, March 13, p. 12E.

Heer, D. M. (1966), 'Negro-White marriage in the United States', *Journal of Marriage and the Family*, August.

Heiss, J. (1960), 'Premarital characteristics of the religiously intermarried in an urban area', *A.S.R.*, February.

Johnson, C. S. (1943), *Patterns of Negro Segregation*, New York.

Kimura, Y. (1957), 'War brides in Hawaii and their in-laws', *A.J.S.*, July.

Kitano, H. H. L. (1969), *Japanese Americans*, Englewood Cliffs, N.J.

Klineberg, O. (ed.) (1944), *Characteristics of the American Negro*, New York.

Larsson, C. M. (1965), *Marriage Across the Color Line*, New York.

Little, K. (1954), 'The position of colored people in Britain', *Phylon*, First Quarter.

Mangum, C. S. Jr. (1940), *The Legal Status of the Negro*, Chapel Hill, N.C.

Mittlebach, F. G. and Moore, J. W. (1968), 'Ethnic endogamy—the case of Mexican Americans', *A.J.S.*, July.

Myrdal, G. (1944), *An American Dilemma*, New York.

Rosenthal, E. (1963), *Studies of Jewish Intermarriage in the United States*, The American Jewish Committee.

Roy, P. (1962), 'The measurement of assimiliation: the Spokane Indian', *A.J.S.*, March.

Schmitt, R. C. and Souza, R. A. (1963), 'Social and economic characteristics of interracial households in Honolulu', *Social Problems*, Winter.

Schnepp, G. J. and Yui, A. M. (1955), 'Cultural and marital adjustment of Japanese war brides', *A.J.S.*, July.

Sklare, M. (1964), 'Intermarriage and the Jewish future', *Commentary*, April.

Sklare, M. and Greenblum (1967), *Jewish Identity on the Suburban Frontier*, New York.

Strauss, A. (1954), 'Strain and harmony in American war bride marriages', *Marriage and Family Living*, May.

Stuckert, R. S. (1958), 'The African ancestry of the white American population', *Ohio Journal of Science*, May.

Yuan, D. Y. (1966), 'Chinatown and beyond: the Chinese population in metropolitan New York', *Phylon*, Fourth Quarter.

Select Bibliography

The following bibliography is, of course, in no sense exhaustive. A number include passages which, given more space, the editors would wish to have included in their selection. Others offer a more extended and comprehensive treatment of issues raised in the book. It is hoped that teachers, students and research workers will find this a useful initial guide to the race relations literature.

Part 1 Sociological Perspectives

Banton, M. (1967), *Race Relations*, London.
Barth, A. E. and Noel, D. (1972), 'Conceptual frameworks for the analysis of race relations: an evaluation', *S.F.*, vol. 50.
Blalock, H. (1967), *Towards a Theory of Minority Group Relations*, New York.
Fanon, F. (1965), *The Wretched of the Earth*, London.
Frazier, E. F. (1947), 'Sociological theory and race relations', *A.S.R.*, vol. 12, no. 3, pp. 265–71.
Horton, J. (1966), 'Order and conflict theories of social problems as competing ideologies', *A.J.S.*, vol. 71, pp. 701–13.
Hughes, E. (1963), 'Race relations and the sociological imagination', *A.S.R.*, vol. 28, no. 6, pp. 879–90.
Lieberson, S. (1961), 'A societal theory of race and ethnic relations', *A.S.R.*, vol. 26, no. 6, pp. 902–10.
Little, K. (1947), *Negroes in Britain*, London.
Lockwood, D. (1969), 'Some notes on the concepts of race and plural society', paper delivered to the British Sociological Association.
Montagu, A. (1972), *Statement on Race*, 3rd ed.
Moore, R. (1971), 'Race relations and the rediscovery of sociology', *B.J.S.*, vol. 22, no. 1, pp. 97–104.
Noel, D. L. (1968), 'A theory of the origin of ethnic stratification', *S.P.*, pp. 157–72.
Reuter, E. B. (1945), 'Racial theory', *A.J.S.*, vol. 50.
Rex, J. (1969), 'The concept of race in sociological theory', paper delivered to the British Sociological Association.

Rex, J. (1973), *Race, Colonialism and the City*, London.
Rex, J. and Moore, R. (1967), *Race, Community and Conflict*, London.
Richmond, A. H. (1972), *Readings in Race and Ethnic Relations*, London.
Richmond, A. H. (1961), 'Sociological and psychological explanations of racial prejudice', *Pacific Sociological Review*, vol. 4, no. 2.
Shibutani, T. and Kwan, K. M. (1965), *Ethnic Stratification*, New York.
Simpson, G. E. and Yinger, M. (1972), *Racial and Cultural Minorities*, 4th ed., New York.
Smelser, N. (1963), *Theory of Collective Behavior*, New York.
Tumin, M. (ed.) (1969), *Comparative Perspectives on Race Relations*, Boston.
Van den Berghe, P. L. (1967), *Race and Racism*, New York.
Westie, F. R. (1965), 'The American dilemma: an empirical text', *A.S.R.*, vol. 27, no. 3, pp. 527–38.

Part 2   Ethnic Stratification

Banton, M. (1972), *Racial Minorities*, London.
Banton, M. (1967), *Race Relations*, London.
Baran and Sweezey (1966), *Monopoly Capital*, Harmondsworth.
Baxter, P. and Sansom, B. (1972), *Race and Social Difference*, Harmondsworth.
Berthoud, R. (1973), *West Germany's 'Guest Worker' System*, London.
Blumer, H. (1965), 'Industrialization and race relations', in S. Hunter (ed.), *Industrialization and Ruce Relations*, London.
Castles, S. and Kosack, G. (1973), *Immigrant Workers and Class Structure in Western Europe*, London.
Cox, O. C. (1959), 'Caste, class and race', *New York Monthly Review*, vol. 8.
Deakin, N. (ed.) (1972), *Immigrants in Europe*, London.
Deighton, H. S. (1959), 'History and the study of race relations', *Race*, vol. I, no. 1.
Dollard, J. (1949), *Caste and Race in a Southern Town*, New York.
Eisenstadt, S. N. (1954), *The Absorption of Immigrants*, London.
Fanon, F. (1970), *A Dying Colonialism*, Harmondsworth.
Fanon, F. (1965), *Wretched of the Earth*, London.
Fanon, F. (1970), *Black Skin, White Masks*, London.
Franck, T. (1960), *Race and Nationalism*, London.
Frazier, E. F. (1947), 'Sociological theory and race relations', *A.S.R.*, vol. 12, no. 3.
Furnival, J. S. (1956), *Colonial Policy and Practise*, New York.
Hayes, M. (1972), *Community Relations and the Role of the Community Relations Commission in Northern Ireland*, Runnymede Trust, London.
Henriques, F. (1966), 'The sociology of immigration' in G. E. Wolstenholme and M. O'Connor (eds.), *Immigration: Medical and Social Aspects*, London.

Hughes, E. C. and H. M. (1952), *Where Peoples Meet: Racial and Ethnic Frontiers*, Glencoe, Ill.

Hunter, G. (1965), *Industrialization and Race Relations*, London.

Jones, K. and Smith, A. D. (1970), *Commonwealth Immigration: the Economic Effects*, Runnymede Trust, London.

Jordan, W. (1968), *White over Black*, Chapel Hill, N.C.

Kleinberg, O. (1935), *Racial Differences,* New York.

Kuper, L. and Smith, M. G. (eds.), *Pluralism in Africa*, Berkeley.

Lester, A. (1972), *Citizens without Status*, Runnymede Trust, London.

Lévi-Strauss, C. (1956), 'Race and history', in UNESCO, *The Race Question in Modern Science*, Paris.

Lewis, O. (1967), *La Vida*, London.

Lieberson, S. (1961), 'A societal theory of race and ethnic relations', *A.S.R.*, vol. 26, no. 6.

Logan, R. W. (1957), *The Negro in the United States*, New York.

Marden, C. F. and Meyer, G. (1968), *Minorities in American Society*, New York.

Minority Rights Group (1973), *Religious Minorities in Soviet Russia*, MRG 1, London.

Minority Rights Group (1972), *The Two Irelands*, MRG 2, London.

Minority Rights Group (1971), *Japan's Outcasts*, MRG 3, London.

Minority Rights Group (1971), *The Asian Minorities of East and Central Africa*, MRG 4, London.

Minority Rights Group (1973), *The Crimean Tartars, Volga Germans and Mesthetians*, MRG 6, London.

Minority Rights Group (1971), *The Position of Blacks in Brazilian Society*, MRG 7, London.

Minority Rights Group (1972), *The Basques*, MRG 9, London.

Minority Rights Group (1972), *The Chinese in Indonesia, the Phillipines and Malaysia*, MRG 10, London.

Minority Rights Group (1972), *The Biharis in Bangladesh*, MRG 11, London.

Minority Rights Group (1972), *Israel's Oriental Immigrants and Druzes*, MRG 12, London.

Minority Rights Group (1972), *East Indians of Trinidad and Guyana*, MRG 13, London.

Minority Rights Group (1973), *The Rom: the Gypsies of Europe*, MRG 14, London.

Minority Rights Group (1973), *What Future for the Amerindians of South America?* MRG 15, London.

Nakane, C. (1970), *Japanese Society*, London.

O'Brien, J. (1972), *Brown Britons: the Crisis of the Ugandan Asians*, Runnymede Trust, London.

Pettigrew, T. F. (1964), *A Profile of the American Negro*, New York.

Reuck, A. de and Knight, J. (1967), *Caste and Race: Comparative Approaches*, London.

Rose, A. M. (1969), *Migrants in Europe*, Minneapolis.

Rose, P. I. (1964), *They and We: Racial and Ethnic Relations in the USA*, New York.

Segal, R. (1966), *The Race War*, London.

Shibutani, T. and Kwan, K. M. (1965), *Ethnic Stratification*, New York.

Shils, E. (1957), 'Primordial, personal, sacred and civil ties', *B.J.S.*, vol. 8.

Simpson, G. E. and Yinger, J. M. (1965), *Racial and Cultural Minorities*, New York.

Thompson, E. T. and Hughes, E. C. (1958), *Race: Individual and Collective Behavior*, Glencoe, Ill.

Van den Berghe, P. L. (1967), *Race and Racism*, New York.

Wagley, C. (1963), *An Introduction to Brazil*, New York.

Wagley, C. and Harris, M. (1970), *Minorities in the New World*, New York.

Warner, W. Lloyd and Srole, L. (1945), *The Social Systems of American Ethnic Groups*, Yale.

Waughray, V. (1960), 'The French racial scene: north African immigrants in France', *Race*, vol. 2, no. 1.

Weingrod, A. (1965), *Israel—Group Relations in a New Society*, London.

Woodward, C. Vann (1966), *The Strange Career of Jim Crow*, New York.

Part 3 Institutions

Antonovsky, A. (1964), 'The social meaning of discrimination', in Rosenberg, Gerver and Howton (eds.), *Mass Society in Crisis*, New York.

Banton, M. (1969), 'What do we mean by racism?', *New Society*, no. 341, pp. 551–4.

Bayley, D. H. and Mendelsohn, H. (1968), *Minorities and the Police*, New York.

Bosanquet, N. (1973), *Race and Employment in Britain*, London.

Bowker, G. (1967), *Education of Coloured Immigrants,* London.

Bowker, G. (1971), 'Interaction, intergroup conflict and tension in the context of education', *International Social Science Journal*, vol. 23, no. 4.

Brandon, D. (1973), *Not Proven*, London.

Butterworth, E. (1967), 'The presence of immigrant school-children: a study of Leeds', *Race*, vol. 8, no. 3.

Clarke, K. (1968), *Dark Ghetto*, London.

Coard, B. (1971), *How the West Indian Child is made Educationally Subnormal in the British School System*, London.

Coleman, J. S. *et al.* (1966), *Equality of Educational Opportunity*, Washington.

Deakin, N. (1971), *Colour and the British Electorate*, London.

Dentler, R. A. (1961), 'Equality of educational opportunity', *Urban Review*, vol. 1, pp. 27–9.

Deutsch, M., Katz, I. and Jensen, A. (eds.) (1968), *Social Class, Race and Psychological Development*, New York.

Ellison, R. (1953), *The Shadow and the Act*, New York.

Evans, P. (1971), *Attitudes of Young Immigrants*, London.

Eysenck, H. J. (1973), *The Inequality of Man*, London.

Eysenck, H. J. (1971), *Race, Intelligence and Education*, London.

Foot, P. (1966), *Race and Immigration in UK Politics*, Harmondsworth.

Glass, R. and Pollins, H. (1960), *Newcomers*, London.

Hernton, C. C. (1969), *Sex and Racism*, London.

Hodge, R. W. and Trieman, D. J. (1966), 'Occupational mobility and attitudes towards Negroes', *A.S.R.*, vol. 31, no. 1, pp. 93–102.

Hunter, G. (ed.) (1965), *Industrialization and Race Relations*, London.

Jensen, A. R. (1969), 'Response: Arthur Jensen replies', *Psychology Today*.

Jensen, A. R. (1969), 'How can we boost I.Q. and scholastic achievement?', *Harvard Educational Review*, vol. 39, pp. 1–34.

Jones, C. (1971), *Race and the Press*, London.

Jones, K. (1961), 'Immigrants and the social services', *National Institute Economic Review*, no. 41, pp. 28–40.

Krausz, E. (1973), 'Factors of social mobility in British minority groups', *B.J.S.*, vol. 23, no. 3.

Lambert, J. R. (1970), *Crime, the Police and Race Relations*, London.

Leggett, J. C. (1968), *Class, Race and Labour*, London.

Lieberson, S. (1970), *Language and Ethnic Relations in Canada*, New York.

Mack, R. (1968), *Race, Class and Power*, 2nd ed., New York.

Mathews, A. S. (1972), *Law, Order and Liberty in South Africa*, Berkeley.

Oakley, R. (ed.) (1968), *New Backgrounds*, London.

Patterson, S. (1963), *Dark Strangers*, London.

Patterson, S. (1968), *Immigrants in Industry*, London.

Rainwater, L. (1971), *Behind Ghetto Walls*, Chicago.

Richardson, K., Spears, D. and Richards, M. (eds.) (1972), *Race, Culture and Intelligence*, Harmondsworth.

Rose, P. (1969), *The Ghetto and Beyond*, New York.

Rosenthal, R. and Jacobson, L. (1968), *Pygmalion in the Classroom*, New York.

Rossi, P. H. (1969), 'The education of failure or the failure of education', *Journal of Negro Education*, p. 332ff.

Rossi, P. H. (1970), *Ghetto Revolts*, Chicago.

Sims, V. M. and Patrick, J. R. (1936), 'Attitudes towards the Negro of northern and southern college students', *Journal of Social Psychology*, vol. 7, no. 2.

Singer, B. (1973), 'Mass society, mass media and the transformation of minority identity', *B.J.S.*, vol. 24, no. 2, pp. 140–50.

Smithies, B. and Fiddick, P. (1969), *Enoch Powell on Immigration*, London.

Squibb, P. G. (1973), 'The concept of intelligence—a sociological perspective', *S.R.*, vol. 21, no. 1, pp. 57–75.

Taylor, J. H. (1973), 'Newcastle upon Tyne: Asian pupils do better than whites', *B.J.S.*, vol. 24, no. 4, pp. 431–47.

Tumin, M. (1963), *Race and Intelligence: a Scientific Evaluation*, New York.

Watson, G. (1970), *Passing for White*, London.

Whitten, P. and Kagan, J. (1969), 'Jensen's dangerous half-truth', *Psychology Today*.

Wirth, L. (1928), *The Ghetto*, Chicago.

Wright, P. L. (1968), *The Coloured Worker in British Industry*, London.

Acknowledgements

For permission to reprint copyright material the editors and publishers are indebted to the original publishers for the following articles and extracts:

1. R. E. Park, *Race and Culture.* © Macmillan Publishing Company Inc. 1950.
2. Reprinted from pages lxxi–lxxiii and lxxiv–lxxv in *An American Dilemma* by Gunnar Myrdal. © 1944, 1962 by Harper and Row, Publishers Inc. By permission of the publishers.
3. S. N. Eisenstadt, *The Absorption of Immigrants*, Routledge and Kegan Paul.
4. Oliver Cromwell Cox, *Caste, Class and Race.* By permission of the author.
5. Andrew Asheron, 'Race and politics in South Africa', *New Left Review*, vol. 53, Spring 1969, pp. 53–8.
6. From pages 53–75 in *Racial Oppression in America* by Robert Blauner. © 1972 by Robert Blauner, reprinted by permission of Harper and Row, Publishers, Inc.
7. R. A. Schermerhorn, *Comparative Ethnic Relations: A Framework for Theory and Research.* © 1970 by Random House, Inc. Reprinted by permission of the publishers.
8. Alfred Schutz, 'The stranger: an essay in social psychology', *American Journal of Sociology*, vol. 49, no. 6, 1944, by permission of the University of Chicago Press.
9. John Rex, *Race Relations and Sociological Theory*, reprinted by permission of George Weidenfeld & Nicolson Ltd., and Schocken Books Inc. © 1970 by John Rex.
10. Winthrop D. Jordan, 'Modern tensions and the origins of American Slavery', *Journal of Southern History*, vol. xxix, (February 1962), 18–30. © 1962 by the Southern Historical Association. Reprinted by permission of the Managing Editor. Extensive development of argument has been deleted from the notes. A modified and much more complete description of the origin of American slavery appears in Winthrop D. Jordan, *White Over Black: American Attitudes to the Negro, 1550-1812* (Chapel Hill, 1968).

11. S. Elkins, *Slavery*. © 1959 University of Chicago Press.
12. E. D. Genovese, 'Materialism and idealism in the history of Negro slavery in the Americas'. © 1971 by Peter N. Stearns. Reprinted from the *Journal of Social History*, vol. iv, no. 4, pp. 333–56, by permission of the editor.
13. W. Lloyd Warner, 'American caste and class', *American Journal of Sociology*, vol. 42, 1936, pp. 234–7, by permission of the University of Chicago Press.
14. Gerald D. Berreman, 'Stratification, pluralism and interaction', in A. V. S. de Reuck and J. Knight (eds.), *Caste and Race: Comparative Approaches*, Ciba Foundation, 1967.
15. Oliver Cromwell Cox, *Caste, Class and Race*. By permission of the author.
16. E. R. Leach, 'What should we mean by caste?', in E. R. Leach (ed.), *Aspects of Caste in South India*, Cambridge University Press, 1969.
17. Michael Banton, *Race Relations*, Tavistock Publication Ltd. and © 1967 by Michael Banton, Basic Books Inc., Publishers, New York.
18. St. Clair Drake and H. Cayton, *Black Metropolis*. © 1946 by St. Clair Drake and Horace C. Cayton, renewed, 1973, by St. Clair Drake and Susan C. Woodson. Reprinted by permission of Harcourt Brace Jovanovitch, Inc.
19. M. G. Smith in L. Kuper and M. G. Smith (eds.), *Pluralism in Africa*. Originally published by the University of California Press, 1969. Reprinted by permission of the Regents of the University of California.
20. M. Lofchie, 'The Plural Society in Zanzibar', in L. Kuper and M. G. Smith (eds.), *Pluralism in Africa*. Originally published by the University of California Press, 1969. Reprinted by permission of the Regents of the University of California.
21. Reprinted from N. Glazer and D. Moynihan, *Beyond the Melting Pot*, by permission of M.I.T. Press, Cambridge, Massachusetts. © 1970 N. Glazer and D. Moynihan.
22. From *Tally's Corner* by Elliot Liebow, by permission of Little, Brown & Co.
23. W. W. Daniel, *Racial Discrimination in England*, Political and Economic Planning.
24. *Colour and Citizenship* by E. J. B. Rose and associates. Published for the Institute of Race Relations by the Oxford University Press, 1969. © Institute of Race Relations, 1969.
25. Charles E. Silberman, *Crisis in Black and White*, Jonathan Cape Ltd. and Random House Inc. © 1964. Reprinted by permission of the publishers.
26. Leo Kuper, *An African Bourgeoisie*, Yale University Press Ltd.
27. Ira Katznelson, *Black Men, White Cities*, published for the Institute of Race Relations by the Oxford University Press, 1973. © Institute of Race Relations, 1973.

28. Harry Brill, *Why Organizers Fail: the Story of a Rent Strike*. Originally published by the University of California Press. Reprinted by permission of the Regents of the University of California.

29. Reprinted with permission of Macmillan Publishing Co. Inc. from *Ethnic Stratification* by T. Shibutani and K. Kwan. © Copyright 1965 by Macmillan Publishing Co., Inc.

30. Lee Rainwater, *Behind Ghetto Walls: Black Families in a Federal Slum*, Allen Lane 1971, by permission of Penguin Books Ltd. © copyright 1970, Lee Rainwater; and Aldine Publishing Company.

31. T. F. Pettigrew, 'Race and equal educational opportunity', *Harvard Educational Review*, vol. 38, Winter 1968, 66–76. © 1968 by President and Fellows of Harvard College.

32. Murray and Rosalie Wax, 'Federal programs and Indian target populations' from Norman R. Yetman and C. Hoy Steele, *Majority and Minority: the Dynamics of Racial and Ethnic Relations*. © 1971, Allyn & Bacon, Inc, Boston. First published as 'Cultural deprivation as an educational ideology', in the *Journal of Indian Education*, Aldine Publishing Company.

33. A. Little, C. Mabey and G. Whitaker, 'The education of immigrant pupils in Inner London primary schools', *Race*, vol. 9, no. 4, 1968, pp. 439–52, by permission of the Institute of Race Relations.

34. C. Bagley, 'The educational performance of immigrant children', *Race*, vol. 10, no. 1, 1968, pp. 91–4, by permission of the Institute of Race Relations.

35. 'Intermarriage: interracial, interfaith and interethnic' (pp. 488–516) in *Racial and Cultural Minorities*, 4th edition by George Eaton Simpson and J. Milton Yinger (abridgement). © 1953 by Harper and Row, Publishers, Inc. © 1958, 1965, 1972, by George Eaton Simpson and J. Milton Yinger. By permission of the publishers.

Name Index

General Index

.